Operations Management

Operations Management

Professor V.P. Gupta

Ms. Ila Sinha

RESEARCHCO BOOK CENTRE

NEW DELHI-110005

First Published 2007

ISBN : 81-89614-04-5

Published by :

Researchco Book Center
25B/2, New Rohtak Road
(Near Liberty Cinema)
Karol Bagh
New Delhi-110005

Printed at :

Salasar Imaging Systems
New Delhi

CONTENTS

UNIT-I

UNIT-II

UNIT-III

UNIT-IV

UNIT-V

Operations Management

UNIT—I

1

Introduction

Production and operations management concerns itself with the conversion of inputs into outputs, using physical resources, of as to provide the desired utility/utilities-of form, place, possession or state or a combination thereof-to the customer while meeting the other organizational objectives of effectiveness, efficiency and adaptability. It distinguishes itself from the other functions such as personnel, marketing etc. by its primary concern for 'conversion by using physical resources'. Of course, there may be and would be a member of situations in either marketing or personnel or other function which can be classified or sub-classified under production and operations management. For example, (i) the physical distribution of items to the customers, (ii) the arrangement of collection of marketing information, (iii) the actual selection and recruitment process. (iv) the paper flow and conversion of the accounting information in an accounts office, (v) the paper flow and conversion of data into information usable by the judge in a court of low, etc. can all be put under the banner of production and operations management. The 'conversion' here is subtle, unlike manufacturing which is obvious. While in case (i) and (ii) it is the conversion of 'place' and 'possession' characteristics of the product, in (iv) and (v) it is the conversion of 'state' characteristics. And this 'conversion' is effected by using physical resources. This is not to deny the use of other resources such as 'information' in production and operations management. The input and/or output could also be non-physical such as 'information', but the conversion process uses physical resources in addition to other non-physical resources. The management of the use of physical resources for the conversion process is what distinguishes production and operations management from other functional disciplines. Table 1.1 illustrates the many facets of the production and operations management function.

Often, production and operations management systems are described as providing physical goods or services. Perhaps, a sharper distinction such as the four customer utilities and physical/non-physical nature of inputs and/or outputs would be more appropriate. When we say that the Central Government Health Service provides 'service' and the Indian Railways provide 'service', these are two entirely different classes of utilities, therefore criteria for reference will have to be entirely different for these two cases. To take another example the Postal Service and the Telephones Service are different because the major inputs and major outputs are totally different with different criteria for their efficiency and effectiveness.

Also, a clean demarcation is not always possible between operations systems that provide 'physical goods' and those that provide 'service' , as

Table 1.1. Production and Operations Management-Some Cases.

Sl. No.	Case	Input	Physical Resource/s Used	Output	Type of Input/Output	Type of Utility Provided to the Customers
1.	Inorganic chemicals production	Ores	Chemical Plant and equipment, other chemicals, use of labour, etc.	Inorganic chemical	Physical input and physical output	Form
2.	Outpatient ward of a general hospital	Unhealthy patients	Doctors, nurses, other staff, equipment, other facilities	Healthier	Physical input and physical output	State
3.	Educational institution	'Raw' minds	Teachers, books, teaching aids, etc.	'Enlightened' minds	Physical (?) input and physical (?) output	State
4.	Sales office	Data from market	Personnel, office equipment and facilities, etc.	Processed 'information'	Non-physical input and non-physical output	State
5.	Petrol pump	Petrol (in possession of the petrol pump owner)	Operators, errand boys, equipment, etc.	Petrol (in possession of the car owner)	Physical input and physical output	Possession
6.	Taxi service	Customer (at railway station)	Driver, taxi itself, petrol	Customer (at his residence)	Physical input and physical output	Place
7.	Astrologer/ palmist	Customer (mind full of questions)	Astrologer, Panchange, other books, etc.	Customer (mind with less questions hopefully	Physical input and physical output	State
8.	Maintenance	Equipment gone 'bad'	Mechanics, Engineers, repairs equipment, etc.	'Good' Equipment	Physical input and physical output	State and form
9.	Income tax office	'Information'	Officers and other staff, office facility	Raid	Non-physical input and physical output	State (posses sion?)

an activity deemed to be providing 'physical goods' may also be providing 'service' , and vice versa. For example, one might say that ' the food in the Southern Railways is quit good' however, food is not the main business of the Railways. To take another example: A manufacturing firm can provide good 'service' by delivering goods on time. Or, XYZ Refrigerator Company not only makes good refrigerator, but also provides good 'after sales service'. The concepts of 'physical goods production' and 'service' provision' are not mutually exclusive; in fact, in most cases these are mixed, one being more predominant than the other.

Similarly we may also say that the actual production and operations management systems are quite complex involving multiple utilities to be provided to the customer, with a mix of physical and non-physical inputs and outputs and perhaps with a multiplicity of customers. Today, our 'customers' need not only be outsiders but also our own 'inside staff'. In spite of these variations in (i) input type (ii) output type, (iii) customers serviced, and (iv) type of utility provided to the customers, production and operations management distinguishes itself in terms of 'conversion' effected by the use of physical resources such as men, materials, and machinery.'

Criteria of Performance for the Production and Operations Managenent System

Three objectives or criteria of performance of the production and operations management system are

(a) Customer satisfaction
(b) Effectiveness
(c) Efficiency.

The case for 'efficiency' or 'productive' utilization of resources is clear. Whether, the organization is in the private sector or in the public sector, is a 'manufacturing' or a 'service' organization, or a 'profit-making' or a 'non-profit' organization, the productive or optimal utilization of resource inputs is always a desired objective. However, effectiveness has more dimensions to it. It involves an optimality in the fulfillment of multiple objectives, with a possible prioritization within the objectives. This is not difficult to imagine because modern production and operations management has to serve the so-called target customers, the people working within, as also the region, country or society at large. In order to survive, the production/operations management system, has not only to be 'profitable' and/or 'efficient', but, must necessarily satisfy many more 'customers'. This effectiveness has to be again viewed in terms of the short-and long-time horizons (depending upon the operations system's need to remain active for short or long time horizons)-because, what may seem now like an 'effective' solution may not be 'all the effective in the future'. In fact, the effectiveness of the operations system may depend not only upon a multi-objectives satisfaction but also on its flexibility or adaptability to changed situations in the future so that it continues to fulfil the desirable objectives set while maintaining optimal efficiency.

Table 1.2. Jobs of Production and Operations Management

Long Time Horizon	**Intermediate Time Horizon**	**Short Time Horizon**
• Product design • Quality policy • Technology to be employed • Process selection • Site selection • Machinery and plant selection • Plant size selection-phased addition • Manpower training and development-phased programme • Long-gestation period raw material supply projects-phased development • Warehousing arrangements • Insurance spare • Design of jobs • Setting up work standards • Effluent and waste disposal systems • safety and maintenance systems	• Product variations • Methods selection • Quality implementation, inspection and control methods • Machinery and plant loading decisions • Forecasting • Output per unit period decision • Deployment of manpower • Overtime decisions • Shift-working decisions • Temporary hiring or lay-off of manpower • Purchasing policy • Purchasing source selection, development and evaluation • Make or buy decision • Inventory policy for row material, work-in-progress, and finished goods • Transport and delivery arrangements • Preventive maintenance scheduling • Implementation of safety decisions • Industrial relations • Checking/setting up work standards and incentive rates	• Production scheduling • Available materials allocation and handling • Scheduling of man-power • Breakdown maintenance • Progress check and change in priorities in production scheduling • Temporary Manpower • Supervision and immediate attention to problem areas in labour, materials, machines, etc.

Jobs/Decisions of Production/Operations Management

- Typically, what are the different decisions taken in production and operations management? As a discipline of 'management' which involves basically planning, implementation, monitoring, and control, some of the jobs/decisions involved in the production and operations management function are as mentioned in Table 1.2

Nature and Scope of Production & Operations Management

Nature of Production

Among all the functional areas of management, production is considered to be crucial in any industrial organization. *Production is the process by which, raw materials and other inputs are converted into finished products.* The other word synonymously used with production is manufacturing. Some people try to draw distinction between the two terms: production and manufacturing. Manufacturing is understood to refer to the process of producing only tangible goods, whereas production includes creation of both tangible goods as well as intangible services. Though, distinction of this type is sought to be made, we use these tow terms synonymously in this book.

Nature of production can be better understood, if we view the manufacturing function from three angles: production as a system, production as an organizational function and decision making in production.1

Production as a System

A system is understood as a whole which cannot be taken apart. It must be studies as a whole. While looking from this perspective, we may note that , there are three systems: (i) production system, (ii) conversion sub-system, and (iii) control sub-system. Read Table 1.3 for definitions of the three concepts.

Table 1.3. Production System Concepts

Concept	Definition
1. Production system	A system, whose function is to convert a set of inputs into a set of desired outputs.
2. Conversion sub-system	A sub-system of the larger production system where inputs are converted in to outputs.
3. Control sub-system	A sub-system of the larger production system where, a portion of the output is monitored for feedback signals to provided corrective action, if required.

Production system receives inputs in the form of materials, personnel, capital utilities and information,. These inputs are changed in a conversion sub-system into desired products and services, which are called the output able in terms of quantity, cost and quality. If the out and services, which are called the Outputs. A portion of the output is maintained in the control sub-system to determine if it is acceptable in terms of quantity, cost and quality. If the output is acceptable, no changes are required in the system. If, however, the appropriate standards are not met, managerial corrective action is required. The control sub-system ensures a uniform level of system performance by providing feedback information so that corrective action may be taken by managers Fig.1.1 illustrates the production system.

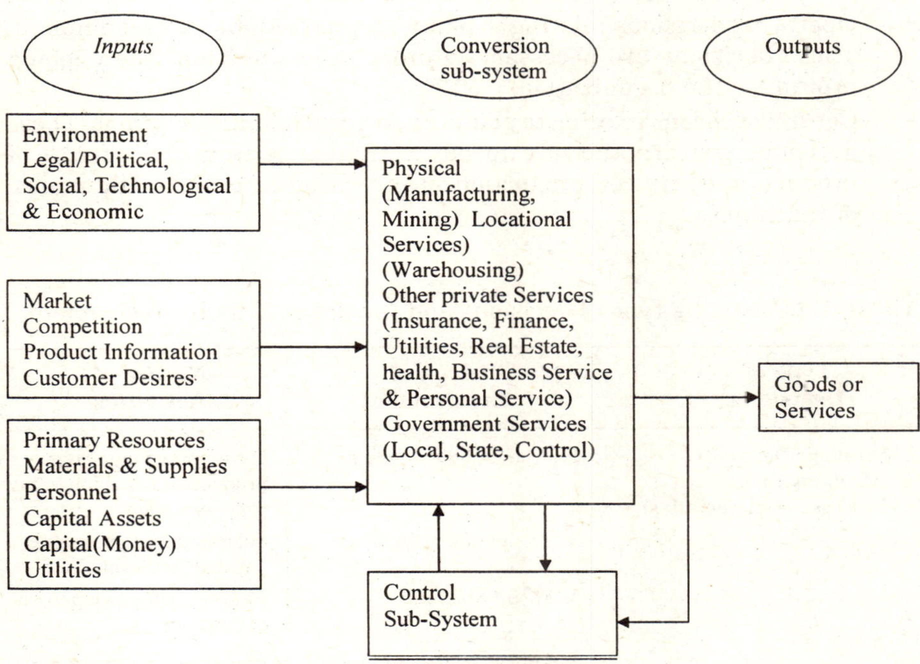

Fig. 1.1. A production System Model

Production as an Organisation Function

The core of a production system is its conversion sub-system. wherein workers, materials and machines are used to convert inputs into products and services. This process of conversion is at the heart of production function and is present in some form in all organizations. It may be stated that every organization, irrespective of its purpose, has a production function where be stated that every organization, irrespective of its purpose, has production function where departments and personnel plan a central role in achieving the objectives of the organization.

Decision-making in Production

Operations managers are required to make a series of decisions in the production function. They plan, organize, staff, direct and control all the activities in the process of converting all the inputs into finished products. At each level, operating managers are expected to make decisions and implement them too.

The decisions made by operations managers about the activities of production systems tend to fall into three general categories viz;

- Strategic decisions relating to products, processed and manufacturing facilities. These decisions are major ones, having strategic importance and long-term significance for the organization.
- Operating decisions relating to planning productions to meet demand. These decisions are necessary in order to ensure that, the ongoing profits for the organization.
- Control decisions relating to planning and controlling operations. These decisions concern the day to day activities of workers, quality of products and services, production and overhead costs and maintenance of machines.

Table 1.4. Lists the type of decisions and the areas of their involvement.

Type of Decisions	Area of Involvement	Nature of Activities
I. Strategic Decisions (Planning Products, Processes and Facilities)	1. Production Processes	Developing long range production plans including process design.
	2. Production Technology	Selecting and managing production technology
	3. Facility Layout	Planning the arrangement of facilities.
	4. Allocating Resources To Strategic Alternatives	Planning for the optimal distribution of scarce resources among product lines or business units.
	5. Long Range Capacity Planning and facility Location	Answering the how much and where questions about long range production capacity.
II. Operation Decisions (Planning Production to Met Demand)	1. Production Planning Systems	Aggregate planning and master production scheduling
	2. Independent Demand Inventory Systems	Planning and controlling finished goods inventories
	3. Resource Requirements Planning systems	Planning materials and capacity requirements.

Table 1.4. *(Contd.)*

Type of Decisions	Area of Involvement	Nature of Activities
	4. Shop floor Planning and Control	Short range decisions about what to produce and when to produce at each work center
	5. Materials Management	Managing all facts of materials system
III. Control Decisions (Planning and controlling Operations)	1. Productivity and Employees	Planning for the effective and efficient use of human resources in operations.
	2. Total Quality Control	Planning and controlling the quality of products and services.
	3. Project Planning and control Techniques.	Planning and controlling projects.
	4. Maintenance Management and Reliability.	Planning for maintaining the machines and facilities of production.

Importance of Production Function

It needs on exaggeration to say that production makes significant contribution to society's well being. The standard of living of people depends on production of goods and services. Well being. The standard of living of people depends on production of goods and services. More the production. Higher then standard of living of the people. Alexander solzhenitsyn in his novel August 1914 beautifully sums up the importance of production. One of the characters in the work is Suyataslav Iakintovich Obodovsky. A former anarchist. Who maintains the following position.: "As for industry. Anyone who has created something with his own hands knows that production is neither capitalist nor socialist but one thing only, it is what creates national wealth, the common national basis without which no country can exist."

Having reached that conclusion, Obodovsky went on to say. "Before, I was most concerned with how to distribute everything that other people had created without my help. Now, my main preoccupation is how to create. The best brains and hands in the country should concentrate on doing that; we can safely leave distribution to the second-raters. When enough has been built and made, then even if distribution is less than perfect, no one will be left completely without his share."

Competitive advantage of companies is highly talked about these days. It is believed, that a firm, strong in competitive advantage, is well poised to succeed whatever may be the constraints or restraints. Firms look to production function to achieve competitive advantage.

Production function can offer competitive advantage, is well posed to succeed whatever may be the constraints or restraints. Firms look to production function to achieve competitive advantage.

Production function can offer competitive advantage to a firm in the following areas. Shorter new-product lead time.

More inventory turns.
Shorter manufacturing lead time.
Higher quality.
Greater flexibility.
Better customer service.
Reduced wastage.

Many causes that deny competitive advantages to any firm can be attributed to manufacturing function-specifically to poor quality and reliability, delayed deliveries, high production costs and lack of adequate inventory at the right time.

It has long been recognized that, high productivity is one of the keys to high standard of a greater standard of living of Japanese may be attributed to high productivity. It may be stated that the production function offers vast scope for achieving productivity with effective management of materials and lead time, and with better control of cost, a firm will be able to bring out more output from a given input at reasonable cost. Table 1.5 shows the different areas of achieving productivity.

Production Management

Production management refers to the application of management principles to the production functioning a factory. In other words, production management involves application of planning, organizing, directing and controlling to the production process.

The application of management to the field of production has been the result of at least three developments. First is the development of factory system of production. /Until the emergence of manufacturing, there was no such thing as management as we know it. It is. It is true that people operated business of one type or another, but for the most part, these people were owners of business and did not regard themselves as managers as well. He second, essentially stems from the work of many the pioneers of scientific management who were able ȯ demonstrate the value. From a performance and profit point of view, of some of the techniques they were developing.

Table 1.5 Production function- Areas of Productivity

1. Improving volume of production
2. reducing rejection rate
3. Minimising re-work rate
4. Maintaining delivery schedules
5. Controlling idle machine and manpower hours
6. Establishing/updating/improving /setting industrial engineering norms
7. Updating processes and procedures
8. Maintaining accuracy and timeliness of MIS
9. Decreasing machine set-up time
10. Controlling overtime
11. Good house-keeping
12. Checking absenteeism, thefts/pilferage and misconduct
13. Eliminating accidents
14. Effective grievance-handling
15. Efficient training and team building
16. Minimising inventory and achieving better yields
17. Enhancing customer satisfaction
18. Total Quality Management (TQM)
19. Business Process Re-engineering (BPRE)
20. Automation

Operations Management

Operations management is often used also with production management in literature on the subject. It is therefore, useful to understand the nature of operations management. Operations management is understood as the process whereby resources r inputs are converted into more useful products. A second reading of the sentenced revels that, there is hardly any difference between the terms production management and operations management. But, there are at least two points of distinction between production management and operations management is more frequently used where various inputs are transformed into intangible services. Viewed from this perspective, operations management will cover such service organizations as banks, airlines, utilities, pollution control agencies, super bazaars, educational institutions, libraries, consultancy firms and police departments, in addition, of course, to manufacturing enterprises. The second distinction relates to the evolution of the subject. Operations management is the term that is used now a days. Production management precedes operations monument in the historical growth of the subject.

The two distinctions not withstanding, the terms production management and operations management are used interchangeably. We also allow the same approach in this book.

Scope of Production and Operations Management

The scope of production and operations management is indeed vast. Commencing with the selection of location, production management covers such activities as acquisitions of land, constructing building, procuring and installing machinery, purchasing and storing raw materials and converting them into saleable products.

Added to the above are other related topics such as quality management, maintenance management, production planning and control, methods improvement and work simplification and other related areas. As subsequent pages in tins book, show, all these topics have been discussed in greater detail.

Evolution of production Function

In order to trace the evolution of production function, we identify six historical developments the Industrial Revolution, scientific management, the human relations movement, operations research, computers and advanced production technology and the service revolution. A brief explanation of each stage follows.

The Industrial Revolution

Since times ancient production systems were used in one form or another. The Egyptian Pyramids, the Greek Parthenon, the great wall of china and the aqua ducts and roads of the Roman Empire, dams and anicuts built by the chola Kings attest to the ingenuity and industry of the people of ancient times. But the ways the people in the ancient days produced goods were different from the production methods of today. Production systems prior to the 1700s are often referred to as the cottage system, because the production of goods took place in homes or cottages, where craftsmen directed apprentices in performing hand work on products.5

From 1770 to the early 1800s, series of events took place in England which together are called the Industrial revolution. Industrial Revolution resulted in two major developments: widespread substitution of machine power for human power and establishment of the factory system.

The events that took place from 1770 to the 1800s are characterized by great inventions. The great inventions were eight in number, with six of them having been conceived in England, one in France and one in the United States. The eight inventions are- Hargreaves Spinning engine, Berthollet's Chlorine Bleaching Discovery, Mandslay's Screw-cutting Lathe and Eliwhitney's Interchangeable Manufacture,

As observed from eight inventions, most of them have to do with the spinning f yarn and weaving of cloth. This is logical from the point of view that clothe was the principal export commodity of England at the time and was in short supply owing to the considerable expansion of England's colonial empire and its commercial trade.

The availability of machine power greatly facilitated the gathering of workers in factories that housed the machines. The large number of workers congregated in the factories, created the need for organising them in logical ways to produce goods. The publication of Adam Smith's The wealth of Nations in 1776 advocated the benefits of the division of labour of specialization of labour, which broke production of goods into small specialized tasks that were assigned to workers on production lines. Thus, the factories of late 1700s not only had developed production machinery, but also ways of planning and controlling the output of workers.

The impact of the Industrial Revolution was first felt in England. From here, it spread to other European courtiers and to the United States.

The Industrial Revolution advanced further with the development of the gasoline engine and electricity in the 1800s, the old cottage system of production had been replaced by the factory system. As days went by, production capacities expanded, demand for capital grew and labour became highly dependant on jobs and urbanized. At the commencement of the 20th century, the one element that was missing was management- the ability to develop[and use the existing facilities to produce on a large scale to meet massive markets of today.

Scientific Management

The missing input, viz., management, was ably provided by Scientific Management-a philosophy which was propounded by business leaders, consultants, educators and researchers. Table 1.6 presents the players and their parts in Scientific Management.

The essential principles of Scientific Management are:

1. Developing a science for each element of a person's work, which would replace the old rule-of thumb method;
2. Selecting workers scientifically and training and developing them;
3. Cooperating with workers so as to ensure that all the work would be done according to the principles of science that have been developed; and
4. Dividing work and responsibility almost equally between management and workers. Management should take over all the work for which, it is better fitted than the workers.

Scientific Management become a powerful force as it contributed to increased efficiency in industrial establishments. This force was so successfully applied during the US build up of output for War I and after the war, European countries imported Scientific Management methods to develop their factories.

Table 1.6. Contribution to scientific Management.

Contributor	Life Span	Contributions
1. F.W.Taylor	1856-1951	Scientific Management Principles, Exception Principle, time study,mentodsanalysis, standards, planning and control.
2. Frank B. Gilbreth	1868-1924	Motion study, methods, therbligs, construction contracting, consulting.
3. Lillan M. Gilbreth	1878-1973	Fatigue studies., human factor in work, employee selection and training.
4. henry L.Gantt	1961-1919	Gantt charts, incentive pay systems, humanistic approach to labour, training.
5. Carl G. Barth	1960-1939	Mathematical analysis, slide rule, feeds and speeds studies, consulting go automobile industry.
6. Harrington Emerson	1885-1931	Principles of efficiency, million dollars-a-day savings in rail roads, methods control.
7. Morris L. cooke	1872-1960	Scientific Management its application to education and government.

Scientific Management has dramatically affected today's management approaches. Table 1.7 lists a few modern management concepts and practices the t find their genesis in Scientific Management. Its struggle to find the one best way to operate factories leads logically to a questioning attitude on the part of managers in every phase of production system. The questioning attitude and analytical investigations are perhaps Scientific Management greatest legacy to modern management.

However, the main thrust of /scientific Management was workers at the shop floor, foremen, superintendents and lower middle management. Taylor and his associates concentrated on the shop level because it was here that management problems of the day were found. What was needed was production and efficiency, which means doing things right and implies focusing on the details of operations. Scientific Management methods met the challenge. Later, focus was shifted on developing the overall organisation's effectiveness, which meant doing the right things.

The human relations movement

The term human relations refers to the ways in which managers interacts with their employees. When people in management stimulates more and

Table 1.7. Scientific Management Legacy: Some practices and concepts found in today's organizations.

Organisation Function	**Concept and Practices from Scientific Management**
Management	Exception principle
	Identifying management tasks that are distinctly different from worker tasks
	Placing responsibility for organizational performance on management
	Formal education of managers
	Staff experts
	Control systems as sensing mechanisms
	Decision making based on analysis
	Cost and budgeting systems
Industrial Engineering	Time study
	Motion study
	Workplace layout and design
	Work sampling
	Standardisation of tools and work methods.
	Slide rules and mnemonic devices
	Assemble lines and mass production methods
Personnel management	Incentive pay systems
	Scientific selection of employees for jobs
	Employee training
	Co-operation between workers and management
Operations Scheduling and Control	Labour and materials standards
	Graphic scheduling devices
	Planning departments
	Standardisation of product designs

better work, the organization has effective human relations; when morale and efficiency deteriorates, its human relation are said to be ineffective. The human relations movement arose from early attempts to systematically discover the social and psychological factors that would create effective human relations.

Before describing the human relations movement in detail, it would be useful to recollect the environment in which workers were operating. Factory workers of the Industrial Revolution were uneducated, unskilled indiscipline and starving peasants straight from farms. These peasants abhorred factory jobs, but they were essentials for them, otherwise starvation was the consequence. Factory managers developed rigid controls to force workers to work hard. This legacy of a work environment structured around rigid control carried over into the 1800's and early 1900's.basic to this management philosophy, was the assumption that workers were to given jobs, where they would work hard and efficiently.

Towards the mid 1900's, a realization dawned on the job-givers that, workers deserve to be treated as human beings, while on their respective jobs .the human relation movement begin in Illinois with the work of Elden Mayo. J.RothlisBerger, T.N.Whitehead and W.J Dickson at the Hawthorne, Illnois, plant of Western Electric Company in 1927-1932 period .the Hawthorne Studies were initially begun by industrial engineers and were aimed at determining the optimal level of lightning to get maximum output from workers when these studies produced confusing results about the relationship between physical environment and worker productivity, the researchers realized that human factor must be affective productivity this was perhaps ,the first time that researchers and managers alike, recognized that psychological and social logical factors affected not only employee motivation but their productivity as well.

Operation research

Popularly known by its acronym OR, operations research refers to the use of mathematical techniques to solve management problems table 1.8 brings out the characteristics of OR clearly.

OR has interesting history. At the beginning of World War II, Great Britian, desperatively needed to solve a number of new and complex problems in warfare. With there survival at stake, the British formed the first OR teams by polling the expertise of mathematician physicists, and other scientist. With such team, the British were able to achieve significant technological and tactical breakthrough.

When the war over, the applicability of OR to problems in the industry gradually became apparent. New industrial technologies were being in to use transportation and communication were becoming more complicated. These developments brought with them, a host of problem that could not be solved easily by conventional means. Increasingly, OR specialist were called in to help the management come up with answers to these new problem.

Although scientific Management, human relation and Operation Research have affected the ways that managers in production manage today, perhaps no other development is as important to these managers as the growing presence of computers in there jobs

Table 1.8. Characteristics of OR.

- OR approaches problems solving and decision making from the total system prospective
- OR draws on technique from varied disciplines such as biology, physics, chemistry, mathematics and economics and applies the appropriate technique from each field to the system being studied
- OR dosen't experiment with the system itself but, constructs a modal of the system upon which to conduct experiments.
- The primary focus is on decision-making
- Computers are used extensively

Computers and Advance Production Technologies

Ever since 1954,when the first computer was put to use the no. Of computers and their areas of application and business have increased enormously. In the beginning computers were used for clerical duties such as payrolls, billings, inventory transaction and cost reports, as on today, computer are used as Decision Supports System (DSS), Experts system and artificial intelligence analyzed and managers now used computer to analyzed problem and obtain solution, what would be the shape and use of computers 10 or 15 years hence, is almost impossible to predict,

The Service Revolution

One of the starting developments of our time is the mushrooming of service in every economy. Table1.7 shows the list of services and the organization that offers them. In our economy too, the share of the services sectors (also called tertiary sectors) in the GDP is much higher than that of industry or agriculture.

The impact of this explosion of services organization on production management has been enormous. It is a challenge for manufacturing managers, that they should evolve strategies and action to manage services areas for better productivity, quality and competitiveness.

One should wait for the type of action that would emerge in future for managing service economics effectively. In the mean time, it is useful to bring out characteristics of the systems that produce services.

In the factory of the future there will be a great role for professional like design engineers, computer operators and production planners. It is these people who will have a greater say in the production process.

With increasing customization and product variety, the services component of a product will assume more importance. Days are not far off when a customer will be able to walk into an automobile dealership, order a car based on his reference for color, style and the like, and arrange all necessary financing using a computer terminal. The order will be relayed to the factory, where a car meeting the customer's specific requirement will be manufactured and readied for delivery in a short time. Obviously, corporate profitability depends on how best the service component is

Table 1.9. Services and Organization.

Services	Organization
Airlines	-Indians Airlines, Jet Airways, NEPC Skyline, East West, Sahara
Banks	-State Bank of India, CanaraBank Global Trust Bank, Vysya Bank, Corporation Bank
Fashion Retailing	-Parks Avenue, Zodiac, Ven Heusen
Food Distribution	-MTR .RK, Vasu
Drug Distribution	-Cash Pharmacy, Janata Bazaar, Khodays, Hosmat
Health Care	-Jindal, Malaya, Manipal, Hospital
Hosing/Real Estate	-Raheja's, Ranka, VGP, HDFC
Eating Places	-Rice Bowl, Peacock, Pizza Hut, KFS
Entertainment	-Funland, Jawahar Lal Bhawan, Century Club, Best Club, Doordarshan, ABCL, Star Plus
Hotels/Motels	-Taj, Oberiao, Welcome Group, ITDC
Financial Services	-Lloyds Finance, Shriram Finance, Kanban Factoring
Insurance	-Peerless, Shriram Chits
Saving And Loans	-DBS, Classic Business Service, Business Connection
Business Services	-AIR, Vivid Bharti
Broadcasting	-NIIT, Aptech, Wipro, Infosys
Computer Services	-Land Amy, ECC (L&T).
Construction/ Engineers	-Mandovi, Solar, Kaveri, Ford.
Industrial Distribution	-Airflows Engineers, Airstreams System, Bass Pollution, Control System, Ducon Environment.
Pollution Control	-Co lour Splash, Eye to Eye Production, Image Makers, Prakirti Films, Redifussion Advertising
Advertising	-Himalaya Publishing house, Tata McGraw-Hill, Prentice Hall
Publishing	-Indian Railways, Best
Rail Roads	-CDOT, Siemens, Mobilink
Telecommunications	-KSRTC, BMTC, Sharma Transport, VRL
Transportation	-LIC And GIC
Trucking	-Prakash Road lines, Patel Roadways, TVS Group, K.G.Brothers
Utilities	-KEB, BWSSB

integrated in to the product. Table 1.10 clearly brings out the distinction between systems to produce products and systems to produce services.

Characteristics of Modern Production and Operations Function

The production management of today presents certain characteristics, which make it look totally different from what it was during the past. Specially, today's production system is characteristics by basically four features.

1. Manufacturing as Competitive Advantages: In the past, production was considered to be like any other function in an organization. When demand was high and production capacities were inadequate, the concern was to somehow muster all inputs and use them to produce goods that would be grabbed by the potential market. But today's scenario is contrasting. Plants have excess capacities, competition is mounting and firms look and gain competitive advantage to survive and success. Interestingly, production system offer vast scope to gain a competitive edge and firms intend to exploits the potential. Total Quality Management (TQM), Time-Based Competition, Business Process Reengineering (BPRE), Just Time (JIT), Focused factory (Revised), Flexible Manufacturing System (FMS), Computer Integrated Manufacturing (CIM) and Virtual Corporation are but only some technique, which the companies are employing to gain competitive advantage.

2. Services orientation: As stated earlier v, the services sector is g gaining greater relevance these days. The production system, therefore, needs to be organized, keeping in mind the peculiar requirements of the service component, as was shown in Table 1.8, the entire manufacturing needs to be geared to serve (i) intangible and perishable nature of the services (ii) constant interaction with the clients or customers, (iii) small volumes of production to serve local market and (iv) need to locate facilities to serve local market. There is increased presence of professional on the production idea, instead of techniques and engineers.

3. Disappearance of smokestacks: Commencing from the Industrial Revolution till the middle of the 20th century, production system was dominated by smokestacks, these smoke stacks (the term used by Alvin Toffler in his book power shift) represented industrial establishments which ejected thick smoke, polluting the environment around. Smokestacks not only disgorged reek, they produced nauseating smell, generated dust, created sound and in general, were resembling ghost. Not that they have become extinct, but they are disappearing gradually

Protective labor legislation, environmental movement and gradual emergence of knowledge-based organization, have brought total transformation in the production system. Today's factories are aesthetically designed and built, environment friendly - in fact, they are, a home away from home. Going to factory everyday is no more an excruciating experiences; it is [illegible]ening work with a healthy perspective. A visit to ABB, L&T or

Table 1.10. Charaterics of system to produce products versus systems to produce services.

Products	Services
Tangible	Intangible and perishable; consumed in the process of their production
Can be produced to inventory for 'off the-shelf availability	Availability achieved by keeping the productivity system open for services
Minimal contact with ultimate consumer	High contact with clients or customers
Complex and interrelated processing	Simple processing
Demand on system variable on weekly, monthly and seasonal basis	Demand commonly variable on hourly, daily and weekly basis
Market served by production system are regional, national and inter national	Markets served by production system are usually local
Large units that can take advantage of economics of scale	Relatively small units top serve local markets
Location of system is in relation to regional, national and inter national markets	Location depends on location of local customers, clients and users

Smith-Kline and Beecham should convince the reader about the transaction, that has taken place in the wealth creation system

4. Small has Become Beautiful: It was E.F Schumacher who, in his famous book Small is Beautiful, opposed giant organization and increased specialization. He advocated instead, intermediate technology based on smaller working units, community ownership and regional work place utilizing local and resources. For him, small was beautiful. Businessmen all over the world did not believe in Schumacher's philosophy. Inspired by the economics of scale, industrialists went in for huge organization and mass production systems

The wheel has turned its full circle. If not for the reasons advanced by Schumacher, we find small and tiny manufacturing units sprouting everywhere. Increasing customization, flexible manufacturing system and similar other developments have made economics of scale outdated and giant organization irrelevant. Days are not far off when the giants of today like, Hindustan Aeronautics Limited Telephone Industries will be decomposed in o antiquity. These organizations are already showing signs of decay. In their place, tiny units owned and managed by family members, started just a couple of years back, are doing roaring business.

Why be Interested in Study?

Why general readers should study production and production management is a relevant question .the following paragraph answer the question. Factories occupy a unique place in our country. They are the temples of modern India, shouldering the stupendous task of lifting our economy from its traditional and agrarian fold to a modern and industrial one. Next to agriculture, it is the factories, which are the largest employers. Thousands of families look up to the plants for support ands sustenance. It is industrial establishments, which produce the various goods and services for our day-to-day consumption. Factories are great institute, which brings about desired changes in our social-economic out look. Our incomes. Factories influence living standards, wants motives, thought, actions, life style and patterns. It is desirable that one should be knowledge about factories - their nature and scope, and their functions and problems.

A study about factories helps us appreciate the role played by people in producing goods and services. When a product is turn out by a plant, it is the result of fusion of the efforts and services of scientists, engineers, technicians, managers, workers and janitors. Factory is not merely building and machines. Factory is people. The best of automation may result in the reduction of numbers of people working in a plant, but the presence and contribution of human beings cannot be completely dispensed with. Neither factories, nor products should be divested of people. They are the common ingredients of all activities that take place in factories.

The total picture the about factory becomes clear by a close study of the subject. Contrary to the popular belief, factory is not a sinner that has annihilated the handicrafts. Factory is not a monster out to disrupt ecology. Not a Satan that has destroyed the traditional values that we once held dearly. Neither factory is a scourge that result in migration of people from village to cities. Nor factory is bad neighbor who disturbs our sleep early morning by blowing sirens. Systematic study of factory management reveals its interesting psychological, social, political, technical and artistic phases all of which lend color, characters and genuine splendor to the activities which permeate an industrial enterprise.

Factory study helps in selecting a carrier. As mentioned earlier, factories are potential employers. They offer attractive position for effective executives, brilliant scientist financial wizard creative artists, skilled technicians and hard-working women. First step in selecting a carrier is to understand the various positions available and what they demand, in term of qualification and experience. Next step is to evaluate one's fitness in relation to the requirements of the job. Submitting application and attending interviews will follow later.

Taking a close look at the subject by practicing managers helps them in at least two ways. First, it has been recognized that, high productivity has been one of the keys to the high standard of living. Productivity is the backbone of a nation's economics progress, particularly those countries, where productivity is high and living standard is also high. Increasing productivity should be a national challenge, and it behaves all managers to do their utmost to achieve ever increasingly levels

Second, the managing of manufacturing firms today presents a greater challenge than ever before. Top managers of companies are presented with endless streams of problems that arise from continuing inflation energy crises, high taxes, government regulation and intense foreign competition. To get some idea of the magnitude of these problems, one needs, but pick up a daily newspaper or news-magazine and read effort to offset price increase, to secure plant modernization, to increase productivity, to meet foreign competition and so forth. Knowledge about the ways of managing production and operation management will be strategically useful to the executives.

Project Management

What is a project?

Minor repair work in a plant facility or building a dam and irrigation network are both projects. Any work that has a well defined objective or goal to the sequence of the multitudinous activities required to be performed can be defined as a project. In short, a project has an end. Technically speaking the 'end' is termed as the 'sink'. The various starting points of the project are called the sources. A project can have a number of sources, but only one sink.

The technical definition aside, the management of projects on a scientific basis is gaining continuous acceptance in India. It has received Government approval since the last two decades or so, when the Planning Commission stipulated the a sanction for any project costing over Rs.20 crores, should be accompanied by scientific project network and other analysis.

Element

Project management is a scientific way of Planning, implementing, monitoring and controlling the various aspects of a project such as time, money, materials, manpower and other resources. The objective of such an exercise is to achieve the basis objectives or goals set forth while formulating a project. Project management, in fact, comprises various elements such (i) identification of the project, (ii) technical and financial appraisal of the project, (iii) economic or socio-economic appraisal of the project when necessary, (iv) proper formulation of the project,(v) plan for implementation of the project, (vi) actual implementation of the project, (vii) monitoring the implementation to see that the project has not deviated considerably from the pre-defined targets and budgeted resources and time, (viii) control action/rectification action for the deviations, and (ix) evaluation either at the end of the project or few years after the completion of the project to gain hindsight as to what went right or wrong vis-à-vis the predefined objectives of the project and what lessons can be learnt so as to transmit the same knowledge to other similar or related projects to be executed in future.

Project Management in India

Project management as a science seems to have evolved around the Second World War and got much importance due to the various nuclear, aerospace, and other defense programmes of the United State in the 1950s and 1960s. The principles underlying project management have been utilized also by industry and by various public systems in the developed countries. Project management in India started gaining momentum around the mid 1960s. It is yet to gain full-fledged acceptance by industry, and more so by our public systems.

Although we are approaching the year 2000, still many project feasibilities in large private industries and in public systems are done without the necessary attention to the basics, and lacking in adequate rigour and attention to details. A feasibility study gone wrong is a perennial source of problems for the project during its implementation and its operation. There may be delays in completion and cost over runs. There may be problems in scales and operating revenues, break-even volumes, actually available capacities and profits before tax. Other problems could be concerning continuation of the availability of raw materials, appropriate quality of manpower, proper strategic alliances, proper technology transfer, and adaptation and adsorption. In public systems, the proposed benefits of the project may not reach the intended people.

Element of feasibility analysis

The first step of project management is project identification and appraisal which is also often called project feasibility analysis. This comprises the following elements:

1. Generation of project ideas
2. Screening of the generated ideas
3. Detailed evaluation of the screened project ideas.

Generation of Project Ideas

This first step, besides providing an inventory of ideas, also facilitates the basis structuring process, so that only the 'right' projects enter into further detailed analysis. The generation of project ideas can come only through the objectives which need to be achieved by the authorities planning the investment in the project. The basis structuring process is provided by the "objectives" of the nation or a region or an organization. Unless a clarity of the objectives (either long-run or short-run) is achieved, the crucial project ideas may not be considered. The resources available are limited whether it is a small organization, or a region or a nation. Therefore, a thorough exercise right in the beginning of the generation of project ideas is absolutely essential, if the limited resources are to be properly utilized. A project is generally heavy-investment and long-term proposition unless it happens to be short-term project such as a maintenance project. For instance, a nation has to be clear whether it want to invest in heavy industry which will yield fruits only after a very long term, or whether it wants to invest heavily in short-term yielding and labour-intensive projects in agricultural or rural development. Even in agriculture, one may think of either a major irrigation or minor irrigation projects in terms of their relative emphasis. The overall and specific objectives of the national or regional or organizational policy drive the ideas-generating machine.

A company has to ask, for instance, 'What kind of business am I in.' because the company cannot have a number of business due to imitation of monetary resources. A proper target-market orientation or market-segmentation probably needs to be done in a broad manner right in the beginning of the exercise of project management. The public works projects may be the result of two broad categories of policy objectives: (1) socio-economic policy objectives (2) internal and external security policy objectives. The former objective of socio-economic policy could by brought about by: (i) providing extension of market and achieving higher level of utilization of resources, and (ii) by increasing factor and product mobility. The second objective of improving internal and external security can be brought about by the Public Works Department by providing extended facilities for the mobility of security resources. Such objectives need to be concretely spelt out and the priorities amongst the objectives should be established; otherwise the idea generation may be an exercise in the wilderness.

During the idea-generation stage, the ideas arising within the objectives need to be tempered or filtered simultaneously by the constraints present for the nation or the region or the organization. The constraints are of the following types:

1. Constraints of physical resources,
2. constraints of human resources and organizational (structural/cultural) constraints, and
3. Constraints of financial resources.

The various project ideas must lie within the limits defined by the constraints. The effect of this is to limit the number of ideas to a feasible minimum.

Screening

The process of generating ideas should, so far, have been carried out without any inhibitions and preconceived notions, excepting the guiding and creative influence of objectives and constraints. This process should, by now, provide the analyst with enough ideas to work on.

Not all project idea need to be analyzed in detail, though. At a point of time, for a particular region, society, nation, or for an organization certain things are of higher priority than others. For instance, in the border areas of our country, the priority is for security against external aggression. Development of the economy of the region would be of second priority. Of course, much depends upon the particular time, the internal and external political affairs of the region or state, or the environment in which the organization or company may be working, etc. But it should be understood that the measures of priorities, however, crude will provide the analyst with a means to find out clearly which project idea needs to be primarily considered and which should not be of secondary or tertiary interest. These primary projects provide us with a shorter list of project-ideas that need to be evaluated further in much detail.

Another screening which needs to be applied to this short-list is the detailed analysis of the existing facilities thus eliminating project ideas which would essentially be duplications of the existing ones. In this analysis the following criterion may be applied.

The criterion is that of effective capacity, which is weighing various element of the existing facilities to determine how adequately the priority objectives are being met. A new project should be considered to the extent the existing facilities fall short of the demand for the particular priority objective. The criterion of effective capacity can be easily understood for the public systems projects. For commercial organization these may need to be supplemented by a thorough study of the market. Three questions are important:

1. How big is the market?
2. How much is it likely to grow?
3. How much of it can the project accommodate?

For new projects, one may study import statistics, the existing indigenous production, the end-use for which the product or the derived products might be but, the demand for related or substitute products, the market competition, the demographic and economic factors, etc. The possibilities of expanding the market by improvement in the quality of the product, or by generation cost economies through the use of cheaper raw materials, cheaper labour; or the cost advantages due to particular location should be borne in mind while answering these market-oriented questions. Such analysis of the market will eliminate or screen some of the projects from further detailed final considerations.

Detailed Evaluation

This essentially involves the following steps:

1. Analysis of technical feasibility
2. Measurement of cost
3. Measurement of benefits
4. Comparison of the benefits and costs

Technical Feasibility

Technical feasibility is broad-level, to start with, to determine what kind of technology would be needed for the different earlier screened project-ideas. The questions could be for example : Is there enough water to construct a dam and a power station? What is the rain fall in the catchments area? What kind of terrain is it? Therefore, what kind of dam could be constricted? In it technically possible to construct a dam and power station in that region? What seepage is expected in irrigation-canals? If it is a road-building project, then one may investigate: What is the topography of the region? Are these flood in that region (washing out or blocking the road periodically)? etc. Therefore, is it technically feasible to construct such a road? Such analysis should be done with the help of engineers or scientists in the field who have the competence and up-to-date knowledge to assess the technology available. If a project is found to involve such technical requirements which may not be indigenously available or may be available at only a very high premium from foreign countries, it can be avoided keeping in view the objectives and priorities of the nation, region or organization. Speaking of Government projects or national or regional level projects, one may be justified in experimenting with new technology or very high prices imported technology, but, such justification may not be there for projects of the profit-oriented private industry. The private industry may avoid experimental or obsolescent projects. New process or machinery, although apparently quite well tested under laboratory or pilot-plant conditions, may not produce the desired results under commercial mass production conditions. Commercial criteria and governmental or public systems criteria may often be quite different.

Capital and Operating Costs

After having done a preliminary technical feasibility survey, one may proceed with the measurement of costs, benefits and their comparison for different projects.

To a private organization, costs include capital as well as operating expenses. The costs may be that of land, housing, machinery, raw material, fuel, power, labour, water, transportation, etc. These different aspects of costs need to be investigated not only for one but several alternate locations, including cost on delivery of imported items. It should be remembered that the costs include not only equipment and other fixed costs, input materials and labour, but also transportation and other aspects. Therefore, a plant or site location problem is inevitably connected with a cost feasibility or financial feasibility analysis.

While investigating the proposed plant sites, the estimates of the total production costs in several alternative output sizes should be calculator. Sometimes, there may be a conflict between the plant size needed for meeting the economic demand and the size needed to obtain the optimum cost of production. In such cases a size which would be some what larger than the existing market can justify, and somewhat smaller than that required for lower cost production is recommended. This financial feasibility phase of investigation involves a considerable amount of field work but the extent of such an analysis should not exceed 1 to 2% of the total possible project cost.

The working capital requirements may also be estimated on the basis of the volume of production expected and the estimated production cost, the length of time cycle from the moment the raw material enters the plant till the customer pays for the goods the payments for the supplies and labour which must be made during this span of time, etc.

The benefits for the private organizations are the sales revenues which could be estimated after the estimation of sales volume based on production capability, product quality, size of the market, amount of competition in the market, product price and many other internal and external environmental factors. It should also be noted that the full capacity can be achieved over a period of time, and also that the market can be created only slowly. Therefore, the slow growth of production capacity as well as that of the market capacity should be taken into account while calculating either the revenues or costs.

Especially for the private organizations, it is imperative that in addition to the cost-benefit analysis, a rigorous cash-flow analysis is done for the short-term and long-term future. Because, many a time the profitability may be good but the but the timings of the cash outflows and inflows and their magnitudes may not match.

Social cost-benefit analysis

For public system projects, particularly involving projects with social objectives and Government projects, the market is the society at large. For instance, for railway projects, the market comprises passengers and the freight transport user. Therefore, the considerations of market could be quite different from that of private organizations. In addition, not all costs or benefits can be measured only in financial terms, they should be viewed in terms of the disadvantages and advantages to the society over a long range of time. Such an analysis which keeps in view the larger interest of the society is termed as Social Cost-Benefit Analysis and is an integral part of any public systems project formulation procedure.

For Social Cost-Benefit Analysis the costs expressed at market prices need many adjustments to reflect the real cost. The taxes, fees, cess, duties, etc. on various commodities have to be excluded from the costs. The market price may not reflect the opportunity costs of labour due to various wage laws. The real costs of unskilled labour may be less than the market wages, and those of the skilled labour may be more than that of the market wages. If the labour employed on a project has no other employment possibility, then the cost of the labour in social terms may be zero. Only those costs need to be considered where the scarce resources are being weaned away form other areas of the economy or other projects. The cost of environmental damage should also figure in the social cost-benefit analysis. Extraction of either iron ore or the mining of coal might seem to be lucrative financial projects; but some of them might to such considerations, the strip-mining of coal has been totally abandoned. USA is one such example. The foreign-exchange component cannot be costed by the pegged value of the exchange rate. It may need to be costed at a higher rate which reflects the true conditions in the foreign exchange market.

Similar to the measurement of cost, the measurement of benefit is fraught with a number of difficulties while dealing with social cost-benefit analysis. There are direct benefits as well as indirect benefits and many of them cannot easily be expressed in monetary terms as they are non-marketable public goods and have no price equivalence. For instance, the major benefits of a public-works highway project are: (1) greater mobility for people and goods thus leading to economic development, (2) benefits of fast, cheaper, comfortable and reliable transport facility with fewer expenses less damage to goods.

The major benefits (for the above public works highway project), which are direct, can be calculated in terms in terms of increase in income due to: (a) increase in movement of various commodities, (b) increase in passenger traffic. In case of the 'new road, it may be calculated with the following equation: $y = x\ L\ e$, where Y= Income

x = Average number of vehicles per annum both ways

L = Length of new roads

e = Average earnings per vehicle kilometre

The income for goods and passengers can be estimated separately as the values of x and e are likely to be different in each case. The indirect benefit such as the comforts, convenience, reliability, etc. cannot be well expressed monetarily and are therefore quite often excluded from the analysis.

Conceptual Problems and Difficulties

The conceptual problems and difficulties in doing a social cost-benefit analysis can be summarized:

1. Some benefits and costs are not measurable in monetary terms.

2. When it is a situation of multiple projects, which is true in the case of many governmental or public systems, it is difficult to apportion or allocate the expected benefits amongst the different projects. This is so because the exact component of the expected benefits may not be directly attributable to each individual project. The benefit expected may be as a result of the integrated development mental projects. For example, we all know that rural development is the result of various projects such as major irrigation, minor irrigation, providing infrastructure facilities, credit facilities, provision of fertilizers and seeds, development of rural industries, and the integration of a host of other such development projects to get the desired beneficial effect. In such cases, the location of the developmental benefits to any one of the projects is definitely a difficult exercise.

3. Public systems projects, which are development-oriented projects, may alter the income distribution of the people who make use of these projects. This redistribution of income may alter the price structure significantly from what it was at the time of the initial project feasibility analysis.

4. We have seen in Chapter 4 that a particular discount rate of interest is assumed in the calculations. This assumed rate of interest of the comparison of costs and benefits, is actually as assumption regarding the public's time preference rate of interest: which means that it is the rare of interest to be charged for the future flow of benefits which will come as a result of the sacrifice of current consumption by the consumers (i.e. public). This expression of time-preference also raise questions regarding the entire cost-benefit comparison and feasibility analysis.

Inspite of such difficulties of applying the cost-benefit principles to public systems projects, the objective of such analysis is sound. In the absence of such analysis, we shall only be disregarding the effect of various public projects on the people for whom it is primarily meant. Moreover, for many public projects for instance, road building, there is little or no financial return to be gained. In such case, there is no alternative but to resort to social cost-benefit analysis since financial analysis is either out of the question or not of much help.

The cost-benefit information can be used to rank the technically feasible projects and thus select projects optimally. The analysis may be Financial Feasibility Analysis and/or Social Cost-Benefit Analysis. The principles of capital budgeting and the choice of project under limited availability of funds.

Projects which look financially feasible, may need to be looked at more rigorously through Technical Feasibility Analysis. The idea is to screen the project initially with a broad technical and financial analysis. Those that are obviously not very good ideas may thus be rejected and rigorous analysis of technical and financial of economic feasibility can be applied to the remaining project-ideas.

Project Formulation

Although project formulation and appraisal process was mentioned in a step-wise or sequential fashion. It should be emphasized that there is much feedback or to and-fro interaction in the entire project formulation process. The processes of considering financial, manpower, organizational or other resource constraints, the process of technical feasibility and the processes of the financial, and socio-economic feasibility all have various feedbacks. There are various grey areas within all these considerations and there are many flexibilities within the constraints and therefore the entire project formulation and appraisal process is a multi-round exercise where all the relevant aspects of checking the feasibility within the constraints and therefore the entire project formulation and appraisal process is a multi-round exercise where all the relevant aspects of checking the feasibility and relative comparison of the projects are taken care of.

Long Term & Short Term Problems of Operations Management

Product Safety & Increasing Consumerism

The great majority of organizations provide us with goods and services which perform as expected, and are of good value, and are safe in use. However, there will always be some goods and services which are unsatisfactory and possibly unsafe in certain applications.

The upsurge in consumer safety consciousness which we are still seeing today had its biggest boost from the publication of Ralph Nader's book, Unsafe at Any Speed, which referred to General Motors' subcompact car, the Corvair. This book, published in 1965, in fact, only made the point that small cars are not as safe as large cars. Nonetheless, it shocked the automobile industry and drove the Corvair off the market. Among its immediate effects was the passage of new automobile safety laws which required considerable redesigning of automobiles.

This interest in consumer safety quickly spread out in many directions. Very soon people were calling attention to the hazards in use of any number of other products. Instances were found where toys which children often put in their mouths and chewed on were painted with lead based paint, which could give them lead poisoning. Other toys were found to have sharp edges which could cause cuts, and realistic toy cookstoves were found which could burn children.

The food industry also came in for attention. Questions were raised over the possible health hazards of artificial coloring matter, of sweeteners, and of preservatives put into foods. Ecologists and environmentalists joined in with their interest in reducing air and water pollution and in the preservation of wildlife.

The public has, on the whole, been favorable and has supported these actions. Consequently, manufacturers and service organisations are redoubling their efforts to comply with the regulations and to improve their products and services.

The point to these examples is that the design of products and services is no longer wholly a matter of an organization's managers responding to the needs of the market place, as they see such needs. They have to manage within the framework of the requirements that society imposes on them through government regulations and pressures from consumer and environmental groups.

Negative aspects of regulation

From a managerial point of view, there are two serious negative aspects to the consumer protection wave. First is the cost of complying with the regulations. Maruti Udyog reports that today's automobiles each cost Rs. 21,000 more to make because of all of the extras required by emission and safety regulations. Thermal Power Stations spend many millions for "scrubbers" to keep particulate matter out of their smoke chimneys. The government regulators often ask for near perfection when something less would be satisfactory and could be achieved at much lower cost.

The second negative is the wave of lawsuits claiming damages from injuries from products which are claimed to be faulty. These have increased in recent years, and judges have been awarding large claims which were not awarded before the consumer protection wave. Today it almost certain that consumer courts take the view that if an accident has happened it is the fault of the maker of the product or provider of the service.

In any case, manufacturers need to do their best to be sure that their products are safe to use, just as service people must try to render good service. Product designers need to use safe materials and to put in appropriate safety guards. Both designers and lawyers should probably decide upon warning labels and look over advertising claims to be sure that they are not misleading in any way and that they include appropriate warnings of dangers. Records also need to be kept of complaints and of responsive actions, and appropriate liability insurance should be carried.

Nor are the makers of products relieved from their obligation to do their best to keep the users of their products from having accidents by the fact that it is really unfair to blame product manufacturers for most accidents. Peopl cause accidents far, far more often than products cause accidents. According to the National Safety Council, unsafe practices by people are involved in perhaps as many as 90 percent of all accidents.

People don't get their brakes fixed and then have accidents from faulty brakes. Or they drive their cars too fast or after drinking too much alcohol (For example, Lady Diana's death in 1997 in a similar car accident). Or they smoke in bed. Or they leave open bottles of aspirin around children. Or the housewife goes away and leaves the electric iron turned on. Or people misuse a product, or use it for purposes for which it was never intended, and then. if it fails, they blame the manufacturer.

None of these acts of carelessness, however, excuse the manufacturers from making the safest product they can. In some cases this means that cheaply made flimsy products will have to be discontinued even if they are in demand since such products are likely to be dangerous in use.

2

Automation and Operations Management

Introduction

Selection, acquisition and management of production technology is a significant part of production and operations management. A detailed discussion of automation, its nature, types of automated machines, automated production systems, factories of the future and other related automation issues are discussed in this unit.

Nature of Automation

Traditionally, automation has been understood as mere replacement of labour by machines. This perception has now changed. Today, automation projects are initiated not just for labour cost savings, but also for improved product quality, fast production and delivery of products and increased product flexibility.

Simply stated, automation refers to the technique of operating or controlling a productive process by electronic devices and reducing human intervention to the minimum. Human contribution to production comprises two kinds of effort – physical and mental. The physical contribution or muscle power was taken over by machines which came to be increasingly used after the Industrial Revolution. The 'mental' contribution to production is now taken over by electronic devices, chiefly computers, which are often known as giant brains. With the advent of automation, the second Industrial Revolution has begun.

In a fully automated plant, all the aspects of manufacturing, that is feed, production, information and control, are carried on by computers, watch-dogged by only a few men who glance occasionally at a control panel or sweep the cuttings. However, the extent of automation varies from plant to plant, and depends on the willingness and capacity of the management cooperation of the workers and their trade unions, and the general economic conditions of the country. *"In the simplest sense"*, writes Ruddell Reed, *"automation is nothing more than the extension of the principles of mechanization to the integration of machines, one with another in such a manner as to have the group operate as an individual processing and control unit".* At the other extreme, automation is the application of electronic digital computer control systems, which not only read the individual measurement devices but analyse the data as received from the devices, reach a decision, and adjust the control values or motors to proper settings for projected optimum results. Between these extremes are a number of levels of levels of application of *automation techniques and principles".*

In practice, automation may assume three distinct forms, namely, *integration, feedback control and computer technology. Integration* involves processes in which the finished product is moved automatically, untouched by human hands, from one state to another; for example industries handling liquids, gases, powdered goods such as oil and chemical industries. *Feedback control* is mainly an electronic process by which any error or diversion of the machine from a planned performance is automatically corrected. These controls, called *'servo mechanisms',* are highly developed in chemical industries and operate the multitude of mechanisms involved in these industrial processes. Third, the *computer technology* depends on the use of electronically operated machines capable of recording and classifying information, and when required, drawing conclusions from this information.

Automation and Mechanisation

The terms *automation* and *mechanisation* are often understood as synonymous in their meaning. But there is a difference between the two. Mechanisation, as mentioned earlier, only replaces the muscle power of labour but not the labour itself. The use of a pressure cooker to cook food in the house eliminates the labour of the housewife; but she has to be there before the cooker is placed on the stove and after it is removed in order to complete the process of cooking. The use of a bicycle, too, is an example of mechanization. A bicycle may eliminate physical walking and increases the speed at which a person travels; but the rider is not dispensed with. In a factory, *feed, inspection, information and control* – these aspects of manufacturing may be looked after by labour, though mechanization attends to the production aspect. But, in automation, all the aspects of manufacturing, as mentioned earlier, are carried on by computers. The human contribution is reduced to the minimum. The worker in an automated plant simply observes the work of the machines, even as a traffic constable merely stands and observes the traffic at a busy traffic island or intersection while its actual regulation and control are governed by the automatic signaling system. Nevertheless, mechanization and automation go together, for automation presupposes the use of machines on a large scale.

Automation and Rationalisation

In the same way, there is a difference between rationalisation and automation. In its simplest sense, *rationalisation* refers to doing things on a rational and scientific basis. It does not necessarily involve the replacement of labour by machines. If the loan application of a customer in a branch of a bank is considered by the branch manager himself and not forwarded in a time consuming and wasteful procedure to the head office, this is rationalisation. But *automation,* as observed earlier, involves an increasing and large-scale use of machines and the consequent displacement of labour. Though rationalisation and automation may be regarded as two separate concepts, the effect they have on employment and labour is similar, though not of the same magnitude. In a sense, automation may be considered a part of the wider concept of rationalization. It is possible to conceive of rationalisation taking place in an establishment without any significant resort to automation and capital-intensive devices; but automation will necessarily be the higher reach of rationalisation. Both will depend upon the nature of the technological development and the considerations which are consciously brought to bear upon practical policy in the matter of the choice of techniques.

Scope of Automation

A question often raised is: In what kinds of activities should the new technology be applied? Automation may be applied to almost all the activities – to manufacturing, insurance, banks, wholesale and retail distribution, communications, educational institutions and so forth. The only exception is a firm which is faced with seasonality – where production consists of short runs of varying items or where operators lead the machines and apply a great deal of skill and judgment (as in the garment industries) – then the idea of automation is far off. Add to this factor, the inability of smaller firms to raise money easily and the lack of specialised staff assistance – then automation recedes still further as a goal.

Proliferation of Automation

The field of automation is mushrooming, particularly in the advanced countries. In the US for example, the number of robots increased to 100,000 in 1990 from 19,000 in 1995. The US is far behind Japan in this respect, The Japanese manufacturers of automated production systems are much ahead of their US counterparts.

Automated Machines

The mushrooming of industrial automation has brought a myriad of automatic machines with diverse features. Particular emphasis needs to be made about machines attachment, numerically controlled (NC) machines, robots, automated quality control inspection, automated identification systems (AIS) and automatic process controls. Table 1.1 describes each type with examples.

Machine Attachments

These are usually inexpensive add-ons to machines that reduce the amount of human effort and time required to perform an operation. These appendages represent the oldest technology in automation and are generally found in all production systems.

Table 1.11. Types of Automatic Machines.

	Types of Machines	Description	Examples
1.	Machine attachments.	Machines that reduce human effort with machine effort and typically perform from one to a few simple operations.	Magazine feed attachments, quick cutting and grasping devices for lathes, strip feeders for stamping machines, vibrating hoppers with scales that drop charges of chemicals into waiting containers.
2.	Numerically controlled (N/C) machines	Machines with control systems that read instructions and translate them into machines operations.	Lathes, boring mills, tire building machines, curing machines, weaving machines
3.	Robots.	General – purpose, reprogrammable, multifunction manipulators that possess some human like physiological characteristics.	Machines that weld, paint, assemble, inspect for quality, grasp, transport and store.
4.	Automated quality control inspection	Automated machines that perform part or all of the inspection process.	Electronic circuit checks, computer driven checks, weighting robots, flexible inspection.
5.	Automatic identification systems (AIS).	Technologies used in automatic acquisition of product data for entry into a computer.	Bar-coding systems, inventory counting, data entry for shop floor control, systems for adjusting settings of production machines.
6.	Automated process controls	Computer systems that receive data on the production process and send adjustments to process settings.	Control systems for rolling mills in the manufacturing, calendars in plastic film processing, cracking units in oil refineries.

Numerically Controlled (NC Machines)

These machines are pre-programmed through microcomputers to perform a cycle of operations repeatedly. The machines have a control system that reads the instructions and then translates them into machine operations. Machine settings are achieved by the control system rather than by human beings.

In computer numerically controlled machines (CNC), information storage is transferred from the punched tape to the flexible memory of a computer.

Advantage of CNC machines Over NC machines.

1. Instructions may be stored and handled more efficiently with a data cartridge or floppy disc memory.
2. The microcomputer system may be programmed to perform functions, beyond simple controlling of the machines.
3. Real-time and off-line diagnostic possibilities may be built into the CNC system.
4. Machining data and operator instructions may be displayed on a screen as part of the system.

Direct Numeric Control also known as Distributed Numerical Control (DNC) places a battery of machines under the control of a single computer (Central main frame computer). Machines can be of different types and programmed to carry out different tasks.

The central main frame computer supplies the part programs to the individual CNC machines through communication lines which also provide for feedback of production and machine tool status from the shop floor.

DNC systems provide rapid, real-time feedback on problems as they occur enabling immediate corrective action to be initiated. The ability to store massive data on programmes and to retrieve the data quickly is another significant advantage of DNC system.

Robots

Robots are human like machines that perform production tasks. Specifically, robot is a programmable machine, which means that a sequence of moves can be preset to be repeated time after time, then reset again to perform another set of moves. The brain is a micro computer which guides the machine through its predetermined operations. Robots replace human beings for some very heavy, dirty, dangerous, unpleasant or monotonous tasks. The science of selecting robot for various used – and knowing when not to use them – is called *robotics.*

Robots are advantageous as they not only relieve human beings from the burden of attending to dirty and dangerous tasks; they can also produce products of better quality than workers can do. Robots can produce better quality products because they are more predictable and perform the same operations precisely and repeatedly without fatigue.

Automated Quality Control Inspection

Quality control inspection systems are machines that have been integrated into the inspection of products for quality control purposes. These systems perform a wide range of tests and inspections and are found in many industries. They can be used to take physical dimensions of parts, compare the measurements to standards, and determine whether the parts meet quality specifications. Similarly, these machines can be used to check the performance of electronic circuits. For example, in the computer industry, computers are checked by software that tests every function that the computers must perform. These automated machines ensure 100 present inspection which in turn guarantee improved product quality.

Automated Identification System (AIS)

These comprise bar codes, radio frequencies, magnetic stripes, optical character recognition, and machine vision which help sense and feed data into computers. Data are read from products, documents, parts and containers without the need for workers to rear or interpret the data. AIS are becoming more commonplace in warehouses, shop floors of factories, retailing and wholesaling and a variety of other applications. While the cost of the AIS hardware is not high, the cost of developing computer software and computer data base is high, and such software is needed to make AIS effective.

Automated Process Controls

Automated process controls use sensors to obtain measures of the performance of industrial processes, they compare these measures to standards within stored computer software programmes, and when the performance varies significantly from standards, they send signals that change the settings of the processes. Such systems have been in use for many years in the chemical processing, petroleum-refining and paper industries.

With the increasing use of computer-aided design and computer aided manufacturing (CAD/CAM) systems, automated process controls have become important in other industries as well. Even in discrete-unit manufacturing, the settings of individual machines and groups of machines can now be sensed and changed as necessary to provide products of uniform dimensions and other characteristics.

CAD/CAM Systems

Computer Aided Design (CAD) is the use of computers in interactive engineering drawing and storage of designs. Programmes complete the layout, section views of a part and its relationship with other parts.

CAD is concerned with the automation of certain phases of product design and its use is growing as more and more powerful software is being developed.

Advantages of CAD :

(a) Increased productivity of designers
(b) Improved quality of designs
(c) Improvement in product standardization and design documentation.
(d) Creation of a manufacturing database.

Computer Aided Manufacturing (CAM) is concerned with automating the planning and controlling of production. CAM controls the machine tools on the shop floor. The machines perform a variety of operations and receive instructions from a computer on the sequence and specification of operations. The computer programs can be stored in the manufacturing database, retrieved, updated and revised as components are added or redesigned and transmitted electronically in house or externally by satellite to other divisions/facilities.

Benefits from CAM :

(a) Instructions from a computer are more reliable than those from a skilled operator.
(b) Product quality is more consistent from unit to unit.
(c) Close tolerances can be obtained.
(d) Lowe labour costs because of less operator time.

CAD/CAM implies a merger of CAD and CAM and the interaction between the two systems. The important result of this merger is the automation of the transition from product design to manufacturing. New products can be designed quickly as market demands change. And because these new products designs are store in a common database, through CAM, the new products can be introduced into production much more quickly and with less expense. Thus, CAD/CAM promises greater product flexibility, lower production costs and improved product quality.

Automated Production Systems

The technology of automation has indeed spawned newer and non-sophisticated machines. Increasingly, these machines are getting lined up for broader purposes. Four categories of machines are discernible : automated flow lines, automated assembly systems, flexible manufacturing systems, automated storage and retrieval systems.

Automated Flow Lines

In this, several automated machines are linked together by automated parts transfer and handling machines.

The individual machines on the line, use automated raw materials feeders and automatically carry out their operations without the need for human intervention. As each machine completes its operations, partly completed parts are automatically transferred to the next machine on the line in a fixed sequence until the work of the line is finished. These systems are generally used to produce an entire major component, for example, rear axle housings for trucks. They are common in the automobile industry.

Automated flow lines are also called as fixed automation or hard automation in as much as the lines of machines are designed to produce one type of component or product. These demand high investment and are highly inflexible. Hence, these machines are justified when demand for the product is high, stable and predictable. But the demand is never stable. Shortened product life cycles and changes in production technology render the fixed automation lines unpopular and call for flexible manufacturing systems.

Automated Assembly Lines

Here, the automated assembly machines are linked together by automated materials-handling equipment. Materials are automatically fed to each machine, which is some type of robot, which joins one or more materials, parts, or assemblies. Then the part-completed work is automatically transferred to the next assembly machine. This process is repeated until the whole assembly is completed. The purpose of these systems is to produce major assemblies or even completed products.

Product-design modifications are essential to make the automated assembly system successful. Table 1.12 shows the principles to be observed while redesigning products for automated assembly

Three advantages are claimed in favour of automated assembly systems. First, these systems can provide manufacturers with low per unit production costs, improved product quality, and quicker production rates.

Table 1.12. Principles of Product Redesign.

1.Reduce the amount of assembly required.
2.Reduce the number of fasteners required.
3.Design components to be automatically delivered and positioned.
4.Design products for layered assembly and vertical insertion of parts.
5.Design parts so that they are self-aligning.
6.Design products into major modules for production.
7.Increa se the quality of components.

Second, because some of the machines tend to be standard robots that are available at competitive rates, initial investment is not high. Third, these robots can be reprogrammed to other products and operations, thereby reducing the dependence on stable product demand.

Flexible Manufacturing Systems (FMS)

FMS are groups of production machines, arranged in a sequence, connected by automated material handling and transferring machines and integrated by a computer system. To elaborate, FMS is a computer controlled system. It contains several work-stations, each geared to different operations. Work-station machines are automated and programmable. Automated materials-handling equipment move components to the appropriate work-station, then on to the programmed machines that select, position and actuate the specific tools for each job. Hundreds of tool options are available. Once the machine has finished one batch, the computer signals the next quantity or component, and the machine automatically repositions and retools accordingly. Meanwhile, the just finished batch is automatically transferred to the next work station its routing.

An FMS is generally appropriate when.

1. All products are variations of a stable basic design;
2. All products utilise the same family of components;
3. The number of components is only moderate (10 to 50);
4. The volume of each component is moderate (1,000 to 30,000 units annually), but in lot sizes as small as one unit.

FMS technology can help produce moderate variety of products in modest volumes, that too quickly and with high quality. Operating costs also can be reduced with and FMS; lower direct labour costs lead to lower manufacturing costs. But FMS require very large investments in equipment, planning and control systems, and human resources.

Automated Storage and Retrieval Systems (ASRS)

These are systems meant for receiving orders for materials from anywhere in operations, collecting the materials from locations within a warehouse, and delivering the materials to work stations in operations.

ASRS has three major elements :

1. *Computer and communication systems :* These systems are used for placing orders for materials, locating the materials in storage, giving commands for delivery of the materials to locations in operations and adjusting inventory records showing the amount and location of materials.

2. *Automated materials handling and delivery systems :* These systems are automatically loaded with containers of materials from operations and deliver them to the warehouse. Similarly, the are automatically loaded with orders of materials at the warehouse and deliver orders to work stations in operations.

3. *Storage and retrieval systems in warehouse :* Warehouses store materials in standard size containers that contain fixed amounts of each material. For example, a container of a particular type of plastic moulding would always contain 100 parts. These containers are arranged according to a location address scheme that allows the location of each material to be precisely determined by a computer. A storage and retrieval (S/R) machine receives commands from a computer, gets containers of materials from a pick-up point in the warehouse, delivers materials to their assigned location in the warehouse and places them in their location. Similarly, S/R machines locate containers of materials in storage, remove containers from storage and deliver containers to a deposit point in the warehouse.

The benefits of ASRS are increased storage capacity, increased system throughput, reduced labour cost and improved product quality.

Automation Issues

Automation poses several issues. The major area requiring decisions are (a) high tech, mid-tech, or law-tech production, (b) building manufacturing flexibility, (c) justifying automation projects, (d) deciding among alternatives and (e) managing technological change.

High-tech, Mid-tech or Low-tech Production

One of the issues to be resolved relates to high-tech, mid-tech or low-tech production. This is a serious problem, because, there are factories using very old technology but doing well. There are others with latest technology but performing poorly. This does not mean that production technology has no impact on a company's profitability. The following conclusions are relevant in this context :

(i) Automation, however advanced it may be, cannot be substitute for good management.

(ii) Is not technically feasible to automate some operations. For example, in garment industry cutting, assembling and sewing are not yet automated.

(iii) Some automation projects may prone to be failure. Companies which embark on automation may poorly manage the implementation of the automated machinery. Consequently, they prove to be worse off than they were before automation.

However, it may be concluded that all companies must keep their production processes updated as production technology advances. To do otherwise, means that the future of the companies would be in jeopardy, because they must assume that the competitors will seize the strategic advantage offered by switching to advanced technology.

Building Manufacturing Flexibility

Manufacturing flexibility refers to all types of equipment and production systems that provide the ability to respond to changing market needs. Manufacturing flexibility is advantageous as it enables quick execution of customer orders; production capacity can be developed and introduced into production quickly and inexpensively in response to shifting market needs.

The following machines of production systems make the manufacturing system flexible:

1. N/C machines.
2. Programmable and reprogrammable robots.
3. Automatic quality control inspection.
4. Automatic identification system (AIS).
5. Automated process controls.
6. Automatic assembly systems.
7. Flexible manufacturing systems (FMS).
8. Automatic storage and retrieval systems (ASRS).
9. CAD/CAM.
10. Computer integrated manufacturing (CIM).

These machines and production systems represent the core of manufacturing flexibility. They involve huge investments. Such huge investment is worth because the machines and systems help achieve low unit cost and high profitability.

Justifying Automation Projects

Till now, traditional capital-budgeting techniques such as payback period, net present value, internal rate of return and the like have been used to evaluate and decide upon investment in new capital projects. These techniques have tended to lead managers to expand present facilities with existing technology, rather than build new facilities with new production technology. Carrying the approach to its extreme, companies end up with huge unwieldy, highly centralised production facilities based on outdated production technology.

From now onwards, decisions on new projects should not be based on conventional appraisal techniques. Rather, investing in new technology must be seen as a long-term strategic choice for the company. These choices like other major strategic business decisions, cannot be based solely on a simple payback formula. Although returns on investment will continue to be an important criterion for new investment decisions, the term *return* should take extended meaning. Improved product quality, faster delivery of customer orders, increased manufacturing flexibility, reduced production costs, increased market share and other advantages will have to be factored into the future capital budgeting decisions. Investment in new technology must be seen as a way of changing the factory into a competitive weapon that assists the corporation in achieving its strategic objectives.

Deciding among Automation Alternatives

Three approaches that are commonly used in the industry today are economic analysis, rating scale approach and relative aggregate scores approach :

(i) Economic analysis involves cost comparisons of processing alternatives, the concept of operating leverage, break-even analysis and financial analysis.

(ii) Rating scale approach. Important factors that must be considered are:

   (a) Economic factors which provide with some idea of the direct impact of automation alternative on profitability. The focus is on cash flows, annual fixed costs, variable cost per unit, average production cost per unit or total annual production costs at the forecasted production levels but the intention is to determine the direct impact on profitability. Break-even analysis and financial analysis are frequently used.
   (b) Effect on market share.
   (c) Effect on product quality.
   (d) Effect on manufacturing flexibility.
   (e) Effect on labour relations.
   (f) Amount of time required for implementation.
   (g) Effect of automation on on-going production.
   (h) Amount of capital required.

   A five point rating scale is used with score of 5 for excellent, 4 for good, 3 for average, 2 for below average and 1 for poor.

   The rating scale approach requires decision makers to weigh the factors for each alternative.

(iii) Relative aggregate – scores approach.

This approach requires that, managers state the factors, that will be considered in the decision and the weights of each factor before the decision is made. Only the alternative that are fundamentally sound and feasible should be included in the analysis.

Relative scores approach can be best illustrated by the following table:

Managing Technological Change

Any change is resisted and technological change is not exception. Management will find that automating a plant is more expensive and more difficult than expected. The following suggestions, however, help implement raw projects with less difficulty and least resistance.

Table 1.13. Relative Aggregate Approach to Compare Automation Alternatives.

Automation Factors	Factor weights	Automated Flow Line			FMS		
		Economic data	Scores	Weighted scores	Economic data	Scores	Weighted scores
Unit production costs	0.30	Rs.59.40	1.00*	0.300	Rs.63.02	0.943	0.283
Market share	0.10		1.00	0.100		0.800	0.080
Product quality	0.10		0.80	0.080		0.800	0.080
Product flexibility	0.20		0.40	0.080		0.800	0.060
Volume flexibility	0.05		0.80	0.040		0.400	0.020
Labour relationship	0.05		0.60	0.030		0.600	0.030
Implementation time	0.10		0.60	0.060		0.800	0.080
Existing operation	0.05		1.00	0.050		1.000	0.050
Capital requirements	0.05		0.60	0.030		0.700	0.035
Total	1.00			0.770			0.818

$$\text{*Scores for FMS for unit production cost} = \frac{59.40}{63.02} = 0.943$$

1. Have a master plan for automation. The plan should indicate what operations to automate, when and in what sequence to automate each area of the business, and how the organisation and its products, marketing and other business units will have to change because of automation.
2. Recognise that there are risks in automation. Two risks which need recognition are the risk of radical obsolescence and the danger that competitors will easily copy new technology.
3. Have a separate technology department. This unit will disseminate information about new technology; become an advocate for new technology adoption; lead the way in educating and training others about new technology, and provide the technical assistance necessary for the installation and implementation of advanced technology equipment.
4. Allow enough time for learning how to install, tool, debug, programme and otherwise get an automated machine upto production speed. Do not rush through the completion of automation projects.
5. Automating everything at once is not wise. Phasing out installation is advantageous so that what is learnt from one project can be applied to another project. By allowing plenty of time, the frequency of missed scheduled dates, organisation frustration and pressure to compress the schedule are somewhat reduced.
6. Realise that it is the people who can make automation projects successful. Educating and training of employees must be an ongoing

activity. Participation of all employees is a must. Union representation is essential in any automation.

7. Finally, if companies move too slowly in adopting production technology, they are likely to be left behind. An advice that companies need to be cautious about automation does not mean that they must go slow. Any delay in implementation is sure way of giving in to the competitors.

Advantages and Disadvantages of Automation

'Automate or die' is the slogan of many producers all over the world. Increased production and productivity, reduced cost, better quality, elimination of wastage and inefficiency etc. — these are the essential requirements for any owner of an industrial establishment so that he may successfully face competition. Those days are gone when whatever was produced found a ready market; in times to come, only the producers with the best performance will survive, and the best performance will be possible only through automation.

Moreover, technological change is historical inevitability; and automation is the ultimate stage which Aristotle dreamt of when he said in his *Politics: "There is only one condition in which we can imagine managers not needing subordinates and masters not needing slaves. This condition would be such that each instrument could do its own work at a word of command or by intelligent anticipation".*

Specially, the advantages of automation are :

Increased Output and Enhanced Productivity

Automation results in enhanced productivity and production because it increases the speed of production, eliminates production bottlenecks, reduces 'dead time' (the time a machine is not working caused by such controllable factors as lack of cutters, fixtures or materials).

Improved and Uniform Quality

The quality of production is immeasurably improved because the entire production process, beginning with raw materials and ending with end products, is handled by machines. There is uniformity in the quality of the products – a factor which earns or spoils the customers' goodwill.

Reduced Cost

Automation results in reduced total cost per unit of output. This is indicated in Table 1.14.

It is evident from Table 8.4 that after automation, the manufacturing cost is reduced by 34 paise per unit. This saving in the cost is mainly due to the virtual elimination of labour.

Table 1.14. Effect of Automation.

	Before Automation Rs.	After Automation Rs.
Material	1.00	1.02
Labour	0.38	0.04
Overheads	0.57	0.55
Manufacturing cost	1.95	1.61
Sales and administrative profit	0.08	0.0
(to yield 20% return on investment)	0.17	0.34
Selling price	2.20	2.03

Fewer Accidents

Automation results in a virtual elimination of labour and therefore the number of accidents to workers.

Better Production Control

Automation results in better control of the speed and flow of production as a result of highly mechanical sequencing.

Lost Prerogatives Gained

Fortunately or unfortunately for society, the greatest attraction is that machines can be controlled better than men. Management is attempting to regain some of its traditional prerogatives lost through successive years of union contract negotiations.

Dangerous and Unpleasant Tasks

The tasks like cutting work on the lathe which produces an ear-splitting noise, painting which requires the workers to cover their whole face except their eyes, tasks in a machinery plant where oil seeps right through the clothes to the skin etc., are now handled by robots instead of by men. It is predicted that robots will be performing many public and welfare services within the next few years. These will fight fires, work in garbage dumps, remove snow and take the place of nurses in lifting patients out of their beds. The day is not far off when the robot will step outdoors to carry out tasks under dangerous conditions.

Others

The other advantages which flow from automation include reduced inventories, greater operating flexibility, reduced lead time, reduced scrap, improved reliability and design freedom.

Disadvantages

Automation creates certain problems which must be borne in mind by the management. These problem are:

Heavy Capital Investment

Automation involves higher capital outlay, and the consequential problems of the cost of capital, depreciation, power consumption, etc. Automation is therefore, a luxury for small firms.

Displacement of Labour

In spite of assurances to the contrary, automation does result in worker replacement, and often in management replacement as well. Workers in unionised concerns oppose the move for automation. The Life Insurance Corporation (LIC) wanted to introduce five computers in 1965. Trade unions raised a hue and cry and successfully stalled the introduction of four computers, although one was introduced in the Bombay office. Trade unions also saw to it that no LIC employee was retrenched because of automation. They are still unhappy because, with the introduction of the computer in the Bombay office, future employment opportunities have been closed in that office.

Benefit of Employee Suggestion Lost

Labour being displaced, the benefit of suggestions from employees is lost. This is an irreparable loss to the management.

Tighter Specification May be Needed

In an unautomated factory, when there are slight deviations from the specifications of the materials that have been received, workers are still able to use them after making minor adjustments. This can never be done in an automated plant because machines are not as flexible as human beings. Inevitably, increasing automaton will bring demands on suppliers to adhere more rigidly to specifications. This may raise the costs of purchased materials slightly. It may also increase the probability of supply failure due to poor quality.

Costs of Supply Failure Increase

If the supplier fails to deliver the goods in time and if the stock of the materials is also exhausted, the inevitable result is to shut down the plant. The cost of a shutdown in an automated plant is many times greater than the cot of a shutdown in a non-automated plant. In the latter case, workers can be sent home; but, in the former, less can be saved by sending them home because there are very few of them. Substituted for the workers is a tremendous investment in the equipment that goes right on depreciating, whether it is being used or not.

Slack Season Would be Disastrous

Automation results in increased production. If increased production does not find a ready market, the prices will fall and the result will be disastrous. The management should, therefore, be sensitive to demand. Automation based on hopeful market expansion is a direct road to bankruptcy.

Dehumanisation

Automation, carried to its logical end, dehumanizes the plant and generates a peculiar atmosphere in it. True, it offers several advantages. It is also true that an automated plant frees the management from labour troubles. T the same time, it should not be forgotten that the employment of thousands of persons in a single plant carries its own charm, and give a sense of pride and satisfaction in achievement which hundreds of computers and robots cannot.

Problems of Developing Countries

Automation poses certain peculiar problems for developing countries. These countries are characterised by a high rate of unemployment, scarcity of foreign exchange, shortage of highly skilled personnel, shortage of capital, etc. All these are impediments to the introduction of the new technology. Not that automation has no relevance in developing countries. In fact, it has a definite role to play in these countries as well. It is expected to stimulate agricultural, industrial and other development, because mass production will create more demand for raw material and components, and in the process, will help generate employment in the long run. Goods and services will produced at lower unit costs, prompting greater consumption and improved levels of living. But developing countries cannot, for some more time to come, afford the luxury of automation as it is understood and introduced in highly developed countries. Selective automation to ensure accuracy, if not speed, may be more relevant in the developing countries, where 'automation without tears' is a cry which should be needed and respected for some time to come.

Factories of the Future

Factories of tomorrow will present certain contrasting features. They are:

1. There will be stress on high product quality.
2. Greater emphasis on flexibility.

3. Customer orders will be executed and delivered fast.
4. There will be changed production economics. Fixed costs will become variable and variables shall turn fixed.
5. CAD/CAM will be the basis for product design and process planning. CIM will integrate all phases of the business from a common database.
6. Organisations will undergo structural changes with line staff becoming staff personnel and vice versa. Maintenance, product quality, engineering, management of technology change, software development and maintenance, and robotics and automation projects will become mainstream activities of the organisation.

The factory of future will have digital computers as driving force. Popularly called as the computer-integrated manufacturing (CIM), the digital computers provide shared data base for four primary manufacturing functions: engineering design, manufacturing engineering, factory production and information management. The shared database is the glue that synchronises the four functions, thereby yielding gains in productivity. The database stores all product and process related information required to produce a component or a product. It contains information about machines, tools, materials, manufacturing steps, quantities demanded, due dates and vendors.

CIM is not a reality yet, but a vision of things to come. Some elements of CIM are found in factories today. They are CAD/CAM and robots. Robots were explained earlier. Coming to CAD and CAM – these (along with robots) are computer-based systems that integrate the entire product development process – from concept to market.

Computer-Aided Design (CAD)

This involves the use of computers in creating or modifying the product design. The designer makes full use of computer interactive graphics. The computer is employed to display pictures, symbols or data. In so doing the designer is able to sit at the console of a computer terminal and make any changes in the product design. The details of the design are stored in the computer's memory and can be withdrawn at any time in a copy of the design.

Computer-Aided Manufacturing (CAM)

CAM is understood as the effective utilisation of computer technology in the management, control and operations of the manufacturing facility through either direct or indirect computer, interfaced with the physical and human resources of the company. Applications of CAM involve the monitoring and controlling of manufacturing operations as well as any indirect applications where the compute is used.

CAD and CAM are generally merged and the important result of this merger is the automation of the transition from product design to manufacturing. New Products can be designed quickly as market demands change. And because these new product designs are stored in a common database, through CAM, the new products can be introduced into production much more quickly and with less expenses. Thus, CAD/CAM promises great product flexibility, low production costs and improved product quality.

Mechanisation & Productivity

When you buy a light bulb. you know it will screw into the socket because light bulb bases are standardized (only a few kinds of bases are made). But an Indian light bulb will not fit into a socket in Europe, or vice versa, because their bases are different. Or, if you buy a new hosepipe to water your lawn. you don't have to wonder if it will screw onto the water tap because the size of the pipes and screw threads are standard.

Also, most people probably never think about a light bulb's voltage because, in the India, 230 volts is standard in homes. But again, Europe is different; several voltages are used there. An Indian traveler in Europe using an electric shaver has to buy an adapter. We have used the word " standard" as meaning that only certain specific sizes are made and sold. Some people prefer to call this process of limiting the number of sizes "simplification." "Standardization." these people would say, is something else; it is the process of specifying the size, shape, performance, and other characteristics of the items being made. These two concepts are so closely related, however, that we will use them here as being nearly the same.

Standardization (including simplification) usually means that nonstandard items will not be made except when a customer orders them specifically (and pays extra for them).

Sometimes standards have been enacted into law for safety or health reasons. Automobile windshields, for example, must be made of safety glass (which does not shatter and make jagged edges on impact). Although standardization has largely been voluntary in the past, today's product safety laws are making it mandatory in many areas. The glass now used in eyeglasses, for example, must now be very resistant to breakage. It is standardized at a high-quality level.

Most industries, even those producing consumer products where there are no legal regulations, can and do standardize extensively on a voluntary basis. This holds true in the setting of shoe sizes, photographic film. automobile tire sizes, nails, pipe, and even razor blades.

Duties & Responsibilities of Operations Manager

Our picture so far of production managers in operation has been confined largely to internal organizational matters. This is proper in that this is where most of them operate. Usually only top managers deal with broad social matters.

But high-level managers are in a dual position. They try to serve their employers, who are the company's stockholders or legislative bodies. But at the same time they operate in a social system and owe obligations to society. Many of these obligations to society are written into laws, but others in the production area, such as trying to maintain stable employment, to pay fair wages, to serve customers well, and to maintain or increase productivity, are less formal.

Social obligations are not altogether stable but are often dynamic. Recent years have seen a shift and tile emergence of a strong consumer consciousness, particularly as it concerns the design of products and services so that they are safe for customers to use and so that working conditions will be safe for employees. Besides this, environmental considerations have also become very important.

Only a few years ago, an enterprising organization could design a product or provide a service in accord with its managers' views of whether or not the market would want it and whether the company could make money doing it. The only considerations were economic, and, so far as quality and safety were concerned, all that was required was to satisfy customers. If they were satisfied, they bought the product or service, and, if they were dissatisfied, they didn't buy it a second time.

Today this has changed. Managers, in both private and governmental organizations, have to pay more attention not only to what their customers might buy, but also to increasing governmental regulation and also to consumer and environmental protection groups. Such groups take them to task if their products or services are unsatisfactory, or if they cause people to get hurt, or if people have their health impaired, or if they do harm to the environment by polluting the air or water, or if they waste scare natural resources.

Nowadays there are frequent newspaper accounts about lawsuits against manufacturers, doctors, accountants, and transportation companies. And there are frequent stories about a ban on the use of a drug or food preservative or about the public ban of a product in the market on findings by public service laboratories. (For example Coke and Pepsi being found to contain Pesticides).

Much of the criticism in such actions is related to the quality of the product or of the service being rendered. These are areas where the remedial actions to correct the unsatisfactory conditions are often in the domain of production managers and their staff.

Operations Management

UNIT—II

3

Work Standardization and Process

Introduction

Industry everywhere has been striving hard to discover new work methods and techniques which could help produce goods of required quality at reasonable costs. The search has resulted in finding techniques such as work simplification, job design, value analysis and the like. All these are collectively called 'methods engineering' or 'industrial engineering'. The other names used are 'work design', 'work study', 'methods analysis' and 'operation analysis'. Methods engineering is closely affiliated with the functions of work measurement (or time study) and method study. This unit is devoted to a detailed discussion of these approaches.

For the sake of simplicity or for avoiding confusion, we us the term *'work study'*, which comprises two techniques known as 'method study' and 'work measurement', throughout this chapter.

Work Study

Definition of Work Study

Work study is defined as that body of knowledge concerned with the analysis of the work methods and the equipment used in performing a job, the design of an optimum work method and the standardization of proposed work methods. Work study has contributed immeasurably to the search for better methods, and the effective utilisation of this management tool has helped in the accomplishment of higher productivity. Work study is a management tool to achieve higher productivity in any organization, whether manufacturing tangible products or offering services to its customers.

Work study is also understood as a systematic, objective and critical examination of the factors, affecting productivity for the purpose of improvement. It make use of technique of method study and work measurement to ensure the best possible use of human and material resources in carrying out a specific activity.

To give a clear and better understanding of this chapter, definitions of various terms are listed in Table 2.1.

Table 2.1. Definitions of Terms often Used.

	Term	Definition
1.	Work Design or Work System Design	Systematic investigation of contemplated and present work systems in order to formulate, through the ideal system concept, the easiest and most effective systems and methods for achieving the necessary functions/goals/purposes.
2.	Work Study	The generic term used for those techniques, particularly method study and work measurement, which are used in the examination of human work in all its contexts and which lead systematically to the investigation of the facts which affect efficiency and economy of the situation being reviewed, in order to effect improvement
3.	Methods Engineering	The body of knowledge concerned with the analysis of the methods and the equipment used in performing a job, the design of an optimum method and the standardization of the proposed methods, are frequently referred to as 'Work Study'.
4.	Industrial Engineering	Concerned with the design, improvement and installation of integrated system of men, materials and equipments to improve productivity.
5.	Method Study or Methods Analysis or Operations Analysis	The systematic recording and critical examination of existing and proposed ways of doing work as a means of developing and applying easier and more effective methods and reducing costs.
6.	Motion Study or Motion Analysis	Detailed study of the manual and/or body motions used in a work-task or at one work area often involving comparative analysis of right hand and left hand motions. (Part of method study)
7.	Work Measurement	The application of techniques, designed to establish the time for a qualified worker, to carry out a specified job, at a defined level of performance.
8.	Work Simplification	Involves improvements in work methods or work flow initiated and developed by workers or supervisors on the job as a result of methods training and/or economic incentives. It is an organised use of common sense to find and apply better ways of doing any work at lesser cost.
9.	Time Study	A technique of work measurement used for determining as accurately as possible from a limited number of observations, the time necessary to carry out a given activity at a defined standard of performance. A stop watch is used for the purpose of recording the actual time taken by the worker under observation to perform various elements of the work or task.

Importance of Work Study

In today's competitive business environment, it is necessary that the employees work harder, be more productive so that, production costs can be kept low to met global competition. Operations managers have to continuously strive for low production costs, high product quality and improve every facet of manufacturing. In this direction, improving labour productivity and reducing costs by improving work methods and simplifying the work, needs special attention by operations managers. To facilitate this, the work study technique (now known as industrial engineering) has been developed over a period of time.

Objectives of Work Study

1. To analyse the present method of doing a job, systematically in order to develop a new and better method.
2. To measure the work content of a job by measuring the time required to do the job for a qualified worker and hence to establish standard time.
3. To increase the productivity by ensuring the best possible use of human, machine and material resources and to achieve best quality product/service at minimum possible cost.
4. To improve operational efficiency.

Benefits of Work Study

1. Increased productivity and operational efficiency.
2. Reduced manufacturing costs.
3. Improved work place layout.
4. Better manpower planning and capacity planning.
5. Fair wages to employees.
6. Better working conditions to employees.
7. Improved work flow.
8. Reduced material handling costs.
9. Provides a standard of performance to measure labour efficiency.
10. Better industrial relations and employee morale.
11. Basis for sound incentive schemes.
12. Provides better job satisfaction to employees.

The purpose of work study is to determine the best or most effective method of accomplishing a necessary operation or function. The criteria for the best method could be an increase in job satisfaction and individual morale, reduction in physiological fatigue, decrease in number of accidents and personal injuries, minimization of material usage, tool breakage or usage of consumable supplies and increase in productivity by reduction of performance time. Every operation/activity in an organization contains to a certain degree, of mechanical, physiological, psychological and sociological factors. The purpose of work measurement is to quantify these factors.

Relationship of Time and Motion Study to Work Study

Both time study and motion study which resulted from the integration of concepts and practices developed by F.W. Taylor and by Frank B. and Lilian M. Gilbreth, are concerned with the systematic analysis and improvement of manually controlled work situations. However, time study is a quantitative analysis leading to the establishment of a time standard whereas motion study is a qualitative analysis of a work station leading to the design or improvement of an operation/activity. Fig. 2.1 illustrates the relationship between motion and time studies as a part of the total work study procedure.

Work study as a discipline is concerned with:

a. Better ways of performing jobs/tasks, and
b. Exercising control over the output in respect of those jobs/tasks by setting standards for performance (i.e., for output/work) with respect to time.

The former technique is known as method study (also known as method analysis or operation analysis) and the latter technique is known as work measurement (or time study).

Fig. 2.1 illustrates the steps involved in work study, comprising the techniques of method study and work measurement.

Method study and work measurement are closely linked. Method study is concerned with reduction of work content while work measurement is concerned with the investigation and reduction of the *ineffective time* and the subsequent establishment of time standards for the task or job or operation on the basis of the work content established by the method study. Usually method study should precede work measurement. However, when time-standards for output are being set, it is often necessary to use an appropriate work-measurement technique such as activity sampling (also known as work sampling) in order to determine the ineffective time or idle time. This will facilitate corrective action to be taken by the management before going for method study. On the other hand, time study may be used to compare the effectiveness of alternative work methods or operations.

Basic Work Study Procedure

There are eight basic steps involved in a work study procedure. Some of them are common to both method study and work measurement. These steps are:

1. *Select* the job or the process of the operation to be studied.

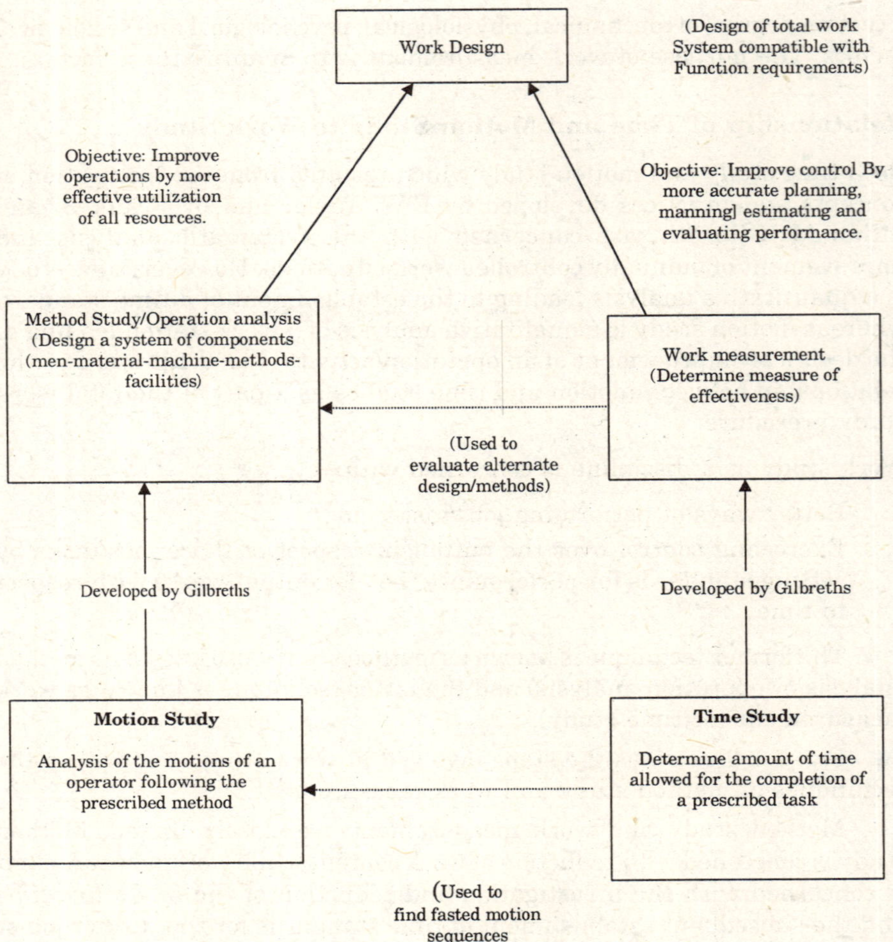

Fig. 2.1. Relationship of motion and time study to work design

2. *Record* all relevant facts about the job or process or operation using suitable charting techniques such as operation process chart, flow process chart, flow diagram, SIMO chart (simultaneous motion chart) and man-machine chart.
3. *Examine* critically all the recorded facts, questioning the purpose, place, sequence, person and the means of doing the job/process/operation.
4. *Develop* the new method for the job/process/operation.
5. *Measure* the work content and establish the standard time using an appropriate work-measurement technique, viz; time study using stop watch, synthesis method, analytical estimating method, pre-determined motion time system and work sampling.
6. *Define* the new method for the job/process/operation.

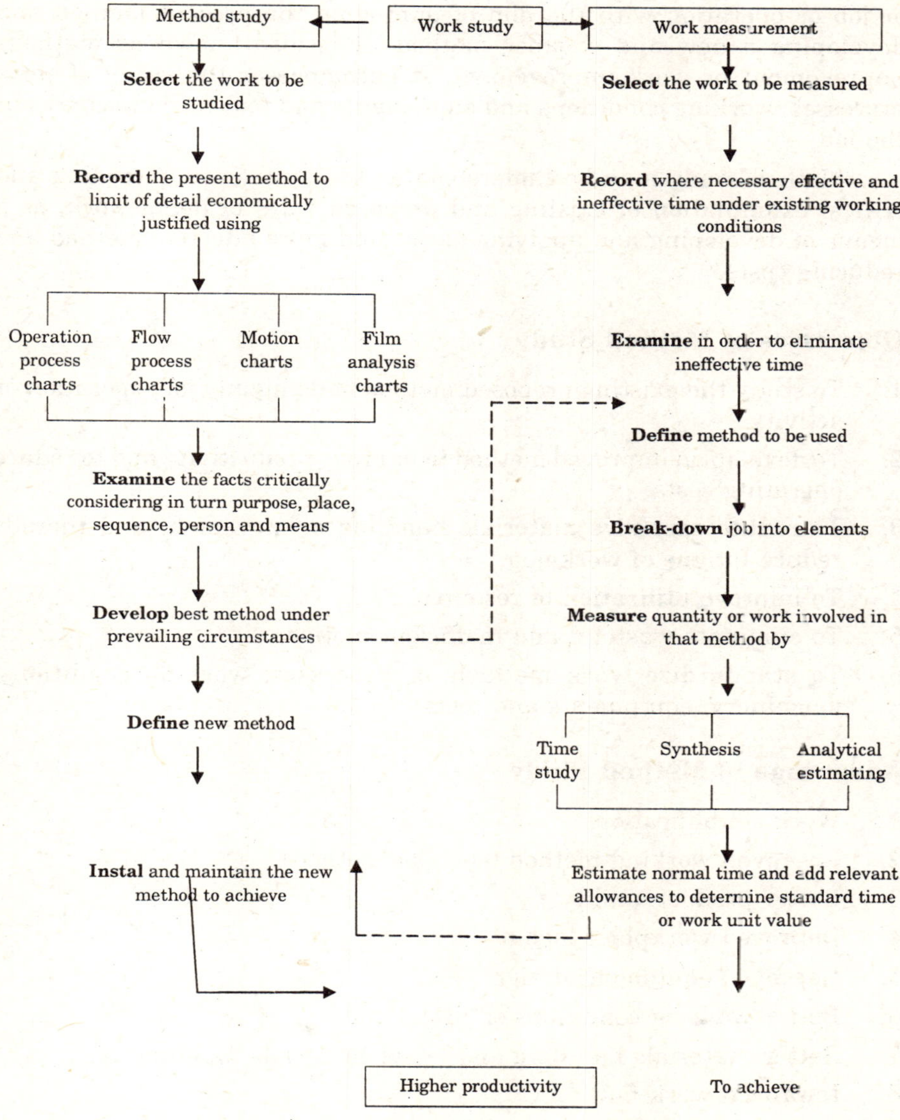

Fig. 2.2. Steps involved in work study

7. *Install* the new method as standard practice.
8. *Maintain* the new method for the job/process/operation.

Method Study or Methods Analysis

Work methods analysis or method study is a scientific technique of observing, recording and critically examining the present method of performing a task or job or operation with the aim of improving the present method and developing a new and cheaper method. It is also known as methods improvement or work improvement. It encompasses the study of work processes, working conditions and equipments and tools used to carry out the job.

Method study may be understood as the systematic recording and critical examination of existing and proposed ways of doing work, as a means of developing and applying easier and more effective method and reducing costs.

Objectives of Method Study

1. To study the existing/proposed method of doing any job, operation or activity.
2. To develop an improved method to improve productivity and to reduce operating costs.
3. To reduce excessive materials handling or movement and thereby reduce fatigue of workmen.
4. To improve utilization of resource.
5. To eliminate wasteful and inefficient motions.
6. To standardize work methods or processes, working conditions, machinery, equipments and tools.

Advantage of Method Study

1. Work simplification
2. Improved working method (cheaper method)
3. Better product quality
4. Improved workplace layout
5. Improved equipment design
6. Better working conditions/environment
7. Better materials handling and lesser materials handling cost
8. Improved work flow
9. Less fatigue to operator
10. Optimum utilization of all resources
11. Higher safety to workmen
12. Shorter production cycle time
13. Higher job satisfaction for workmen
14. Reduced material consumption and wastages
15. Reduced manufacturing cost and higher productivity

Factors facilitating Method Study

1. High operating cost
2. High wastage and scrap
3. Excessive movement of materials and workmen
4. Excessive production bottlenecks
5. Excessive production bottlenecks
6. Excessive rejections and rework
7. Complaints about quality
8. Complaints about poor working conditions
9. Increasing number of accidents
10. Excessive use of overtime

Method Study Procedure

The various steps involved in method study are:

1. *Select* the work or job to be studied and define the objectives to be achieved by method study. The job selected to have maximum economic advantage, shall offer vast scope for work improvement through reduction of excessive materials handling and fatigue of workmen, offer scope for improving the working conditions and improving the utilization of resources.

2. *Record* all the relevant facts or informations pertaining to the existing method using the recording techniques such as –

(a) *Process charts*
  - (i) Outline process chart
  - (ii) Operation process chart
  - (iii) Flow process chart–material type, man-type and machine type/ equipment type.
  - (iv) Man-machine chart
  - (v) Two handed process chart
  - (vi) Multiple activity chart
  - (vii) Simultaneous motion chart (SIMO chart)
  - (viii) Motion chart
  - (ix) Film analysis chart.

(b) *Diagrams such as*
  - (i) Flow diagram
  - (ii) String diagram
  - (iii) Cycle graph
  - (iv) Chronocyclegraph

3. *Examine* the recorded facts critically, challenging everything being done and seeking alternatives, questioning the purpose (What is achieved?), the means (How is it achieved?), sequence (When is it achieved?), place (Where is it achieved?), and the person (Who achieves it?).

Table 2.2 illustrates the questioning attitude of method analysis

Table 2.2. The Questioning Attitudes of Methods Study.

1.	What is done? What is the purpose of the operation? Why should it be done? What would happen if it were not done? Is every part of the operation necessary?
2.	Who does the work? Why does this person do it? Who could do it better? Can changes be made to permit a person with less skill and training to do the work?
3.	Where is the work done? Why is it done there? Could it be done somewhere else more economically?
4.	When is the work done? Why should it be done then? Would it be better to do it at some other time?
5.	How is the work done? Why is it done this way?

4. *Develop* the improved method by generating several alternatives and selecting the best method. The factors to be considered while evaluating alternatives and selecting the best method are:

(a) Cost of implementation.
(b) Expected savings in time and cost.
(c) Feasibility.
(d) Producibility.
(e) Acceptance to design, production planning and control, quality control, production and sales departments.
(f) Reaction of employees to the new method.
(g) Short term or long term implication of the alternative.

Establish the new method by providing suitable equipment design, mechanical aids, jigs and fixtures, tools, working conditions, material handling equipments, workplace layout and work planning and control techniques.

5. *Install* the improved (new) method in three phases — planning, arranging and implementing phases. In the first two phases, the programme of installation and a schedule (i.e. time table) are planned and necessary requirements such as resources, equipments, tools, operating instructions to workers are provided. The implementation phase involves the introduction of the developed method as standard practice to achieve the desired results.

6. *Maintain* the new method by ensuring that the installed method is functioning well. This is done by periodic checks and verifications at

regular intervals. Proper control procedures are used to ensure that the new method is practiced to achieve the benefits of methods study and also to achieve higher productivity.

Recording Techniques Used in Method Study

Some of the useful recording techniques used in method study are process charts, flow process charts, multiple activity charts, man-machine charts, flow diagram and string diagram.

To facilitate the charting process, some symbols are used such as those illustrated in Fig. 2.3.

Standard Symbol	Name of Activity	Definition of Activity
○	Operation	Modification of an object at one work place. Object may be changed in any of its physical or chemical characteristics, assembled or disassembled or arranged for another operation, transportation, inspection or storage.
⇨	Transportation or movement	Change in location of an object from one place to another.
□	Inspection	Examination of an object to check on quality or quantity characteristics.
D	Delay/Temporary storage	Retention of an object in a location awaiting next activity.
▽	Storage	Retention of an object in location in storage which is protected against unauthorized removal.
□ ⇨	Combined activity	A combined activity occurs when two activities occur simultaneously. Various combinations of simultaneous occurrence of two activities could be possible.

Process Charts used in Method Study

1. *Outline process chart :* An outline process chart records an overall picture of the process and records only the main events sequence-wise. It considers only the main operations and inspections.

2. *Operations process chart :* The basic process chart, an *operation process chart,* is understood as a graphic representation of the points at which the materials are introduced into the process and of the sequence of inspections and all operations except those involved in materials handling. It includes information considered desirable for analysis such as time required to carry out the operation and the location.

3. *Flow process charts* are graphic representations of the sequence of all operations, transportation, inspections, delays and storages occurring during a process or a procedure and include information considered desirable for analysis such as, time required and distance moved.

The flow process chart could be of three types, viz.,

(i) Flow process chart material or product type.

(ii) Flow process chart–man type.

(iii) Flow process chart machine type of equipment type.

Material or product type flow process chart records what happens to the material or product i.e., the changes the material or product undergoes in location or condition (includes operation and transportation). Man type process chart records the activities of a worker or operator i.e., what a worker or operator does, whereas equipment or machine type flow process chart records the manner in which an equipment or machine is used.

4. *Two handed process chart :* In this chart, the activities of a worker's or operator's both hands or limbs are recorded chronographically.

5. *Multiple activity chart* : In this chart, the activities of more than one subject (worker, machine or equipment) are recorded on a common time scale to show their inter-relationship.

6. *The man machine chart or worker-machine chart :* This is a variation of multiple activity chart and illustrates the operation and delays of the operator and the machine which he operates. An example of man machine chart may be one worker running two machines simultaneously.

7. *Flow diagram :* The flow diagram is a drawing or diagram drawn to a scale to show the relative position of a machine or equipment, jigs and fixtures, gangways or isles and shows the path followed by materials or machines.

8. *String diagram :* It is a scale plan or model on which a string or a thread is used to trace and measure the path of workers, materials or equipments during a specified sequence of events.

9. *SIMO chart :* The simultaneous motion cycle chart (SIMO) is a type of two handed process chart in which the micromotions (therbligs) of both hands are recorded.

Motion Study

Motion study is the science of eliminating wastefulness, resulting from using unnecessary; ill-directed and inefficient motion. The aim of motion study is to find an o\perpetuate the scheme of the least waste methods of a labour.

Micro motion study provides a valuable technique for making minute analysis of those operations that are short in cycle, contain rapid movements and involve high production over a long period of time. For example, sewing of garments and assembling small parts. Micro-motion study may be used for the following purposes in addition to its primary use for job-analysis work :

(i) To study the inter-relationship among the members of a work group.
(ii) To study the relationship between an operator and the machine which he operates.
(iii) To obtain the time for an operation.
(iv) To establish a permanent record of the method of doing a job.

The usual procedure of performing a micro-motion study is to take motion picture of the operations, analyse the film and to prepare a SIMO chart from the results of the film analysis. In analyzing the film, very small time values (commonly 1/2000 minute) may be obtained by reading a clock (micro-chronometer) that appears in each of the motion pictures.

The film is analyzed by breaking the job cycle into micromotions or *therbligs* which indicate the basic body motions of the worker.

Therbligs indicate the basic motions consisting of three parts, viz;

(i) When the motion begins.
(ii) The nature of the motion.
(iii) When the motion ends.

The examples of therbligs are

1. *Search (Sr) :* That part of the cycle during which, the eyes of the hands are hunting or groping for the object. Search begins when the eyes or hands begin to hunt for the object and ends when the objects have been found.

2. *Select (St) :* The choice of one object from among several. Select refers to the hunting and locating of one object from among several.

Example : Locating a particular pencil in a box containing pencils, pens and miscellaneous articles.

3. *Grasp (G) :* Taking hold of an object, closing the fingers around it, preparatory to picking it up, holding it or manipulating it.

Example : Closing the fingers around a pen on the desk.

4. *Transport Empty (TE) :* Moving the empty hand in reaching for an object.

5. *Transport Loaded (TL) :* Moving an object from one place to another.

6. *Hold (H) :* Retention of an object after it has been grasped, no movement of the object taking place.

7. *Release Load (RL) :* Letting go of the object. Release load begins when the object starts to leave the hand, and ends when the object has been completely separated from the hand or finger.

8. *Position (P) :* Turning or locating an object in such a way that it will be properly oriented to fit into the location for which it is intended.

Example : Lining up a door key preparatory to inserting it in the key hole.

9. *Pre-position (PP) :* Locating an object in a pre-determined place or locating it in the correct position for some subsequent motion.

10. *Inspect (I) :* Examining an object to determine whether or not it complies with standard size, shape, colour or other qualities previously determined.

11. *Assemble (A) :* Placing one object into or on another object with which it becomes an integral part.

12. *Disassemble (DA) :* Separating one object from another object of which it is an integral part.

13. *Use (U) :* Manipulating a tool, device or piece of apparatus for the purpose for which it was intended

14. *Unavoidable Delay (UD) :* A delay beyond the control of the operator.

15. *Avoidable Delay (AD) :* Any delay of the operator for which he is responsible and over which he has control.

16. *Plan (Pn) :* A mental reaction which precedes the physical movement, i.e., deciding how to proceed with job.

17. *Rest for overcoming fatigue (R) :* A fatigue or delay factor or allowance provided to permit the worker to recover from fatigue incurred by his work.

18. *Find (F) :* Mental reaction at the end of search.

Motion Economy and Work Efficiency

Most workers do not enjoy making unnecessary or wasted motions, particularly if they result in unnecessary fatigue. In addition to providing some social and psychological rewards, a job should be reasonably efficient Motion study helps to reduce fatigue and waste motions.

Principles of Motion Economy

The rules of motion economy and efficiency which referred to hand motions of operators were developed by Gilbreths. The principles of motion economy are divided into three groups, viz;

(a) Effective use of the operator
(b) Arrangement of the workplace
(c) Tools and equipment

Table 2.3 lists twenty two principles of motion economy as developed by Barnes.

Table 2.3. Principles of Motion Economy.

a.	*Rules concerning use of human body*
1.	The two hands should begin as well as complete their motions at the same time.
2.	The two hands should not be idle at the same time except during rest periods.
3.	Motions of the arms should be made in opposite and symmetrical directions, and should be made simultaneously.
4.	Had and body motions should be confined to the lowest classification with which it is possible to perform the work satisfactorily. (a) Finger only. (b) Fingers and wrists. (c) Fingers, wrists and lower arms. (d) Fingers, wrists, lower and upper terms. (e) Hands, arms and body.
5.	Momentum should be employed to assist the worker wherever possible, and it should be reduced to a minimum if it must be overcome by muscular effort.
6.	Smooth, continuous curved motions of the hands are preferable to straight line motions involving sudden and sharp changes in direction.
7.	Ballistic movements are faster, easier and more accurate than restricted or controlled movements.
8.	Work should be arranged to permit easy and natural rhythm wherever possible.
9.	Eye fixation should be as free and as close together as possible.
b.	*Rules concerning arrangement of the work place.*
10.	There should be a definite and fixed place for all tools and materials.
11.	Tools, materials and controls should be located close to the point of use.
12.	Gravity feed bins and containers should be used to deliver material close to the point of use.
13.	Drop deliveries should be used wherever possible.
14.	Materials and tools should be located to permit the best sequence of motions.
15.	Provisions should be made for adequate conditions for seeing. Good illumination is the first requirement for satisfactory visual perception.
16.	The height of the work place and the chair should preferably be arranged so that alternate sitting and standing at work are easily possible.
17.	A chair of the type and height to permit good posture should be provided for every worker.
c.	*Rules concerning the design of tools and equipment*
18.	The hands should be relieved of all work that can be done more advantageously be a jig, a fixture or a foot-operated device.
29.	Two or more tools should be combined wherever possible.
20.	Tools and materials should be pre-positioned whenever possible.
21.	Where each finger performs some specific movement such as in type-writing, the load should be distributed in accordance with the inherent capacities of the fingers.
22.	Levers, cross bars, and hands wheels, which should be located in such positions that, the operator can manipulate them with the least change in body position and with the greatest mechanical advantage.

Through the application of the principles of motion economy, it is possible to greatly increase the output of manual labour with a minimum of fatigue.

An Example of Application of Motion Economy Principles These principles can be applied to a simple situation (an example) of assembling a nut and a bolt to form an assembly. If the nuts and bolts are kept on the work table on the two sides of the worker, so that they are kept within easy reach, facilitating smooth curved symmetrical motion of both hands (to be done simultaneously), are stacked or kept in such a way as to eliminate search, a fixture provided to eliminate grasp by a hand while assembling, a chute provided to eliminate transport and release by hand, then we have used some of the above principles to improve the method and productivity.

Process Flow Charts

Just as the motion of hands are studied by classifying into certain fixed categories of micromotions, any job or process can be studied for methods improvement by recording all the events. For the study of the process, therefore, 'process-charts' are used giving the sequence of event occurring in the process from the beginning to the end. The ASME symbols which are universally accepted are:

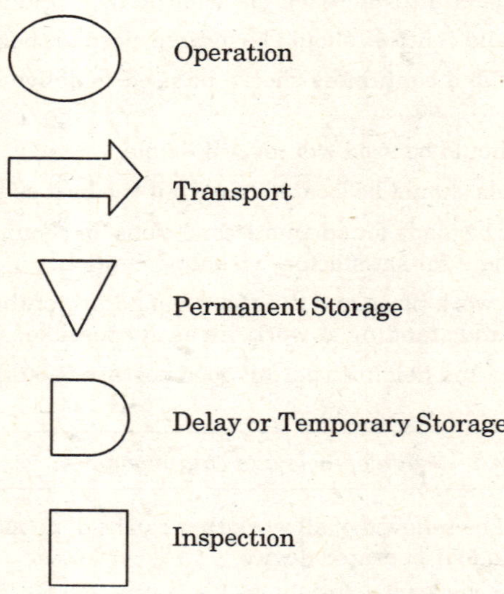

Fig. 2.4. An example of Process in Chart

Process charts are generally drawn for the material which goes from the raw material stage to the finished goods stage. Sometimes they may refer to the activities performed by the worker in getting a certain process done; in such a case the 'transport' refers to the movement of the man, the 'delay' refers to his waiting involved, etc. Process charts do not refer to the material and man or machine simultaneously.

Such charts give a clear picture of the process and help in analyzing whether the efforts are utilized in accomplishing the job or whether they are wasted. Each one of the activities can then be analyzed to find whether it could be

(i) eliminated, or
(ii) reduced in time, or
(iii) substituted by some other activity, or
(iv) put elsewhere in the sequence of activities, etc.

The ultimate goal is to simplify the procedure to minimize the man/ machine effort and reduce avoidable wastage of time resulting in minimization of the process costs.

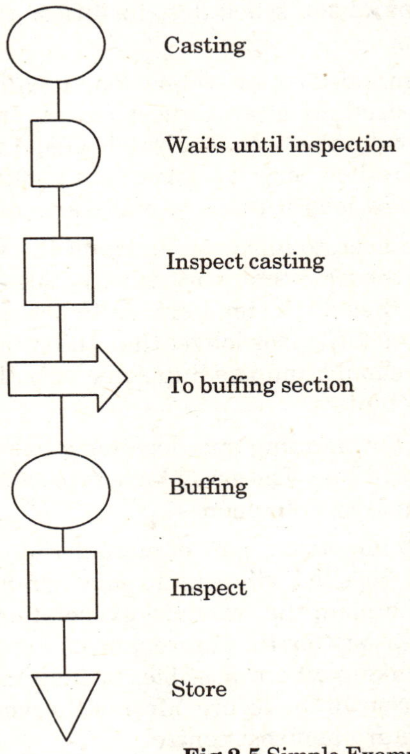

Fig.2.5 Simple Example of Process Chart

Memomotion Study

Memomotion study which originated by M.E. Mundel, is a special form of micro-motion study in which motion pictures are taken at slow speed using a motion picture camera. Sixty frames per minute and one hundred frames per minute are most common.

Memomotion study has been used frequently to study the flow and handling of materials, new activities and multi-man-and machine relationships and activities of department store clerk. In addition to all the advantages of micro-motion study, it can be used at relatively low film cost and permit rapid visual review of long sequences of activities.

This technique is not usable unless the work is restricted to a general area which can be covered by a motion picture camera. If the person under observation moves from place to place, it could be difficult to use this study.

Work Simplification and Work Standardisation

STANDARDS are highly desirable for almost every kind of organized work. Managers need to have some idea of how long work will take, how many employees will be needed, and what it will cost. Only with this information can they make intelligent decisions about schedules, facilities, people needed, and costs and selling prices.

Holiday Inn (a 5 star hotel chain) needs to know how long it will take to clean a room and change the bedclothes after a guest leaves. Indian Airlines needs to know how long it will take to unload the baggage when an airplane lands. HCL needs to know how long it takes to put together a PC, and Tata Steel needs to know how long it takes to make a steel rail.

In all of these cases, managers need to have some idea of the times it takes to do things. They measure the time that work usually takes and set standards so they can plan. But they don't stop here. After the event, they check to see if the standard was met. If it look longer than the standard called for, then it cost more than it should and used up some of both the time and money needed for other activities.

So the first use of standards is for planning and deciding what to do and what not to do and what things will cost. The second use is to compare what does happen with what is supposed to happen.

This leads to a third, and a very important, part of managerial work. The comparison between actual and expected will usually show a number of discrepancies. Most of the time the plan, the standard expectations, is not accomplished in all respects. Reasons for the discrepancies are then investigated and remedial actions taken, where possible, to help insure that expected accomplishment will occur in the future. Most of the work in this area falls in the realm of budgetary and cost control.

Here we are interested in the standards themselves. Sometimes reasonably good standards can be set just by looking back at what has been done in the past. Holiday Inns. Indian Airlines, HCL, and Tata Steel can look to the past and get rough answers to the questions we posed.

Yet setting standards for work just by looking back is not a very good way to do it. There is no "plus" in if. The time taken to do things in the past includes the method used as well as the casual pace so often found in unorganized work. Unless the job has been studied and a good method worked out, then the time taken in the past is almost surely more than it should be. It includes all of the inefficiencies of poor methods, and it includes all of the waste times that uncontrolled work always includes.

Properly set production standards specify the time it should take to do work when it is done in the best way. Such standards can be set only after the job has been analyzed and the best way determined and timed when performed by a normally proficient worker.

Saying that production standards are needed and that operations will be more effectively controlled if they are used is not to say that they are always used. Managers don't always use all of the managerial tools, including production standards, which are at their disposal. Furthermore, production can be accomplished without standards. Workers working on machines and materials will get something done. They will produce products, but without standards rarely will they produce as much as they would with standards. And, lastly, desirable though it is to have production standards, some kinds of work are not susceptible to measurement, so good standards cannot be set.

The discussion here will be centered on production standards as they are set and used in factory operating situations because these are usually well worked out. Sometimes, too, these same techniques can be anticipated and used for determining standards in other settings, such as offices, banks and services provided by governmental units.

In factories, production standards are most often set by time study methods with a stopwatch being used to time the work. In many companies the end product, the time standard, is used in setting job work rates for job workers.

There are also other important reasons for wanting standards. Consequently, many companies, which do not use piecework incentives, use time study and set up time standards. And conversely, a few companies which use incentives set their time standards without using time study.

Production standards and time standards are the same thing. One says that a worker ought to do the job 20 times in an hour, and the other says that the job is a 3-minute job. Occasionally, when a standard is stated as a quota, the quota actually represents the quantity of production needed in a given period of time in order to keep unit costs down to the figure used in setting selling prices.

Aside from piecework, production standards are needed in order to find out what the work ought to cost, to estimate the cost of new jobs, and to determine what it costs to do work in alternative ways. Standards are needed in order to know how much work machines will turn out, and for scheduling work as well as for setting quotas for machine-paced work. They are also needed for work along assembly lines so that assemblers' work may be divided equally. And they are needed, too, for planning the number of machines and workers needed for future production.

Concept of Methods Engineering

A production standard embodies a concept of normality and reasonableness. Almost all jobs can be done fast, or slow, or in between. The idea of a standard implies choosing a particular rate as being reasonable and expected. Other performance is then regarded as better than standard or poorer than standard. The process of choosing and deciding normal times is implicit in standard setting, as is the fact that choosing means judging. Standards, therefore, always contain a subjective clement of judgment. Standard setters cannot escape having to judge normality as they try to set fair and reasonable standards.

To illustrate how important this is, we might consider the simple task of walking a mile. If several men were to walk a mile, some of them would finish before the others. Perhaps the fastest man would finish in 15 minutes, the slowest man would lake 30 minutes, and the others would be spread out in between, with most men taking 10 or 20 minutes.

If it were cold weather or if rain was imminent, the average time would probably be less. The men would have an incentive not to dawdle. The same would be true if those who finished the mile in 20 minutes or less were to get a reward, probably almost everyone would make it and be rewarded. But. if only those who finished in less than 16 minutes were to be rewarded, fewer of the men would make it. A person has to hurry to walk a mile in 16 minutes, and to some of the men the incentive might not be enough to cause them to hurry this much.

Several points are involved here which are pertinent to setting production standards. The casual workaday pace of people differs, and their best performance capabilities also differ. So does their response to incentives. Furthermore, performances differ both because of chance variations (some of our walking men might have had to wait for traffic or a traffic light) and the effort a person is willing to exert. A person can go faster or he can slow down. as he wishes. All of these variations exist on production Jobs. The time it takes workers to do jobs varies and for similar reasons.

It might seem that the proper way to set production standards would be to see how long a job takes in the overall and use that time as the standard. But this time observed would depend wholly on who was observed and his performance during the period of observation. Returning to our walking men, the man we happened to pick to observe might be the one who walked a mile in 15 minutes or it might be the one who look 30 minutes. Of course, neither 15 nor 30 minutes would be reasonable to use as a standard. More certainty of reasonableness is needed than accepting the time observed as standard.

The next step in the way of improvement in standard setting would seem to be to see how long a job takes on the average over several performances and with several workers. This method is much better than using the time taken on one performance as the standard. Yet it is still not perfect as a standard setting procedure because the workers observed might all be fast (or slow), and, if this is so. their average time would not be a reasonable standard. If the workers observed were all very good, an average of their times would not allow enough time for the standard.

Using the average of the observed times is an imperfect solution also because workers have control over their work pace. If the time a worker takes is to become the standard, he would be working against his own best interest if he performed the task in his minimum time. It would only be human nature for him to slow down and stretch out the time. Furthermore, he would have few friends among his fellow workers if he did not try to get loose, easy to meet, standards. The surprising thing is that workers don't always slow down when standards are being set. There is enough slowing down, however, to make it unwise to accept observed times, even an average of several observed times, as being reliable for standards setting purposes.

It becomes necessary, therefore, not only to rather data on how long it takes to perform jobs but also to "pace rate" (judge the normality) the performances observed. If 10 men were observed walking 1 mile and they all did it between 15 and 17 minutes, their average would be 16 minutes, but this average is better than normal and should be rated as such by the standards setter. The pace rating should indicate that this is let us say, 125 percent of standard. Thus the standard, when it is set, will allow more time than the 16 minutes actually taken, in this case 1.25 as much time, or 20 minutes in total.

Or, at the other extreme, the men observed could have walked very slowly and averaged, perhaps. 25 minutes. If this were so, the standard setter's pace rating should be below 100. This time, when he calculates the standard time, he should arrive at something less than the average of the times observed. If their performance was rated at 80, then 8 of the time observed will become the standard and 8 X 25 = 20 minutes. Again, a 20-minute mile would be regarded as the standard.

As we said, it is necessary for the standards setter to judge the normalcy of the pace observed, but the concept of normal is somewhat abstract. As applied to factory jobs. it should he the pace, or time, that it would take an ordinary, experienced worker to do a job while applying himself in a normally diligent fashion (but not his pace when he is really pressing himself).

This concept of normality is particularly important where wage incentives are used because the production standard is the basis on which a worker's bonus is calculated. If a job is regarded as a 5-minute job, then the worker is expected to perform the job 12 times in an hour before he starts to earn a bonus. Production of 15 units would earn him a 25-percent bonus. Should 6 minutes be regarded as the standard time, however, the worker would get a bonus for all production in excess of 10 an hour. If he could get up to 15 units, he would get a 50-percent bonus.. Thus, the reasonableness of the standard is very important.

Problems In Setting Production Standards

Most of the problems in setting production standards center on situations where the analyst has to use judgment. And of these, "pace rating" (also called leveling) is probably the most open to question. It is apparent that some particular pace ought to be thought of as reasonable and that this pace should not be either a worker's best or poorest performance. Yet, it is hard to convince everyone that the end result, the time standard, is exactly right when everyone knows that the times allowed contain an adjustment reflecting the analyst's judgment of normal.

No better way seems to be available than to have the standard setter make such a leveling judgment. Some companies try to refine this by having the analyst make several pace 'ratings', one for each element, and adjust each element's average time to "normal" before summing up the times to get the whole-job standard. A very few companies even try to have their analysts rate every occurrence of every element. Probably such extra effort on their part produces a better standard, yet, the process is still one of judging.

It might seem that the need to judge pace could be reduced or even eliminated by studying all the members of a group and using their average time as the standard. But we have already noted that this is unfair to groups of good workers who turn out more work than a fair standard should call for. And we also noted that such a standard would be equally wrong if it were an average of slow performers. There is the added difficulty that there are only one or two workers on a good many jobs. And there is the still greater difficulty that workers who are being studied usually slow down somewhat, be they one or ten in number. As was said earlier, there is no safety in numbers.

Judgment must also be exercised in the matter of how often certain things should be done. An operator may have to stop the operation in order to gare the material, or sharpen a tool, or replace a broken or worn tool. But. how often must he stop the operation to sharpen the tool? When has it become dull enough to need sharpening? It is a matter of judging. In occasional cases, there is even a question of whether certain elements are really needed at all as part of the job. Sometimes the work is really someone else's work. Again, judging plays a part in the selling of the standard.

Limitations to use of Methods Engineering

Production standards can be and are used in many instances where the work itself cannot be timed. Most such production standards, however, are only approximations. Rarely are they as poor as time study standards; yet, approximate standards are usually better than none. The weaknesses of time study as a method for setting production standards can be enumerated as follows:

1. An analyst can time only what he can see. This eliminates the time of the thinking parts of jobs and leaves only manual jobs.
2. If an analyst times a job, it has to be a specific job with starting and stopping points and separable into units so that it is possible to count how many times it is done. This cannot be done with, say, the work of a administrator, or plant guard, or with most office jobs.
3. It doesn't pay to set standards for some jobs because they are not repetitive enough. The pain from setting standards for a small job that will be done only once or twice in the future won't pay for the analytic work. Standards setting by time study is limited to repetitive jobs.
4. Nor does it pay to time jobs and set standards on them when workers do a great many things. A maintenance department carpenter, example, does too many things to have standards for all of them (his daily work report would sometimes be several pages long). Also, it is too costly to verify what he says he did. And when no one checks reports, many workers on piecework will report that they have turned out more work than they did.
5. It usually doesn't pay to have standards for only part of an operator's work. If it isn't possible to put all of their work on standards, some workers will exaggerate the time they report spent on daywork (for which they get paid by the hour) and so keep their earnings up. A worker may have spent four hours on piecework and four on day-work (not in single stretches of time but all mixed up during the day), but he may report that he did the piecework in three hours and the day work in five hours, and no one can prove that he didn't. It looks as if he did nine hours work in the day (four hours of piecework [done in three hours] plus five hours of daywork) instead of eight. The foreman is put on the spot of having to give him nine hours of pay or arbitrarily. If quality is hard to define (as in polishing a surface), standards and production incentives may cause quality to fall off. The operator may say that he has done the job well enough when he hasn't.

   The analyst should think twice before accepting this criticism of production standards, though. If a worker is not on piecework but is on daywork instead, he might, and if he it allowed to, may be will, shine a polished surface all day and he proud of the fine job he does. Unfortunately, he cannot be allowed to spend so much time on an operation that it makes the cost go way up. Jobs where quality is hard to define are exactly the places where production standards, as well as quality standards, are needed.

6. Unions often oppose time study and where a union is opposed and where it is very strong, it may be able to stop or preclude time study work. Standards might be set by other methods but not by time study. Process Charts

A *process chart* is understood as a graphic representation of events and information relating to them during a series of actions or operation.

Operation process charts are similar to assembly charts except that they include specifications for the components as well as operating and inspection times and thereby provide more instruction on how to produce an item.

The operation analysis and routing sheets or simply the route sheets specify precisely how to produce an item by identifying the equipment and tools to be used, the operations to be carried out and their sequence to be followed and the machine set up and the run-time estimate.

Purpose of Process Charts

Process charts can present a picture of a given process so clearly that, every step of the process can be understood by those who study the charts.

Process charts may be effective in process analysis and may help in detecting inefficiencies of the processes currently adopted.

Types of Process Charts

Process charts can be classified as operation process charts, flow process charts, worker-machine/man-machine charts and activity charts or multiple activity charts.

4

Standard Time and Value Engineering

Introduction

Once the method is established, the next thing to do would be to set the standard times for the work. This aspect of Work Study is called the 'Time Study'. The 'standard time' by its very meaning should be a consistent and truthful measurement of the time required to perform the job or components of the job with the established method, incorporating established number of adequately skilled and healthy human beings, their actions, machines, materials and work place conditions. The consistency of the time standard should hold good for the same job done day after day without any harmful physical effects.

Uses of Time Study

The utility of the Time Study comes in:

(i) determining the work content and thereby setting wages and incentives;

(ii) arriving at cost standards per unit of output for the various jobs used for cost control and budgeting for deciding on sales price;

(iii) comparing the work efficiency of different operators;

(iv) arriving at job schedules for production planning purposes;

(v) manpower planning;

(vi) aiding in the method study

(a) to appropriately sequence the work of an operator and the machines or that of a group of workers,

(b) to highlight time consuming elements, and

(c) to compare costs of alternative methods.

(vii) product design by providing basic data on costs of alternative materials and methods required to manufacture the product.

Three Basic Systems of Time Study

The setting of time standards is done basically by following three methods:

(a) Using a stop-watch
(b) Using synthetic time standards
(c) Using statistical sampling.

In the first, the actual performance is studied by collecting data while the worker/s are working, and the data so obtained are synthesized into the time standard. In the second, any work is sub-divided into certain standard components for which the standard times are available from previously established time-studies; and these predetermined times are totaled, with appropriate allowances to compute the standard time for the job as a whole. Much of the skill of the time study man lies here in identifying the standard components of a job; the rest is arithmetical computation on paper. The third method is different from the previous two in that it relies on statistical sampling.

Steps Involved in a Stopwatch Time Study

Stopwatch Time Study makes direct observations by means of a simple stopwatch measuring, generally, to the precision of 0.01 minute. The observation equipment consists of the stopwatch, the recording board, the observation sheet and a pencil. The steps involved in such a study are:

1. Subdivide the job into observable and distinct elements.
2. Choose 'acceptable' operator/s for study.
3. Make direct observations of the work elements (while the operator is actually performing the job) and record the time of each element. Make a statistically adequate number of repeated measurements and record each time.
4. Performance rate each element and record.
5. Calculate the 'normal' Time.
6. Establish 'allowances'.
7. Compute the 'standard' Time.

The key step in a stopwatch time study is that of subdividing the job into component elements. One should take care that the elements are distinct or well defined and therefore amenable to repeated measurements. Also, the elements should be as short as possible without losing accuracy of measurement; the practical minimum is generally 0.02 or 0.03 minute the time required to read and record being 0.027 minutes or 45 TMU (Time Measurement Unit which will be explained subsequently in this chapter). The following are the uses of this breakdown into elements:

(a) It helps in separate performance rating of each of the job elements, instead of performance rating the whole job (which may lead to much error in the Time Standard).

(b) If a job method changes in terms of only one or two elements, the revised time standard can be easily established in the future. Unnecessary time studies are, therefore, eliminated. Standards for similar or related jobs can also be easily established.

(c) It highlights the work element which consumes excessive time, and this can then be subjected to a critical examination to eliminate/ substitute the element.

(d) Element/s with large variation in time can be examined for necessary changes in the job design or method.

(e) It highlights the inconsistency in working conditions.

(f) Such division into elements provides a detailed method description which can be used for training new workers.

A few points may be mentioned regarding elementalization:

1. One must separate the machine time from the worker time. At certain times the worker may appear to be working slow, but in actuality he may be waiting for a machine element to complete. Obviously, the worker cannot be performance rated low for this element.
2. While studying a job, elements of work other than the usual cycle may be encountered frequently. For instance, once in every 10 cycles the operator may clean the tool; or once in every 40 cycles the operator may have to replace the tray filled with finished work-pieces with an empty tray; or he may get the raw material once in a few cycles. These elements have got to be included in the time analysis since they are an integral part of the work. But since these elements are outside the routine cycle, they are called 'foreign' elements. There may be some genuine foreign elements such as when the worker is talking to a fellow employee or some other interruption which is not a part of the work. The Work Study analyst must note all the foreign elements as and when they occur.
3. It may also help if the analyst separates the constant elements from the variable elements.
4. Also, there is no unique method of subdividing a job into elements. Much depends upon the particular job being studied, the type of jobs encountered in the plant, and finally the judgement of the analyst. Only the precautions of distinctiveness and appropriate shortness of elements and of differentiating between constant and variable elements and man-or-machine elements needs to be observed.

For the Time Study one has to choose an 'acceptable' operator. He is one amongst many operators who are trained sufficiently in the job to be performed and are healthy and capable of performing the job at an acceptable pace day-in and day-out. He is not an abnormally fast or slow worker but one amongst the many who fall in between who might qualify for doing the job. The theme is to:

(i) eliminate the extra-ordinary (in either sense), and
(ii) to time study only those jobs that have received sufficient learning or training (reaching saturation in terms of 'learning) and in general all the working conditions are well established/settled.

Two Methods of Stopwatch Reading The observation and recording of the element times are done by two methods:

(a) Continuous
(b) Snap-back

In the continuous method the stopwatch is allowed to run continuously and observations on successive elements are recorded. The times for individual elements are obtained later by successive subtractions. The 'snapback' method involves measuring each element separately and snapping the watch back to zero for timing the next element (Fig.2.6).

One of the criticism of the snap-back method is that the analyst may forget to take into account any foreign elements. Also the direct recording of the individual element times may make the analyst tend toward recording more uniform readings. Moreover, the error due to observing a job and reading a watch simultaneously is not small enough to be ignored in the snap-back method. It is of the extent of 3 to 9% on an element of 0.06 minute duration and the error could be larger if the elemental time is shorter.

Performance Rating Each of the element is performance rated. For this, the analyst's concept of what is the 'normal' pace of working is important. Although this may sound very judgemental, speed rating techniques as used in the Society for Advancement of Management (SAM) rating films and in the Lowry, Maynard and Stegemerten (LMS) system are available to adjust/improve the judgement towards more uniformity amongst various raters. The LMS system gives weights to Skill, Effort, Conditions and Consistency on a Super, Excellent, Good, Average, Poor scale. Of course, the judgmental element or mental concept of what is 'average' is always there.

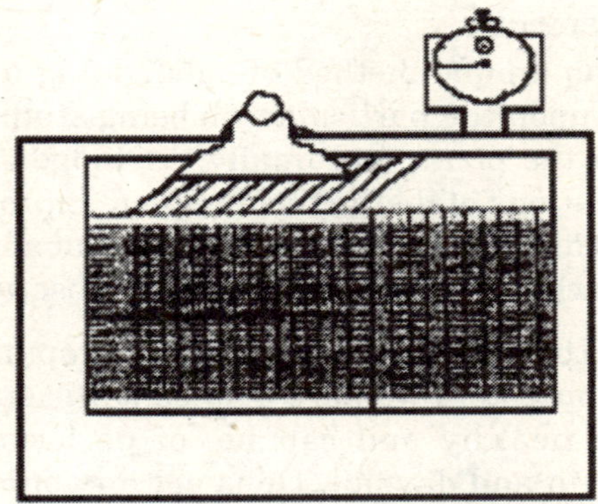

Fig. 2.6. Stopwatch Time Study Equipment

Each element should be timed repeatedly a number of times before arriving at the usable figure for the elemental times. For this, generally, an arithmetical average of the readings is taken. But, how many such readings should be taken? Or, what is the adequate sample size from which to take an average? This question has been answered by statistical principles. The formula (not derived here; the reader may refer to books on statistics) for having 95 chances out of 100 that observed average will be within 5% of the true average for the element for the pace at which it was performed, is:

$$N_{reqd} = \left(\frac{40.\sqrt{N_{taken}.\sum x^2 - (\sum x)^2}}{\sum x} \right)^2$$

Where

N_{reqd} = Required number of readings or sample size

N_{taken} = Number of readings taken based on which data, the sample size is being determined.

X = Individual reading or elemental time

Σ = Sum of

The sample size computations are done for each element and the element having highest degree of variability, will determine the sample size required for that job.

Computation of Normal Time and Standard Time

The 'Normal time' for the job is the sum of the 'normal times' for all of its elements. The normal time for an element is given by:

$$\left(\begin{array}{l}\text{Arithmetical Average}\\ \text{of the Recorded Times}\end{array}\right) \times \left(\begin{array}{l}\text{Performance Rating experessed in}\\ \text{percentage with 100\% as the 'accepted'}\\ \text{performance}\end{array}\right) \div (100)$$

Thus, if an element is rated as 120% and the actual readings are (in minutes):

0.05 0.06 0.05 0.05 0.05 0.06 0.06 0.05 0.06 0.06

(arithmetical average = 0.055)

$$\text{Normal Time for the element} = \frac{0.055 \times 120}{100} = 0.066\text{min}$$

This is so, provided the sample size of 10 is the proper one (statistically required). We can check this.

$$N_{\text{reqd}} = \left(\frac{40 . \sqrt{10 \times 305 - 3025}}{55} \right)^2$$

$$= . \quad 12.2 \approx 13$$

Therefore, if we take three more readings we have the adequate sample size. Let these be 0.06, 0.06, 0.05 min.

Now, arithemetic average of the 13 readings

$$= \quad 0.0554 \text{ min.}$$

Normal Time for the element = $\frac{0.055 \times 120}{100} = 0.066$ min.

$$= \quad 0.06648 \quad = 0.066 \text{ min.}$$

Allowances 'Standard Times' are derived from the Normal Times by applying appropriate 'allowances' for Personal Time, Fatigue and Unavoidable Minor Delays (outside the control of the worker).

A worker needs time to attend to personal physical needs such as drinking water, etc. which is reflected in the Personal allowances added to the Normal Time. These are generally not less than 5%.

At the end of the day a worker tends to work at a slower pace which is due to muscular as well as mental fatigue caused by noise, vibration, need for concentration, rapidly changing directions of motion, heat, etc. This allowance normally is given to the extent of 5 to 10%, but much depends upon the particular conditions of work prevailing.

During the day there are usually some interruptions in the operator's activity over which the operator has no control, for example a delay in the availability of material. Work Study analyst must analyze the extent of such time losses and add appropriate allowance to the Normal Time.

Although to some extent these allowances can be estimated by a proper and extended analysis, these need to be agreed to by the workers' unions.

Determination of the Standard time

The first step in setting the standard from the raw data is to subtract the elements' ending times from their starting times. This was done in Figure above, producing the actual time that each element look. These times are in italics and are the figures used in the calculation from this point on.

There are several readings for each element, and it can be seen in the Figure above that the individual times vary somewhat. In this analysis we used a simple arithmetic average of the clement times observed, except that the times in parentheses were omitted as not typical.

These averages appear in Figure below as the element time figures. Next, these times were multiplied by how often the element occurs per unit of output. When our sample study was taken, the analyst timed putting on the skate's front wheels and tightening the axle bolt as different from assembling the back wheels, but these turned out to he identical activities; so, in the write up in Figure below, putting wheels on appears as only one element but is said to occur four times per pair of skates.

After each element's time was multiplied by how often it occurred, the typical cycle time was totaled up as 3.027 minutes. To this was added a 12-percent allowance for fatigue and personal time. Next. the 110 per cent performance rating was used, causing the addition of 10 percent more time and a total time standard of 3.729 minutes per pair of skates.

This study was done in a college classroom as a demonstration and with only the skate key for a tool. Obviously, this work would go much faster when done in a factory on a repetitive basis and with appropriate tools used at a properly designed work place by an experienced worker.

		Time in Minutes	
			Time per pair
Element	**Frequency**	**Element time**	**of skates**
Preassemble toe clips	2	.123	.246
To be clips on frame	2	.203	.406
Assemble two wheels	4	.148	.592
Tighten axle nut	4	.108	.432
Attach frame halves	2	.197	.394
Tighten frame nut and bolt	2	.233	.466
Pack two skate into carton liner	1	.308	.308
Insert liner into carton and aside	1	.183	.183
Total average cycle time observed			3.027
Add 12% for fatigue and personal time			.363
			3.390
Adjust for performance rating of 110%			.369
Time standard in minutes per pair			3.729

Standard hourly output: 60 3.995 = 16.1 pairs per hour

Piece rate at $4.50 an hour :$4.50 16.1 = $.28 per pair

This method, as described here, is typical of how time standards are set. Personal and fatigue allowances are sometimes set a little lower, perhaps at 10 percent.

Many factory jobs, of course, are more complicated than assembling roller skates. If they have quite a few miscellaneous elements that are done irregularly, this makes it difficult to find out how much time to allow for them. One way is to take a much more extended time study and handle such elements on a proportional basis, just as we did with putting the skates into cartons.

This, however, may take a long time to do well because of the infrequency of many such elements. Sometimes, therefore, the analyst turns to "work sampling". If an operator is observed performing miscellaneous tasks one fifth of his time and main elements four fifths of his time, it is assumed that miscellaneous elements take one fourth as much time as main elements and they are therefore given one fourth the time of main elements.

Machine Time Within Work Cycles

Many factory machines are semiautomatic; once they are set up and the material is inserted, the machines perform all the operations. All that the operator does is take out the product just finished and put in the next one. While the machine works, there is nothing for the operator to do, so there is a question of how the element "wait for machine" should be handled in the production standard. If the wait is short or if the machine needs watching, "wait for machine" should be listed along with all of the other elements and incorporated into the standard. If a job takes 2 min to unload and load and then a 1/2 minute wait while the machine runs, this would be a 2 1/2 minute production standard. But if unload and load time is 2 minutes and then the machine runs by itself for 10 minutes, this job probably should be considered a 2-minute, not a 12-minute, job. The operator is given other work to do during his idle 10 minutes - possibly operating other machines.

Setup and Change Time

Machines nearly always have to be "set up" for each job or changed over from the previous job. The tools, tool holders, material holders, and so on all must be put in place and adjusted. But before that starts, the old setup from the last job has to be torn down and its tools and gadgetry put away. Besides this, the operator usually has to make a trip to the tool crib to return his last-used tooling and get the next tooling, and perhaps a drawing. Along the way he rings out on his old-job time card and rings in for his new job.

Work Measurement

Method Study and work measurement are two techniques of work study. Whereas method study or methods analysis is a tool for standardizing the methods of doing a job, work measurement establishes the work content of a job. Work content of a job can accurately be established only after the method of doing a job is standardized. Hence, it is needless to mention that method study should precede work measurement.

Both, method study and work measurement are important elements in achieving higher labour productivity. The overall productivity of an organisation is the result of the productivity achieved by all components of the organisation such as capital assets, labour, material, and plant and equipment. Hence, managers must be concerned about the productivity of all resources and at the individual worker level, labour productivity is determined by work measurement.

Definition of Work-measurement

Work measurement is defined as the application of techniques designed to establish the work content of a specified task by determining the time required for carrying out the task at a defined standard of performance by a qualified worker.

Qualified Worker

"A qualified worker is one who is accepted as having the necessary physical attributes, possessing the required intelligence and education and having acquired the necessary skill and knowledge to carry out the work in hand to satisfactory standards of safety, quantity and quality" definition by International Labour organization (ILO). In short, work measurement may be defined as the techniques applied to determine the amount of time necessary for a qualified worker to perform a particular task. The amount of time that a job is expected to take is expressed as time standard, work standard, labour standard, production standard or standard time. The standard time is the amount of time a qualified worker, working at a normal rate of speed, will require to perform the specified task. It may be expressed as minutes per unit of output or units of output per hour (i.e., standard output).

Work measurement is concerned with measuring the work content of any activity under study with a view to assess the human effectiveness or to compare one method with another or to develop labour standards that will be used for planning and controlling operations and thereby achieving high labour productivity.

Objectives of work measurement can be to achieve:

1. Improved planning and control of activities or operations;
2. More efficient manning of the plant;

3. Reliable ideas for labour performance;
4. Reliable basis for labour post control;
5. Basis for sound, incentive schemes.

Benefits of Work-measurement

Work measurement helps

1. To develop a basis for comparing alternate methods developed in method study by establishing the work content in each method of doing the job.
2. To prepare realistic work schedules by accurate assessment of human work
3. To set standards of performances for labour utilization by establishing the labour standards for an element of work, operation or product under ordinary working condition.
4. To compare actual time taken by the worker with the allowed time (standard time) for proper control of laour.
5. To assist in labour cost estimation.
6. To provide information related to estimation of tenders, fixation of selling price and assessment of delivery schedule.

Techniques of Work-measurement

The main techniques used to measure work are:

1. Direct Time Study.
2. Synthesis Method.
3. Analytical Estimating.
4. Pre-determined Motion Time System (PMTS).
5. Work sampling or Activity Sampling or Ratio Delay Method.

Fig. 2.8 summarises the various techniques that may be used to establish standard time values.

Steps in Work-measurement

The various steps are :

1. Break the job into elements.
2. Record the observed time for each element by means of either time study, synthesis or analytical estimating method.
3. Establish elemental time values by extending observed time into normal time for each element by applying a rating factor.
4. Assess relaxation allowance for personal needs and physical and mental fatigue involved in carrying out each element.

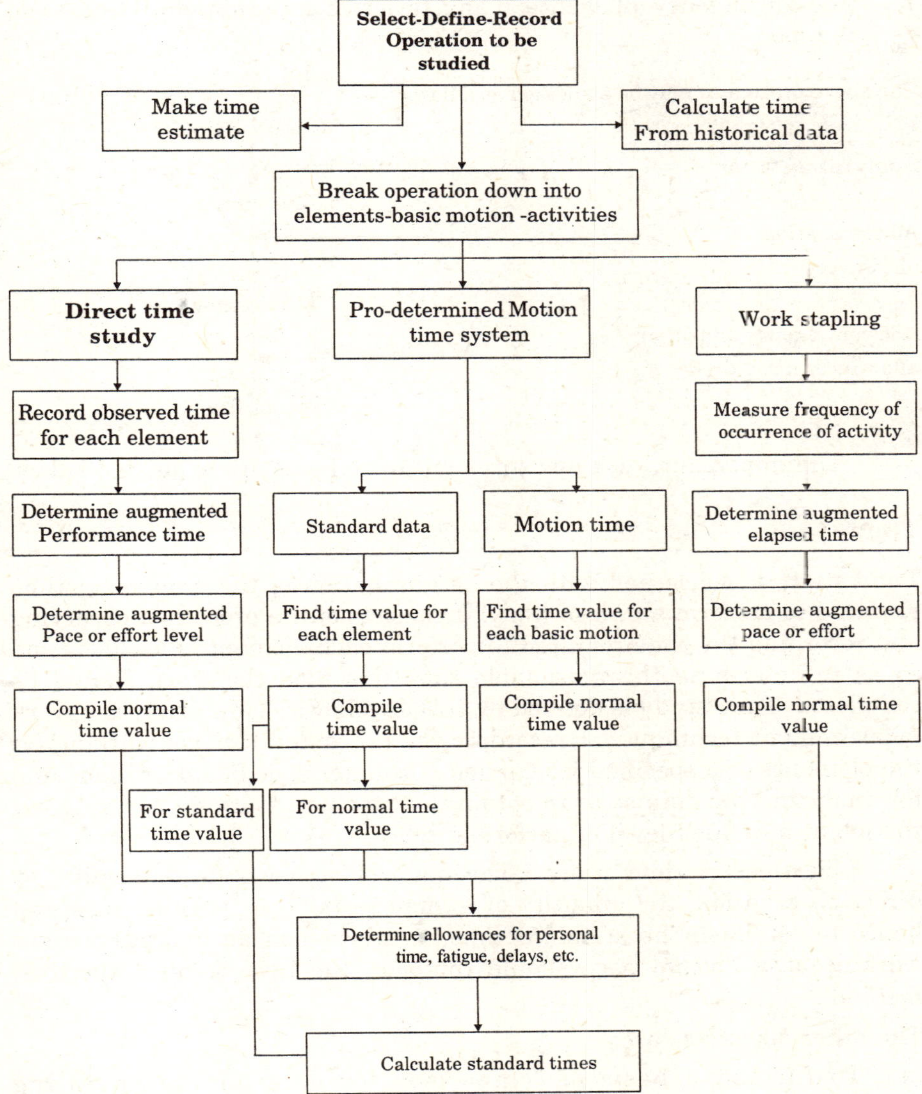

Fig. 2.8. Techniques for determining standard time values for an operation.

5. Add the relaxation allowance time to the normal time for each element to arrive at the work content.
6. Determine the frequency of occurrences of each element in the job, multiply the work content of each element by its frequency (i.e., number of time the element occurs in the job) and add up the times to arrive at the work content for the job.

7. Add contingency allowance, if any, to arrive at the standard time to do the job.

The above procedure may be explained as follows:

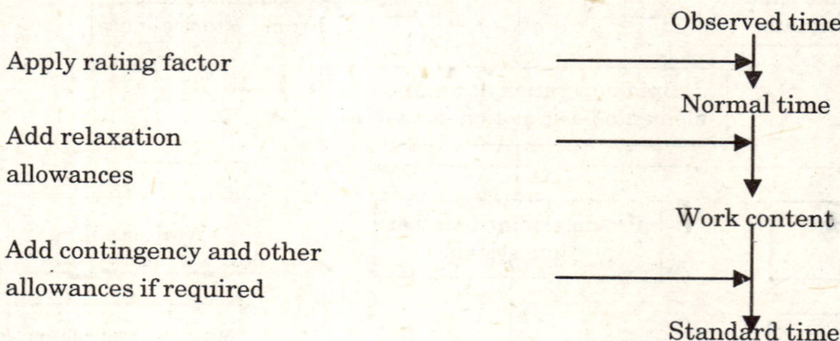

The important work measurement techniques are explained below:

Time study

Time study is concerned with the determination of the amount of time required to perform a unit of work. It consists of the process of observing and recording the time required to perform each element of an operation so as to determine the reasonable time in which the work should be completed. Time study is defined by ILO as follows: 'Time study is a work measurement technique for recording the times and rates of working for the elements of a specified job carried out under specified conditions and for analyzing the data so as to obtain the time necessary for carrying out the job at a defined level of performance'.

Objectives of time study : The main objective is 'to determine by direct observation, the quantity of human work in a specified task and hence to establish the standard time, within which an average worker working at a normal pace should complete the task using a specified method'.

The other objectives are:

(a) To furnish a basic of comparison for determining operating effectiveness.
(b) To set labour standard for satisfactory performance.
(c) To compare alternative methods in method study in order to select the best method.
(d) To determine standard costs.
(e) To determine equipment and labour requirements
(f) To determine basis times/normal times.
(g) To determine the number of machines an operator can handle.
(h) To balance the work of operators in production or assembly lines.
(i) To provide a basis for setting piece rate or incentive wages

(j) To set the completion schedules for individual operations or jobs.
(k) To determine the cycle time for completion of a job.

Time study by stop watch : The steps involved are -

Select the job to be studied

The reason for selecting a job for time study are -

(a) New job taken for production.
(b) Chance in manufacturing method.
(c) Design change.
(d) Change in raw material or components used for a job.
(e) Complaint about inadequacy of allowed time.
(f) For bottle neck operations.
(g) When labour cost is high.
(h) To establish standard time as a basis for incentive scheme.
(i) When new tools, jigs and fixtures are used.

Select the worker to be studied

The ideal worker would be the 'qualified worker', as defined earlier in this chapter. Since the ideal worker or qualified worker may not be available in the organization, the best available worker is chosen and his rating is determined as compared with the qualified worker.

Conducting stop watch time study

In this step, the various activities involved are -

(a) Obtain and record all information available about the job, operator and working conditions.
(b) Record the method of doing the job and break down the job into elements.

An element is a distinct part of a specified job selected for convenience of observation, measurement and analysis.

The various type of elements involved in a job are:

(i) Repetitive element : which occurs in every work cycle of the job. e.g. picking up a component from the container before assembly operation.
(ii) Occasional element : which occurs at intervals e.g., setting a tool on a machine.
(iii) Constant element : for which the basic or normal time remains constant, whenever it is performed: e.g. measuring a dimension
(iv) Variable element : for which the basic or normal time varies
(v) Manual element : which is performed manually

(vi) Machine element : which is performed automatically by a machine

(vii) Governing element : which occupies a longer time than any other element in a job.

(viii) Foreign element : which is found to be an unnecessary element of a job e.g. unexpected breakage of a tool.

(c) Examine the various elements to ensure that the most effective motions are used in the elements of job performed.

(d) Measure the actual time taken by the operator to perform each element of the job, using a stop watch.

A stop watch may be of the following types

(i) Non-fly back (ii) Fly-back (iii) Split-hand

(i) The non-fly back stop-watch is preferred for recording continuous timing. Pressing of the winding knob first, starts the watch and long hand begins to move. If the winding knob is pressed second time, the long hand stops and with the third pressing, the hands return to zero position.

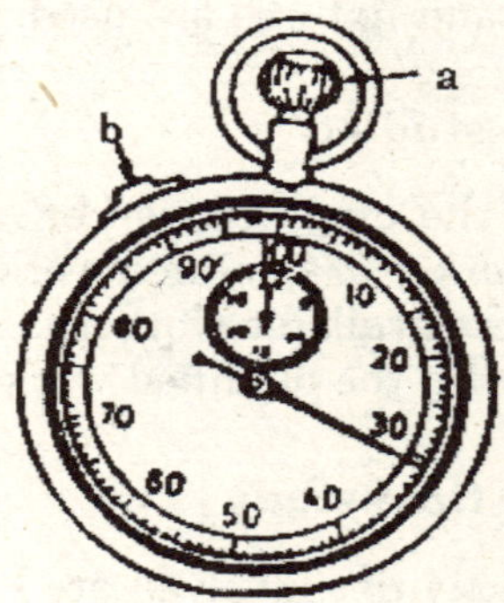

Fig. 2.9. Contaminate stop-watch.

The decimal-minute stop-watch has a long hand making one revolution per minute (100 divisions) and the small hand makes one revolution in 30 minutes.

(ii) In fly back stop-watch, the watch is started and stopped with the help of the slide (item b in Fig. 2.9) Pressing the winding knob brings the hands back to zero, but they do not stop but start immediately moving forward again. The slide is used to stop the hands at any point.

(ii)Split hand type of stop-watch gives higher accuracy in reading when two elements are to be timed successively. As one element is completed, pressing the winding knob makes one hand to stop while the other hand keeps moving. After the time taken for the first element is recorded on the time study observation sheet, a second pressing of the knob restarts the stopped hand and the two hands move together. (The first hand catches up with the other moving hand immediately after pressing the knob).

(e) Assess the effective speed of working of the operator with respect to the time study observer's concept of the speed of working of the qualified worker who is assumed to have a standard rating.

Rating factor or leveling factor is determined by comparing the actual pace of speed of working (of the worker studied) with the standard pace or speed of working (if the qualified worker).

Rating scale : The commonly used rating scales are:

(i) 60-80 Scale (ii) 75-100 Scale (iii) 100-133 1/3 Scale

These three rating scales are compared as below :

Rating assigned in the scale			**Level of performance**	**Corresponds to walking speed**
60-80	**75-100**	**100-133?**		
0	0	0	No activity	Nil
40	50	67	Very slow, clumsy, no interest to do	2 mph
60	75	100	the job Normal, steady, unhurried performance	3 mph
80	100	133?	Businessman – like, brisk performance of a qualified worker	4 mph
100	125	167	Very fast, incentive motivated	5 mph

$$\text{Rating factor} = \frac{\text{Rating of the observed worker}}{\text{Rating of the qualified worker}}$$

(f) Determination of normal or basic time: Once a particular rating scale is chosen and the rating of the worker under observation is assessed as compared to the standard rating of the qualified worker (for e.g. In a 75-100 scale, the qualified worker's rating is 100),

$$= \text{observed time} \times \text{Rating factor}$$

$$= \text{observed time} \times \frac{\text{Observed rating}}{\text{Standard rating}}$$

The observed time for each element is calculated as follows:- A number of readings are taken for each element, depending on the degree of accuracy desired and the length of the work cycle. The average observed time for each element is calculated by dividing the total of the element times by the number of cycles for which the element times are recorded.

(g) Determine the relevant allowances : Once the basic time per cycle required by the qualified worker to perform each element at standard rate of working is determined, the next step is to determine the time allowance to be given to the operator for relaxation, fatigue, contingency etc. Usually these allowances are taken as a percentage of basic or normal time. The various type of allowances are:

(i) *Relaxation allowance (RA)* : This is also known as personal, fatigue and delay allowance (PFD allowance), This allowance is given to the worker to overcome the fatigue due to physical exertion, posture, concentration, working condition and personal needs such as going to toilet, drinking water, attending phone calls etc., It usually varies from 10% to 20% of normal or basic time.

(ii)*Contingency allowance (CA)* : This allowance is give for infrequent or non-repetitive activities such as obtaining special materials from stores, sharpening of tools, getting a special tool from the tool stores, and consultation with the supervisor. It is usually about 5% of normal or basic time.

(iii) *Process allowance* : Allowance given to the worker to compensate himself for enforced idleness due to the nature of a process or operation, for e.g., working on automatic machine, electroplating etc., during which the worker is forced to be idle during a part of the work cycle.

(iv) *Special allowances* :

(a) Interference allowance given to a worker when he/she is looking after 2 or 3 machines. One machine may idle when the worker works on another machine for a short period and allowance has to be given to the worker for this loss of production.

(b) Periodic activity allowance - for activities carried out periodically during a work cycle e.g., setting up a tool on the machine.

(h) Determine the standard time by adding the relevant allowance to the normal or basic time

Standard time = Normal time + all relevant allowances

Fig. 2.10 shows the conversion of observed time to standard time.

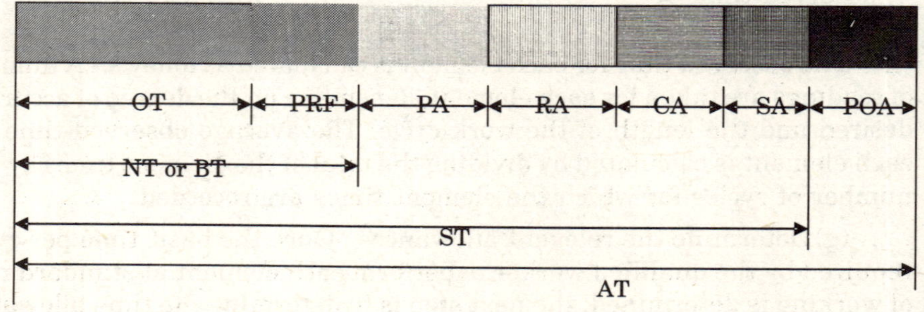

OT = Observed time
PA = Process Allowance
SA = Special Allowance
PRF = Performance Rating Factor
POA = Policy Allowance
ST = Standard Time
NT = Normal Time
RA = Relaxation Allowance
AT = Allowed Time
BT = Basic Time
CA = Contingency Allowance

Fig. 2.10. Computation of Standard Time

Synthesis Method

Synthesis is a technique of work measurement for building up the time required to do a job at a defined level of performance by synthesizing or totaling elemental time values obtained from previous time studies on other jobs containing similar job elements or from standard data or synthetic data or built-up time standards.

Standard data : Standard data is a catalogue of 'normal' or 'basic' time values for different elements of jobs. This catalogue is prepared by compiling the timings of a number of standard elements. Since many similar elements or motions are involved in many jobs (for e.g. drilling holes), if time study is to be conducted for a new job, it is wasteful to re-time those elements of the new job which are in common with the previously timed jobs. In such cases, it is always economical to use the previously timed and complied data known as standard data. Once the standard data catalogue is built up, one required to list the job elements of an operation, refer to the standard data catalogue and obtain the elemental time values from the standard data catalogue and add them up (i.e. synthesize). The total time thus obtained, give an estimate of normal time for a job which can then be converted into standard time by adding relevant allowances.

Advantage of Synthesis Method

1. Reliable as the built-up time values of the 'standard data' catalogue, are based on data derived from a large number of time studies.
2. Economical as less time is required when compared to 'stop-watch' time study.
3. Used for estimating labour times for preparing cost estimates for new jobs for which the selling price has to be quoted to customers.

Applications of Synthesis Method

(a) To estimate standard time for new jobs
(b) To estimate production time for determining the prices of products to be sold.
(c) Used as a basis for designing incentive schemes.

Analytical Estimating

This technique of work measurement is used to determine the time values for jobs, having long and non-repetitive operations. The time values are determined by using synthetic data or on the basis of the past experience of the work study engineer, when no synthetic or standard data is available. It is essential, that the estimator must have adequate experience of estimating, motion study, time study and the use of standard data (or synthesized time standards).

Procedure of analytical Estimating

The various steps involved are:

(a) Find out the job details such as job dimension, standard procedure to do the job, and the job conditions, such as poor illumination, high temperature, hazardous environments, availability of jigs, fixture or tools, etc.,

(b) Break the job into its elements

(c) Select time values from the standard data catalogue for as many elements as possible. (i.e. use synthetic data wherever available)

(d) Estimate the time values for the remaining elements (for which synthetic data is not available) from past knowledge and experience

(e) Add the time values obtained by steps (c) and (d) to get the total 'Basic' or 'Normal' time (for 100% rating)

(f) Add the appropriate blanket relaxation allowance (say 10% to 20% of total normal or basic time). Note that in analytical estimating, the relaxation allowance is not added to time values of individual elements. The blanket relaxation allowances depends on the type of the job and the job conditions.

(g) Add any other allowances if applicable, to arrive at the standard time for the given job.

Advantages of Analytical Estimating Technique

(a) Offers the same advantages enjoyed by synthesis method.

(b) Helps in planning and scheduling the production.

(c) Provides a basis for fixing the labour rate for non-repetitive jobs.

(d) Steps to improve labour control.

Disadvantages

Since analytical estimating technique relies upon the judgement of the estimator, the time values obtained may not be as accurate and reliable as that estimated by the stop-watch time study.

Applications of Analytical Estimating Technique

(i) For non-repetitive jobs, jobs having long cycle times and jobs having elements of variable nature. For such jobs the stop-watch time study proves to be uneconomical.

(ii)For repair and maintenance work, job production, one time large projects, office routines, tool room jobs and engineering construction works.

Predetermined Motion Time System (PMTS)

Predetermined motion time system is defined as a work measurement technique by which normal or basic times are established for basic human motions and these time values are used to build up the time for a job at a defined level of performance.

PMTS is an improvement over motion study because, besides affording detailed analysis of the motion, it makes it possible to set a measure of the time, that a series of motion ought to take.

Predetermined time standards are standard data for wide variety of basic body motions which are common in many industrial operations. For example, some of the basic or elementary human body motions are - 'move', 'position' etc. Predetermined time standards contain table of standard time values for such basic motions.

Advantages of PMTs

1. Affords fine analysis and improvement of work methods.
2. Since the time for each basic motion is predetermined, the computation of standard time for a job or an operation is faster and more economical than time study using stop watch.
3. Offers a precise means of recording time, avoiding subjective judgement or bias of the rater.
4. Involves no interference in the normal work routine and hence faces little resistance from workers.
5. More effective and economical tool for work measurement for repetitive jobs of short duration.

Disadvantages

1. Such standards are not available for each and every human activity
2. Limited to only uninhibited work in its application, i.e. for the work which does not involve motions, restricted by the process
3. Has limited application in non-repetitive and office activities.
4. Fairly long period of intensive training under expert guidance is necessary to use this technique.

Despite their limitations, PMTs represents the most accurate time estimates as it is based on careful analysis of the motion required to perform a job.

Types of Predetermined Motion time Systems

(i) Methods Time Measurement (MTM) : In this method, predetermined time values for basic motions or therbligs such as reach, move, turn, apply pressure, grasp, position release and disengage etc. are established in terms of TMU's (i.e. Time measurement Units). One TMI = 10-5 hour or 0.00001 hour or 0.0006 minutes or 0.036 seconds. The time values are listed in tables in terms of TMU's for basic motions and may be applied to any type of operations that may be resolved to the basic motions, thus eliminating the use of stop-watch.

Application of MTMs Technique

MTM has been used for:

(a) Developing effective methods in advance of beginning the production.

(b) Improving existing methods.

(c) Establishing standard time data.

(d) Estimating labour time and cost.

(e) Training supervisors to be method-conscious.

(f) Choosing between alternative methods.

(ii) *Work-Factor :* This technique is based on basic motions which are modified elements of difficulty, all of which tend to make movement slower. These features or work factors are weight or resistance, change of direction, need for care, stopping a motion and manual control. Each of these features is known as a 'work factor' and it modifies the basic time value.

(iii) *Basic Motion Times (BMT) :* In this system, the times were derived from laboratory experiments and were carefully checked against a variety of factory operations before being accepted for general use. BMT data are based on basic motions. A basic motion occurs every time a body member which is at rest moves and again comes to rest. For example, the action of knocking on a door, requires two basic motions for every knock - one to draw the hand back and another to move the hand forward and knock.

Basic motions are classified as : finger, hand and arm motions, foot and leg motions and miscellaneous body motions. The motions of finger, hand and arm are further classified as 'class A' motions, 'class B' motions and 'class C' motions, depending on the use of muscular control in stopping the motions 'class A' motions are stopped without muscular control by impact with an object, 'class B' motions are stopped entirely by the use of muscular control and 'class C' motions are stopped by the use of muscular control both to slow down the motion and to end it in grasping or placing action.

Work Sampling or Activity Sampling or Ratio-Delay Method

Work sampling is a work measurement technique that randomly samples the work of one or more employees at periodic intervals to determine the proportion of total operations that is accounted for in one particular activity.

These studies are frequently used to estimate the percentage of time spent by the employees in unavoidable delays (commonly called ratio-delay studies), repairing finished products from an operation and supplying material to an operation.

Uses of Work Sampling Technique

1. To estimate the percentage of a protracted time period consumed by various activity states of a resource such as equipment, machines or operator.
2. To determine the allowances for inclusion in standard times.
3. To indicate the nature of the distribution of work activities within a gang operation.
4. To estimate the percentage of utilization of groups of similar machines or equipment.
5. To indicate how materials handling equipments are being used.
6. To provide a basis for indirect labour time standards.
7. To determine the productive and non-productive utilization of clerical operations.
8. To determine the standard time for a repetitive operation as an alternative to the stop watch method.

Work Sampling Procedure

In work sampling study, the works study engineer takes a great number of observations of a worker or machine random times throughout the working shift or day. He records precisely what the worker or the machine is doing (i.e. working or idle) at the time of observation. No stop-watch is used. The objective is to find the frequency of occurrence of every work element.

The technique is based upon the laws of probability. It is based on the statistical premise that, the occurrences in an adequate random sample observations of an activity will follow the same distribution pattern that might be found in a lengthy, continuous study of the same activity.

Algebraically put,

$$P = \frac{x}{N} = \frac{\text{Number of observations of the activity}}{\text{Total number of observations}}$$

Thus, the work sampling method, as stated above, consists of taking a number of intermittent, randomly spaced instantaneous observations of the activity being studied and from this determining the percent of time devoted to each aspect of the operation.

In order to set a standard by the work sampling procedure, it is necessary to level or rate the performance of the worker being studied (as with stop watch time study) and to count the actual number of units produced during the period under study.

Finally it may be stated that the accuracy of the approach depends on the number of observations made. Higher the number of observations, greater is the occurrence.

Steps in Work Sampling

The work sampling study consists of essentially the following steps:

1. Determine the objective of the study, including definitions of the states of activity to be observed.
2. Plan the sampling procedure including:
   (a) An estimate of the percentage of time being devoted to each phase of the activity
   (b) The setting of accuracy limits
   (c) An estimation of the number of observations required
   (d) The selection of the length of the study period and the programming of the number of readings over this period
   (e) The establishment of the mechanics of making the observations, the route to follow and the recording of data
3. Collect the data as planned.
4. Process the data and present the results.

Principles involved in Work Sampling

Work sampling is based on statistical theory of random sampling and probability of normal distribution and confidence level associated with standard deviation. This is best illustrated by the following example.

Let x = number of observations of the activity in a pilot study

n = Total number of observations of the activity in the pilot study. Then the

$$\text{proportion of activity } P = \frac{x}{N}$$

The proportion of 'no activity' = 1 - p = q (say)

The total of the two states which are mutually exclusive is 1, i.e., p + q = 1.

Where p = probability of an occurrence (e.g. Working)

q = probability of no occurrence (e.g. not working or idling)

This expression may be extended to include several observations (N) and then becomes,

$$(p + q)^N = 1$$

If this expression is expanded by the binomial theorem, the first term of the expression will have a probability that , x = 0, the second term x = 1 and so forth. The distribution of these probabilities will follow the binomial distribution and will have a mean $\sqrt{Npq}$ value equal to Np and a standard deviation equal to . As N becomes larger, the binomial distribution approaches the normal distribution and we may use the normal distribution as a satisfactory approximation.

In order to use the normal distribution approximation, we need to divide both mean and the standard deviation by N, thus we have the mean equal to and the standard deviation

$$\sigma_p \frac{\sqrt{Npq}}{N} = \text{where } q = 1 - p$$

$$\text{Thus, } \sigma_p = \frac{\sqrt{Npq}}{N} = \sqrt{\frac{pq}{N}} = \sqrt{\frac{p(1-p)}{N}}$$

On the basis of the sampling theory, we cannot expect the 'p' determined by an estimate to be the true value of p. However, on the basis of normal distribution, we can expect the true p to be within ±3sp' approximately 99% of the time. In view of this relationship, if we wished to evaluate p so that the sampling error is reduced to the point where we may say the chances are 95 out of 100, that 'p' is correct to within ±5% of the true value of p, then,

$$2\,\sigma_p = 0.5 = 2\sqrt{\frac{p(1-p)}{N}}$$

$$\therefore \sqrt{\frac{p(1-p)}{N}} = \frac{.05}{2} \text{ or } \frac{p(1-p)}{N} = \left(\frac{.05}{2}\right)^2 = \frac{(.05)^2}{4}$$

$$\frac{4\,p(1-p)}{(0.05)^2}$$

In general, if E is the absolute error (%), then $N = \frac{4\,p(1-p)}{(E)^2}$

Where N is the number of observations needed for work sampling study to get a result within the error of ± E% and a confidence level of 95% for which the standard deviation under normal distribution curve is + $2\sigma_p$.

Similarly, if a confidence level of 99% is needed with an absolute error of E (%) than 3 σ_p = E = 3

$$\sqrt{\frac{p\,(1-p)}{N}}$$

$$\text{or } E^2 = \frac{9\,p\,(1-p)}{N} \text{ or } N = \frac{9\,p\,(1-p)}{(E)^2}$$

If we assume that C is a constant, corresponding to the confidence level, then values of C will be 1 for 68.3% confidence level, C = 2 for 95.45% (or 95%) confidence level and c = 3 for 99% confidence level. Then the number of observations needed for the work sampling study to get the result within an absolute error of ±E (% age) is $N = \dfrac{C^2\,p\,(1-p)}{E^2}$

If is the relative error or accuracy desired as a decimal fraction of, true proportion p, then absolute error E = s × p

$$\text{and } N = \frac{C^2\,p\,(1-p)}{(sp)^2} \text{ or } \frac{C^2\,p\,(1-p)}{E^2} \text{ or } \frac{C^2\,p\,q}{E^2}$$

where

p = percentage or true proportion of activity or idling which is being observed based on pilot study,

s = relative error of the true proportion ‘p’.

c = constant having values of 1, 2 and 3, corresponding to the confidence level of 68.3%, 95% and 99% respectively.

Advantages of Work Sampling over Conventional Work Measurement Methods

1. Economical to use and usually costs considerably less than a continuous time study
2. Can be used to measure many activities that are impractical to measure by time study
3. Not necessary to use a trained work measurement analyst to make the observations
4. Work sampling measurements may be made with a pre-assigned degree of reliability

5. Measures the utilization of people and equipment directly.
6. Eliminates the necessity of using stop-watch for measurements.
7. Provides observation over a sufficiently long period of time to decrease the chance of day to day variation affecting the results.

Limitations of Work Sampling

1. It is of 'little value in helping to improve work methods and doesn't offer some of the opportunities for methods analysis that accompanies time study methods.
2. Statistical work sampling may not be understood by workers
3. If random sampling is not done, the results may be biased.

Solved Problems

1. For a certain element of work, the basic time is established to be 20 seconds. If for three observations, a time study observer records ratings of 100, 125 and 80 respectively, on a '100-normal scale', what are the observed timings?

Solution

$$\begin{pmatrix}\text{Observed}\\\text{time}\end{pmatrix}\times\begin{pmatrix}\text{Observed}\\\text{rating}\end{pmatrix}=\begin{pmatrix}\text{Basic or}\\\text{Normal time}\end{pmatrix}\times\begin{pmatrix}\text{Standard}\\\text{rating}\end{pmatrix}$$

$$\therefore \text{Observed time} = \frac{(\text{Basic or Normal time}) \times (\text{Standard rating})}{\text{Observd rating}}$$

Data : Basic or Normal time = 20 seconds

Given Standard rating = 100

For observation No. 1, Observed rating = 100

$$\therefore \text{Observed time} = \frac{20 \times 100}{100} = 20 \text{ seconds}$$

For observation No.2, $\text{Observed time} = \frac{20 \times 100}{125} = 16 \text{ seconds}$

For observation No.3, $\text{Observed time} = \frac{20 \times 100}{80} = 25 \text{ seconds}$

2. An 8 hours work measurement study in a plant reveals the following: Units produced = 320 nos. Idle time = 15%. Performance rating = 120%. Allowances = 12% of normal time. Determine the standard time per unit produced.

Solution

Observed time for 320 units = Working time - Idle time

= 8 - 8 × 0.15 = 8 - 1.2

= 6.8 hours

= 6.8 × 60 = 408 minutes.

$$\text{Observed time per unit} = \frac{408}{320} = 1.275$$

$$\text{Normal time per unit} = \frac{\text{Observed time / Unit} \times \text{Observed rating}}{\text{Standard rating}}$$

= Observed time/unit x Performance rating

= minutes

Standard time/unit = Normal time/unit + Allowances

= 1.53 minutes + 12% of 1.53 minutes

$$= 1.53 + \frac{1.2}{100} \times 1.53$$

= (1.53 + 0.184) minutes

= 1.714 minutes

Man-Machine Diagrams

Other types of charts used are the Man-Machine charts, which on a vertical time scale indicate the various activities done by man and machine both on the same chart, for carrying out a certain operations by the man-machine team. An example is given in Fig.2.11.

Similar graphic charts are sometimes constructed for multi-man-machine situations and some to purely show the coordination (or lack of it) between the left and right hands of the operator (called Simo Charts).

The basic idea behind such charts is to visually aid in highlighting the possibility of:

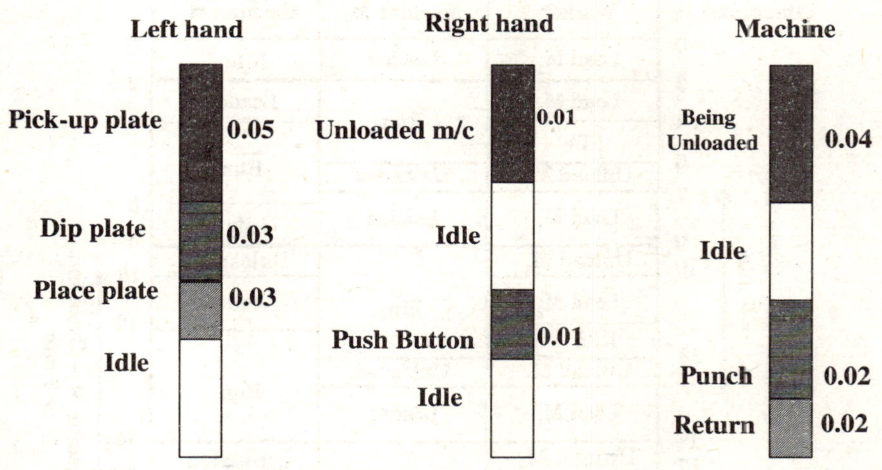

Fig. 2.11. An Example for Constructing a Man-Machine Chart, showing Left and Right Hand and the Punching Machine Activities

(i) better coordination between man and machine,

(ii) reduction/elimination of idle times of man and machine to improve the utilization, and

(iii) exploration of alternative man-machine arrangements suitable to the plant conditions.

Worker-Machine Chart or Man-Machine Chart or Multiple Activity Chart

Worker-machine charts or man-machine charts are a graphical representation of simultaneous activities of a worker and the machine or equipment he or she operates. These charts help identify idle time and costs of both workers and machines. Alternative worker-machine combinations can be analysed to determine the most efficient arrangement of worker-machine interaction for carrying out a job.

Worker-machine charts show the time required to complete tasks that constitute a work cycle. A cycle is the length of time required to progress through one complete combination of work activities. Fig. 2.12 illustrates a worker-machine chart.

Process Design Procedures in General for a Typical Industry Manufacturing Consumer Durable Home Appliances

The major steps involved are :

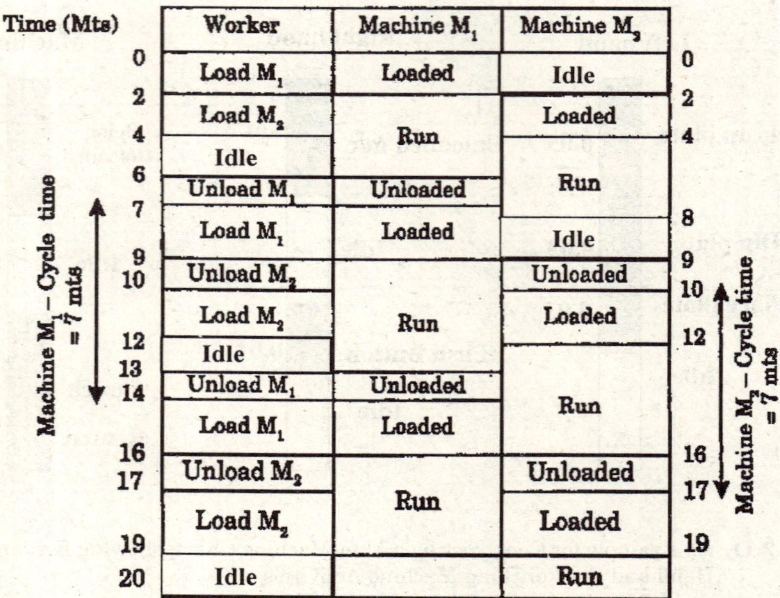

Fig. 2.12. Worker-Machine chart

Step No. 1 : The product designer and the process engineers need to work in close co-operation during the design of the part to ensure that all possible manufacturing problems are taken into consideration as the component part design is developed. This will also ensure economic manufacture of the component parts and for the product as a whole. Besides, the design changes that may be required at a later date to accommodate the manufacturing process, will also be minimum.

Step No. 2 : Determination of the three basic factors of volume, quality and the availability of manufacturing equipment is possible once the design of the component part is completed. Purchase or development of new or more modern equipments may be considered.

Step No. 3 : The next step is the decision to 'make' or 'buy'. Comparison of the purchase price for a component part, with the estimated manufacturing cost, as determined by the process engineer, enables the decision maker to decide, whether to make or buy the component part. Other factors such as, maintenance of employment levels, optimum utilization of plant facilities and relationship with vendors, also enter into the consideration.

Step No. 4 : Assuming that the decision is taken to make the part in-house, the next step is to consider all the work that is necessary to bring the part from the raw material stage to the completely processed part stage, which is ready for assembly.

Step No. 5 : Determination of the various operations to be carried out and their sequence is the next step. The basic factors of volume to be produced, the required quantity of the product and the capabilities of the equipment available are carefully considered in this step. Each operation is assigned to the type and size of the machine or work station that will perform the job, most economically.

Step No. 6 : The last step in operation analysis is to arrange the operations in proper sequence for the most economical manufacture.

Value Analysis/Value Engineering

Another important job of the purchasing executive, is that of finding proper substitutes for raw materials. For this, a management technique developed during the Second World War period called Value Analysis (VA) or Value Engineering (VE) might be of much help. It is a systematic method of thinking about substitutes. It basically consists of studying in detail the 'value' of the material. The value could be due to the functional characteristics (i.e. performance) of the product or due to other considerations of value such as the 'esteem' value. In organizational purchasing we largely do not encounter the latter kind of value. The idea behind Value Analysis is to find a substitute giving the same functional value, yet costing the same or less.

Step 1 - Information Stage

Here, all the relevant information regarding raw material and the finished production in which it is incorporated, such as the cost, the manufacturing method, the performance characteristics, etc. is gathered. The more detailed the information gathered in this initial stage; the better will be the Value Analysis. Here one may ask questions in detail, such as what, where, when, how and why (for each of them).

Step 2 - Functional Analysis

At this stage, the functions that the material performs are listed in terms of basic function and secondary functions. It is advised that the functions be described in two words - a very and a noun - as far as possible. This is to avoid long winding descriptions of the functions. After having listed the functions, each of these functions is given the value points or the weightages in terms of its importance or desirability. If the value (or worth, as it is alternatively called) is expressed in terms of 0-100 points, then the total for all the functions of a material should add to 100 points. Alongside, we also mention the cost incurred (or price paid) for each of the functions. Placing the cost and the value points side by side immediately reveals those areas of the material where much money is spent for little value. These high cost-to-worth functions are the focus of our attention in suggesting a substitute design of a bought-out part or a substitute material. If the value of a function is small, then that function can be dropped altogether in the substitute product.

Step 3 - Brain Storming

Having done the analysis of the functions and costs of the material, we are now ready to third of various alternative possibilities for the material. The main idea, here, is to encourage creativity. Many of the suggestions may seem like wild guesses. Still, these are recorded even if all suggestions are not feasible. The idea is to break away from rigid thinking and encourage creativity. Some systems of brain-storming start idea-generation from such widely differing 'triggers' as politics and geography, and develop them further so as to apply to the problem at hand (which could be finding an alternative product design). For such idea-generation, a heterogeneous group is preferred.

Step 4 - Evaluation Phase

Each of the ideas is evaluated again in terms of a functional analysis, i.e. by finding the various functions that the substitute can perform-to what extent and at what cost for each of those functions. Such as analysis will indicate a few of the alternatives which might offer similar functional value as the earlier material, but at a reduced cost. We may even find some substitutes with enhanced important functional values.

Step 5 - Implementation

In this phase, the selected substitutes, or new ideas are discussed with the appropriate departments for their implementability. It is possible that some will be screened out and only one or two ideas might be implementable.

Such a systematic analysis of the functional values of input material along with their cost structure will help the purchasing executive in finding alternative materials of equal functional value or better value while reducing the procurement costs. Value analysis, of course, should be done as a team work since it involves a lot of creative and interdisciplinary thinking.

Operations Management

UNIT—III

5

Operation Planning Technique

Introduction

Production planning/Operations planning involves the organization of an overall manufacturing/operating system to produce a product.

The various activities involved in production/operations planning are designing the product, determining the equipment and capacity requirements, designing the layout of physical facilities and materials handling system, determining the sequence of operations and the nature of the operations to be performed along with time requirements (standard times) and specifying certain production quantity and quality levels.

Objectives of production planning is to provide a physical system together with a set of operating guidelines for efficient conversion of raw materials, human skills and other inputs into finished products.

Factors determining Production Planning Procedures

The production planning procedures used varies from company to company. Production planning may begin with a product ides and a plan for the design of the product and the entire production/operating system to manufacture the product. It also includes the task of planning for the manufacturing of a modified version of an existing product, using the existing facilities. The wide difference between planning procedures in one company and another is primarily due to the differences in the economic and technological conditions under which the firms operate. The three major factors determining production planning procedures are:

Volume of Production

The amount and intensity of production planning is determined by the volume and character of the operations and the nature of the manufacturing processes. Production planning is expected to reduce manufacturing costs. The planning of production in case of custom order job shop is limited to planning for purchase of raw materials and components and determination of work centers which have the capacity of manufacturing the product. In high volume operations, extensive production planning is necessary in planning for the design of both the product and the production processes in order to achieve substantial cost reduction when a larger number of products are produced.

Nature of Production Processes

In job shop, the production planning may be informal and the development of work methods is left to the individual workman who is highly skilled. In high volume production, many product designers, equipment designers, process engineers and methods engineers are involved and they put enormous amount of effort in designing the product and the manufacturing processes.

Nature of Operations

Detailed production planning is required for repetitive operations., for example, in case of continuous production of a single standardized product.

The variants in manufacturing approach are:

(a) Manufacturing to order which may or may not be repeated at regular intervals.

(b) Manufacturing for stock and sell (under repetitive batch or mass production). Example: manufacture of automobiles, watches, typewriters etc.

(c) Manufacturing for stock and sell, (under continuous process manufacturing). Example: chemical and food products, soap, synthetic yarn etc.

The degree to which production planning is carried varies with the nature of the process.

Production Planning System

There are two inter-related sub-system in the production planning system namely:

1. Product planning system and
2. Process planning system.

The inter-relationship between these two sub-systems is shown in Fig.3.1

Operations Planning

When Liberty builds a plant to produce shoes, its managers have some idea of the number of pairs of shoes the plant will be capable of turning out.

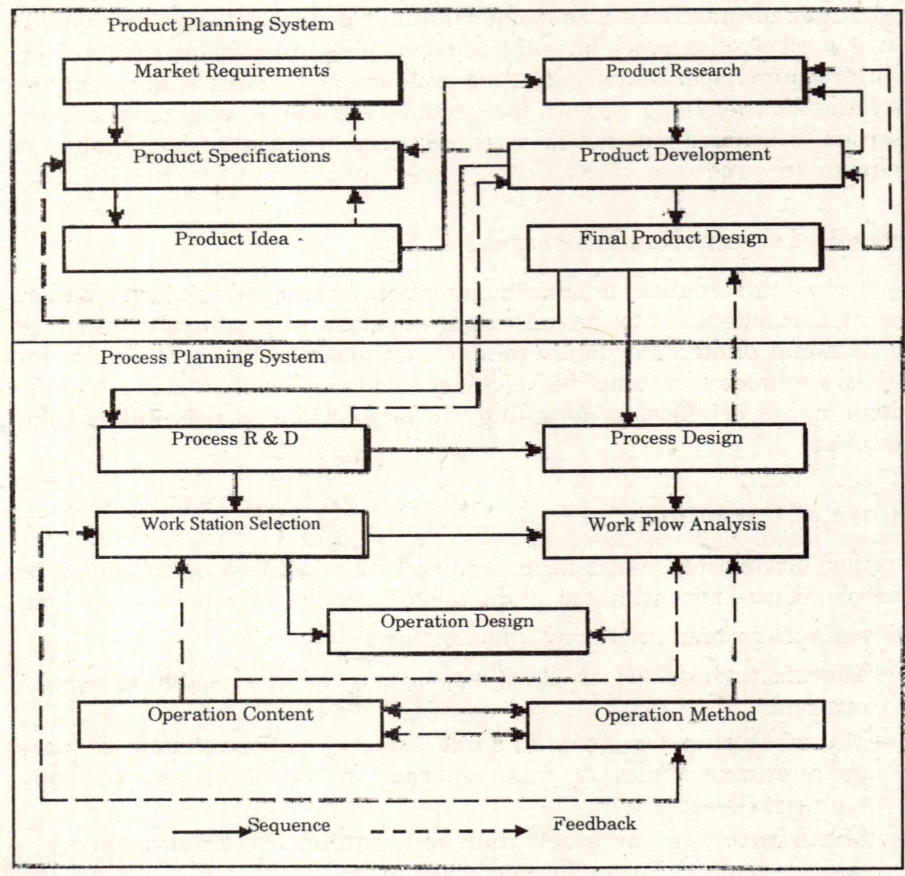

Fig. 3.1. Production planning system

When General Motors builds an automobile assembly plant, its managers have certain expectations concerning the number of cars the plant will be able to produce. A hospital is built to house a specified number of beds. and a school's enrollment is limited by the number and size of classrooms. These facilities are all built to a size that has certain "capacities."

The Concept of Capacity

The capacity of a factory is an ambiguous concept. It is not like the capacity of a milk bottle which will hold one quart of milk and no more under any circumstances. Capacity is a rate of output, a quantity of output in a given time, and it is the highest quantity of output that is possible during that time. Yet, capacity is at the same time a dynamic concept which is subject to being changed and managed. To some extent, it can be adjusted to meet fluctuating sales levels.

The unit of output

One problem with the capacity concept is the unit of output. An automobile tire factory turns out tires, but tires come in many varieties. A tire factory can turn out more of some kinds and sizes of tires than other kinds and sizes. So its capacity when expressed in the number of tires is ambiguous.

In a one-product factory there would not be this kind of ambiguity, but single-product factories are almost unknown. Even a Kellogg's corn flake factory turns out several kinds of breakfast cereals. Oil refineries turn out different kinds of gasolines and oils. Book printing companies turn out large books and small books and in various quantities. Fire departments put out big fires and little fires. It is possible to express a refinery's capacity as so many barrels or gallons of oil or gasoline, and it is possible to express a book printer's capacity us so many books, but neither would be wholly accurate because the number would differ according to the mix of the kinds of products being made. The units of production are not homogeneous.

The matter of product mix is important when planning for the future. Sometimes, when a company's top administrators approve plans to spend money for added capacity, they express the new capacity only in terms of Rupees worth of sales. They leave it to the industrial and process engineers to develop a prospective product-mix breakdown. After doing this, these same engineers then have to calculate the kind and number of machines needed to produce the expected rupee volume for the mix they anticipate.

Time

Time poses another problem. A person talking about capacity is talking about a quantity of output in a given amount of time, but how much time? Some kinds of manufacturing processes require continuous operation. A steel rolling mill must operate continuously, 24 hours a day, or not at all. When it is not operating, the furnaces cool down (unless extra money is spent to keep them hot though idle), and they must be relined with new fire bricks at high cost. The only way a steel mill can change its scale of operation is to open up or close down furnaces. When talking about the capacity of a steel mill, a manager probably would be thinking about the lot -- the amount of steel it can roll out while operating all of its furnaces 24 hours a day, 7 days a week. On the other hand, the capacity of a book binder would probably include only daylight hours.

Most operations do not operate around the clock; instead, they operate from 9 to 5 daily, Monday to Saturday. Their capacity is regarded as being their normal output in a 48-hour work week. But a 48-hour week is not their maximum capacity. It is usually possible to work more hours a day or more days a week. In most cases, the maximum possible capacity is considerably more than the 48-hour output.

Capacity, Inventories and Steady Production Rates

Capacity should never be considered by itself but rather as part of a bigger picture. Often, because of sales volume variations, a company has to choose between increasing or decreasing its production levels or carrying inventories, both of which are costly. Diwali is a time of heavy sales in department stores, Holi is a busy period for automobiles, and Umbrellas sell well in the monsoon. But sales dip for many items in off seasons. Such variations make it difficult to operate efficiently.

If the facility's managers were to expand and contract production with sales, their plant's capacity would have to be big enough to take care of peak sales, but the plant would not work at top capacity very much of the time. Operating this way is usually impractical because it is impossible to keep an efficient work force with off-and-on employment. A factory's normal production capacity probably should be set at a point well below its peak needs.

Operating steadily is fine from the production point of view, but, if sales are irregular, other costs must be considered. Management could choose to produce at low volumes continually and pass up the extra sales during high sales periods. This might be a costly solution to the problem because of the sales which would be lost. Another alternative would be to produce at a higher level, but this would probably cause inventories to build up during slack periods. But carrying inventories can also be costly.

In the case of automobiles, for example, the monsoon and winter months are two lean months, followed by a heavy festival demand. It would be very expensive for Maruti to make 50,000 extra cars in June, July and August just to keep producing steadily. By the end of August it would have 150,000 extra cars on hand. Even at Rs. 200,000 each, Rs. 3000 crores would be needed to carry the inventory. Farms and fair grounds would be needed as parking lots for all of these cars.

Besides the staggering investments, there is a danger of a poor sales year. If car sales in the Diwali season did not come up to what was expected, production would have to be cut back. Such miscalculations can bankrupt companies. Stockpiling finished products is dangerous because no company knows for sure just what volume it will sell in the future.

There are, however, some things a company can do to regularize production. It can change its capacity by increasing or decreasing work hours. And, although it is not a happy solution, the organization can change its capacity by hiring extra employees or laying off people as sales go up and down. And it can change its capacity by subcontracting non-core work during peak periods and doing all the work itself in slack periods. It can also do a little stockpiling and try to stimulate sales in off seasons. Possibly, too, it can try to hold back some peak-season business, promising later delivery and hoping that business will not be lost. And, as a long-run policy, a company can try to diversify into related product lines whose seasonal demands are opposite to that of existing products.

No one of these measures can, by itself, be carried far enough to eliminate all changes in production rates. A little of each, however, carried on at the same time, will accomplish quite a bit of leveling out of production.

Finally, it is well to note that idle plant capacity is a tremendous incentive to try to increase demand. It might stimulate sufficient extra sales effort to generate enough added demand to alleviate much of the problem.

Planning Overall Operations

In order to adjust a factory's capacity up and down to respond to the demands of the marketplace, it is necessary to forecast sales expectations and to plan for the needed capacity changes. Otherwise changes are likely to be sudden and drastic and, consequently, costly to make.

Forecasting is particularly important where products are made to be stocked rather than to fill customers orders already on hand. Almost all makers of products that are sold to final consumers make them to stock. Products are made for expected sales, but they are neither ordered nor sold until after they are made and put into finished goods stock.

It is necessary to forecast, at least roughly, the sales of every important product and of groups or classes of minor products and to do this month by month. This has to be done in order to tell the factory what to make and to check the future capacity demands against the capacity available. The problem is to foresee what and how many products the customers will buy (and customers are for the most part an unpredictable lot). This is an area where computers are being very helpful even though they do not produce perfect forecasts.

In addition to the unreliability of forecasts are the equally important irregularities of sales. It could easily be, for example, that a sales forecast would show that the sales of product A for the next three months will be in the range of 15,000, then 25,000, and, finally, in the last month, 10,000. Almost always it would be uneconomical to make the necessary capacity adjustments to match such an extremely irregular demand pattern. At the 25,000 level, the plant would probably be on a 10-hour, 6-day week schedule, whereas, at a 10,000 rate, it would be on short hours, would have some people laid off, and the plant would be half idle. Managers have to try to operate more steadily than this.

Yet, if operations are steadier, this will mean that there will be times when more products are being produced than are being sold, so inventories will build up. There will be other times when the reverse happens, and inventories are drawn down. The existence of inventories allows production and sales to be "decoupled" so that production can be carried on economically while at the same time the irregular demands of customers are taken care of by filling orders out of stock. Inventories cushion differences between production and sales.

This is one situation where optimizing one factor, in this case inventories, should not occur. Optimal inventories, considered by themselves, almost always are small inventories. But holding down inventories often neglects the total picture and would sometimes be poor inventory control from the total operations viewpoint.

Capacity as a lower-limit constraint

The discussion so far has emphasized how a factory's lack of capacity sets top limits to production schedules. But capacity also serves as a lower level constraint. During slow sales periods it is almost always desirable to produce more products than are currently being sold because it is so uneconomical to reduce capacity drastically when it is highly probable that sales will soon again pick up.

Capacity as a limiting constraint to production schedules at the low end is different from the way it works at the upper end. At high levels it becomes a very positive limiting factor. No more can be produced. At the low end it is a managerial decision constraint. Physically, it is possible to stop production altogether, but this would usually be so uneconomical that managers impose a managerial decision constraint requiring a certain amount of production even when some of the production is not needed and has to go into inventories.

Overtime for Expanding Capacity

Although workers in the automobile industry almost always work short hours in the winter, in the spring they are usually on overtime. Management plans it this way. Yet, when we say that management plans it this way. we do not mean that management wants the short hours. We mean that companies plan for overtime in the spring rather than planning to hire large numbers of extra employees who would soon have to he laid off. Similar decisions are also common in other industries with large seasonal variations in sales.

Planned overtime to meet seasonal peaks has many advantages. It increases the employee's pay and usually more than offsets the lowered earnings during seasonal lulls, so most of the employees like it. It minimizes the need for hiring more people and laying them off later. Jumping employment up and down usually results in low productivity. Besides, this would increase unemployment taxes when the new workers were laid off. And sometimes a company cannot find enough people with the right skills to hire anyway.

Furthermore, in autos. steel, and many other industries, full work crews are needed for many of the operations, it is not possible to get, say, 10 percent more output by adding 10 percent more workers. Longer hours for regular crews is often the only way to get 10 percent more output. Also, much of the work is paced by conveyors or by equipment work cycles. Consequently, fatigue from the long hours does not result in lower output (quality, however, might suffer).

Overtime is not, however, without its problems. One is that workers incomes go up and down because the overtime is not regular and continued. Another problem is the lowered production pace when the work is not machine or paced by fixed-speed conveyors. Obviously, if production drops off drastically during overtime hours, labour costs during these hours become prohibitive.

Important, too, is the drop in a worker's pay when overtime stops. A cut from a 55 - hour week to a 40 - hour week pares a person's pay 28 per cent (from 55 to 40 hours' pay). Most workers would not like 28 percent pay cuts. So, if they have any notion that operations are going down to 40 hours and if they are not machine paced, they sometimes drag out their work. It may be necessary to continue the overtime just to get a normal 40 hours of work done.

We are saying that workers want to work overtime because of the quite high pay. Sometimes this is so. When only a few people are asked to come in on Saturday and work overtime, workers frequently use their seniority to be among those chosen.

Yet, in some cases, the reverse happens. Workers do not want to work overtime. If they have been working overtime for a long time, they may prefer shorter hours. In particular, they often object to surprise decisions, such as a foreman asking them at 3:30 in the afternoon to work until 8 or 10 P.M.

Normally, workers can be disciplined for refusal to do the work assigned, so it is not surprising that the question of being allowed to refuse to work overtime is covered in the labour contract, meaning that managers are not wholly free to make overtime decisions. Today's labour contracts often give workers a right to refuse to work overtime unless they are told ahead of time and unless the whole department works extra hours.

This has a curious effect on assembly line work. If it is decided on short notice to work a line overtime, some of the workers will surely say no. Then the foreman has to recruit people from other jobs for the overtime on the line. He ends up with a mixed crew of workers, some of whom are on jobs strange to them. Yet, production continues because of the fixed pace of the line. If these jobs are difficult to learn quickly, quality may suffer. On the other hand, if the tasks are relatively simple, quality is usually not affected.

Overtime and operating efficiency

Long workweeks are fatiguing, so gains in output from long hours are not proportional to the extra hours because hourly output slides off. And since overtime hours cost an extra half in pay, the direct labour costs of the extra units produced by the overtime are quite high.

No studies seem to have been made in recent years of the effects of long hours on productivity; however, scattered reports from industry support the results reported in studies made a number of years ago. The results of

Hours per week	Hours percent of 48 (Normal work)	Output as percent of 48 hour production	Index of hourly production
48	100 %	100 %	100
56	117.5 %	115 %	97.5
64	133 %	122 %	86.75

the studies are found in table above. These figures are, of course, only approximate and cannot be used as exact relationships. The actual decline in any specific case would depend on a great many things. The decline is more pronounced on heavy than on light work, more pronounced for women than men, more after weeks of overtime than at first, more on employee-paced work than on machine paced work, and more when workers are paid by the hour than when they are on piece work. Absenteeism and accidents also increase a little with continued long hours.

For men, according to the one study, total output reaches its peak at about 56 hours (less on heavy jobs). Above 56 hours the dropoff in hourly output from fatigue more than offsets the production in added hours, so total production goes down. For women, the peak is somewhere around 52 hours.

Hours per week	Production per Hour	Total Production in week	Labour cost (@ Rs.10 Normal and Rs. 15 per hour Overtime)	Average Cost per Unit	Extra Production	Extra Cost	Cost per unit for extra costs
48	100	4800	480.00	0.10	0	0	0
56	97	5432	600.00	0.11	632	120	0.18
64	87	5568	720.00	0.13	768	240	0.31

For low labour costs per unit, a company probably should stick to 48 hours. Figure above shows how much more the production from the added hours can cost. It shows that by going from 48 to 56 hours a week, total production (in a hypothetical case) might be expected to go from 4,800 units to 5,432, but. because of overtime costs and slightly lowered hourly output, the unit costs for the extra units are much higher.

The extra 768 units produced by going from 40 to 64 hours cost Rs.. 0.31 each extra (direct labour costs only) or 30 % extra unit cost for production in a 48-hour week.

Figure above does not, however, tell the whole story. It exaggerates the costs of production during overtime because certain other costs, such as the company's hourly contribution to the supplemental unemployment benefit fund and other costs of fringe benefits, do not go up 50 percent for overtime hours as does the direct pay for hours worked. Nor do workmen's compensation taxes. Also, PF are based on only the base pay of a person's earnings. Should workers' earnings go above that there is no further PF for the year?

But, even more important, some charges, such as for general plant overheads, do not go up any at all. They are taken care of in the 8-hour a day operating costs. If they amount to as much as 50 percent of direct labour costs (and this is common), then the costs of overtime hours are about the same as for regular hours. The only extra costs are those stemming from fatigue-caused lower production. Thus, the total costs of producing on overtime may not be nearly so much as Figure above suggests.

It is possible also that working long hours today will not cause as much decline in productivity as was found in the older studies cited above. The pace of work in today's factories is less demanding than it used to be. Affluent workers, who can easily get jobs elsewhere, often do not push themselves very hard. Absentee rates, for example, are higher than they used to be and may even go to 10 percent or more on Mondays and Saturdays. When this is so, the work pace during the regular 48 hours may be leisurely enough that long hours may not result in any substantial reduction in hourly output.

In fact, it is now customary in many organizations to have a few extra "floaters," (employees to fill in for absentees). It is not unknown for such workers to come to work and be kindly told to "just do nothing." On days of excellent attendance there is simply nothing for them to do. In a sense these floaters are an "inventory safety stock of labour." If they are not needed, then idle "labour inventory" costs are incurred.

It is interesting to note that during the recession of the 1980s, many organizations retained skilled employees rather than lay them off even when they had little for them to do.

Capacity and the 40-Hour Week

A small plant, operated day and night, can turn out just about as much as a larger plant operating only one shift. So, when a company plans its operations, it can choose whether to put up a small plant and use it intensively or a larger plant and use it less intensively.

Most manufacturing companies can operate 8, 16, or 24 hours a day. A plant with operations 8 hours a day needs to be nearly 3 times as large as one in 24-hour operation in order to produce the same daily output. Similarly operations can be carried on for 4, 5, 6 or 7 days a week. The fewer hours worked, the more physical plant capacity is needed for a given output.

At first, operating a small plant long hours looks like the best arrangement because the overhead costs per unit of product are reduced. Most of the time. however, it costs less to operate a larger plant fewer hours. Common practice is to have a plant large enough to take care of normal needs when it operates 8 hours a day and 5 days a week.

Although single-shift production requires a larger plant and more machines than 24 hours-a-day production, equipment depreciation costs per unit of product may, in the long run. be about the same either way. Three shift operations permit one machine to produce almost as much as three machines would produce in one shift, but a machine that is used 24 hours a day lasts only about one third as long as a machine that is used 8 hours a day. Over the years, a company may have to buy about the same number of machines in either case.

Many overhead expenses, such as building depreciation, insurance, taxes, interest on investment, and obsolescence of machinery, are reduced when a small plant is used intensively. But three-shift operation has certain costly disadvantages which often more than offset the gains. Second and third-shift employees get higher hourly pay rates (commonly 5 percent extra on the second shift and 10 percent on the third shift). And unless they are paced by production lines, night shift workers are a little less productive than first-shift workers. Night shifts often have more new employees than day shifts because most people like the day shift, and, as soon as they can they use their seniority to transfer to first-shift work. There is also usually a little more turnover and more absenteeism among night-shift workers. Also, night-shift people often do too many things during the day and come to work tired, and so are less productive.

In any case and as a consequence of all these factors, night-shift workers may be no more than 90 percent as efficient as their day-shift counter-parts. Products made on the night shift are likely to cost 10 percent more than products made on the day shift, depending, of course, on how important labour costs are in total manufacturing costs.

Maintenance is also easier with one-shift five-day operation than with three-shift, seven-day operation. In the former case, most repairs can be done in off hours with no interference to production. Less intensive use of the plant also permits production to be expanded during peak periods with little increase in overhead costs because adequate plant capacity is already available.

Many companies use parts of their plants intensively (16 or 24 hours a day) and other parts extensively (8 hours a day) at the same time. They buy the smallest possible number of very expensive machines and operate them two or three shifts, while other machines work only the normal first shift.

Detroit's auto companies, GM, Ford, and Chrysler, in USA, usually plan for their automobile assembly factories to operate, during their busy periods 53 hours a week (five 9-hour days plus one 8-hour day). They do not plan to use second shifts even during seasonal peaks because there are just too many problems and cases involved in hiring large numbers of people for short periods of time in USA. And the auto companies have found that work weeks of more than 53 hours cause too much absenteeism. People just don't show up for work.

Automobile companies do not, however, put in enough capacity to handle their peak sales volumes in 53-hour weeks. Rather, they set the 53-hour capacity at 75 to 80 percent of their peak needs. This means that they are not able to fill all orders from new production during sales peaks. So during peak seasons, some customers have to wait. To avoid losing too many sales, the companies do a little stockpiling ahead of the peaks, and they try to get their dealers to do the same. By setting capacity production below their peak needs, they can operate at capacity for a good portion of the year.

Yet everybody has seen automobile plants lighted up and operating at night, so there is obviously some second-shift operation. This, however, is usually confined to parts-making departments, where machines are costly. In such cases, normal parts-making "capacity" is the output of two shifts. The capacity of second-shift parts-making plants equals the one-shift needs of the assembly plants.

Break-Even Charts and Capacity

When a factory is operating at or below capacity, the relationships among costs, sales, and profits are as they are shown in the break-even chart in Figure A given below. But there are times when demand exceeds capacity. If such an excess demand appears to be temporary, capacity should probably be expanded by working overtime in spite of the extra costs. Such a company's break-even chart would be shown in Figure 3.2. So long as the new profit spread, "A" (in Figure 3.2), exceeds the old "B" profits (in Figure 3.2), this would be a paying action.

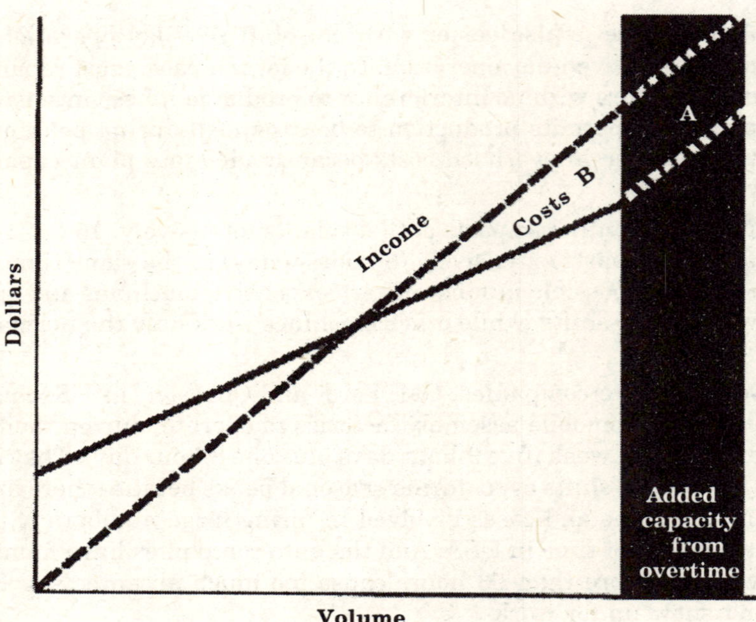

Fig. 3.2

Should, however, the larger sales volume appear to be permanent, then perhaps the capacity should be expanded by adding more machines rather than using overtime. Such a change would result in a new break-even chart: Figure 3.3 below. The new higher level of fixed costs would move the break-even point a little to the right (a higher volume would now be required). But since considerably higher volume is expected, the profit spread should be greater than before.

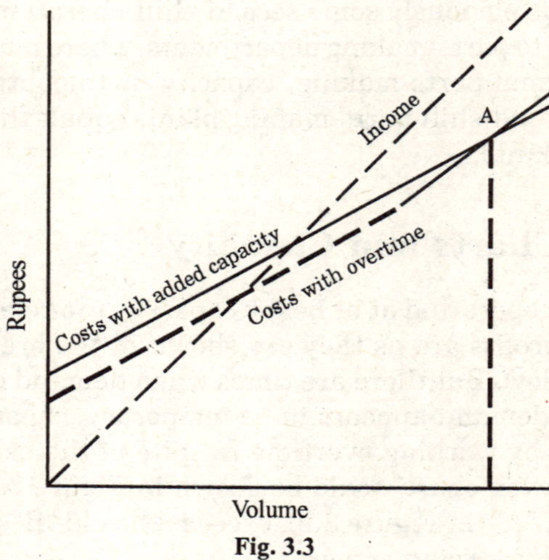

Fig. 3.3

Even if today's above-normal-capacity demand is only seasonal, it may still pay to make the permanent additions to capacity indicated in Figure B. This would be true, for example, if the extra amount of available profits, even though available for only part of a year, were greater than the reduction in profits during the rest of the year when operations return to the old capacity level. Whether or not such permanent capacity should be added can be calculated.

Let us say that:

Old profits at old capacity are Po,

New profits at new capacity are Pn.

Profits with new capacity but at old capacity levels are Pr

The fraction of the year when operations will be at new capacity are F1.

The fraction of the year when operations will be at old capacity are F2.

Then the new capacity should be installed any time such that

$(Pn \times F1) + (Pr \times F2) > Po$.

Although it may not often be wise, another choice open to managers when demand exceeds capacity is to raise prices and so hold volume down. Such an action would raise the income line but would decrease the volume. The proper decision would depend on the expected profits at the two different volume levels. Competition and elasticity of demand also come into the picture here.

Work Force Capacity

We have been making the point that it is quite uneconomical to increase and decrease the work force with every sales increase and decrease. This might sound as if we were saying that a given number of employees is a fixed capacity resource.

But this is far from true. Substantial adjustments can be made without having to resort to hiring more people and then having to lay them off.

An example will show how this could work. Suppose that the labour requirements needed to make all of the company's products while working a normal 6-day, 48-hour week produces the following expectation of number of employees needed:

June 300
July............................. 400
August........................ 600
September.................. 450
October........................ 400

The labour load in August is double that of June. Actually, however, the figures on the number of people needed are for "equivalent employees."

There is a need for the work that this number of employees would do in 48-hour week. But, as we have suggested earlier, the hours per week can be changed, and so can the amount of work sent to outside contractors. And, by doing a little stockpiling, some of the work from peak months can be transferred to earlier months, as shown earlier.

Here is a feasible plan for factory work hours to take care of the sales needs while holding the work force constant.

Month	Number of people	Hours per week	Equivalent people contracted outside
June.................	350	34	----
July....................	350	46	----
August...............	350	58	92
September..........	350	51	----
October..............	350	46	----

Whether to go to overtime, or to vary the work force more, or to send out more work, or to build inventories are obviously largely managerial decisions (except where the labour contract provides otherwise) and depend, as before, on the relative costs of the alternatives.

Our example demonstrates that a factory's capacity, so far as labour power is concerned is susceptible to considerable change without the need either of hiring more employees or laying people off.

Labour power planning has many more minor facets which need to be allowed for. We did not, in our example, allow for any loss in production from fatigue during long workweeks, which would probably be substantial during the 58-hour workweeks planned for August. Nor have we allowed, in our example, for any stockpiling with inventories to be carried over.

Nor are all months alike. Some have as few as 20 and some as many as 23 work days. So a given workload per month is not the same employee load in different months. Absences also need to be figured in. It takes at least 105 people on the payroll to keep 100 people on the job. And it takes even more in the summer when everyone takes vacations (presumably, because of summer train rush, employees in this company would take their vacations at other times during the year). Labour turnover may also need to be considered. There is always a loss in production when an employee leaves and is replaced, so if there is a significant turnover this needs to be allowed for.

Indirect labour to support the work of direct workers needs to be planned just as much and perhaps more than direct labour. This is partly because some "indirect" people are technical employees and are sometimes hard to find and partly because it is hard to know just how many indirect workers are needed. Most companies try to get an idea of how many indirect workers they need by using some kind of a ratio of indirect workers to direct workers or to the factory's work load. They do not, however, continually increase and decrease indirect employment in proportion to factory work load changes.

Machine Capacity Balance

For companies that make varied products, the mix of products shifts all the time, and this places unequal loads on different machines and work centers. Also, some machines are slower than others; consequently some equipment will always be working full time while other equipment is sometimes idle. Some work centers will be working overtime while others are on short hours.

Long-term trends cause part of the problem because yesterday's products often required machines which are not needed as much today. At the same time, today's products call for heavy use of certain other machines. About all that can be done is to add more machines where today's demand consistently required costly overtime work and where this demand seems likely to continue. Old machines -- those no longer used -- can be retired. By making such changes continuously, a reasonable balance of capacity for doing various kinds of work can be maintained.

It is also possible to work on controlling the demand side. If some department is not busy, the sales force can try harder for the kind of business which will use its machines. Or, if departmental capacities are out of balance, jobs formerly sent out to subcontractors can be brought back in-house, as is IBM's policy. Similarly, work in overloaded departments can be sent outside or delivery dates to customers can be changed.

Bottleneck limitations

When machine capacities are out of balance with needs, it is the bottlenecks which hurt because they limit what can be done. Often a bottleneck can be loosened by improvisation's which expand the capacity of bottleneck machines temporarily. They can be operated through lunch periods and they can be worked overtime. Normal overhauls can be postponed by running the machines until they break down. Or they can be speeded up and run as fast as they will go, even if this is hard on the machines and tools. Three people, instead of one, can be assigned to do setups and repairs to speed them up.

The supervisor can also try to get people who operate bottleneck machines to hold down their coffee breaks. And, if a person has to be away from the machine during the day, the supervisor can have someone else keep the machine running. Also, it is not unknown for supervisors to "roll up their sleeves" and pitch in and help if union rules allow it, that is (usually they don't). Finally, it may be possible to supplement the bottleneck machine's capacity by doing some of the work on older, less efficient machines. Or perhaps part of the work can be sent out to other companies.

Most of these improvisations are only expediencies, however, and they do not solve imbalances between operations permanently. And because individual machines' capacities differ and the work loads generated by sales keep shifting, there will always be a few bottleneck spots.

A plant's capacity is therefore limited by the capacity of its bottleneck operation. If this operation can be changed, this single change affects the capacity of the whole plant or department. It may even be economical to redesign the bottleneck machine so that it will run faster, or maybe a second machine of this kind should be bought.

The gain in total capacity, however, will not be equivalent to the improvement in the bottleneck operation. If the latter's capacity is increased by 25 percent, the increase in a department's capacity might come to, say, only 5 percent, because now some other operation becomes a bottleneck.

This will be illustrated in our discussion of machine use in PERT & CPM. Capacity expansion becomes a matter of handling a succession of bottlenecks.

Resource Allocation

Free Float and Total Float are extremely useful in the allocation of resources, particularly when there are constraints on their availability and usage. In the developing countries, shortage of commodities such as cement, steel, or explosives at onetime or another is common. Also capital shortage is not unusual. Under such conditions it may not always be possible to complete the project in the planned time. Rescheduling the start of various activities, taking advantage of their floats, might relieve the pressure on the requirements of the resources at different points of time.

Resource Analysis

With the pattern of availability of resources being constrained, with the best of reallocation we may not be able to complete the project in the planned time, but at least the delay will me minimized. Such an exercise of rearranging activities, by taking advantage of their floats, in order to cause minimum delay to the project from availability and usage constraints on resources is called "Resource Analysis". This is a very important component of network analysis.

There are two types of resource problem:

(i) There may be a ceiling on the availability of the resources in a particular period of time. For instance, only Rs.125 lakh, per annum may be available to the projects and, if unutilized during the year the remaining amount lapses. The particular resources analysis used, for this case, is termed as Resource Smoothing.

(ii)A resource may be required to be used in a uniform manner. For instance, in the present day labour situation, one cannot have 100 labourers yesterday, 30 today and 80 tomorrow. Once a labourer is hired, it is difficult to fire him. The rate of usage of labour has to be uniform. Resource Analysis used for this category of problem is called Resource Levelling.

In order to illustrate the Resources smoothing problem, let us consider Fig. 3.4. It is time scaled network, which means, the length of the arrow is proportional to the duration of that activity and the entire network is squared within any oblique arrows. Moreover, the network is drawn with all activities starting at there earliest. The broken part of the arrow represents the float (in this case, Free Float). In Fig.3.4, the number on top of an arrow represents not only the duration of the activity in days but also the requirements of unskilled workers on any day for that activity. The requirement of the workers on different days can be easily computed as shown in fig. This is the early start requirement of workers. It has a peak requirement of 12 workers on days 3, 4 and 5.

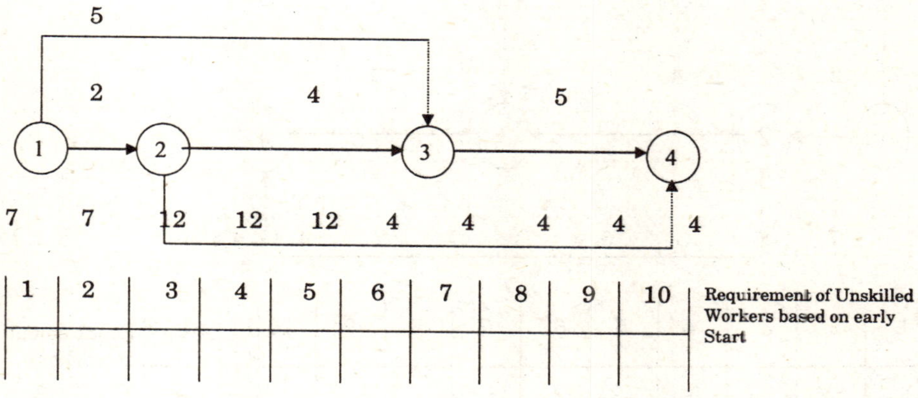

Fig. 3.4. Time-scaled Network, Depicting Floats, Accompanied by Calculations on the Minimum Requirement of the Unskilled Workers on Different Days

Now if there is a constraint on the availability of labourers, the maximum available o any day being 9, can the project still be completed on time (i.e. in 10 days)?

As Fig. 3. shows, the project can still be completed in1 0 days, by rescheduling activity (2, 4) to start on the 6th day and curtailing its float to 2 days (from the original 5 days.) Thus, the 'floats' of the activities are useful in rescheduling and in the reallocation or resources.

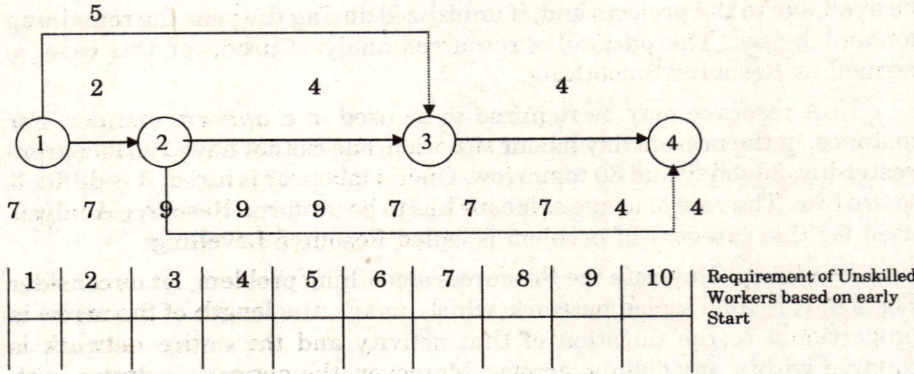

Fig. 3.5. Network Rescheduling for the Availability of Maximum 9 Workers on Any Day

Figure 3.6 shows rescheduling when the resources are constrained to the level of 7 workers (maximum) available on any day. Under such a drastic constraint, the project has to be delayed by at least 3 days.

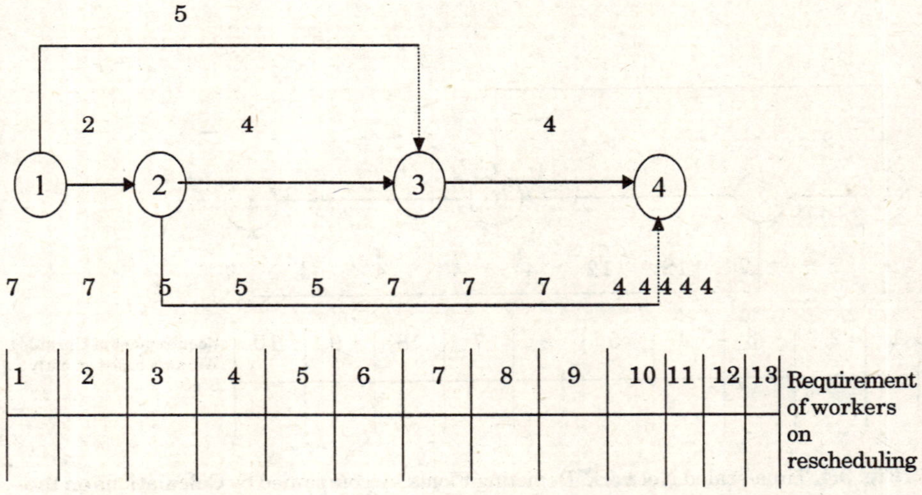

Fig. 3.6. Network Rescheduling for the Availability of Maximum 7 Workers on Any Day

(NOTE: In Figs. 3.4 to 3.6 it has been assumed that the activities, once started, cannot be interrupted moreover, higher or lower amount of application of resources does not reduce or enhance the time duration of the activities).

Uses of Heuristics in Resources Analysis

We see from the above example that making use of floats available and shifting activities (rescheduling them) to correspond the resource availability in such a way as not to delay the project or in cases where it is impossible not to delay the project, to delay the project as little as possible is the crux of Resources analysis. There is no formula or any easy analytical or mathematical model to indicate the optimal shifting of activities from the early stat schedule, taking advantage of the total and free floats. What we have are certain thumb rules or a set of thumb rules. These thumb rules or heuristics' do give, if not optimal, near optimal results. One of the heuristic procedures fro leveling of the resources is by Burgess, a modified versions of the same is given below:

Leveling of Resources Step 1 List the project activities in order or precedence by arranging the arrow head numbers in ascending order, and when two or more activities have he same head numbers, list them so that the arrow tail numbers are also in ascending order. Next prepare a bar chart for the activities showing their total and free slack and heir current schedule which should be as early as possible. If certain activities have schedules fixed by previous resource allocations or total projects duration time constraints, they should be drawn on the chart with no slack.

Step 2 Starting with the last activity (the one at the bottom of the diagram), a schedule it to give the lowest total sum of squares of resource requirements for each time unit. If more that one schedule gives the same total sum of squares, then schedule the activity as late s possible to get as much slack as possible in all preceding activities.

Step 3 Holding the last activity fixed, repeat step 2 on the next to the last activity in the network, taking advantage of any slack that may have been made available to it by the rescheduling in step2. In general, this slack availability check is made by observing the scheduled start times of all activities having a tail number equal to the head number of activity in question, these activities will always be found below the one in question. The earliest of these observed scheduled start times is then the latest allowable finish time of the activity in question.

Step 4 Continue Step 3 until the first activity in the list has been considered, this completes the first rescheduling cycle.

Step 5 Carry out additional rescheduling cycles by repeating Steps2 through 4 until no further reduction in the total sum of squared or resource requirements is possible, noting that only movement of an activity to the right (schedule later) is permissible under this scheme.

Step 6 Make final adjustments to the schedule taking into account factors not considered in the basic scheduling procedure.

The above procedure was for ensuring, as far as possible, a constant rate of usage of resource and hence the concept of the least sum squares was quite appropriate. But when there are constraints or ceilings on the availability or resources, a very different kind of heuristic or algorithm is to be used. Most of the resources allocation algorithms schedule the job in each period (day or week, etc.) only up to the limit of the resources, and then postpone any remaining jobs until resources are sufficient for scheduling them. The resources are allocated on a period by period basis to some subset pf the available jobs - these whose predecessors have been completed. The approach is to use the jobs which are most critical. One of the heuristic presented by Wiest and Levy is given below:

Resource smoothing

1. Allocate the resource serially in time, i.e. start on the first day and schedule all the jobs that are possible, then do the same for the second day, and so on.
2. When a number of jobs compete for the same resources, give preference to the jobs that have the least slack.
3. Reschedule non-critical jobs, if possible, and free resources for scheduling critical or non-slack jobs.

It should be emphasized once again that this heuristic, or any heuristic for that matter, may not produce optimal results, but definitely, near optimal results can be achieved with this expenditure of less energy and time. Analytical procedures are to some extent available and they guarantee optimality. Analytical procedures might involve Linear programming, Integer Programming etc. but again, these analytical methods are feasible for only very small projects. For the present, heuristic programmers are that only possible procedure for dealing with the problem of large projects and multiple constrained resources.

To sum up, resource allocation is a way of utilizing the available floats of the activities and rescheduling the activities in such a way as not to exceed the given ceiling on the resources (or to achieve as m much constant rate of usage of the resources as possible if that is what is needed) and to do this with limited delay in project completion. Resource allocation/ analysis is also a very valuable planning exercise. It can provide alternative schedules by trying out different resource patterns. Various assumed conditions can provide different scenarios for the project manager's decision-making.

6

Liner Programming Problem

Introduction

Linear Programming is an Operations Research technique which originated during the early 1950s. Having diverse practical applications, this technique has benefited immensely various organization in their production and other operations. Prof. G.B. Dantzig is one of the pioneers in formulating the procedure of Linear Programming.

This technique can be applied in various situations: long range planning, production planning, warehousing decisions, physical distribution decisions, marketing and product-mix decisions, fluid-blending problems, exploration of oil deposits, purchasing decisions, quality control decisions, material utilization decisions, etc.

Linear Programming Problem

Definition

The basic problem solved by Linear Programming is that of optimizing either profit or total costs or some other utility function. It takes into consideration the limitations or constraints on the availability or usage of different resources such as manpower, machinery, materials, time and money as also other limitations and constraints such as those existing in the market (e.g. only so many units of a product could be sold) or specification for quality such as the maximum or minimum limit on the performance characteristics of a particular product, etc. In short, Linear Programming deals with optimizing a desired objective under a situation where there are various constraints. Most of the management problems are optimal decision-making problems made under the various limitations. Therefore, Linear Programming rightly attracts the attention of practicing executives.

LINEAR programming is a widely used operations research method which is a member of a family of techniques called mathematical programming. In general, mathematical programming methods are designed to allocate limited resources among competing alternative uses for these resources so that some predetermined objective -- usually maximizing profit or minimizing costs -- is satisfied or optimized.

The term "linear" in linear programming means that the relationships between factors must be linear or the answer will not be valid. Linear relationships means that when one factor changes so does another and by a constant amount. An hourly paid employee's working hours and wages are linear: the more hours, the more total wages. Linearity can also be negative, the more there is of one thing, the less there is of another. If a person starts with Rs. 20, the more he spends on something, the less he has left.

We shall illustrate what Linear Programming means through a simple example. Suppose a Company produces two products X and Y, both of which require a particular raw material and a particular machine. Product X requires 4 machine hours and 3 kg of raw material per unit of the product, and product Y requires 2 machine hours and 6 kg of raw material per unit of the product. Suppose that the availability of the raw material and machine hours is limited. The raw material is available to the maximum extent of only 240 kg per month and the machine hours are available to a maximum extent of only 200 machine hours per month. Each of the products X and Y contribute to the profit margin by Rs.7 and Rs.9 respectively per unit of the product. How many units of products X and Y should the company produce every month?

Formulation of a Linear Programming Problem

In the above problem, the company has to decide on the quantities of X and Y which are the decision variables, and this is to be done so as to maximize the profit margin which is the objective, under the limitations or constraints of resources. Linear Programming problems, typically, have three elements:

(i) Decision variables, the determination of whose value is the problem to be solved.

(ii) Objective function, which is to be either maximized or minimized (e.g. maximization of profits or minimization of total costs, as the case may be).

(iii) Constraints or limitations or conditions related to the decision variables.

The solution of a Linear Programming problem involves:

1. Expressing the objective in an algebraic form involving the decision variables in algebraic notations. This expression is called the Objective Function which is either to be maximized or minimized.
2. Expressing the constraints in algebraic inequalities involving the decision variables in algebraic notations.
3. The above two steps complete the formulation of the Linear Programming problem. This, now, is solved for the determination of

the optimal values of the decision variables by means of a mathematical procedure. Simple Linear Programming problems can be solved as a graphical procedure. The graphical procedure is shown for the solution of our product-mix problem.

Example Let X and Y denote the quantities of the products X and Y. The Objective Function is given by:

Maximize profit contribution, $P \equiv 7X + 9Y$;

Subject to the constraints:

$4X + 2Y \leq 200$ ....constraint for machine hour;

$3X + 6Y \leq 200$ ....constraint for raw material;

and

$$X \geq 0;$$

$$Y \geq 0.$$

The last two constraints express that the quantities of X and Y cannot be negative. These are known as non-negativity constraints which are necessary for all Linear Programming problems.

Having formulated the problem, thus, we shall now try to solve the problem for the decision variables X and Y by means of a graphical technique.

Taking the first constraint of machine hours, let us convert it into the following:

$Y + 2X\ 100$ (1)

Similarly, the second constraint of raw materials can be converted into

$Y + 0.5X\ 40$ (2)

Automobile Manufacture: a Graphic Solution

We will illustrate linear programming by using an example of an automobile assembly factory. To keep the problem simple, we will assume that this factory makes only two models: a two-door six-cylinder car and an eight-cylinder station wagon. We will deal with three manufacturing departments: metal stamping, engine assembly, and final assembly. In the final assembly department there are two assembly lines: one for two-door cars and one for station wagons. Both can operate at the same time.

The stamping department can in a week, turn out enough parts for 7,000 two-door cars or 12.000 station wagons. But it can't do both at the same time. It is possible to do one or the other or to make parts for some two-door cars and some station wagons. It is the same with engines, it is possible to produce 9,000 six-cylinder engines which are used only in the two-door cars. or 6,000 eight-cylinder engines which are used only in station wagons, or to have some six's and some eight's.

The two-door car assembly line can turn out 6,000 cars as a maximum. And the station wagon line's maximum capacity is 4,000. Here, however both lines can operate at the same time. Increasing the output of one line does not require reducing the other.

These limitations impose several "constraints" to the possible choices in production quantities. In summary, these are:

Departments	Maximum number for		Maximum number for
Metal stamping.................................7,000		or	12,000
Engine assembly...............................9,000		or	6,000
Final assembly..................................6,000		and	4,000

No one limitation sets limits for all possible combinations. It is possible, at one extreme, to make 9,000 six-cylinder engines, the kind used in the two-door cars. but there is no need to make this many six-cylinder engines since only 6.000 two-door cars can be assembled. Assembly limitations would rule here.

It is also possible, so far as assembly is concerned, to assemble 4,000 station wagons as well as the 6,000 two-door cars. But actually this can't be done because it is not possible to make enough stamped parts or engines. The stamping capacity will allow making parts for 6.000 two-door cars, but, if this is done, then there is not enough stamping capacity left to make parts for 4,000 station wagons. Nor could enough engines be made to permit making the maximum assembly quantities of each kind of car at the same time.

All of the possible maximum quantity mixes can be defined by using the "linear rate of substitution" between two-door cars and station wagons. For stampings, this rate of substitution is 7,000 / 12.000 or 0.5833. For every one station wagon that we stamp parts for, we could instead stamp parts for 0.5833 two-door cars. Thus, if we stamp enough parts for 6.000 two-door cars, or 1,000 under the maximum of 7,000, we could also stamp enough parts for l,715 stationwagons (1,000 / 0.5833).

Similarly, for engines, for every eight-cylinder engine, we could make instead 9,000 / 6,000, or 1.5 six-cylinder engines. So, if we made 6,000 six-cylinder engines, this would leave enough additional capacity to make 3,000 more six-cylinder engines, or 2,000 eight-cylinder engines (3.000 / 1.5).

These relationships can be stated in the form of constraint equations. If we let T equal the number of two-door cars we can make, and W the number of station wagons, then the stampings department constraint is:

T + 0.5833 W 7,000

For the engine department, the constraint equation is:

T + 1.5 W 9,000

Figure 3.7 below shows the area of feasible solutions for stamping production. The enctosed area encompasses all possible combinations of two-door cars and station wagons which can be stamped. The diagonal sloping line is the constraint and defines the "linear rate of substitution" between the two models. Any combination of numbers of two-doors and station wagons which falls on the diagonal line will keep the stamping department fully occupied. Combinations within the enctosed area are also possible but will not keep the department fully busy.

Figure 3.8 shows the solution feasibilities for the engine department. Again, the diagonal line sets off the maximum production combinations. And again, lesser combinations are feasible even though they would not keep the engine department busy, so slack would occur. The two other constraints, the assembly capacity for each kind of car, are shown in Figure 3.8. These constraint lines are not mutually dependent on each other, and one cannot be substituted for the other so there is no rate of substitution. Again, the enclosed area encompasses the feasible combinations so far as these two constraints are concerned. The constraint equations for the two assembly lines are:

$T \leq 6{,}000$

$W \leq 4{,}000$

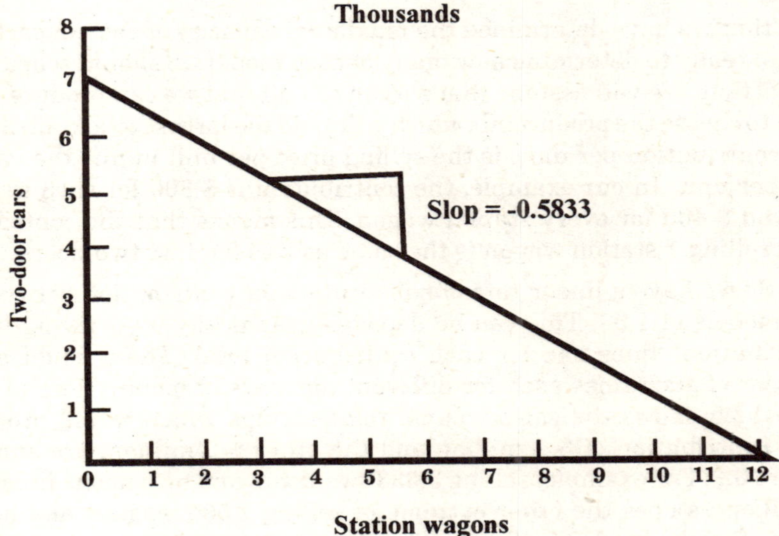

Fig. 3.7

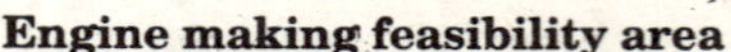

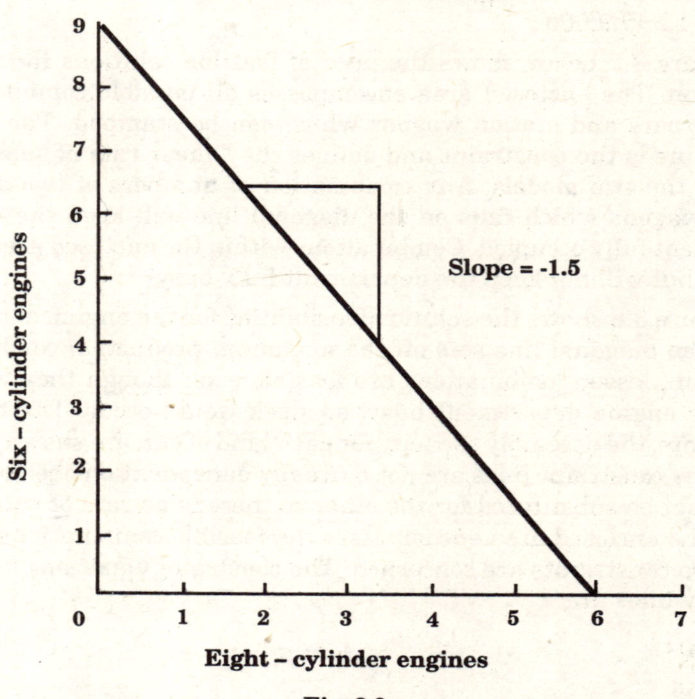

Fig. 3.8

Now that we have determined the maximum capacity of each department, we are ready to determine how many of each model we should schedule for production. We will assume that we can sell all that we can produce and so want to choose the product mix which will yield the largest total contribution. The contribution per unit, is the selling price per unit minus the variable cost per unit. In our example, the contribution is $ 300 for each two-door car and $ 400 for every station wagon. This means that the contribution from selling 1 station wagon is the same as it is for 1.33 two-doors.

So we have a linear rate of substitution for contribution between the two models of 1.33. This can be depicted graphically by drawing in "iso-contribution" lines one for each contribution total. There could be any number of such lines each for different amounts of money. Two of them, one which shows the sales volume relationships which would produce a total contribution of $ 1 million and the other $ 2 million, are shown in Figure 3.9. For example, selling 3,333 two-doors and no wagons produces $ 1 million as does the other extreme of selling 2,500 wagons and no two-doors. Similarly, $ 2 million in total contribution would occur at any combination of two-doors and station wagons along the B line in Figure 3.9.

If, for example, we sold 5,000 two-doors this would bring in $ 1.5 million leaving $ 500 thousand to come from station wagons. At $ 400 each, sales of wagons would have to be 1,250 to produce the $ 2 million.

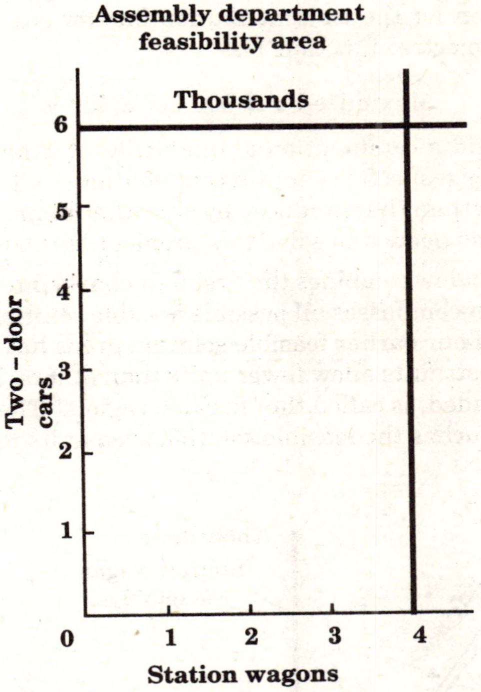

Fig. 3.9

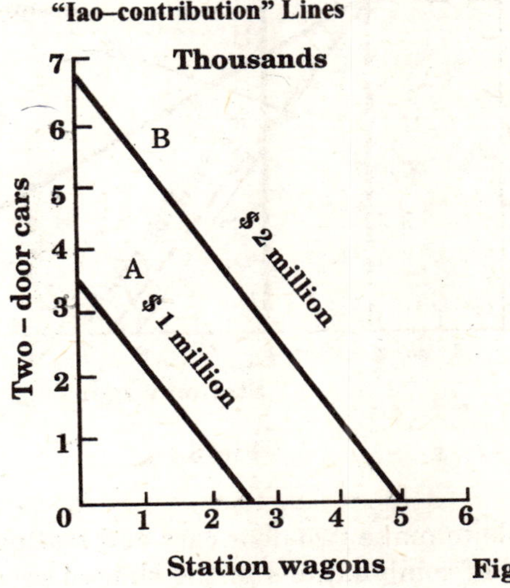

Fig. 3.10

There is a whole family of "iso-contribution" lines for this problem, all having the same slope. The lines closer to the origin produce less total contribution; those farther out, more. Since we wish to maximize the contribution, we want to find how far out (how far to the right) we can draw the iso-contribution line, yet still have it touch one point in the feasibility area. The equation for the iso-contribution line for our problem (which is also called the "objective function") is:

$$\text{Maximize } F = \$\ 300\ T + \$\ 400\ W$$

This says find a combination of quantities of T and W which, when multiplied by their respective per unit contributions, will result in a greater total contribution than that produced by any other combination of T and W. The four equations needed to solve this problem are those shown above.

Figure 3.11 below combines the first four charts into one. The enclosed area A-B-C-D-E encompasses all possible feasible solutions to the problem. Note that some of our earlier feasible solution areas have been eliminated because some constraints allow fewer units than others. This final solution area, which is shaded, is called the "feasible region." The iso-profit line for \$ 2.591 million touches the feasible solution area at its maximum point, C.

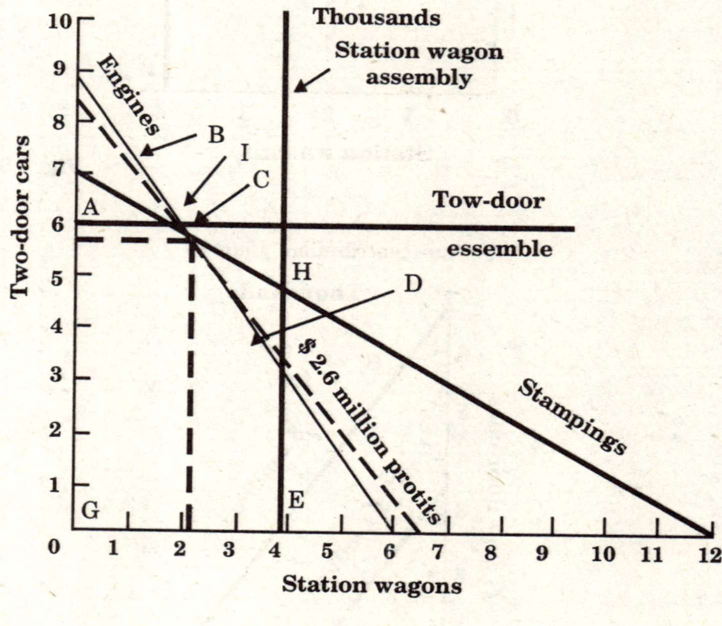

Fig. 3.11

It is feasible to make two-door cars and station wagons in any of the infinite number of combinations in the shaded area. We can make 6,000 two-door cars and no station wagons (point A), or 6,000 two-door cars and anywhere up to 1,715 station wagons (point B). But from there on, in order to get any more station wagons, it will be necessary to reduce two-door cars because the stamping department is up to its capacity. The rate of this substitution as defined earlier is the stop of the line.

For each 0.5833 two-doors we give up, we can stamp parts for 1 more station wagon. By the time we get down to 5,727 two-door cars and up to 2,183 station wagons (point C), we run into engine department limitations. From this point on, as two-doors are cut in order to increase station wagons, engines limit us until we reduce station wagons to 4,000 (point D). By this time we are down to 3.000 two-door cars. From here on station wagons can be increased no more because 4,000 is the maximum limit for assembling station wagons. Even if we cut two-door cars below 3,000, we could not make any more station wagons.

So far, we have seen how the constraints determine the trade-off between two-doors and station wagons. The plant is operating at its full capacity in at least one department at any point on the line connecting the corner points A, B, C, D. and E. At points B, C, and D, the plant is operating at full capacity in the two departments defined by this comer and has excess capacity, or slack, in the other two.

The real goal, however, is not just to keep departments busy but to maximize contributions.

Determining the optimal solution

To determine the optimal solution, we have to find the value of point C in Figure 3.10. This is the point where the stamping department and the engine department lines cross and where both are working at capacity. They are the constraining factors since neither of the assembly lines is working up to capacity. As we already know, the equation for the engines line on Figure 5 is: $T + 1.5\ W = 9{,}000$ and the equation for stampings is: $T + 0.5833\ W = 7{,}000$. To find the value of point C, we have to solve these two equations simultaneously. This we do by multiplying equation (2) by -1 and adding it to equation (1), thus eliminating the T factor from the equations.

$$(1)\ -T + 1.5000W = 9{,}000$$

$$\underline{(2)\ -T -0.5833W = 7{,}000}$$

$$.9167W = 2{,}000$$

At point C : $W = 2{,}180$

Substituting 2,180 into equation (1):

$$T + 1.5(2{,}180) = 9{,}000$$

At point C : $T = 5{,}730$

The solution at point C is therefore to make 5,730 two-door cars and 2,180 station wagons. The total contribution realized from this program will be:

$$\$\ 300\ (5{,}730) + \$\ 400\ (2{,}180) = \$\ 2{,}591{,}000$$

Actually this answer should not be accepted as being the best without checking the total contribution of other corners. Figure 6 shows the contributions from all of the corner points in our problem.

Slack

While the solution defined by point C uses all of the capacity of the engine and stamping departments, slack capacity remains in the two assembly areas. To calculate this slack, we simply subtract the number of each kind of product in the solution from its assembly capacity. At point C, the two-door assembly department is producing 270 cars less than its capacity, and the station wagon assembly department is 1,820 wagons under its capacity. There is, however, no slack in either the engine or in the assembly departments.

This kind of analysis can be used to aid in managerial decision making. Suppose that it is possible to sell more station wagons if the engine making capacity could be expanded. We could then move to point H in Figure 5 and would be assembling 4,000 station wagons.

	Number of		Total contribution		
Point	Two doors	Station wagons	Two -doors ($ 300 each	Station Wagons ($ 400 each)	Both
A............	6,000	0	&1,800,000	0	$1,800,000
B............	6,000	1,715	1,800,000	$ 686,000	2,486,000
C............	5,730	2,180	1,719,000	872,000	2,591,000
D...........	3,000	4.000	900,000	1,600,000	2,500,000
E.............	0	4,000	0	1,600,000	1,600,000

At point H. the limitations of the stamping department come into play and limit the two-door cars to 4,670. Thus, we would need 1,060 fewer six-cylinder engines than at point C. In total the new engine capacity would have to be capable of making 4,000 eight-cylinder engines plus 4,670 six-cylinder engines, or the equivalent of 10.670 six's or 7,110 eight's. This would require an increase in engine making capacity of 11.9 percent.

Suppose that the company's managers were considering making this expansion, and they find that if they do the charges against the First year's operations would be $ 350.000. Should they go ahead? The new sum of the contributions would be 4,000 x $ 400 + 4,670 x $ 300 = $ 3,028,000. The present sum is $ 2,591,000, which shows that this move would increase the contributions by $ 437,000. This is more than the cost of the expansion, so it should be made.

Sensitivity analysis

Often the most important uses of linear programming are not to find single individual problem solutions, but to use the model to analyze a number of trade-offs by asking "what if" questions. This is called "sensitivity" analysis. It reveals how sensitive the solution is to changes in constraints or values. We might ask, for example, what would happen if we had to cut two-door car prices. Or what would happen if we could reduce the costs of making station wagons. Or we might want to know what the effects would be if we could change the method of producing eight-cylinder engines so that so far as capacity is concerned an eight-cylinder engine would equal 1.25 six-cylinder engines instead of 1.5 six-cylinder engines.

This would mean that eight-cylinder engines would require only 25 percent more resources per unit than six-cylinders instead of the present 50 percent extra. The capacity of the engine department would then remain at 9,000 six-cylinder engines, but the eight-cylinder engine capacity would go up to 7,200. And, again, various product mixes would be possible. It would be possible to calculate how much a change might be worth in terms of added contributions and to compare this against its cost to see if this new process should be installed.

Any time that sales volume is being restricted by a capacity limitation of some constraint, it is possible to make comparisons of the cost of relaxing the constraint and the worth of expanding the capacity of the restraining factor.

Mathematical Procedures and Computer Software Packages

A problem cannot be merely solved by a graphical method when there are a large number of decision variables and constraints. Iterative mathematical procedures exist to solve such complex problems. One such procedure is called the Simplex Method. Such procedures for the solution of the Linear Programming problem can be referred to in any book on Operations Research. The idea behind this chapter is to explain the concepts and applications of Linear Programming in the area of Production and Operations Management. The manual solution by Simplex Method may not be difficult when the number of variables and the number of constraints are one-digit numbers. Beyond that, the manual procedure may become laborious and cumbersome. Today there are computers and ready-made Computer Software Packages available to take care of this problem.

Assumptions

The assumptions underlying Linear Programming are:

1. Objective Function and the constraints are all linear relationships. The corollaries of this assumption are that:
   (a) We assume that there are no economies of scale or dis-economies of scale; six units of product Y require six times as much of raw material as required for one unit of Y.
   (b) We assume that there are no interactions between the decision variables; the total raw material required for X and Y was a simple addition of individual requirements for X and Y.
2. There is only one Objective Function. In our product-mix problem there was only one objective and that was to maximize the profit. But, the case is not always so simple in practice. Often, for a particular decision, an organization may have a number of objectives with possibly some priorities between them, all the which need to the considered together. For instance the production planning should be such that both the total costs of production as well as the time delays for delivery of the products need to be minimized. This type of a problem cannot be solved by simple Linear Programming. Linear Programming, therefore, confines itself to a single objective or to a situation where the multiple objectives need to be transformed/modified into a single objective function.

Other Related Methods

There are procedures by which a multiple objectives problem can be transformed to a single objective problem. This can be done by considering the trade-offs between different objectives or by ranking different objectives in terms of priorities and converting the problem to a series of single objective problems. A procedure called Goal Programming can also be used in such a case.

The case where the decision variables cannot take fractional values, a related technique called Integer Programming can be used.

Application of Linear Programming

Linear Programming can be used effectively for Production and Operations Management situations. Usually the objective is to either maximize the profit or minimize the total cost or the delay factor. There are always constraints or limitations on production capacity, the quality of the products and constraints on the saleability of a product in a particular period of time. There may be different constraints related to the decision variables based at different time periods. For instance, in the months of harvest the labour availability is very low, or that in a company, absenteeism is high during the months of summer due to the wedding season. Many of the production problems can be formulated into Linear Programming problems. Thus it is a very useful technique for various planning and other decisions in production operations.

The basic work content in solving a Linear Programming problem is not in its solution per se, but in its formulation. Mathematical formulation of the problem is the first step in Linear Programming. Needless to say, if the formulation is wrong the solution would also be wrong.

Network Analysis

Although a few ranked projects can now be selected, the feasibility analysis cannot be complete unless we apply the Network Techniques. What may emerge after a network analysis, may be different from the earlier result. A technically and financially feasible project may encounter constraints of time; network techniques may clearly bring out certain errors of omission in the earlier analysis.

Network Analysis and Implementation Planning

Once a project has been selected, we move over to implementation planning for the same. This planning involves the time plan of the project (what work needs to be done and when?) the cost plan of the project (how much money needs to be spent and when?), the plan for the materials requirement for the project (what materials are required and when?), the manpower plan for the project and plans for various other resources. In this planning process Network Analysis techniques are used. PERT (Programme Evaluation and Review Technique) and CPM (Critical Path Method) are two such techniques.

As with many management science techniques, the network analysis techniques originated with the Second World War. These techniques are part of Operations Research which were first utilized in the American Polaris Missiles Project. PERT was the first of the network analysis techniques. Over the years, network techniques have gained much acceptance in civilian projects all over the world.

Comparison of Bar Charts and Network Techniques

Network techniques are in essence a modification of the age-old Bar Chart techniques of controlling the various works in a project. The Bar-Chart has certain drawbacks or difficulties, i.e., it is not capable of depicting proper relationships in time between various jobs to be done in a project. Moreover, once the relationship in time of the different jobs in a project is shown in the form of a Bar-Chart, it is difficult to change these Charts. The Bar-Charts are, therefore, somewhat 'static' in character. The network technique helps to overcome this difficulty. PERT and CPM network techniques allow the project planner and implementer to show graphically the proper sequencing and relationships-in-time between different jobs in the project and to concurrently indicate the requirements of time, money, materials, manpower and other resources on the network chart itself.

We shall restrict ourselves to a description of the Critical Path Method (CPM) over here. Later, we shall introduce the related technique of PERT. But it needs to be reiterated here that both these techniques have much in common and they fall under the general category of network techniques.

Whether our purpose is to draw a network for CPM or to draw a bar-chart, the basic requirement for both these graphical techniques is to analyze the various work components of the project and there from get a listing of the jobs to be performed in the project from the beginning to the end of the project. This would help us to proceed in a systematic manner rather than listing the jobs in a haphazard manner. Such a systematic listing of jobs can only produce a systematic graphical representation of these jobs, their inter-relationship with one another with respect to time and their resource requirements.

Operations Management

UNIT—IV

7

PERT and CPM

Introduction

After developing the network, we turn our attention to the control of the project. In the control of the projects, the 'control of time' is undoubtedly very important. For this a procedure called Time Analysis a very helpful. The questions that are addressed by Time Analysis are:

1. What will be the completion time for the entire project?
2. At what points of time can we expect parts/phases of the projects to be completed?
3. What are the activities, which cause bottlenecks and need special management attention?
4. What slacks or free times do different activities have?
5. Is time duration of the projects acceptable? If not, what changes in the logic of the network may be done so as to complete the project within the desired time?

It needs to be mentioned at this point that the Critical Path Method (CPM) uses only one single time estimate for each of the activities, while the PERT techniques uses three times estimates (optimistic, pessimistic, and most likely). Since we are dealing here with the Critical Path Method we shall depend on the single time estimate for the different time activities.

The time duration for the different activities are indicated in the network on top of each of the arrows representing a particular activity. Our first question is: how long will the duration of the project be? Since in the network there are many paths going from the beginning of the project to the end of the project, each of these paths will have a different total in terms of time duration. The project, represented as a network, could be viewed as a flow of different succeeding jobs from the beginning point of the project to the end of the project. Naturally, the longest of these paths, in terms of time duration, will be determine the duration of the project. The longest path is called the Critical Path, and hence the name of this method as the Critical Path Method.

Critical Path

Since the Critical Path is the longest path, all the activities falling on the critical path are "Critical" which means that these activities have no slack. These critical activities, which re the bottleneck activities, need management's special attention since any time delay occurring on any of these activities will delay the project as a whole. The other paths having less time duration will have a certain amount of slack which could absorbs any delays occurring in the activities on these paths. This is an example of the principal of management by exception.

Although in smaller networks it is easy to find visually which is the longest path, and therefore, the 'critical path', is the same is not the case with networks having a large number of activities. There is a systematic method by which one can find out the critical path and as well the slacks available to different activities on non-critical paths. We shall illustrate this method in Fig.3.12

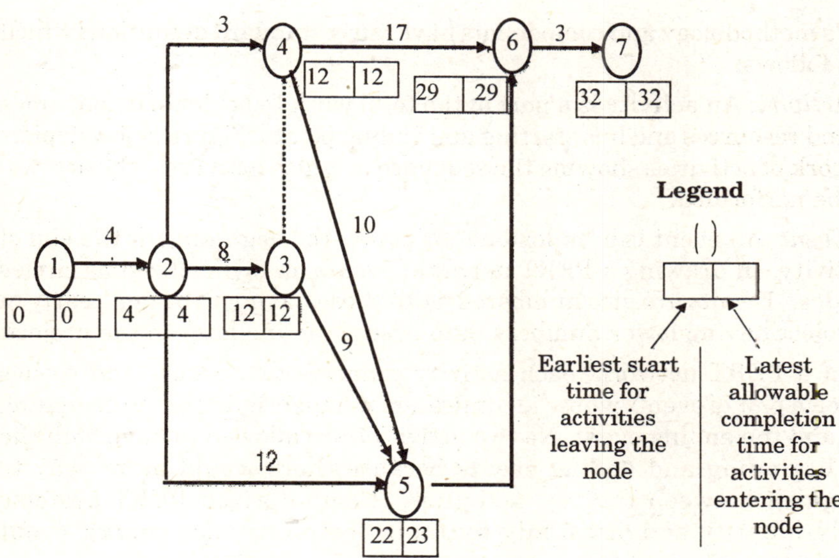

Project planning and control with PERT

SPECIAL projects are continually being planned and produced in all kinds of organizations. For example, the development of new instant cameras in the 1970s was a multimillion Rupee special design project both at Polaroid and at Kodak. Other examples of special projects are: building a space shuttle or opening up a new shopping center.

The management of special projects requires different planning and control techniques than those used for managing repetitive production and service activities.

PERT

The best known and most widely used project planning and control method is called PERT, or Program Evaluation and Review Technique. PERT is an analytical method which is designed to aid in the planning and control of complex projects which require that certain activities be performed in sequence while others may be performed independently of others.

PERT has been used for many kinds of construction activities, for building bridges and unusual buildings such as stadiums, and for coordinating maintenance and installation projects such as refitting ships and installing new computer systems. PERT was used extensively to plan and control the thousands of activities needed in the construction of the Alaskan pipeline for oil. Generally, it is most applicable to rather complex, nonrepetitive projects.

Pert Characteristics and Definitions

PERT's methodology and components have fairly standard definitions which are as follows:

Activity: An activity is a part of the total work to be done: it consumes time and resources and has starting and ending points. Figure below depicts a network of activities showing the sequence in which activities (the arrows) must be performed.

Event: An event is a "milestone"; it marks the beginning or the end of an activity. In drawing a PERT network, events are symbolized as circles or "nodes." Events are also numbered, with those having to be done early in the project having lower numbers than events coming later in the project.

In a PERT network, each activity connects two events and so lies between a pair of events whose identification numbers indicate the beginning event and the ending event. No two activities are allowed to have both the same beginning and ending events because there would be no way to distinguish between the two activities. (Computerized PERT systems usually identify activities only by their beginning and ending event numbers.)

Activity time: PERT uses three estimates of the amount of time an activity might take to complete. These estimates are obtained from people who have some knowledge about the work and how long it will probably take. They are:

a. Optimistic time: The time the activity will take if everything goes well and n delays are encountered.
b. Realistic time: The time the activity will most likely take under normal conditions, allowing for usual delays.
c. Pessimistic time: The time the activity may take if more than the usual delays are encountered.

PERT weights these three estimates to obtain an "expected time" for an activity by:

$$\text{Expected activity time} = \frac{\text{Optimistic time} + (4 \times \text{Realistic time}) + \text{Pessimistic time}}{6}$$

Thus, if an activity in a PERT network for building a building were " pour the concrete floundation" and it had estimates of 2,4 and 12 days, its expected duration wolud be :

$$\text{Expected activity time} = \frac{2 + (4 \times 4) + 12}{6} = 5\text{days.}$$

Precedence requirements: Since some activities cannot begin until others are completed (we cannot pour the concrete foundation until we have excavated and built the forms) and others may be performed independently and/or simultaneously, (we may simultaneously pour the foundation and order lumber), we must develop the immediate precedence requirements of the activities in the project. The easiest way to do this is ask this question of each activity: "Which other activities must be completed immediately before we can begin this activity?"

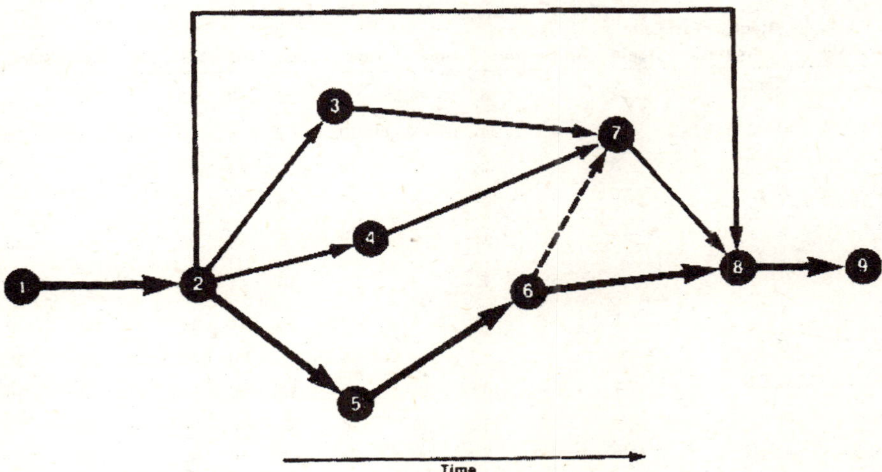

Start and finish times: The earliest time an activity can begin, considering the expected activity times and the precedence requirements of all prior activities, is called the earliest start (ES) time. The latest time an activity can start without delaying the whole project is called the latest start (LS) time. The earliest time that an activity can finish is called the earliest finish (EF). and so is equal to the activity's ES + its expected time. The latest time an activity can be completed without delaying the completion of the entire project is called the latest finish (LF) time. This is equal to the activity's LS + its expected time.

Pert Example

To illustrate how PERT works, let us consider the example whose figures are shown in Figure X and which are depicted in the PERT network in Figure Y. We will suppose that our project has 12 activities (11 real activities and 1 dummy), designated A, B. . .. L; a set of immediate precedence requirements; and the three times estimates for each activity.

A "dummy" activity is not really an activity. It is indicated on a PERT network diagram by a broken arrow line and is there to preserve proper sequences when one activity does not depend directly on another.

Looking just at columns 1, 2 and 3 in Figure X, we can see that activity A is the first activity. It precedes everything else and must be completed before activities B, D, F. and L can begin. This is shown in Figure Y by the "burst" of activities B, D, F, and L not being able to start until after A is completed at node 2 .

(1)	(2)	(3)		(4)	(5)	(6)	(7)	(8)		(9)		(10)
	Immediate precedence Require- ments	Events -------		Opti m.	Real.	Pese.	Erp ect.	Starts -------		Finish -------		Total
Adivily		Begin	End	time	time	time	time	ES	LS	EP	LP	Slack
A.......	None	1	2	3	4	5	4	0	0	4	4	0
B.......	A	2	3	4	7	10	7	4	16	11	23	12
C.......	B	3	7	2	7	12	7	11	23	18	30	12
D.......	A	2	4	3	5	13	6	4	19	10	25	15
E.......	D	4	7	1	5	9	5	10	25	15	30	15
F........	A	2	5	7	8	21	10	4	4	14	14	0
G.......	F	5	6	1	7	7	6	14	14	20	20	0
H.......	G	6	7	-	-	-	-	20	30	20	30	10
I.........	C,E,G	7	8	10	10	10	10	20	30	30	40	10
J.........	G	6	8	15	20	25	20	20	20	40	40	0
K.......	L,I,J	8	9	2	7	12	7	40	40	47	47	0
L.......	A	2	8	10	15	20	15	4	25	19	40	21

Fig. 10

At the other end of the project, activity K is the last activity, and it cannot begin until activities L, I, and J have been completed. This is shown in Figure Y by a merge of these three activities before K can begin. Using only columns 1, 2, and 3 in Figure X and looking at the graphic representation in Figure Y, one can see that all of the immediate precedence requirements have been met.

Next, columns 4. 5, and 6 in Figure X are the three time estimates for each activity. These have been used to calculate column 7's expected times using the formula given above. These expected times have been entered on the network in Figure Y.

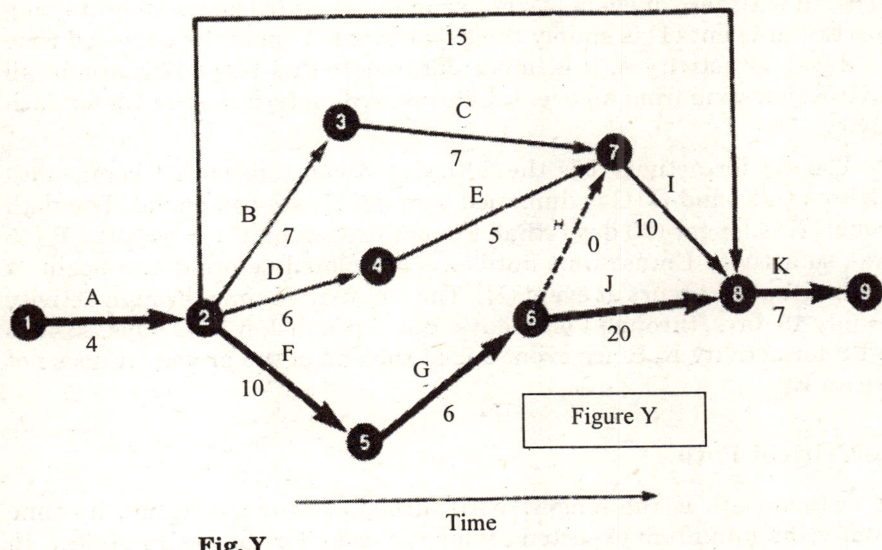

Fig. Y

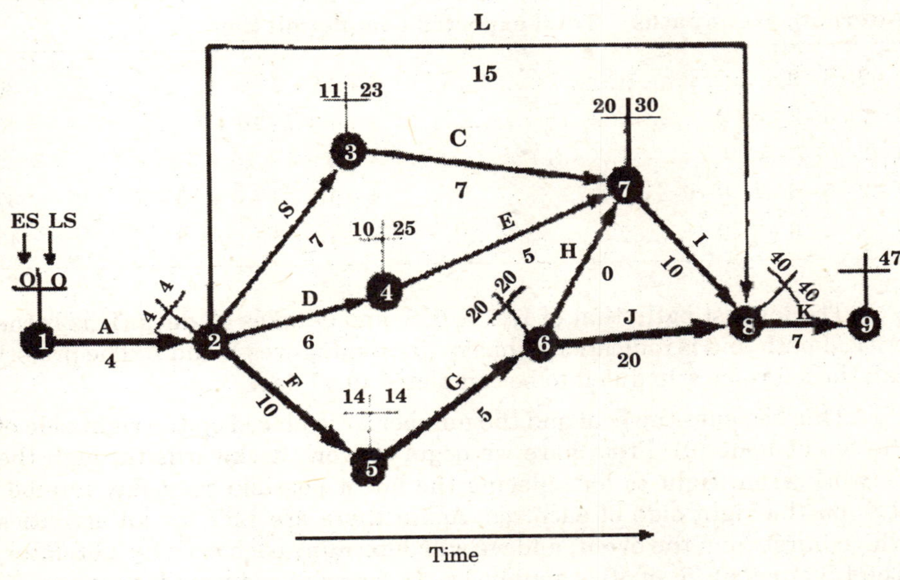

Fig. Z

Figure X. To do this, we turn to the network shown in Figure Z below. This is the same network as before but with more information on it. On this network we first draw a T ("tee") at each node or event. Next, beginning at event (1) and moving to the right in the network, we put the ES for all activities which burst out of each event on the left side of the tee. (Here we will begin with zero at event (1); For example, the earliest possible starting lime (ES) at event (1) is simply the ES at event (1) plus the expected time (of 4 days) for activity A. It is important to note that these ES's are for all activities bursting from an event. Later we will determine the ES for each activity.

The ES for activity I is the 20th day because it cannot begin until activities C, E. and G (G is dummied through H) are completed. The path through H is longer (20 days) than the paths through C (18 days) or E (15 days), so activity I must wait until G is completed before it can begin. A similar situation occurs at event (H). The cumulative time through activity L is only 19 days, through I is 30 days. But through J, it is 40 days, so 40 is the ES for activity K. Since event 9 is at the end of the project, it does not have an ES.

The Critical Path

The critical path is the longest path through the network and its time becomes the minimum expected completion time for the entire project. In our example, the alternative paths and their expected completion times are:

Alternate event paths	Total expected completion time	
1 - 2 - 8 - 9	4 + 15 + 7	= 26
1 - 2 - 3 - 7 - 8 - 9.................................	4 + 7 + 7 +10 + 7	= 35
1 -2 - 4 - 7 - 8 - 9	4 + 6 + 5 + 10 + 7	= 32
1 - 2 - 5 - 6 - 7 - 8 - 9	4 + 10 + 6 + 0 + 10 + 7	= 37
1 - 2 - 5 - 6 - 8 - 9	4 + 10 + 6 + 20 + 7	= 47

The longest path, that of 1, 2. 5, 6, 8, and 9, takes 47 days. This is the critical path and is indicated by heavy lines in Figures Y and Z. The project can therefore be scheduled to be completed in 47 days.

This becomes the goal and the number 47 is placed on the right side of the tee at node (9). From here we begin to work backwards through the network, from right to left, placing the latest possible start day number (LS) on the right side of each tee. Again there are LS's for all activities which burst from the event, and we will determine each activity's LS later. The LS at event (8) of 40 is simply 47 - 7, the expected time for activity K. Similarly, the LS for activity I is 40-10 = 30. This tells us that activity I could start as late as the 30th day and not cause the overall project to be late. Similarly, C could start as late as the 23rd day; E the 25th day; and B and D could also delay their starting.

However, the correct LS for events (6) and (2) require some further analysis. Since the LS at event (6) is for all activities which burst from it, we must choose the most limiting. The LS coming back through H is 30 - 0 = 30: through J it is 40 - 20 = 20. Since the LS through J is smaller, this becomes the LS for event (6). The LS for event (2) is similarly constrained by the path back through activity F and is 14 - 10 = 4. It can be seen in Figure Z that for all events in the critical path, the ES and LS dates are the same. This is always so since activities can't be started any sooner because earlier activities are not completed nor can following activities be started later because then the project will not finish in time.

Slack

Slack is the amount of "play" in the system. When one activity can be finished before the next activity has to start, there is a slack period during which the next activity could be started, but it doesn't have to be started so soon. Slack is thus the time that an activity can be delayed in starting without delaying the completion of the entire project provided that the activities which precede the activity have not been delayed beyond their earliest finish, EF, date. The total slack for each activity is computed as follows: (LS of ending event) - (expected completion time) - (ES of beginning event) = total slack. The slack for each activity in our example is given in the table below:

Activity	LS at ending event		Expected time		ES at beginning event		Total slack
A........................	4	-	4	-	0	=	0
B........................	23	-	7	-	4	=	12
C........................	30	-	7	-	11	=	12
D........................	25	-	6	-	4	=	15
E........................	30	-	5	-	10	=	15
F........................	14	-	10	-	4	=	0
G........................	20	-	6	-	14	=	0
H........................	30	-	0	-	20	=	10
I........................	40	-	10	-	20	=	10
J........................	40	-	20	-	20	=	0
K........................	47	-	7	-	40	=	0
L........................	40	-	15	-	4	=	21

The total slack for all activities on the critical path is always zero if the desired completion time of the project is the same as the earliest expected completion time. In our example, if the desired completion time for the project were 50 days, instead of 47 days, all activities on the critical path would share 3 days of total slack.

Total slack does not often belong solely to one single activity. It is more often shared among adjacent activities along a path. For example, both B and C have slack of 12 days; however, if B is delayed in starling by 4 days or if it goes slowly and takes 4 days extra, then it takes 11 days instead of 7. This uses up 4 days of the 12 days slack and leaves only 8 days of slack for activity C. This also affects I 's slack, reducing it to 6 days. If B's finishing were delayed 4 days and C were delayed by 7 days more, this would reduce I 's slack to - 1, and the whole project would fall 1 day behind schedule.

Determining the ES and LS for each activity

The early start, ES, for each activity is simply the ES on the left side of the tee at its beginning event. The latest start, LS. for each activity is simply the LS at its beginning event (the right side of the tee) plus the activity's slack. These are shown in column 8 in Figure X.

Determining EF and LF for each activity

Now that we have ES 's and LS 's for each activity, EF is simply the activity's ES plus its expected time. Similarly, LF is the activity LS plus its expected time. These are shown in Column 9 in Figure X.

Free slack may also exist in a PERT network. It is the amount of time an activity can be delayed without delaying any succeeding activity's ES. For example, activity C could be delayed until the 13th day without violating activity I's FS at the 20th day. On the other hand. if activity D is delayed even one day. then the ES of activity E is also delayed one day. Thus, there is no free slack in D even though it shares 5 days of total slack with E. Free slack for an aclivity is calculated by subtracting its EF from the ES of all activities to which it is an immediate predecessor.

Probability of meeting PERT schedules

One of PERTs interesting features is that it allows the calculation of the probability that the schedule will be met. Only the critical path is concerned here. For each activity on the critical path, the procedure uses one sixth of the difference between the pessimistic time and the optimistic time as an estimate of the standard deviation of the expected activity time (a range of six standard deviations encompasses virtually all the area in a normal distribution).

Critical path activities	Pessi-mistic time	Opti-mistic time	Differ-ence	Activity's standard deviation	Variance (σ^2)	Cumu-lated variance	Path's standard deviation
A.........	5	3	2	0.33	0.11	0.11	0.33
F.........	21	7	14	2.33	5.43	5.54	2.35
G.........	7	1	6	1.00	1.00	6.54	2.55
J..........	25	15	10	1.67	2.79	9.33	3.05
K.........	12	2	10	1.67	2.79	12.12	3.48

Since we are concerned only with the likelihood of the whole project finishing on time, we have to compute the probabilities of all of the activities in the critical path, taken together, taking more time or less time than the expected time. To do this, we first (in Figure above) square the standard deviation for each activity to get the "variance" and add these variances cumulatively. Then, we take the square root of these cumulated variances and arrive at the standard deviation of the probable variations in the total time for the project. We can also take the square root of the cumulated variance at any intermediate event in the critical path and get the standard deviation of the expected times up to this event. These standard deviations are shown in the figure above.

It is now possible to see how likely it is that the scheduled completion dates for the whole project or for the successive stages in the critical path will be met. The entire project is expected to lake 47 days, and the calculation we just finished tells us that the standard deviation is 3.48 days.

This standard deviation shows that there is a 68-percent probability that the actual time for he project will be between 47 3.48 days, or between 43.52 and 50.48 days. And there is a 95 percent probability that it will be completed in 47 6.96 days. And it is almost certain that the project will be finished in 47 10.44 days.

Suppose that a manager asks the likelihood that the project will be completed in 44 days, or three days ahead of schedule. We can determine the number of standard deviations this is by:

Number of standard deviations = (44-47)/3.48 = - 0.86

Going to Standard deviation tables, (available in any statistics book), we find that - .86 of a standard deviation represents about a 20-percent probability. Thus, there is only a 20-percent chance that the project will be completed in 44 days, unless extra resources are made available to speed things up.

If the manager asks about the chances of the project being completed within 55 days, it would be:

(55-47)/3.48 = +2.29 standard deviation

From Standard Deviation Tables, we find that this results in a likelihood of about 99 percent of the project finishing within 55 days. The purpose in determining these probabilities is that managers may want to increase the chances of finishing early and so to decide to allocate more resources to activities on the critical path. Conversely, if the project is likely to finish earlier than is needed, resources can be diverted to other work without putting the finishing date for this project in jeopardy. Of course, the validity of these probabilities is based on the assumption that the time estimates are realistic and not under or overstated. For this (the possibility that the estimates will be somewhat unrealistic) and other reasons, this aspect of PERT has fallen out of favour and is not used much in practice.

PERT/COST

Although PERT is usually thought of as a means for scheduling the timing of activities required by complex projects, it also provides a framework for cost planning and cost control. Every activity that is carried on costs money; so PERT/time and PERT/cost go hand in hand. When a company plans for and schedules an activity, it also estimates its cost so it has cost estimates for each part of the work.

PERT/cost has become increasingly important over the years as people become more aware of its value. Actually, in many cases managers are more interested in the cost of a project than in exactly when it will be finished. And, as in the case of PERT/time, PERT/cost provides a good control mechanism while projects are under way. Reports of completed activities tell managers when they reach each event point. This gives them frequent opportunities to compare the costs incurred with the expected costs for the work done to date. If the project is running behind on the time schedule or if it is running over the cost estimates, managers learn about it early, perhaps in time to do something to bring the project back on schedule or within the budget.

Time and Resource Trade-Offs

PERT activities are actually work load assignments and are not directly calendar time assignments. Yet, they are usually shown as work which will take a certain amount of calendar time. These times are based on the expected commitment of normally used resources to the activity.

Event milestones with activities shaded to show the kind of resources needed.

There is a problem here, however. One hundred labour-hours of work will take 100 hours of clock time if one person is assigned to do the work. But, if 100 people are assigned, this same activity would become a one-clock-hour job. There is usually, therefore, a possibility of a trade-off between resources committed to an activity and the calendar time it will take.

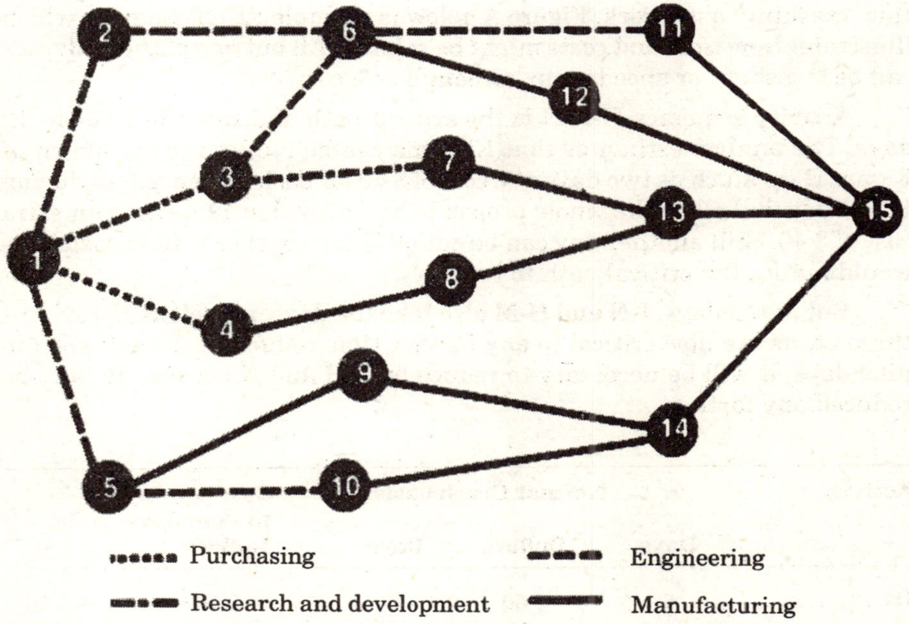

Workers on non-critical path work, for example, might be transferred to critical path activities and thus shorten the calendar time required and possibly at no additional total resource cost. Slowing down the non-critical activity is possible because of the slack in the non-critical paths.

In many cases, unfortunately, resources are not wholly transferable because they are not interchangeable in use. If an activity could use more machines and machine operators, neither of the kind needed may be available.

Another problem is that sometimes both the expected time has elapsed and the money set aside for an activity is spent; yet, the activity is not complete. The work is taking longer and is costing more than was planned. Time slippages can usually be made up if more resources are assigned to the late activity. Ordinarily, almost any activity can be speeded up by assigning more people to it, by working overtime, by using air express to get needed parts or otherwise using more resources. And almost every activity can be speeded up by relaxing some of the technical specifications. And, occasionally, work which was planned to be done in sequence can, in part, be done concurrently.

Cost slippages, on the other hand, usually can be made up only at the cost of a sacrifice in quality in other activities.

Crashing of a project

Sometimes a problem comes up where a manager is willing to trade off the costs of extra inputs against the value of the time saved. Some people call this "crashing" a network. Figure A below is a simple PERT diagram which illustrates how time and costs might be related. All but one of the activities can be “crashed” or speeded up, although at a cost.

Activity sequence H-K-N is the critical path and reouires 3+5+4= 12 days. The analyst estimates that K's time can be reduced (as is shown in Figure B) as much as two days at a cost of $ 40 for each day saved. Reducing K by I day will allow the whole project to be finished in 11 days at an exira cost of $ 40. Still another day can be cut off K for another $ 40 in cost. This would reduce the critical path to ten days.

But at ten days. I-N and H-M also take ten days, as well as H-K-N. All three paths are now critical to any further time reduction. To get down to nine days, it will be necessary to reduce both H and N because K can't be reduced any farther.

Activity		**Normal Crash basis**		**Cost per day to save days**	
	Days	**Dollars**	**Days**	**Dollars**	
H....................	3	$ 50	2	$ 100	$ 50
I.....................	6	140	4	260	60
J....................	2	25	1	50	25
K......................	5	100	3	180	40
L....................	2	80	2	80	-
M.....................	7	115	5	175	30
N.....................	4	100	2	240	70
Total		$ 610		$ 1,085	

Fig. B

Cutting both H and N one day would cost $ 120, but K would then need to be cut only one day, so there would be an offsetting savings of $ 40, making the net added cost become $ 80. To get down to eight days, it would be necessary to cut M and N another day, each at a cost of $ 100. To get to seven days, it would be necessary to cut I, K, and M at a cost of $ 350.

Should the managers make the time cuts proposed for these crash costs? This would depend on the value of the time saved. If we were talking

	Days					
	7	8	9	10	11	12
Cost of repairs...........	$ 1,000	$ 870	$ 770	$ 690	$ 650	$ 610
Cost of Production loss......	420	480	540	600	660	720
Total	$ 1,420	$ 1,350	$ 1,310	$ 1,290	$ 1,310	$ 1,330

about repairing a machine which is out of production and costing $ 60 a day every day it does not operate, then the trade-offs are as follows:

This analysis shows that activity K should be put on a crash program aiming for a ten-day completion. This will hold costs down to $ 1,290, less than the cost of any other program.

Pert System of Networking

PERT, just like CPM, is an activity on Arrow diagram. In fact, the network diagram for PERT and CPM are exactly the same. Where PERT differs from CPM is in its stochastic considerations as against CPM which is deterministic.

For every activity in PERT, three different time estimates are obtained;

Optimistic time (t_o)	:	If everything goes smoothly while performing the activity.
Pessimistic time (t_p)	:	If everything goes wrong, short of natural calamities, while performing the activity.
Most likely time (t_{ml})	:	The time which occurs most frequently

The actual time taken by the activity could fall anywhere between (to) and (tp); and if, hypothetically, The same activity was performed a number of times, it will be complete at tml most number of times.

It is thought that a -distribution would adequately represent this situation. With some approximation, the values of the mea and standard deviation are given as follows:

Mean (i.e. expected) time for the activity,

$$t_e = \frac{t_o + 4t_{ml} + t_p}{6}$$

$$\text{Standard deviation, } \sigma = \frac{t_p - t_o}{6}$$

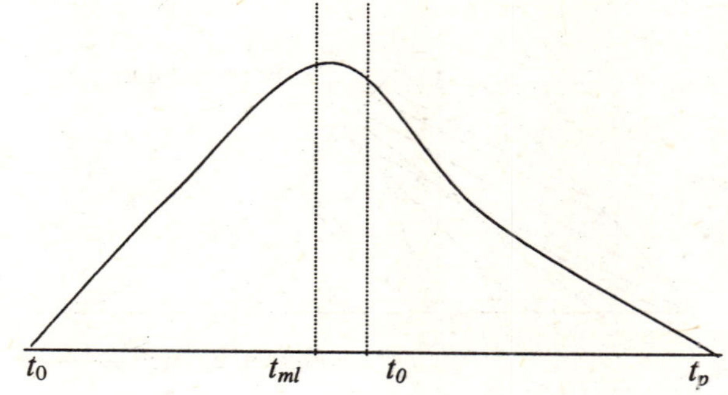

The probability of the completion of a project within a certain time duration can be computed with the help of these data on individual activities. Generally the probability of the completion of the critical path is taken as the probability of completion of the project within any given time. If the number of activities on the critical path is large then one can use the Central Limit Theorem and accordingly assume a Normal Distribution for the path with:

Te (i.e. expected time for the path) = te of all activities on the path Σ and variance (i.e. $\sigma 2$) for the path = activity variance for all activities on the path

Supposing the following are the network and other activity details:

Estimated times, days				Therefore, Calculated	
Activity	**to**	**tml**	**tp**	**te**	**Std. deviation**
1, 2	1	4	7	4	1
1, 3	5	11	17	11	2
2, 4	4	7	28	10	4
2, 3	1	2.5	7	3	1
3, 4	1	4	7	4	1

The critical path is 1-3-4 and the expected project duration is 15 days. Draw the diagram and verify.

Note, that the probability of completing the project in 15 days is 0.50 only. The probability is higher for longer (than 15) project completion times.

Let us compute chances of completing the project in 18 days. The standard deviation for the critical path is 4 + 1 = 5

$$\text{Therefore,} \quad Z = \frac{X - \mu}{\sigma} = \frac{18 - 15}{\sqrt{5}} = + 1.34$$

and the probability of completion of the project = 0.91

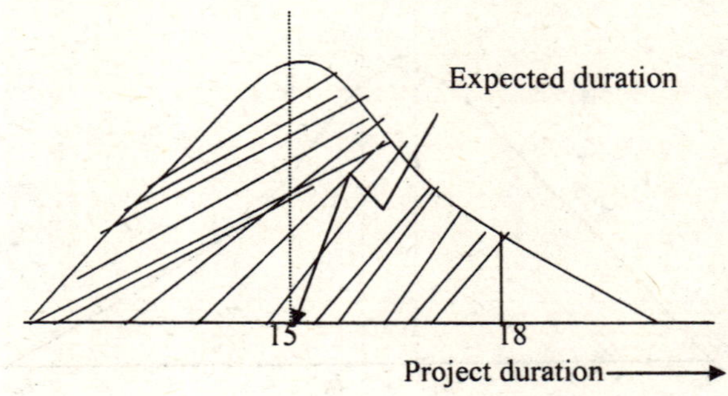

NOTE: Hatched area represents probability of completion within 18 days

Likewise, the various probabilities of the completion of the project within different time durations can be computed. PERT system provides this additional dimension.

However, we should be careful about any false sense of sophistication because even the above computations could be erroneous. We have assumed that for all such computations, considering the (so-called) critical path is enough. In fact, in our example, path 1-2-4 is near-critical (expected duration 14 days) and has a variance much higher (17) than that of the 'critical path' (5).

Let us compute the probability of completing the path 1-2-4 within 18 days:

$$Z = \frac{18 - 14}{\sqrt{17}} = +\,0.971$$

and Probability = 0.835

This is lower than that for the path 1-3-4. So, which path is critical? What could be the definition of 'critical path' in such probabilistic situations?

It would also be worth noting that for a project to e completed, all the activities in the network have to be completed. So really for computing the probability of completion of the given project within 18 days, one has to consider the joint probability of completion of all the paths, which would be significantly less than the probability calculated for the co called critical path.

Although one can analytically arrive at a probability figure for the entire network by combining the statistical distribution for all activities, this analytical procedure is too cumbersome and complex particularly for networks with a large number of activities.

In most cases, therefore, a simulation method helps. It generates thousands of combinations of activity times and computes corresponding critical path lengths. An Index of Critically could be attached to the different paths according to the number of times, during the simulation run, these paths went critical. For instance if path 1-3-4 became critical 400 out of 1000 runs, then the Index of Critically for 1-3-4 is 0.40.

Thus, one may say that there is no one path critical, but each path has an index of critically attached ti it according to its propensity to go critical. These are no critical activities, instead each activity has a probability of being on a critical path.

Although the PERT system appears computationally very precise, it has some serious drawbacks.

1. First of all, the choice of -distribution is not based upon any empirical data. Perhaps, it was chosen because it is unimodal, has finite non-negative end-points, and it needs not be symmetrical. That seems all.

   Also, the jobs do not occur so many times as to provide data to fit a or any other distribution. Many activities occur only once.
2. The formula to calculate the expected times and standard deviations is again an approximation.
3. Moreover, it is difficult in practice to get three time estimates giving a true enough picture of the optimistic, pessimistic ad modal happening for the number of activities on a project. The entire probabilistic analysis depends upon thee estimates.

8

Inventory Management

Introduction

The production control system consists of a group of procedural elements that operates as a whole, to fulfill the four functions listed under importance of control function.

The elements of production control system are :

1. Means of setting the system in motion such as production orders.
2. Methods to determine lead time for production.
3. Methods to control and monitor production operations including means to :
   (a) Determine what and where work is to be done
   (b) Determine when work is to be done
   (c) Issue orders to production shops and ensure that work is completed.
4. Techniques for measuring and recording data on machine utilization, scrap and indirect labour that can serve as a basis for manufacturing action leading to optimum utilization of facilities and low cost operation.
5. An information system for display, recording and retrieval as well as processing and flow of data.

Production Control

Importance of Control Function

The function of production control is to:

(i) Provide for the production of parts, assemblies and products of required quality and quantity at the required time.

(ii) Co-ordinate, monitor and feed-back to manufacturing management, the results of the production activities, analyzing and interpreting their significance and taking corrective action if necessary.

(iii) Provide for optimum utilisation of all resources.

(iv) Achiever the broad objectives of low cost production and reliable customer service.

Benefits of Production Control

1. Improvement in profits through
   (a) Maintenance of a balanced inventory of materials, parts, work-in-process and finished goods.
   (b) Balanced and stabilized production.
   (c) Maximum utilization of equipment, tooling, labour (manpower) and manufacturing and storage space.
   (d) Minimum investment in inventory.
   (e) Reduction in indirect costs.
   (f) Reduction in set up costs.
   (g) Reduction in scrap and rework costs.
   (h) Reduction in inventory costs.
2. Competitive advantage-
   (a) Reliable delivery to customers.
   (b) Shortened delivery schedules to customers.
   (c) Lower production costs and greater pricing flexibility.
   (d) Orderly planning and marketing of new or improved products.

Elements of Production Control

1. *Control of planning :* Assure receipt of latest forecast data from sales and production planning, bill of material data from product engineering and routing information from process engineering.
2. *Control of materials :* Control of inventory and providing for issue of materials to the shop and movement of materials within the shop.
3. *Control of tooling :* Check on the availability of tooling and provide for issue of tools to shop departments from tool cribs.
4. *Control of manufacturing capacity :* Determine the availability of equipment and labour capacities and issue realistic production schedules and provide a means of recording completed production.
5. *Control of activities :* Release order and information at assigned times.
6. *Control of quantity :* Follow-up of progress of production in order to ensure that the required quantities are processed at each production step and to ensure that corrective action is initiated where, work fails to pass each stage of inspection.
7. *Control of material handling :* Release orders for movement of work to ensure availability of material as required at each stage of the operation.

8. *Control of due dates :* Check on the relation of actual and planned schedules and determine the cause of delays or stoppages that interfere with weekly schedules of work assigned to each machine or work centre.
9. Control of information : Distribute timely information and reports showing deviations from plans so that corrective action can be taken and provide data on production performance measurements for future planning.

Factors Determining Production Control Procedures

1. *Nature of production :* The manufacturing firms are classified as intermittent, continuous or composite production firms, depending on the length of processing time without set up changes.

Production control procedure is comparatively simpler in the continuous flow process operation than in intermittent, multi-operation production.

In case of continuous flow process operation, for example, found in petrochemical, soap and synthetic fiber industries, routing is standardised, quality control is highly developed and planning for raw materials, finished goods inventory levels and markets is extremely important. The production control function in such industries, is generally embodied in the process equipment itself. In case of intermittent, multi operation production, found in case of manufacture of hand tools, toys, automobile spares etc, a great variety of material is used in many ways and for many purposes. The products consist of a large number of parts and sub-assemblies. The production control procedures become complex and sophisticated in order to ensure proper sequence of operation and performing these operations at the right time and the right place.

A large number of manufacturing plants include both intermittent and continuous processes and are classified as composite or combination operations. Such a plant may have sub assembly departments making parts in a continuous operation, while the final assembly department works on an intermittent basis. (as in the furniture and custom packaging industries)

1. *Complexity of operations :* Generally, the complexity of production planning and control function increases with the increase in the variety of operations. Factors affecting the complexity of production control procedures are:

(a) Number of ultimate parts in the end product
(b) Number of different operations on each part
(c) Extent to which processes are dependent on the completion of previous operations
(d) Variations on production rates of machines used in the process.

(e) Number of discrete parts and sub-assemblies
(f) Degree to which customer's orders with specific delivery dates occur.
(g) Receipt of many small lot orders.

3. *Magnitude of operations :* The size of operation (i.e. time taken to complete an operation) and the distance traveled by the parts from operation to operation are important in establishing proper production control procedures. Generally, the need is greater for centralized production control organizations and for formal procedures as the size of the operation increases and the dependent operations are more physically separated.

Production Planning/Operations Planning and Control

Production planning and control function essentially consist of planning production in a manufacturing organization befOre Actual Production Activities Start And Exercising Control Activities To Ensure that the planned production is realised in terms of quantity, quality, delivery schedule and the cost of production.

Objectives of Production Planning and Control

1. To deliver quality goods in required quantities to the customer in the required delivery schedule - to achieve maximum customer satisfaction and minimum possible cost.
2. To ensure maximum utilization of all resources.
3. To ensure production of quality products.
4. To minimise the product through-put time or production/manufacturing cycle time.
5. To maintain optimum inventory levels.
6. To maintain flexibility in manufacturing operations.
7. To co-ordinate between labour and machines and various supporting departments.
8. To plan for plant capacities for future requirements.
9. To remove bottle-necks at all stages of production and to solve problems related to production.
10. To ensure effective cost reduction and cost control.
11. To prepare production schedules and ensure that promised delivery dates are met.
12. To produce effective results for least total cost.
13. To establish routes and schedules for work that will ensure optimum utilization of materials, labour and equipments and machines and to provide the means for ensuring the operation of the plant in accordance with these plans.
14. The ultimate objective is to contribute to the profit of the enterprise.

Three stages in production planning and control functions are:

Planning ☞ Choosing the best course of action among several alternatives.

Operations ☞ Execution as per plan.

Control ☞ Maintaining the performance by comparing the actual results with performance standards set and taking appropriate corrective action if necessary to reduce variance.

Role of Production Planning and Control in Operations Management

(Fig. 4.1 shows the production/operations management cycle.)

Operations are at the center of the diagram in Fig. 4.1, because they are the dynamic 'doing' elements of the production process. As the figure shows, planning and control never cease in the production area. There are a variety of production/operations management responsibilities such as :

(i) Product design.

(ii) Job design and process design.

(iii) Equipment selection and replacement.

(iv) Labour skills and training programs.

(v) Input material selection including raw materials and sub-contracting.

(vi) Plant selection and layout.

(vii) Scheduling steps of the plan.

(viii) Implementing and controlling the schedule.

(ix) Operating the production system.

The above are concerned with the design of the production process.

In addition, the control systems to be considered are:

(i) Inventory control policies.

(ii) Quality control policies.

(iii) Production schedule control policies.

(iv) Productivity and cost control policies.

(v) Constructing control systems.

(vi) Implementing and operating control systems.

(vii) Modifying policies and designs.

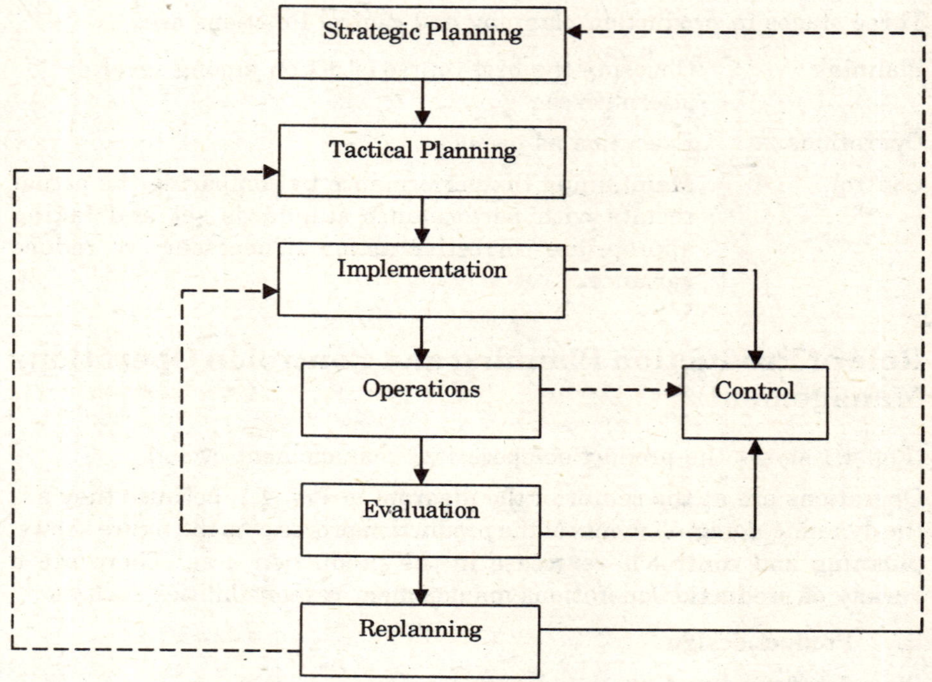

Fig. 4.1. The production/operations management cycle

Fig. 4.2 illustrates the importance of production planning department as the nerve center of the entire productive system.

Production planning and control is a management tool employed for the direction of the manufacturing operations and their co-operation with other activities of the firm.

Scope of production Planning and Control

Production planning and control encompasses the following areas:

1. *Materials* : Planning for procurement of raw materials, components and spare parts in the right quantities and specifications at the right time from the right source at the right price Purchasing, storage, inventory control, standardisation, variety reduction, value analysis and inspection are the other activities associated with materials.

2. *Methods* : Choosing the best method of processing from several alternatives. It also includes determining the best sequence of operations (process plans) and planning for tooling, jigs and fixtures etc.

3. *Machines and equipments* : Manufacturing methods are related to production facilities available in the production system. It involves facilities

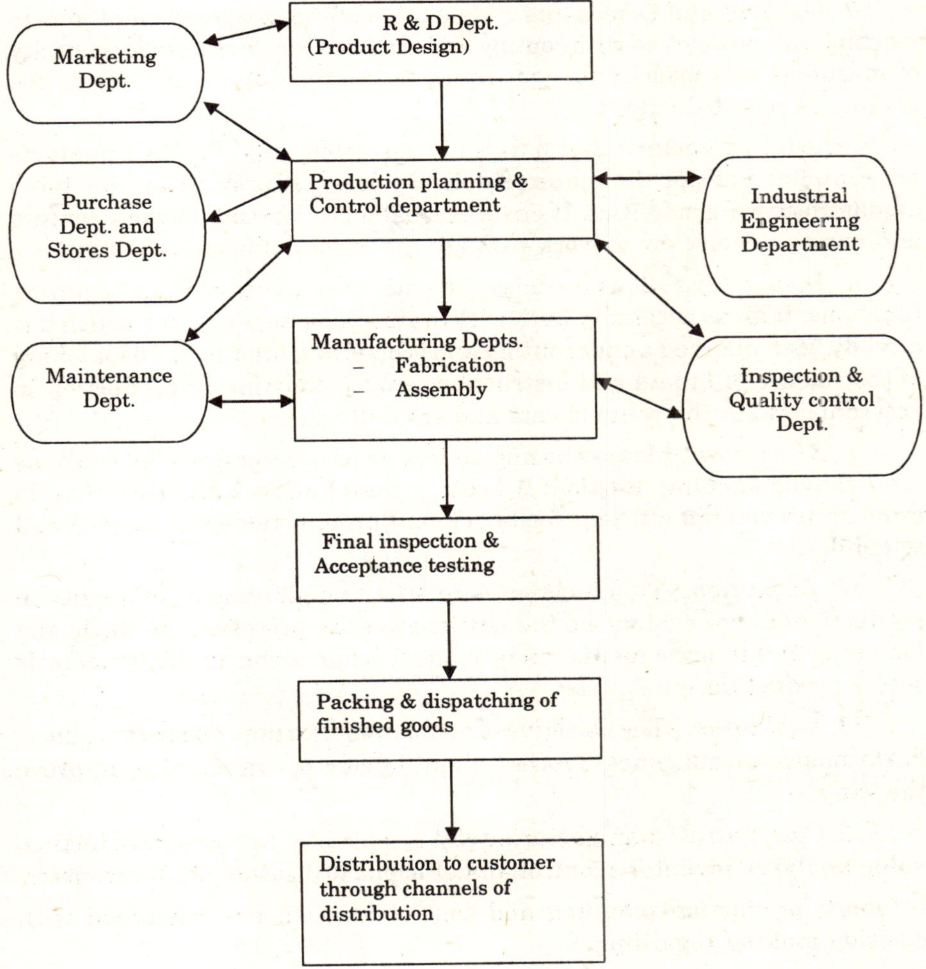

Fig. 4.2. Importance of production planning and control department

planning, capacity planning, allocation and utilization of plant and equipments, machines etc.

4. *Manpower* : Planning for manpower (labour, supervisory and managerial levels) having appropriate skills and expertise.

5. *Routing* : Determining the flow of work, material handling in the plant and sequence of operations or processing steps. This is related to considerations of appropriate shop layout and plant layout, temporary storage locations for raw materials, components and semi-finished goods and of materials handling systems.

6. *Estimating* : Establishing operation times leading to fixation of performance standards both for workers and machines.

7. *Loading and scheduling :* Machine loading is allocation of jobs to machines in conjunction with routing and with due consideration for capacity of machines and priority for jobs in order to utilize the machines to the maximum possible extent.

Scheduling ensures that parts, sub-assemblies and finished products are completed as per the required delivery dates. It provides a time table of manufacturing activities. It ensures a balanced load on all work centers and ensures even flow of work through the manufacturing facilities.

8. *Dispatching :* This is concerned with the execution of the planning functions. It gives necessary authority to start a particular work which has already been planned under routing and scheduling functions. Dispatching is the release of orders and instructions fro the starting or production in accordance with the route-sheets and schedule charts.

9. *Expediting :* Means chasing, follow-up or progressing which is done after the dispatching function. It keeps a close liaison with scheduling in order to provide an efficient feed-back and prompt review of targets and schedules.

10. *Inspection :* This function is related to maintenance of quality in production and of evaluating the efficiency of the processes, methods and labour so that improvements can be made to achieve the quality standards set by product design.

11. *Evaluation :* The objective of evaluation is to improve performance. Performance of machines, processes and labour is evaluated to improve the same.

12. *Cost control :* Manufacturing cost is controlled by wastage reduction, value analysis, inventory control and efficient utilization of all resources. In short, production planning and control function are concerned with decision making regarding.

(a) What to produce → Product planning and development, including product design.

(b) How to produce → Process planning, material planning, tool planning etc.

(c) Where to produce → Facilities planning, capacity planning and sub-contracting planning.

(d) When to produce → Production scheduling and machine loading

(e) Who will produce → Manpower planning

(f) How much to produce → Planning for quantity, economic batch size etc.

Principles of Production Planning and Control (PPC)

1. Type of production determines the kind of production planning and the control system needed.
2. Number of parts involved in the product affects expenses of operating PPC department
3. Complexity of PPC function varies with the number of assemblies involved.
4. Time is a common denominator for all scheduling activities.
5. Size of the plant has relatively little to do with the type of the PPC system needed.
6. PPC permits "management by exception".
7. Cost control should be a by-product of the PPC function.
8. "The highest efficiency in production is obtained by manufacturing the required quantity of a product, of the required quality, at the required time by the best and cheapest method" - PPC is a tool to coordinate all manufacturing activities in a production/operating system.

Phases in Production Planning and Control Function

1. Planning phase : (a) Preplanning (b) Active planning
   (a) Pre-planning activity involves product planning and development, demand forecasting, resources planning, facilities planning, plant planning, plant location and plant layout.
   (b) Active planning involves planning for quantity, determination of product - mix, routing, scheduling, material planning, process planning, capacity planning and tool planning.
2. Action phase : Execution or implementation phase includes the dispatching and progressing function.
3. Control phase : Includes status reporting, material control, tool control, inventory control, quality control, labour output control and cost control.

Main Functions of Production Planning and Control Department

Fig. 4.3. shows the various functions or elements of production planning and control:

Production Planning and Control	
Production Planning	**Production Control**
(i) Estimating	(a) Dispatching
(ii) Routing	(b) Expediting/ follow-up/ progressing
(iii) Scheduling	(c) Inspection
(iv) Loading	(d) Evaluating and corrective action

Fig. 4.3

Levels of Production Planning

Production planning occurs at several levels in the organization and covers different time horizons.

Planning can be classified as strategic planning, tactical planning and operational planning according to the hierarchical levels in which it is done in the organization. Another classification based on time span of planning is long range, intermediate range and short range planning.

Strategic planning : Strategic planning is a process of thinking through the organization's current mission and environment and then setting forth a guide for future decisions and results/

Example: Technology forecasting and choice of appropriate technology for the long range time horizon.

Strategic plans are usually long range plans done at the top management level. For example, the vice-president-operations, together with the top executives of the firm develops long range capacity and facility plans.

The long range plans focus on product lines, divisions, factories, markets and other business units, span several years and reflect the operations strategy of the business. Long range plans focus on the utilization of production facilities in the long run to achieve business objectives. They involve commitment in terms of capital investment, manufacturing process technology, product life and the like. The factors to be taken into consideration in long rage planning are investment capacity of the firm, product life cycle, technology level, market requirements and the like. These plans set in motion activities require to develop facilities and equipment, production processes and major sub-contractors. Long range plans become constraints on how many products can be produced in the intermediate and short range plans.

Objectives laid down by long range planning are:

(a) Production levels (Number of units produced).

(b) Operating capacities.

(c) Inventory policies.

(d) Levels of manufacturing costs.

Tactical Planning : Tactical planning is done over an intermediate term or medium range time horizon, by the middle level management (Operations managers at departmental level). These plans focus on aggregate products rather than individual specific products. These aggregate plans have a time span of 6 to 18 months. They specify the employment plans, machinery and utility plans, the sub-contractor and materials supply plans and facility modification/expansion plans.

Operational Planning : Operational planning is done over a short range time span developed by the junior level management. It is concerned with the utilization of existing facilities rather than the creation of new facilities. It involves proper utilization of key resources such as raw materials, machine capacity, energy etc.

Short term planning takes into account, current customer orders, priorities, material availability, absenteeism rate, cash flows, etc., and it is designed to respond quickly to changes in production levels and market conditions.

Short range planning establishes short range schedules which specify the quantity of specific products to be produced in each week of the planning horizon which varies from a week to a few months.

Example of a short-range plan is master-production schedule, together with materials requirement planning and capacity requirement planning.

Short range production scheduling and shop floor planning involve the day to day issues and decisions related to operations planning.

Table 4.1 illustrates the hierarchy of plans in a production planning system.

Production Planning Functions

The main functions of production planning are:

1. Estimating

Involves deciding the quantity of products to be produced and cost involved in it on the basis of sales forecast.

Estimating manpower, machine capacity and materials required (bill of material is the basis) to meet the planned production targets are the key activities before budgeting for resources (e.g.- production budges is the basis for materials budget, capital equipment budget and manpower budget).

2. Routing

This is the process of determining the sequence of operations to performed in the production process. Routing determines what work must be done, where and how?

Routing information is provided by product or process engineering function and it is useful to prepare machine loading charts and schedules.

Route sheet : A route sheet is a document, providing information and instructions for converting the raw materials into finished parts or products. It defines each step of the production operation and lays down the precise path or route through which the product will flow during conversion process.

Route sheet contain the following information:

Table 4.1. Levels of Planning in a Production Planning System.

Planning Horizon	Inputs	Plans/Schedule	Outputs
1. Long range (strategic planning)	(a) Long range demand forecast (b) Availability of funds and Business analysis (c) Capacity data and analysis	Long range capacity plan	(a) Production facility plans (plant location, layout, size, capacities, etc.) (b) Major sub-contractor plans (c) Major machinery and process plan
2. Intermediate range (Tactical planning)	Intermediate range demand forecast	Aggregate capacity plan	(a) Employment plan (b) Machinery and utility plan (c) Sub-contract and material supply contracts (d) Facility modifications plans (e) Aggregate inventory plans
3. Short range (operational planning)	(a) Short range demand forecasts (b) On-hand customer order (c) Other orders (Intra-company) (d) Availability of material from suppliers	(a) Master production schedules (MPS) (b) Capacity requirement planning (CRP) (c) Material requirement planning (MRP)	(a) Short range production schedules for end products (b) Short range schedule for Parts, components, sub-assemblies and final assemblies (c) Short range plan for purchasing materials (d) Short range shop floor plans.

(a) The operations required and their desired sequence.

(b) Machine or equipment to be used for each operation.

(c) Estimated set up time and operation time per piece (standard time).

(d) Tools, jigs and fixtures required for the operation.

(e) Detailed drawings of parts, sub-assemblies and final assemblies.

(f) Specification, dimensions, tolerances, surface finishes and quality standards to be achieved.

(g) Specification of raw materials to be used.

(h) Cutting speed, feed, depth of cut, etc., to be used on machine tools for the operations to be carried on.

(i) Inspection procedure and metrology tools required for inspection.

(j) Packing and handling instructions during the movement of parts and sub assemblies through the operation stages.

3. Scheduling

Involves fixing priorities for each job and determining the starting time and finishing time for each operation, the starting dates and finishing dates for each part, sub-assembly and final assembly. Scheduling lays down a time table for production, indicating the total time required for the manufacture of a product and also the time required for carrying out the operation for each part on each machine or equipment.

Objectives of scheduling are:

(a) To prevent unbalanced use to time among work centers and departments and

(b) To utilise labour such that the output is produced within established lead time or cycle time so as to deliver the products in time and complete production at minimum total cost.

4. Loading

Facility loading means loading of facility or work center and deciding, which jobs to be assigned to which work center or machine. Loading is the process of converting operation schedules into practice. Machine loading is the process of assigning specific jobs to machines, men or work centers based or relative priorities and capacity utilization.

A machine loading chart (Gantt chart) is prepared showing the planned utilisation of men and machines by allocating the jobs to machines or workers as pr priority sequencing established at the time of scheduling.

Loading ensures maximum possible utilisation of productive facilities and avoids bottlenecks in production. It is important to avoid either over loading or under loading the facilities, work centers or machines to ensure maximum utilization of resources.

Production Control Functions

The control functions are:

1. Dispatching

Dispatching may be defined as setting production activities in motion through the release of orders (work order, shop order) and instructions in accordance with the previously planned time schedules and routings.

Dispatching also provides a means for comparing actual progress with planned production progress. Dispatching functions include:

(a) Providing for movement of raw materials from stores to the first operation and from one operation to the next operation till all the operations are carried out.

(b) Collecting tools, jigs and fixtures from tool stores and issuing them to the user department or worker.

(c) Issuing job orders authorizing operations in accordance with dates and times as indicated in schedules or machine loading charts.

(d) Issue of drawings, specifications, route cards, material requisitions and tool requisitions to the user department.

(e) Obtaining inspection schedules and issuing them to the inspection section.

(f) Internal materials handling and movement of materials to the inspection area after completing the operation, moving the materials to the next operation center after inspection, and movement of completed parts to holding stores.

(g) Returning jigs and fixtures and tools to stores after use.

2. Expediting/Follow-up/Progressing

Expediting or progressing ensures that, the work is carried out as per the plan and delivery schedules are met.

Progressing includes activities such as status reporting, attending to bottlenecks or hold-ups in production and removing the same, controlling variations or deviations from planned performance levels, following up and monitoring progress of work through all stages of production, co-ordinating with purchase, stores, tool room and maintenance departments and modifying the production plans and replan if necessary

Need for expediting may arise due to the following reasons

(a) Delay in supply of materials.

(b) Excessive absenteeism.

(c) Changes in design specifications.

(d) Changes in delivery schedules initiated by customers.

(e) Break down of machines or tools, jigs and fixtures.

(f) Errors in design drawings and process plans.

Benefits of Production Planning and Control Function

Production planning and control function is the nerve center or heart of the production/ operations management function. It co-ordinates all phases of the production/operating system. An efficient production planning and control function results in higher quality, better utilization of resources, reduced inventories, reduced manufacturing cycle time, faster delivery, better customer service, lower production costs and lower capital investment and higher customer satisfaction. Efficient utilization of resources results in higher productivity and economy of production, timely delivery and right quality of goods/services at the right cost will improve customer satisfaction. Minimisation of break-down of machines, plant and equipments minimises idle time of equipments and labour and ensures even flow of work through the plant facilities. This will improve employee discipline and morale in the organisation.

An efficient production planning and control system enables the firm to improve its sales turnover, market share and profitability and provides a competitive advantage for the firm due to balanced inventory levels and higher quality, flexibility and dependability and lower prices which are the performance factors for the firm.

Limitations of P.P.C.

(a) Production planning and control function is based on certain assumptions or forecasts of customers' demand, plant capacity, availability of materials, power etc. If these assumptions go wrong, PPC becomes ineffective.

(b) Employees may resist changes in production levels set as per production plans if such plans are rigid.

(c) The production planning process is time consuming when it is necessary to carry out routing and scheduling functions for large and complex products consisting of a large number of parts going into the product.

(d) Production planning and control function become extremely difficult when the environmental factors change very rapidly such as technology, customers' taste regarding fashion or style of products needed, government policy and controls, change frequently, stoppages of power supply by electricity boards due to power cuts, break in supply chain due to natural calamities such as floods, earthquakes, war, etc.

Measuring Effectiveness of PPC Function

The task of the PPC department is mainly to co-ordinate the activities of various departments which support production departments viz., purchase, stores, industrial engineering, quality control, design, maintenance etc. Hence, the effectiveness of the PPC department can be generally measured by the company's success the meeting the demand and its ability to produce quality products and deliver them in the delivery schedules desired by customers at a reasonable price that is acceptable to customers and thereby achieve and ensure maximum customer satisfaction.

There are four specific areas in which effectiveness of the PPC function can be measured. They are:

1. Delivery : this can be measured by finding out the number of deliveries effected on time and those got delayed over a period of time (usually one year).
2. Inventory levels : The value of average inventory held annually, value of obsolete inventory, value of non-moving and surplus inventories and the inventory turnover ratio, are the indicators of efficiency in inventory management
3. Production/operations management : Comparison of planned and actual production indicates the performance of the PPC function. Number of overtime hours worked, machine utilization ratio, etc., are also indicators of effectiveness of PPC function.

The expenditures incurred for carrying out the various functions of PPC department vis-a-vis the production value and sales revenue realized.

Production Planning and control in different Production Systems

1. PPC in Job Production

Job production involves manufacture of products to meet specific customer requirements of special orders. The quantity involved is usually small. Examples of job production are manufacture of large turbo generators, boilers, steam engines, processing equipments, material handling equipments, ship building etc.

Under job production, we may have three types according to the regularity of manufacture namely:

(a) A small number of products produced only once.
(b) A small number of products produced intermittently when, the need arises.
(c) A small number of products produced periodically at known intervals of time.

When the order is to be executed only once, there is either scope for improvement of production techniques by introducing intricate method studies, special tools or jigs and fixtures unless the technical requirement justifies it. But if the order is to be repeated, jigs and fixtures, tools as well as specially designed inspection gauges should be carefully considered to reduce the manufacturing cycle time.

PPC function is relatively difficult in job production because of the following reasons:

(i) Every job order is of a different nature and have different sequence of operations. There is not standardized routing for job orders.

(ii) Specific job orders are assigned to different work stations as per the availability of capacity

(iii) Production schedules drawn depend on the relative priority assigned to various job orders.

(iv) Scheduling is dependent on the assessment of production times and estimating is based on judgement.

2. PPC in Batch Production or Intermittent Production

Batch production is the manufacture of a number of identical articles either to meet a specific order or to satisfy the continuous demand. The decisions regarding tooling and jigs and fixtures are dependent on the quantities involved in the production batch.

In batch production too, there can be three types namely:

(a) A batch produced only once.

(b) A batch produced repeatedly at irregular intervals, when the need arises.

(c) A batch produced periodically at known intervals, to satisfy continuous demand.

Here again, planning and control become more simplified as quantities increase and as manufacture becomes more regular. Two problems that may arise in batch production are due to the size of the batch and due to scheduling of production.

The solution to these problems depends on whether the production is governed by -

(a) External customer orders only.

(b) Whether the plant is producing for internal consumption i.e., a sub-assembly used in the final product.

If it is the case of external customer orders, the customer order size usually determines the batch size. The timing will also depend on the delivery dates specified by the customers. If it is for internal consumption, both batch size and production scheduling problems are matters for internal management decisions.

The problem of optimal batch size has to take into account the set-up costs which are involved, before each production runs and the inventory carrying costs incurred, when the finished product is held in stock. The batch size determines the length of the production run and affects both the production schedule and batch size considerations of other products.

Characteristics of PPC Function in Intermittent or Batch Production

(a) Before issuing manufacturing orders, need for new raw materials and tools, overloading and under loading of particular machines or work centres must be anticipated.

(b) As products are diversified and several orders are handled simultaneously in different work centres, scheduling and follow-up becomes a difficult task.

(c) Dispatching has to be done efficiently to avoid delays and bottlenecks in the production process.

3. PPC in Continuous Production

Continuous production is normally associated with large quantities of production and with a high rate of demand. Continuous production is justified when the rate of production can be sustained by the market.

Two types of continuous production can be -

(a) Mass production and

(b) Flow production

In mass production, a large number of identical articles are produced, but inspite of advanced mechanization and tooling, the equipment need not be specially designed for the component to be manufactured.

In flow production, the plant and equipment and layout have been primarily designed to manufacture a particular product. A decision to switch over to a different kind of product needs basic changes in the equipments and the layout, especially when special purpose machines and complex material handling systems are used.

PPC in continuous production is usually far simpler than in a job or batch production. Extensive effort is required for detailed planning before production starts, but both scheduling and control need not be elaborate usually. The output is either limited by available capacity or regulated within given limits to conform to production targets, based on periodic sale forecasts.

4. Production Planning and Control in Process industry

PPC in the process industry is relatively simple. Routing is automatic and uniform. Standard processes and specialized equipments are used. As the products are standardised and goods are produced to stock and sell, scheduling is easy. Departmental schedules are derived from master production schedules. Dispatching involves issue of repetitive orders to ensure a steady flow of materials throughout the plant. The main task of PPC in process industry is to maintain a continuous and uniform flow of work at the predetermined rate in order to utilise the plant and equipments fully and to complete the production in time.

Requirements of Effective Production Planning and Control system

1. Sound organizational structure with mechanism for proper delegation of authority and fixation of responsibility at all levels.
2. Information feedback system should provide reliable and up-to-date information to all persons carrying out PPC functions.
3. Standardization of materials, tools, equipments, labour, quality, workmanship etc.
4. Trained personnel for using the special tools, equipments and manufacturing processes.
5. Flexibility to accommodate changes and bottle necks such as shortage of materials, power failures, machine break-downs and absenteeism of employees.
6. Appropriate management policies regarding production and inventory levels, product - mix and inventory turnover.
7. Accurate assessment of manufacturing lead times and procurement lead times.
8. Plant capacity should be adequate to meet the demand. The plant should be flexible in order to respond to the introduction of new products, changes in product-mix and production rate.

Earlier in this chapter, we have discussed three phases in production planning and control function namely, planning phase, action phase and control phase. Pre-planning phase is the first stage in planning phase and it is the interface between product design and process design. One such activity in pre-planning phase is 'make or buy analysis', which is the basis for process planning, capacity planning, facilities planning and plant planning. We will discuss this type of analysis and plant planning in the following paragraphs.

9

Sequencing and Scheduling

Introduction

The materials requirement planning system specifies what production or components are needed in what quantities and when they are required. The production activity control (PAC) or Shop Floor Activity Control (SFAC) directs how, when and where the products/components should be made in order to ensure the delivery of goods as per schedules or due dates. Fig. 4.4 shows the major concerns of production activity control.

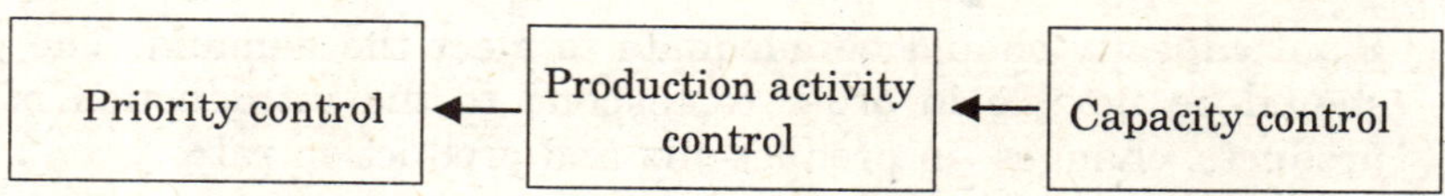

Fig 4.4. Concerns of production activity control

Priority control ensures that the production or shop floor activities are carried out as per a predetermined priority plan. This involves control of orders to vendors/sub contractors and in-house production shops.

Capacity control ensures that, the amount of equipment and labour hours necessary at various work centres to carry out the scheduled work are provided.

The concept of priority control and capacity control can be applied both in production systems and service systems even though the problems associated vary in nature and difficulty.

Objectives of Production Activity Control

1. To know the current status of the job (i.e., what jobs are being processed, at which work center on which machine?)
2. To determine what should be the next job to be processed and in which work centre?)

3. To ensure that the correct quantities of materials are in the right place (machine or work center) at the right time and the required capacity and tooling are provided.
4. To maximize operational efficiency i.e., efficiency of labour and machine utilization.
5. To minimize work-in-progress inventory
6. To minimize set-up costs.
7. To maintain control of operations by monitoring job status and lead times, measuring progress and indicate corrective action when necessary.

The above objectives of a production activity control system help integrate and coordinate the human and machine resources of a production system.

Operations Planning and Scheduling

Scheduling involves developing and assigning specific dates for the start and completion of the necessary tasks or operation in a production shop floor. The output plans indicated in master production schedules must be translated into detailed operational schedules to be implemented on the shop floor on a day to day basis. The operations scheduling and control process includes activities such as priority sequencing, detailed scheduling, loading, expediting and input/output control.

Figure 4.5 shows the operations planning and scheduling system. The various terms used in operations planning and scheduling are described briefly in the following paragraphs.

1. *Loading:* Sometimes known as shop loading or machine loading, is the assignment of jobs to various work centres or machines for future processing, giving due consideration to the sequence of operations as per the route sheet and the priority sequencing and machine/work center utilization. Loading establishes the amount of load (labour hours or machine hours) each work center or machine must carry during the future planning period (weekly or monthly). This will result in load schedules which indicate comparison of labour and machine hours needed to produce the master production schedules with the labour and machine hours actually available in each planning period (week or month) in the short-term planning horizon.

2. *Sequencing* is the process of determining the sequence of processing of all jobs at each work center or machine. It establishes the priorities for processing the jobs which are waiting in the queue at each work center or machine. The priority sequencing is done as per a priority sequencing rule, which will be discussed later in this chapter.

3. *Detailed scheduling* is the process of determining the start and finish times (dates) at each work center or machine for all jobs. Detailed

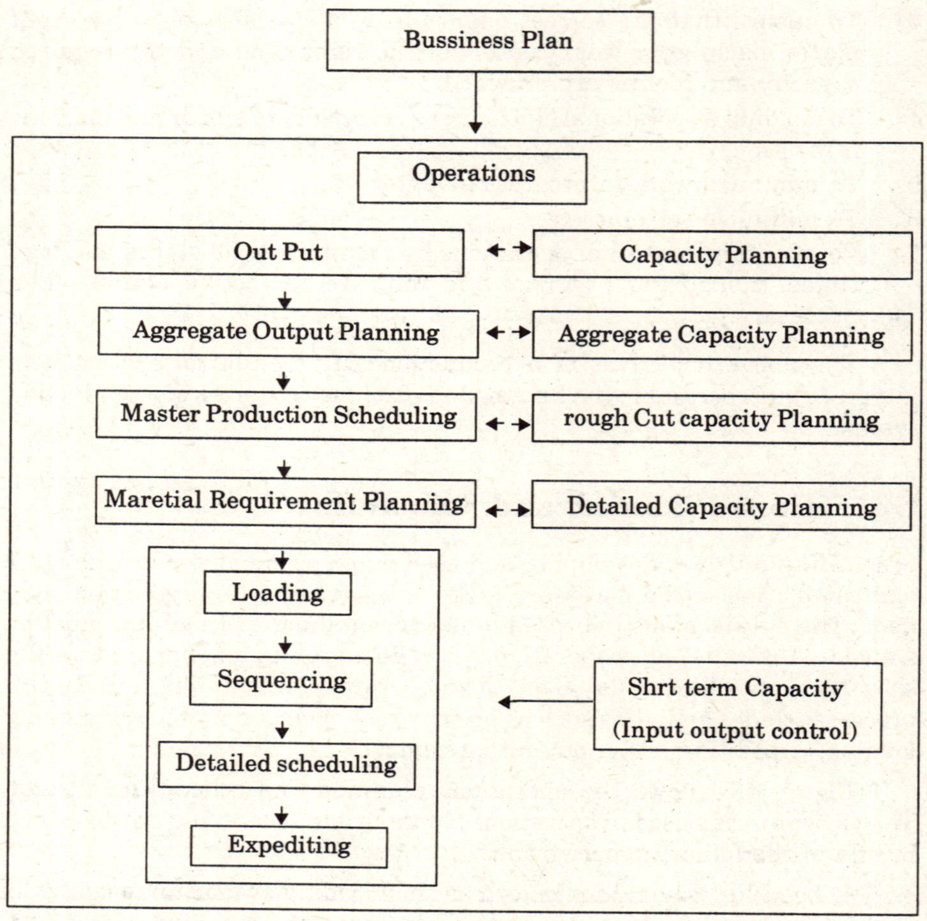

Fig. 4.5. Operations planning and scheduling system

scheduling in possible only after loading and sequencing. By knowing the duration of time each job takes to complete, the operation at each work center/machine and also by knowing the due dates, the detailed schedule indicating the start and finish dates can be established.

4. *Expediting* is the special effort or action needed to keep the job moving through the production facility on time as per the detailed schedule. Disruptions in production due to machine/equipment break downs, non-availability of materials when needed, last-minute priority changes due to special jobs having over-riding priorities, necessitate the expediting action for some important jobs.

This requires operations managers to deviate from the existing plans and schedules.

5. *Input-output control* plans and schedules call for certain levels of capacity at a work center or machine, but actual utilization may differ from what was planned. Input-output control is a key activity that provides detailed information about the actual utilization of a work center or machine's capacity versus the planned capacity utilization. It gives a picture of flow of jobs between work centres. Problems such as insufficient capacity at work stations and problems at upstream work stations can be identified through the input-output control.

Shop Floor Planning and Control

The various activities included in shop floor planning and control are–

1. Assigning a priority to each order which helps in setting the sequence of processing orders at work centres.

2. Issuing dispatching lists to each work center. These lists indicate which orders are due to be produced at a work center, their priorities and completion dates/times.

3. Up-dating the work-in-progress inventory. Informations such as number of good parts coming out of each processing step (operation), amount of scrap, amount of rework required and number of units short on each order.

4. Providing input -output control on all work centres.

5. Measuring the efficiency, utilization and productivity of workers and machines at each work centre.

Scheduling Process-Focused Production Systems

Process-focused production system produce many non-standard products in relatively small batches that flow along different routes or paths through the production facility and require frequent machine change-overs. Such production systems are also known as *intermittent* production systems or jobs shops.

In such production systems, the departments or work centres are organized around the type of equipments or operations. (e.g.: drilling, welding, soldering, etc.) Products flow through work centres in batches corresponding to individual customer orders or batches of economic batch quantities in produce - to stock situations.

Figure 4.6 illustrates scheduling and shop-floor decisions in process - focused operations or job shops.

Scheduling in job shop or process - focused production systems is quite complex because of the following reasons:

(a) Job shops have to produce products against customer orders for which delivery dates have to be promised.

(b) Production lots tend to be quire small and may require numerous machine change-overs.
(c) Possibility of assigning and reassigning workers and machines to many different orders due to flexibility.
(d) In such a flexible, variable and changing environment, schedules must be specific and detailed work center-wise to bring orderliness.

Scheduling Techniques for Job Shop

The type of scheduling technique used in job shop depends on the volume of orders, the nature of operations and the job complexity. Two types of scheduling techniques used are:

1. Forward scheduling 2. Backward scheduling.

A combination of forward and backward scheduling may often be used in practice.

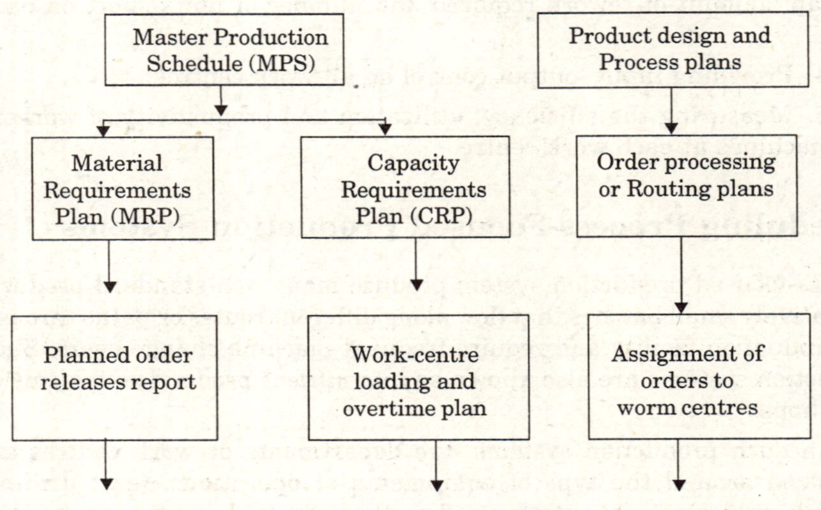

Day-to-day scheduling and shop floor decisions

1. Setting priorities of orders at each work center.
2. Priority sequencing and assigning jobs to machines
3. Shop floor control – dispatching or releasing orders to work centres, expediting orders if necessary, co-ordinating work center schedules and revising as conditions change.

Fig. 4.6. Scheduling and shop floor decisions in process - focused production system

Forward scheduling : In this approach, each task is scheduled to occur at the earliest time that, the necessary material will be on hand and capacity will be available. It assumes that procurement of material and operations start as soon as the customers, requirements are known. The customers place their orders on a 'needed-as-soon-as possible' basis. The earliest completion date, assuming that everything goes as planned, could be quoted to the potential customer. Some buffer time may be added to determine a date that is more likely to be achievable, if it is acceptable to the customer. Forward scheduling is used in many companies such as steel mills and machine tool manufactures where jobs are manufactured to customers orders and delivery is requested on 'as early as possible.' basis, Forward scheduling is well suited where the supplier is usually not able to meet the schedules. This type of scheduling is simple to use, gets jobs done in shorter lead times but accumulates high work in process inventories. Figure 4.7 illustrates forward scheduling.

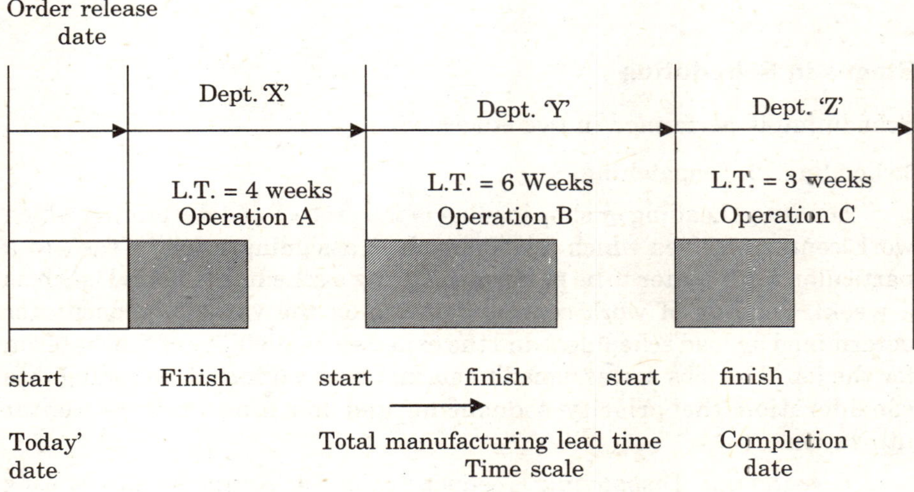

Fig. 4.7. Example of forward scheduling

Backward scheduling: This scheduling technique is often used in assembly-type industries and in job shops that commit in advance to specific delivery dates. After determining the required schedule dates for major sub-assemblies, the schedule uses these required dates for each component and works backward to determine the proper release date for each component manufacturing order. The job's start date is determined by 'setting back' from the finish date, the processing time for the job. By assigning jobs as late as possible, backward scheduling minimizes inventories, since each job is not completed until it is due, but not earlier. Backward scheduling is also known as *reverse* scheduling. (See Figure 4.8)

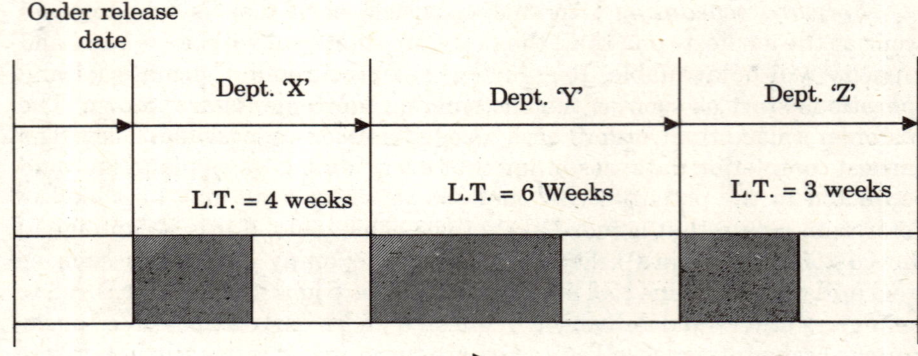

Fig. 4.8. An example of backward scheduling

Stages in Scheduling

Scheduling is performed in two stages, viz.:

1. Loading 2. Dispatching.

Loading : Loading or shop loading is the process of determining which work center receives which job. It involves assigning a job or task to a particular work center to be performed during a scheduling period (such as a week). Loading of work centres depends on the variable capacity (or determined by load schedules) and the expected availability of the material for the job. The jobs are assigned to machines or work centres taking into consideration the priority sequencing and machine or work center utilization.

Dispatching : Dispatching is sequencing and selecting the jobs waiting at a work center (i.e. determining which job to be done next) when capacity becomes available. It is actually authorising or assigning the work to be done. The dispatch list is a means of priority control. It lists all jobs available to a work center and ranks them by a relative priority. When priorities have been assigned to specific jobs, scheduling gets implemented through the dispatch list.

Finite loading and Infinite loading : Loading procedures are categorized as either finite loading or infinite loading. In finite loading, jobs are assigned to work centres by comparing the required hours for each operation with the available hours in each work center for the scheduling period. In infinite loading, jobs are assigned to work centres without regard to capacity (as if the capacity were infinite).

(a) Finite loading : Finite loading system start with a specified capacity for each work center and a list of jobs to be processed at the work center (sequencing). The work centre's capacity is allotted to the jobs by simulating job starting times and completion times. The finite loading system combines loading, sequencing and detailed scheduling. It creates a detailed schedule for each job and each work center, based on the capacity of the work center.

Figure 4.9 shows a finite capacity load profile for a work center having a capacity of 100 labour hours per week.

(b) Infinite loading : The process of loading work centres with all the jobs, when they are required without regard to the actual capacity, available at the work center is called infinite loading. Infinite laoding indicates the actual released order demand (load) on the work center, so as to facilitate decision about using overtime, sub-contracting or using alternative routings and delaying selected orders.

Figure 4.9 illustrates the infinite loading profile for a work center.

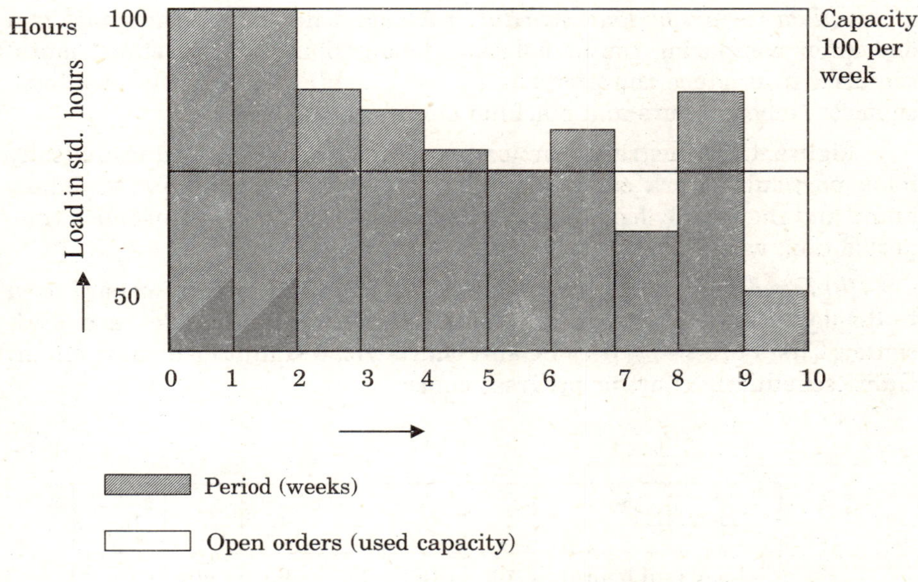

Fig. 4.9. Finite loading

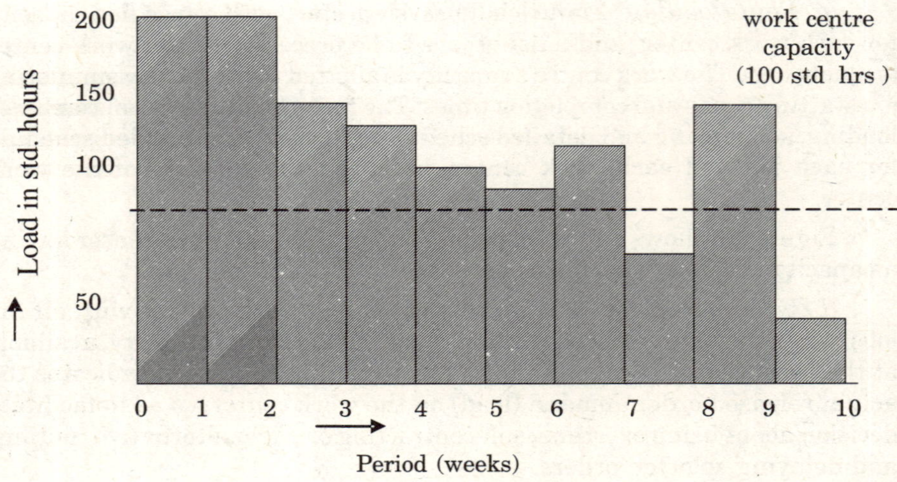

Fig. 4.10. infinite loading

Load Charts and Machine Loading Charts

(a)*Load chart or load schedule :* A load schedule or load chart is a device for comparing the actual load (labour hours and machine hours) required to produce the products as per the MPS against the available capacity (labour hours and machine hours) in each week.

Figure 4.11 illustrates the load schedule or chart shown graphically for a particular work center having a weekly capacity of 100 standard hours and the weekly load for six weeks period. The load against each time period (i.e., week) is as shown:

(b) Machine loading chart (Gantt load chart) : Gantt charts are used to display graphically the work loads on each machine or in each work center. There are two types of Gantt charts viz, i) Gannt load chart and ii) Gantt scheduling chart or progress chart.

Seek NO	1	2	3	4	5	6
Load (std hours)	100	100	80	60	50	70

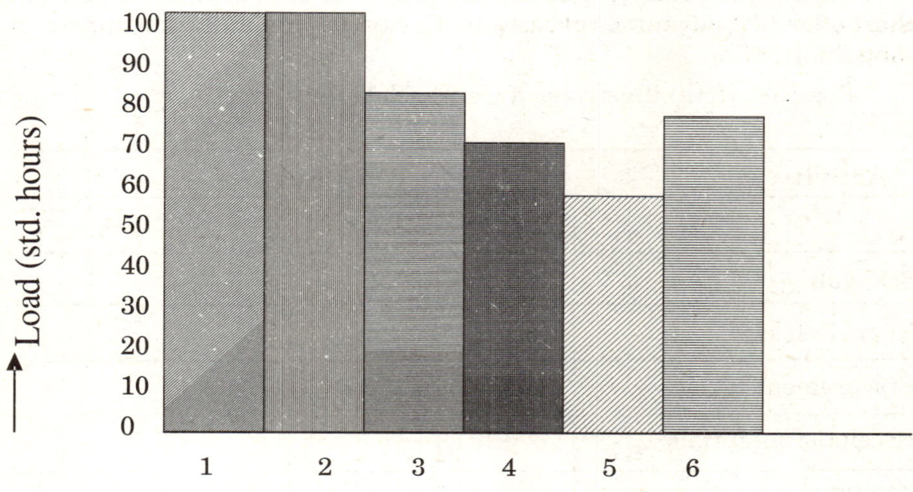

Fig. 4.11. Load schedule

Figure 4.12(a) illustrates a Gantt load chart drawn for a particular week of a particular month.

Dept :			**Week No.**		**Month :**	
Work centre	**Mon**	**Tue**	**Wed**	**Thu**	**Fri**	**Sat**
Fabrication		D	E			F
Machining	C		D	X	E	
Assembly	B	C		D	X	E
Testing		B				O
Packing	A		B	C		

Legend — Actual job progress — Planned job duration — Non– productive i.e., repairs, change over etc.

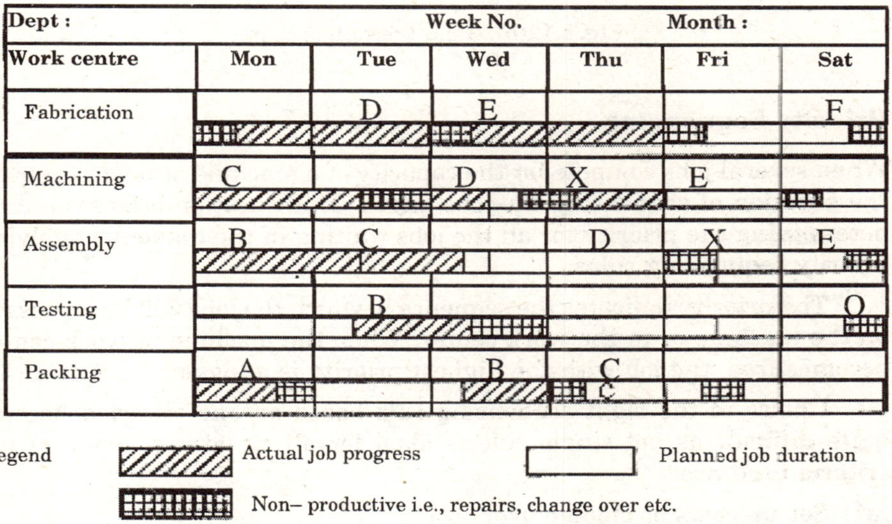

Fig. 4.12(a). Gantt load chart drawn for a particular week of a particular month

Gantt charts simple to devise and easy to understand. The Gantt load chart offers the advantage of ease and clarity in communicating important shop information.

Figure 4.12 (b) illustrates a Gantt scheduling chart

Activity	Week number								
	1	2	3	4	5	6	7	8	9
Scheduling									
Engg. Release									
Procurement									
Receipt of materials									
Tooling									
Fabrication									
Assembly									
Inspection									
Shipping									

Time period (week)

Fig. 4.12(b). Gantt scheduling chart

Priority Sequencing

When several jobs compete for the capacity of a machine or a work center, the question of sequencing the jobs arises. This question is answered by determining the priority for all the jobs waiting in the queue by applying priority sequencing rules.

The priority indicates the sequence in which the jobs will be processed on the machine or in the work center. When the machine or work center becomes free, the job with the highest priority is assigned.

Choice of the right sequencing rule based on one criterion become quite difficult as not single rule is ideal for all situations. Some of the criteria used are:

(a) Set up costs or change over costs.

(b) Work-in-progress inventory cost.

(c) Idle time.

(d) Number or percent of jobs late.
(e) Average job lateness.
(f) Average flow time.
(g) Average number of jobs in the system.
(h) Average time to complete a job.

Single-criterion Priority Sequencing Rules

Some single - criterion priority sequencing rules are:

1. First come first served (FCFS)
2. Shortest processing time (SPT) or shortest operation time (SOT) or minimum processing tie (MINPRT).
3. Longest processing time (LPT) or longest operation time (LOT)
4. Least slack job (LS) first or minimum slack (MIN SLACK) job first.
5. Earliest due date (EDD) job first
6. Truncated shortest processing job first (TSPT)
7. Preferred customer order (PCO) first
8. Random selection (RS)
9. COVERT (Cost over time)
10. Least change-over cost.

The rules of single criterion sequencing are explained in detail in the following paragraphs:

1. First come-first served (FCFS) rule : Jobs are scheduled for work in the same sequence as they arrive at the facility or work center. This rule is commonly applied in service centres such as banks, super bazaars and barber shops.

2. Shortest process time job (SPT) first : The job which has the shortest processing/operation time on the machine or at the work center is given the highest priority to be loaded as the next job for processing. This rule minimises the in-process-inventory, however, at the expense of keeping the jobs having longer processing time for a longer time in the work centre, there-by increasing the job through-put time (i.e. manufacturing cycle time).

3. Longest processing time (LPT) job first : The job with the longest processing/ operation time is scheduled as the first job to be loaded on the machine among the jobs waiting in queue.

4. Least slack (LS) job first : In this rule, the highest priority is given to the job which has the least slack. Slack is the difference between available time and the duration of processing the job. Slack = Available time – Processing time.

5. Earliest due date (EDD) job first : This rule sequences the jobs waiting in the queue at the work centre or machine according to their due dates and the jobs are processed according to their due dates i.e. job having earliest due date is given highest priority while loading the job on the machine (or work centre). This rule does not ensure that all jobs will be completed on time i.e. within their due dates.

6. Truncated shortest processing time (TSPT) job first : This rule sequences the jobs according to the SPT rule, except that the jobs that have been waiting for a time period longer than a specified truncation time are give higher priority than other jobs.

7. Preferred customer order (PCO) rule : Jobs belonging to a preferred customer are given a higher priority than other jobs.

8. Random-selection : This rule is not used normally. It may be used when no other consideration is important.

9. COVERT (cost over time) rule : This rule uses the ratio of expected delay cost (C) to the processing time (T). The job with the largest ratio is given the highest priority.

$$\text{Cost over time ratio} = \frac{\text{Expected delay cost (C)}}{\text{Processing time (T)}}$$

10. Least change-over cost : The sequencing of jobs is done by analyzing the total cost of making all the machines change over between jobs.

Illustration for Sequencing Rules

XYZ Company has received the following jobs at a work centre to be processed. The processing time (in days), arrival date and due date (in terms of shop calendar days) are given. Determine the sequence in which jobs should be processed according to each of the following priority rules viz., FCFS, SPT, LPT, EDD, TSPT, LS and COVERT.

Assume today is day 100 and the jobs cannot be delayed for more than 60 days for TSPT rule. Assume expected cost per delay as Rs. 10 per day.

Job	Processing time (days)	Arrival date (shop calendar day)	Due date (shop calendar day)
A	15	95	185
B	20	110	200
C	10	112	175
D	30	125	235
E	25	125	180
F	18	130	220

Solution:

(a) Priority rule: FCFS ⇨ sequences:

A,	B,	C,	D,	E,	F

(b) Priority rule: SPT ⇨ sequences:

A,	B,	C,	D,	E,	F

(c)Priority rule: LPT ⇨ sequences:

A,	B,	C,	D,	E,	F

(d) Priority rule: EDD ⇨ sequences:

A,	B,	C,	D,	E,	F

(e) Priority rule: TSPT ⇨ sequences:

A,	B,	C,	D,	E,	F

For TSPT rule, it is specified that the jobs cannot be delayed by more than 60 days if we apply the SPT rule. If none of the jobs violates the constraints, the sequence will be identical for the SPT and TSPT rule. To examine this, we should know the wait time of the jobs as per SPT rule, which is determined as below:

Job sequence (SPT rule)	Processing Duration (days)	Arrival date (days)	Start date (days)	Wait time (days)
C	10	112	112	Nil
A	15	95	122	27
F	18	130	137	7
B	20	10	155	45
E	25	125	175	50
D	30	125	200	75

The SPT sequence results in delay of 75 days for job D, which is more than the 60 days specified. Therefore, job D would be scheduled before job E (as per SPT rule) and the sequence would be C, A, F, B, D, E.

f) *Least slack (L.S) rule :*

Job sequence	Processing Duration (days)	Arrival Time (days)	Slack (days)	Sequence (Rank)
A	15	(185 – 95) = 90	(90 – 15) = 75	5
B	20	(200 – 110) = 90	(90 – 20) = 70	3
C	10	(175 – 112) = 63	(63 – 10) = 53	2
D	30	(235 – 125) = 110	(110 – 30) = 80	6
E	25	(180 – 125) = 55	(55 – 25) = 30	1
F	18	(220 – 130) = 90	(90 – 18) = 72	4

Job sequence :

E,	C,	B,	F,	A,	D

g) *Covert Rule :* The covert rule competes possible delays for individual jobs using rule such as FCFS. If one or more jobs are delayed, the ratio of delay cost to processing time (i.e C/T) is computed. Then the jobs are sequenced in the decreasing order of C/T ratio. The calculations are shown below:

Job	Processing Duration (days)	Completion date (days)	Due date (days)	Delay (days)	Expected cost of delay (days)	C/T ratio
A	15	95+15=110	185	Nil	Nil	Nil
B	20	110+20=130	200	Nil	Nil	Nil
C	10	130+10=140	175	Nil	Nil	Nil
D	30	140+30=170	235	Nil	Nil	Nil
E	25	170+25=195	180	15	150	150/25=6
F	18	195+18=213	220	Nil	Nil	Nil

Job sequence :

E,	A,	B,	C,	D,	F

Dynamic Sequencing Rules (Combined Criteria Rules)

(a) Dynamic lack (DS) rule

(b) Dynamic lack per Remaining Operation (DS/RO) rule.

(c) Critical Ratio (CR) rule.

The dynamic sequencing rules are described below.

(a) Dynamic Slack (DS) rule : When the least slack rule is used repeatedly at each machine/work centre for sequencing thejobs, it is known as dynamic slack rule.

(b) Dynamic Slack per Remaining Operation (DS/RO) rule : In this rule, the ratio of total slack time available for the job to the number of operations remaining including the current operation is obtained.

$$\text{DS/RO ratio} = \frac{\text{Total slack time}}{\text{Total number of operations remaining including the current operation}}$$

The job with the smallest DS/RO ratio is scheduled first.

(c) Critical Ratio rule (CR) : The critical ratio rule is designed to give priority to jobs that have the most urgently needed work to meet the shipping schedule.

$$\text{Critical ratio (CR)} = \frac{\text{Due date - Date now}}{\text{Days required to complete the job}}$$

$$\text{or } \frac{\text{Due date - Time now}}{\text{Time required to complete the job}} \text{ or } \frac{\text{D.D - D. N}}{\text{L.T.R.}}$$

where D.D = due date D.N = date now

L.T.R = lead time remaining or processing time

$$\text{or C.R.} = \frac{\text{Days remaining}}{\text{Days required for processing}}$$

$$\text{or } \frac{\text{Time remaining}}{\text{Time required for processing}}$$

The job with the lowest Cr is given highest priority in sequencing.

Scheduling and Controlling Production for Delivery Schedules - Line of Balance (LOB) Method

It is quite common that production systems often produce products as per the commitment to a delivery schedule promised to the customers. These delivery schedules can be part of a purchase order.

In order to ensure that the actual product deliveries match with the planned delivery schedules, a system must be devised to schedule and control all the processing steps of the production system.

Quite often, the firm may be in schedule in terms of deliveries, but may default soon on deliveries because the production pipeline may run out of products sooner or later. When this happens, it may be too late to take corrective action, because the deliveries get affected until the pipeline can again be refilled with products.

Line-of Balance (LOB) technique has been used successfully to schedule and control upstream processing steps in a variety of production systems (LOB) producing goods and services.

LOB Technique

The Line of Balance technique is used in production scheduling and control to determine, at a review date, not only how many (quantity) of an item should have been completed by that date, but also how many should have passed through the previous (upstream) operation stages (processing steps) by that time so as to ensure the completion of the required delivery schedule.

LOB is a charting and computational technique for monitoring and controlling products and services that are made to meet specific delivery schedules. The concept of LOB is similar to the time phased order point system (TROP) and MRP system (Material Requirements Planning). Starting from the delivery schedule (date) for the final product and the quantity, the product structure tree is drawn on a horizontal scale, off-setting lead time on a time scale, reflecting the previous processing steps or stages of production. The processing steps or production stages may include purchased parts, machined parts, sub-assemblies and major assembly operations to support delivery schedule for the finished product. The LOB chart shows the quantity of parts, components, sub-assemblies, major assemblies and end products produced at every stage and at any given review date. It indicates the quantity of goods or services that should have been completed at every production stage or processing step and at any given time, so as to meet the delivery date for the end product.

The LOB technique shows the desired progress as well as the actual progress achieved on the LOB chart. The LOB technique can be best explained with an example as below:

Example

XYZ Company has received customer orders to deliver a product for which the operations program and the delivery schedules are given below:

Delivery schedule

Week No.	Qty. of end product to be delivered
1	5
2	10
3	10
4	10
5	25

Develop a LOB chart and determine the quantities that should have passed through the upstream processing step/stages during the review point at the end of 2nd week.

Solution Method : The five stages required to be followed in LOB technique are

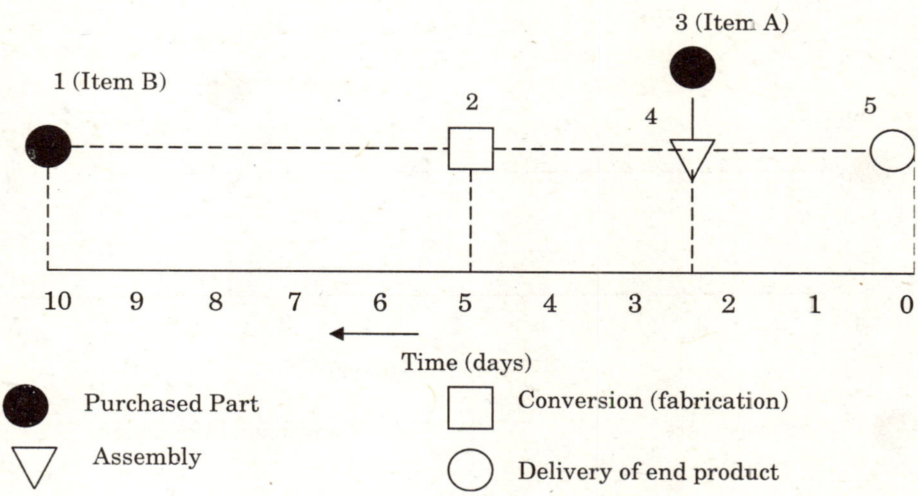

Fig. 4.13. Operations programme

1. Preparation of operation programme or assembly chart.
2. Preparation of cumulative completion / delivery schedule or objective chart.
3. Construction of LOB chart
4. Construction of program progressive chart
5. Analysis of progress and corrective action.

These stages are illustrated below:

Stage 1 : Preparation of operation programme or assembly chart:

The operation programme or assembly chart shows the *'lead time'* for each operation stage/processing step. The 'lead time' is the length of time prior to the completion of the final operation/processing step by which, intermediate operations must be completed.

Fig. 4.14 illustrates an operation programme chart or assembly chart:

The delivery lead time for the finished product (end item) is zero and the time scale indicating *'lead time'* runs from right to left. The operation programme chart indicates that the purchased part A must be combined with the item B in operation stage/processing step 4, three days before the completion of end item.

Item B, prior to combination, has undergone a conversion operation which has to be completed five days before the completion of end item. The purchased part for item B must be available 10 days prior to the delivery date for the end item, which means the longest lead time is 10 days.

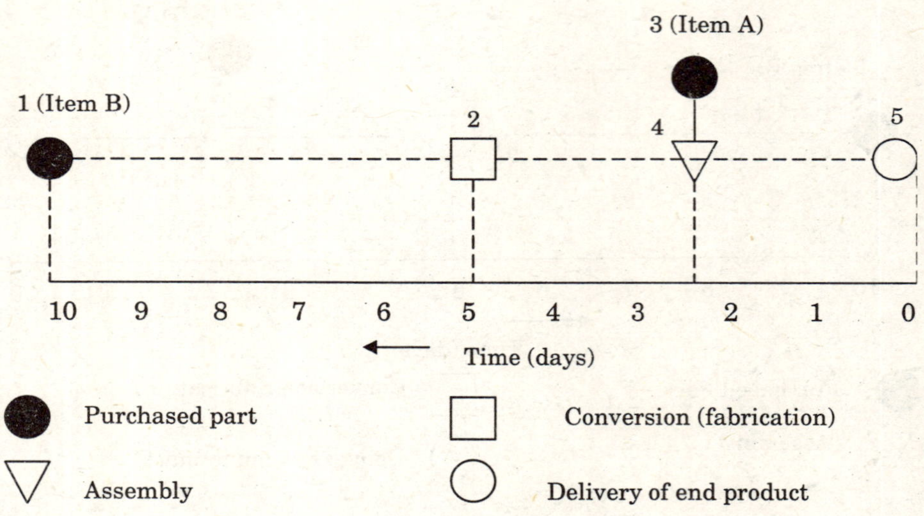

Fig. 4.14. Operation programme chart/Assembly chart

Stage 2 : Preparation of completion schedule (cumulative) or objective chart.

The quantities of the end item to be completed, week by week and cumulatively, are indicated in the cumulative completion schedule and shown in the table below:

The cumulative completion schedule is shown graphically in the objective chart in figure

Stage 3 : Construction of line of balance chart:

The line of balance shows the quantity of item that should have been completed at each operation stage/processing step in a particular week at which, progress will be reviewed so as to meet the delivery schedule for the finished product and to meet the completion schedule quantities cumulatively

Week No.	Qty. of end item to be completed	Cumulative quantity to be completed
1	5 Nos.	5 Nos.
2	10 Nos.	15 Nos.
3	10 Nos.	25 Nos.
4	10 Nos.	35 Nos.
5	15 Nos.	50 Nos.

The line of balance chart can be constructed graphically as illustrated below:

The following steps are required to construct the line of balance chart graphically.

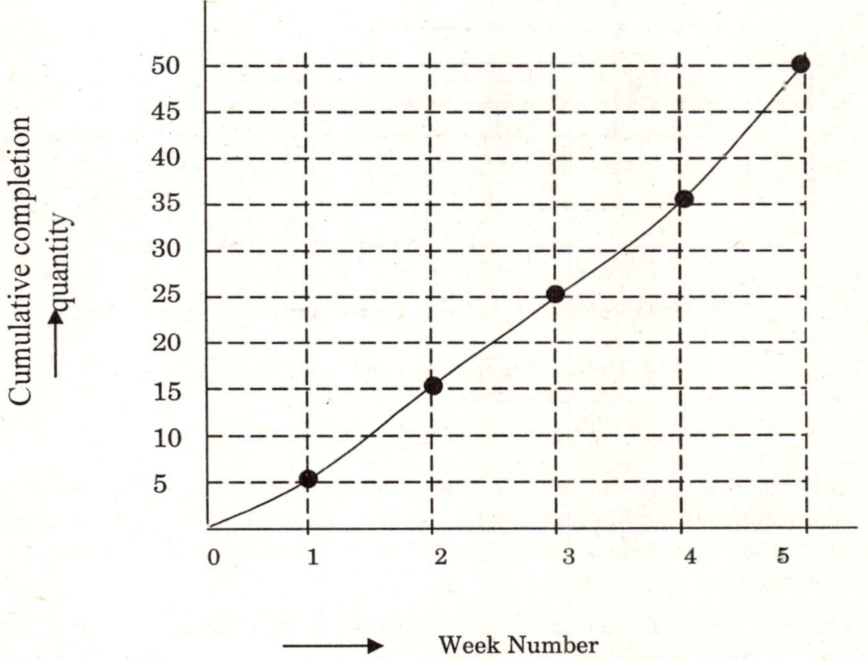

Fig. 4.15 Cumulative completion schedule graph or objective chart

Step No.(a) : Draw the cumulative completion schedule graph as shown in figure 4.16 (a).

Step No.(b) : Draw a vertical line AB on the cumulative completion schedule graph at the week at which the review is to take place (say 2nd week in this example)

Step No.(c) : Draw the line of balance schedule on the right hand side of the cumulative completion schedule graph [refer figure 18.20(b)]. Show by means of vertical bars, the 5 operation stages on the LOB schedule and indicate the quantities of the item that should have been passed through the operation stages/processing steps 1 to 5, by means of height of the vertical bars for each operation stage/processing step. In this example, it is done as below:

Let line A B cut the cumulative completion schedule graph at point 'C'. From 'C'. draw a horizontal line upto the vertical bar at operation stage/processing step No.5. The height of the vertical bar indicates the

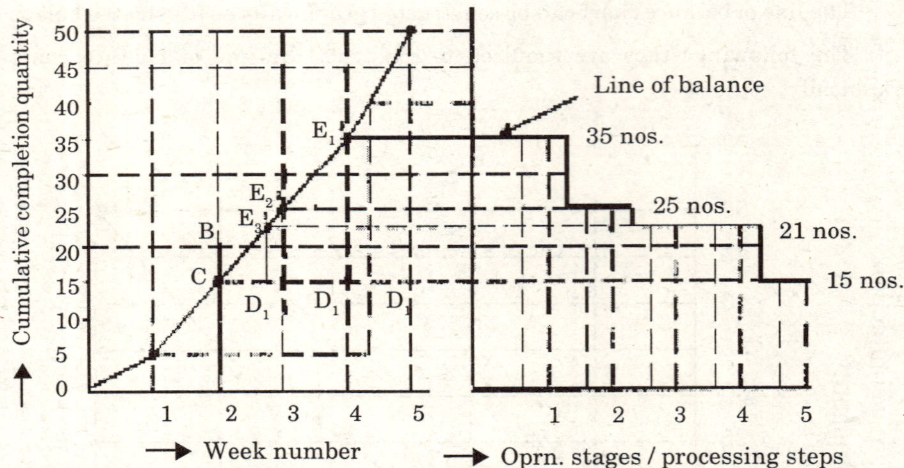

Fig. 4.16(a). Cumulative completions schedule
4.16(b). Line of balance schedule

quantity of the item that should have been completed at operation stage No.5 (i.e. completion of end product). In this example, this quantity of end product that should have been completed by the end of week number two is 15 numbers.

Step No.(d) : For each of the other operation stages/processing step (i.e. operation stages 1 to 4), find out how many should have been completed at the end of week No.2. This will be the total of not only the requirements for the completed end item by the two-week review date, but also the quantity to be completed in the lead time for that operation. This is determined graphically as follows:

Draw a horizontal line C, D_1 from the line AB, such that length C,D_1, indicates the lead time (i.e. 3 days) for operation stages 4 & 3. From D^1, draw a vertical line to cut the cumulative completion schedule graph at E^1. Draw a horizontal line from E_1 extending it upto the vertical bars drawn at operation stage No.4 and 3 (note both operations 4 & 3 have the same lead time of 3 days). The height of the vertical bars at operation stages 4 & 3 indicate the quantities of the item that should have passed through these two stages. In this example, it is 21 numbers. (Analytically calculated as 15 + (3/5) × 10 = 15 + 6 = 21 numbers.)

Similarly, for operation stage no.2, draw a horizontal line CD_2, such that, the length CD_2 indicates a lead time of 5 days (or one week assuming 5 days working per week). Draw a vertical line D_2E_2 to cut the cumulative completion graph at E_2. Draw a horizontal line from E_2 upto the vertical bar drawn at operation stage No.2 on the line of the balance schedule. The height of this vertical bar indicates the quantity of the item that should have been completed at operation stage No.2 at the 2nd review week. (in this case quantity is 25 numbers.)

For operation stage No.1, draw a horizontal line CD_3 such, that the length CD_3 indicates the lead time for operation stage No.1 (in this example it is 10 days or 2 weeks). Draw a vertical line D_3E_3 to cut the cumulative completion graph at E_3. Draw a horizontal line from E_3 upto the vertical bar drawn at operation stage No.1 on the LOB schedule. The height of the vertical bar indicates the quantity of the item that should have been completed at operation stage no.1 (in this case the quantity is 35 i.e. 35 numbers. of purchased part B should have been received by the end of 2nd review week).

Step No.(e) : Draw the line of balance (a stair-case step like line) by joining the tops of the vertical bars for each operation stage.

Stage No.4 : Construction of programme progress chart:

The programme progress chart for the review week (week No.2 in this example) is shown in figure 4.17.

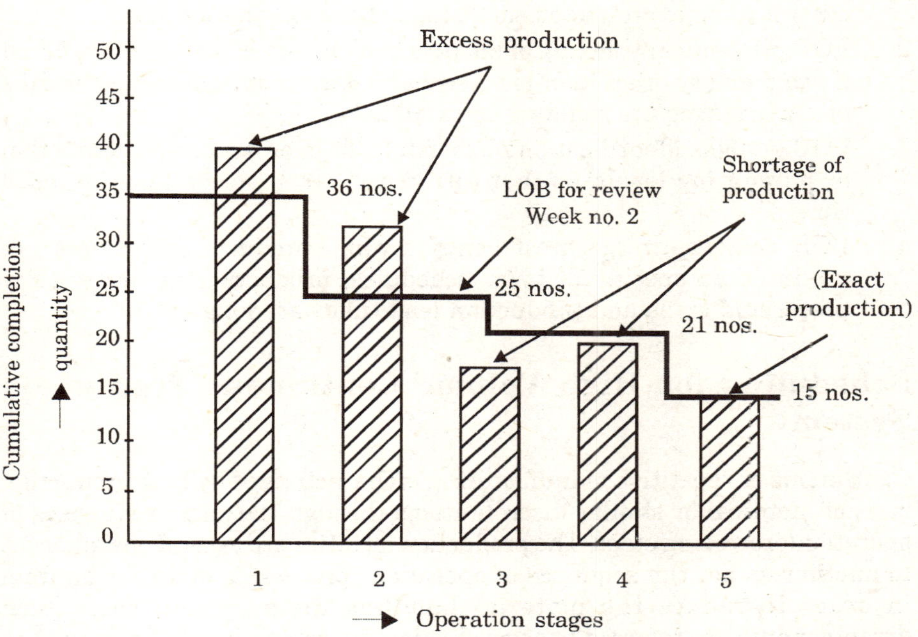

Fig. 4.17. Programme progress chart

In this graph, the actual number of items produced at each operation stage against the quantities that should have been produced as indicated by line of balance are shown on the LOB chart. This chart indicates clearly, the excess or shortage in the quantities of the item at the operation stages, which is illustrated in the figure 4.17. The actual quantities are shown by hatched vertical bars.

Stage No.5 : Analysis of progress and corrective action.

By referring to the programme process chart which is prepared every week, the difference between the desired production (as indicated by line of balance) for the review week (week no.2 in this example) can be compared with the actual production achieved at the end of the review week (shown by height of hatched vertical bars for each operation stage). The excess production or short fall in production can be found out (as shown in Figure 18.20) and appropriate corrective action such as expediting delivery of bought-out item (item B) or production of in-house made items or reducing the production to bring it in line with the line of balance.

Benefits of LOB Technique

1. LOB is a simple planning and control technique, which like network analysis, formalized and enforces planning discipline and enables control to be exercised at each stage of the production line.
2. LOB prevents any feeling of false security which might be engendered if the delivery of an item is on schedule but unappreciated shortfalls at early stages are building up trouble.
3. LOB enables identification of shortfalls or even excessive production or purchasing levels, so that corrective action can be taken in good time.
4. LOB achieves its greatest benefits when products or services are produced to specific delivery schedules, production involves many processing steps and production lead times are long.

Scheduling for High Volume Continuous Production System

Continuous or repetitive manufacturing is characterized by long production runs of identical or similar discrete items through the same sequences of operation/processing steps. The production facilities are located one adjacent to another as per the sequence of operations/processing steps for an item in order to reduce the material handling distance and cost. Such arrangements are referred to as production lines or assembly lines and the manufacturing shops are called as *flow shops.*

The flow shop generally represents a mass production situation (high volume production) and hence, the operations become very efficient. The production control system for continuous production is called as *flow control.*

The production control problem in repetitive production is different from that of job shop. Since the routings are fixed, it is not necessary to plan and prepare individual route sheets. The processing steps, routing and work methods are primarily planned along with the design of the production system.

The waiting time between operations and the work-in-process inventory are both minimal. There are usually no queues of different kinds of jobs waiting at a work centre and there is no need to determine priorities and dispatching at each work centre, is not necessary.

In this type of production, individual parts are not scheduled and tracked unit by unit. It is necessary that every component of a product must be completed at a rate, that is proportional to the quantity of the component used in the end product. Repetitive manufacturing is usually scheduled at daily rates of output.

Control of this type of production system would be simple when only one model of a product is produced at a uniform rat. A special purpose plant with a capacity of the desired out-put rate would meet the requirements. The problem is more complicated if the demand rate varies considerably throughout the year. In such cases, the system may produce at a uniform rate, which may lead to accumulation or depletion of inventory. Alternatively, the output rate can be varied by changing the number of working days per week, the working hours per day or the number of shifts that are worked. Also, it is possible to change the size of the labour force and reassign the work to achieve a different production rate.

However, scheduling and control will become more difficult, when several models are produced on the same line and when demand varies so that, different product mixes must be made from time to time.

Several approaches that high-volume, repetitive manufacturing operations can be used to meet the demand for varying volumes and product mixes are:

(a) To have separate production facilities for each product and to vary the production rate in response to the demand pattern. But this would require a high investment in various facilities that would seldom be fully utilized.

(b) To run one large facility on a product for a while and then change to another product for a while. In this case, the rescheduling and co-ordinating problems could be significant.

(c) To stabilize the product-mix and the production rate for an extended period to so that, many of the advantages of just - in-time production can be achieved.

Estimating the time required to perform jobs, which are standardized, can be simpler as compared to that in job shops. When a sizeable volume of a standard product is produced, the direct labour hours required to produce a unit may decrease considerably as more and more units are produced. This reduction in labour hours is significant enough, so that, it should be taken into account in scheduling delivery rates and in planning capacity utilization. This phenomenon is called *learning curve,* or an improvement curve or a progress curve or a manufacturing progress function.

Controlling Continuous Production

The major problem in flow shop production control (flow control) is to attain the desired production rate with maximum possible efficiency (i.e. max possible utilization of resources) For this, it is necessary to determine the technological process steps (sequence of operations), the required capacity of assembly lines, the number of personnel and the amount of work per person working on the assembly line. This is done by dividing the total work content of the job into elementary or basic operations and group these operations at work stations without violating their pre-determined sequence. The jobs move successively from one work station to another work station till completion. The speed of the assembly line is controlled by the required output rate, the distance between successive work station and the operation time required at each work station. By controlling the speed of the conveyor in the assembly line, the cycle time (i.e. the time for which the job is available at each work station for completion of the operation) is controlled and also the output rate on the production line is controlled.

The technique used in such a production situation where it is necessary to nearly equally divide the work to be done among the workers, so that, the total number of employees required on the assembly line is minimized, is known as *line balancing technique* or *assembly line balancing.*

Line Balancing

Line balancing is, arranging a production line so that, there is an even flow of production from one work station to the next, i.e., so that there are no delays at any work station that will leave the next work station with idle time.

Line balancing is also defined as '*the apportionment of sequential work activities into work stations in order to gain a high utilization of labour and equipment and therefore minimize idle time.*' Balancing may be achieved by rearrangement of the work stations or by adding machines and / or workers at some of the stations so that, all operations take about the same amount of time.

Line Balancing Procedure in Assembly Layouts

Step No.1 : Determine what tasks must be performed to complete one unit of a finished product ad the sequence in which the tasks must be performed. Draw the precedence diagram.

Step No.2 : Estimate the task time (amount of time it takes a worker to perform each task).

Step No.3 : Determine the cycle time (the amount of time that would elapse between products coming off the end of the assembly line, if the desired hourly production were being produced.)

Step No.4 : Assign each task to a worker and balance the assembly line. This process results in determining the scope of each worker's job or which tasks that he or she will perform.

Steps Involved in Combining of the Tasks into Worker's Jobs

1. Starting at the beginning of the precedence diagram, combine tasks into a work station in the order of the sequence of tasks, so that the combined task times approach, but do not exceed the cycle time or multiples of the cycle time.

2. When tasks are combined into a workstation, the number of multiples of the cycle time is the number of workers required at the work station, all performing the same job.

Analysis of Line Balancing Problems

The procedure involves the following steps

1. Determine the number of work stations and time available at each work station.
2. Group the individual tasks into approximately equal amounts of work at each work station.
3. Evaluate the efficiency or grouping.

When the available work time at any station exceeds that, which can be done by one worker, additional workers must be added at that work station.

The key to efficient line balancing is to group activities or tasks in such a way that, the work times at the work station are at or slightly less than the cycle time or a multiple of cycle time, if more than one worker is required in any workstation.

Determination of cycle time (CT)

When the amount of output units required per period (period may be hour, shift, day or week etc.) is specified and the available time per period is given (i.e. the number of working hours per shift, number of shifts per day, number of working days per week etc.) then,

$$\text{Cycle time (CT)} = \frac{\text{Available time per period}}{\text{Output units required per period}}$$

Cycle time is the time interval at which, completed products leave the production line/assembly line.

Determination of the Ideal or Theoretical Minimum Number of Workers Required in the Line.

$$\left.\begin{array}{r}\text{Ideal or theoritical} \\ \text{minimum no. of workers} \\ \text{required in the assy.} \\ \text{line/production line}\end{array}\right\} = \frac{\left(\begin{array}{c}\text{Total operation} \\ \text{or task time}\end{array}\right) \times \left(\begin{array}{c}\text{Output units} \\ \text{required per period}\end{array}\right)}{\text{Available time per period per worker}}$$

$$N = \Sigma\, t \times \left(\frac{1}{CT}\right) = \left(\frac{\Sigma t}{CT}\right)$$

Balancing Efficiency : An efficient the balancing will minimize the amount of idle time.

The balance efficiency can be calculated as

$$\text{(i) } Eff_B = \frac{\text{Output of task time}}{\text{Input by work station times}} = \frac{\Sigma\, t}{CT \times N}$$

Where, = sum of the actual worker times or task times to complete one unit.

CT = cycle time; N = No. of workers or work stations

$$\text{(ii) } Eff_B = \frac{\text{Theoretica l minimum number of workers}}{\text{Actual number of workers}}$$

The grouping of tasks is done with the aid of a precedence diagram. The precedence diagram is divided into work zones or stations and the appropriate activities are grouped under each workstation, until the cycle time is as fully utilized as possible.

Line Balancing Methods

The various line balancing methods or techniques used are:

1. Heuristic methods
2. Linear Programming

3. Dynamic Programming
4. Computer-based sampling techniques.

Heuristic and computer-based techniques are most widely used for solving large scale line balancing problems and the use of linear programming and dynamic programming is limited.

1. Heuristic method

It is a thumb rule method which gives a satisfactory rather than optimal solution to the line balancing problem. Heuristic methods are acceptable when optimizing solutions are not feasible or are too costly to obtain. The trial and error technique used in line balancing is a heuristic method in which, work elements are grouped such that, the cycle time is not violated and the precedence diagram is made use of, to group the activities as per the sequence of operations.

Illustration : The table below shows the number of work stations (N), cycle time (C) and daily production for a product.

Number of work-stations (N)	Cycle time (C) (seconds)	Daily production (in 8 hours shift)
1	120	240
2	60	480
3	40	720
4	30	960
5	24	1200
6	20	1440

If it is desired to have two assembly lines, each producing 720 units per day, the cycle time will be 40 seconds and there will be 3 work stations in each assembly line. He precedence diagram for the activities is shown below. The activity time in seconds are given in bracket for each of the twenty operations involved.

Assuming that activities may be combined within a 'given zone' without violating the precedence relationship, assign the activities into three work stations. This can be done on a trial and error basis by adding activity times upto or nearly equal to the cycle time (i.e. 40 seconds). One such solution is iven in the table :

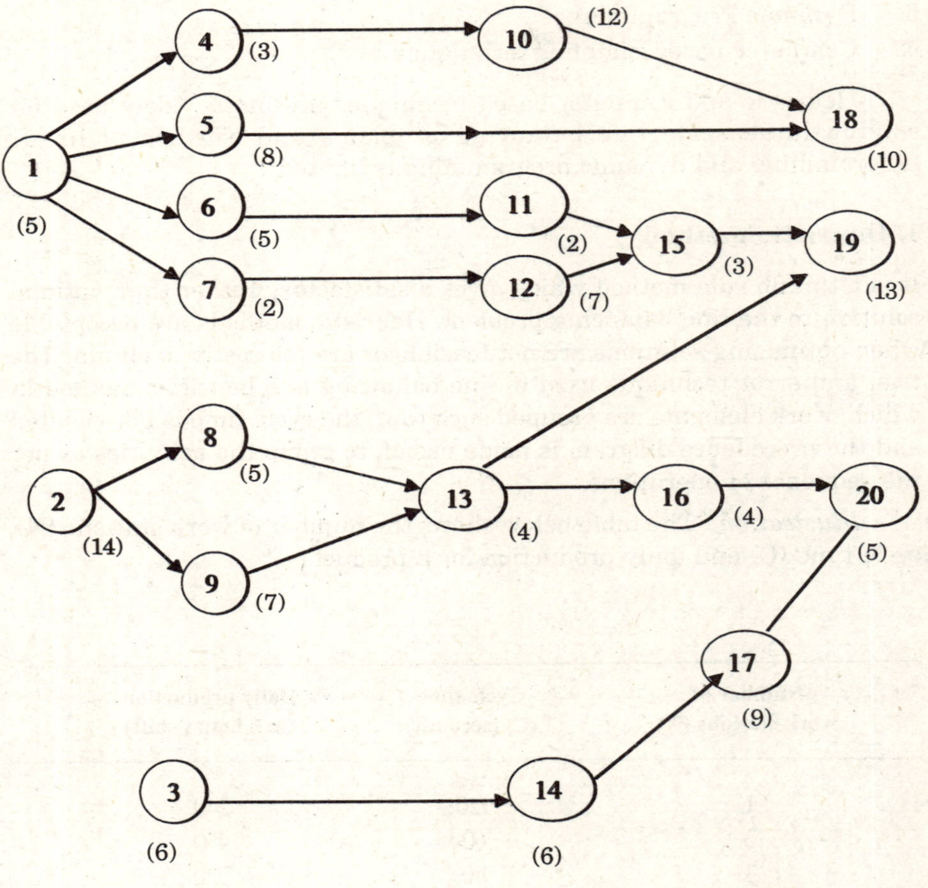

Table

	Activities	Total time for activities (secs)
Work Station 1	1, 6, 7, 2, 8, 9, 11	5 + 5 + 2 + 14 + 5 + 7 + 2 = 40
Work Station 2	4, 5, 10, 12, 13, 3	3 + 8 + 12 + 7 + 4 + 6 = 40
Work Station 3	14, 15, 16, 17, 18, 19, 20	6 + 3 + 4 + 9 + 10 + 3 + 5 = 40

A perfect balance is obtained, since all the work stations have exactly the same work load of 40 seconds. The balance delay is Nil.

Scheduling Services

Introduction : Services are all those economic activities in which, the primary out-put is neither a product not a construction. Value is added to this output by means that cannot be inventoried- i.e., means like convenience, security, comfort and flexibility and the output is consumed as produced.

Some of the examples of services are:

(a) Transportation.
(b) Utilities.
(c) Communications.
(d) Wholesale trade.
(e) Retail trade.
(f) Finance, Banking & Insurance.
(g) Real estate.
(h) Hotel & Restaurant.
(i) Medical services.
(j) Educational services.
(k) Consultancy services.

The characteristics of services are:

1. services are intangible outputs,
2. services cannot be inventoried,
3. services need extensive customer contact,
4. services have short lead times,
5. services are labour intensive,
6. service quality is difficult to determine.

Relationship between Employee's Work and Customers

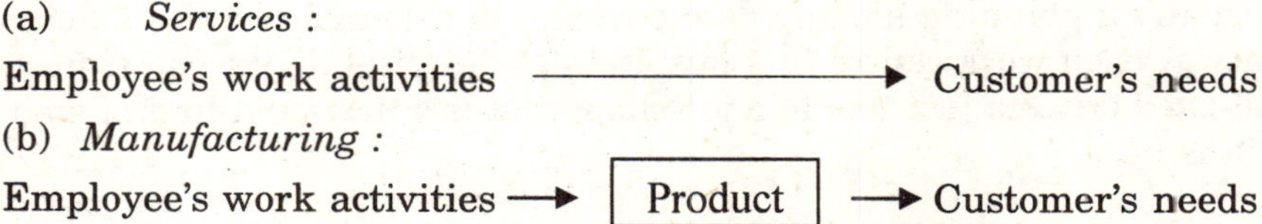

Service Operations

Also known as non-manufacturing operations, service operations are those operations which do not produce tangible products. Service operations can be classified as (a) standard services and (b) customer services. This classification is according to the degree of standardization of the outputs and the process performed by the service systems.

Service systems do not hold finished goods inventories and the demand for their output is highly variable from time to time (e.g., hour to hour, day to day and week to week). Their operations are labour intensive. The principal means of performing the services is through personnel. Hence, personnel scheduling becomes quite complex because the demand for services is highly variable and services are consumed as they are produced.

Service system providing standard services are more like product-focused manufacturing systems. Services are standard for most customers and the processes once begun, are carried through to completion without significant delays. The only difference as compared to product-focused manufacturing is that services are produced according to customers order, rather than for finished goods inventory.

Example of service systems providing standard services are transport companies, fast-food restaurants, postal services, airlines, etc. Sophisticated scheduling such as on-line computer based scheduling systems, are used in the airlines.

Service systems providing customer services are like job shops in their characteristics and hence, their scheduling systems are much like that of job shops. In small services such as doctor's clinics, small retailers and local transport companies, no formal scheduling systems are employed. Simple scheduling devices such as appointment schedules, take-a-number system (i.e., token system) or first-cum-first-served rules are used to assign priorities to the customers. Part-time workers and stand-by equipments are frequently employed during high demand periods.

Service system such as hospitals use more sophisticated scheduling systems than that, found in job shop manufacturing. These systems are also produce-to-order systems and as finished goods inventories cannot be maintained, capacities must be variable to meet wide variations in customer demand levels. Since customer demand is highly variable from time to time (i.e., day to day, or week to week) and services must often be provided on short notice, the scheduling systems work on short planning horizon, (i.e., usually a planning horizon of one week). In setting priorities among patients at each work centre in a hospital, the hospital might use a most critical need criteria just like in a job shop, that is a first-cum-first served criteria is used.

Scheduling Personnel in Services

Four approaches that are usually used by operations managers in service system are

1. Use of waiting lines (based on first-cum-first served priority) as a buffer for the difference between customer demand and system capacity (when demand is more than capacity). This approach enables operation managers to schedule personnel to maintain uniform system capacity from time to time (day to day or week to week).

2. Use of appointment schedules to level out the demand for services. This approach enables operation managers to schedule personnel so that the system capacity is almost uniform. Eg.: appointment schedules are

commonly used in medical, legal and other professional services. Priority systems in hospitals and medical clinics allow emergency patients to be admitted on a priority basis and the remaining patients are admitted by appointment.

3. Personnel schedules are developed to allow system capacities which almost match the pattern of customer demand. The system capacity is varied by varying the number of personnel scheduled to work during each hour of the day. Part time personnel may be employed during periods of peak demand in addition to the full time personnel.

4. For emergency services, such as fire departments or police departments, scheduling of personnel is done for 24 hour full crew coverage. During low-demand periods, the crews perform not only necessary but non-emergency tasks also. During peak demand periods, off-duty personnel are called in and are compensated with overtime payment or compensating time-offs.

It can be seen that operations managers develop personnel schedules based on approximately uniform system capacity or highly variable system capacities. The uniform capacity approach is accompanied by other means of leveling but demand viz., appointment schedules, priority systems and waiting lines (queues). Three general difficulties encountered in scheduling personnel in services are (a) demand variability (b) service time variability and (c) availability of personnel when they are needed.

When the demand is varying very much, the operations managers have two approaches to develop work schedules for employees in service systems designed for variable capacity. The approaches are:

(a) To use full-time employees exclusively and

(b) To use some full-time-employees and some part-time employees in the system

In the first arrangement, more than enough employees may be scheduled in some periods resulting in idle time for employees in these time periods. In other periods when there are not enough employees, overtime may be used or waiting lines will be used (queue) to level out the demand.

In service systems with variable capacity, it is better if part-time employees can be called in at a short notice. This will avoid much of the planned over-staffing and under-staffing to work schedules.

In some services, the use of appointment schedules to level the demand is not very much feasible or desirable. Levelling the demand simplifies the scheduling of personnel to staff the services, but the nature of the service may dictate the extent by which customer-demand can or should be controlled through appointment schedules.

Operations Management

UNIT—V

10

Material Management

Introduction

MOST manufacturing companies spend more than half of the money they take in for materials and component parts that are already made. Maruti spends Rs. 3000 crores a year for materials (59 percent of its sales revenue). CIMMCO spends Rs. 1.3 billion (67 percent of its sales revenue) for bought materials.

Purchasing would seem to be an easy job since it is easier to pay out money than to bring it in. And it is easier to buy cleverly than to make things economically. When buying, a company can get the benefit of effective management just by placing orders with the lowest cost yet reliable suppliers. But. when a company makes its own components, its costs depend on its own operating effectiveness, it is easier to choose an effective source than to be an effective source.

Purchasing is more, though, than just spending money. A person who spends wisely pays less for what he buys. If a company sells Rs. 1 billion (100 crores) worth of products (in 1995, 203 manufacturing companies in India sold more than Rs.1 billion worth of products, but they had to spend more than half of their sales income for bought items), it is selling products which probably contain purchased materials that cost over Rs. 500 million. The difference between a good and a poor job of buying could well be 5 percent or more. At 5 percent, the possible savings would come to over Rs.25 million for such a company. So, even though purchasing is easier than selling, purchasing is still very important.

In some cases the money which can be made (or lost) on inventory can outweigh the eamings-or-loss possibilities from regular operations. The price of cotton and wool varies so much that textile companies can lose heavily by poor buying. Meat packers and flour millers have the same problem.

Purchasing's main job is to get things the organization needs when it needs them and to pay as little as possible considering the quality requirements. But this looks at the job too narrowly. Today most companies say that the purchasing department is responsible for "outside manufacture". This puts a different slant - a managerial slant - on the job. Vendor companies are thought of almost as if they were department of the customer company.

With this view, purchasing becomes more active and less passive. The purchasing agent views his job as more than just placing orders. He becomes interested in the supplier's costs and his quality control procedure should the vendor need it, the buyer even arranges to send his own company's specialists to the vendor's plant to help it become a more effective source of supply.

Materials Managers

Some companies which buy quite large quantities of materials have set up a materials manager job in order to coordinate everything having to do with materials. Purchasing is one of the big activities. And so are the operation of the stores department and inventory control activities. Then activities are closely associated with purchasing, but they are usually not under the direction of the purchasing agent. They would, however, become part of the assignment of a materials manager. The traffic department, too, would probably become part of his domain.

On the other hand, the factory's production control department probably should remain outside his jurisdiction even though it has much to do with materials used and with controlling inventories in process. Production control's closest ties are with the factory's producing departments, not with purchasing.

Problems in Purchasing

No one procedure is satisfactory for buying all of the 50,000 items or so that big companies buy. Some items (like sheet steel for a can maker) are shipped in steadily and, over a period of lime, cost millions. Other items (like the equipment to make automobile motor blocks automatically in a new factory) are one-shot orders that cost millions. Between these extremes steady, high demand or giant one-shot contracts there is every combination of volume, repetition, and variety, clear down to 10-rupee items bought once a year.

Besides variety in kind and quantity, purchasing deals with bulk items (liquids, powders), packaged items, standard items, special items, items always bought, and items sometimes bought and sometimes made (or both).

Steadily used Items bought in large volumes

For important items that are used all the time, the purchasing department gets its authority to make purchase commitments directly from purchase budgets which are based on the approved production schedules for the months ahead. It does not need requisitions from either production control or the stores department. Purchasing has, in its files, lists of all the things to buy. and it knows how much to buy in order to make a single unit of each of the company's major products. All it has to do is look at the scheduled quantities and multiply to tell the amount of material needed. Today computerized systems do most of these calculations.

Most of these items are bought on "blanket" or "open end" contracts which cover a whole year's supply. Blanket contracts leave quantities and times of delivery (and sometimes price) to be set as the materials are needed. The buying company sends out, several months ahead, estimates of its expected volume requirements but which are not specified in detail. They then follow this up by sending out monthly (or even weekly) release orders telling the vendor how many or how much to deliver and when and where. These releases usually go to the supplier directly from the factory's planning department. Purchasing is not active in this part of the contract's operation.

Contracts for these steady-use, high-volume items are not really open to competition in the wide-open sense, except that a company may buy from two sources instead of one just for safety. The buyer-seller relationship is much like that of a company department with a sister department. Supplying companies often keep certain contracts for years. Sunderam Fasteners, for example, made most of General Motors' radiator caps for the 10 years. Goodyear has never failed to get a good share of Maruti's tire business for over 20 years.

These big contracts usually do not "travel around" because the seller takes as good care (price, quality, and service wise) of the customers as anyone else could. Also, these contracts are so big that no competitor could take one on and deliver overnight. He would have to build whole new factories, then tool up, and line up whole new work forces.

One exception is basic raw materials (materials of nature: cotton, wool, rubber, lumber, wheat, and so on). There are many suppliers of such items, and their prices go up and down. Here buyers do not always stick to one vendor but go where they can get the best deal each time they let a new contract. Buyers should not forget, however, that dependable service is important in such items. It is best not to switch a company's whole volume to unknowns, though an unknown might well be given a trial order now and then.

Large special orders

Large special orders are different. They usually are machinery for a newly built factory or equipment for an electric-power dam, or some other construction, or even for a warship. On these projects, months go into planning. Discussions are held with several machinery makers. Alternatives are considered. Sometimes the advance work takes so much engineering work that the customer pays an engineering fee to prospective bidders. Otherwise a prospective vendor may be unwilling to spend Rs. 50,000 on engineering work planning for a job he might not get. Vendors have to bid separately for every one of these large jobs.

Middle-sized orders

Here the buyer in the purchasing department is nearly always buying only after someone else inside the organization has asked him to. He gets a purchase requisition from the production control department or from the stores department. Quite a little of the work done in purchasing departments is for such orders. Production control sends in purchase requisitions for items needed for making the products on the factory's production schedule (except for the heavy and steadily used items discussed above).

Middle-size repeat orders are usually placed with the same vendors. But they don't work like releases against blanket orders. Vendors get specific purchase orders from purchasing for every order. Every new order again describes the product and orders a certain quantity to be delivered by a certain date.

But whether middle-size orders are for old or new items, it is common to ask two or three vendors to bid. Generally the contract goes to the low bidder if he is dependable. Sometimes, if middle-size orders are for standard catatog items (and particularly on rush orders), the buyer may not shop around to try to get the best price but just order the material wherever he can get a good price with an agreement to deliver soon.

Small orders

Small orders are one of the headaches of purchasing. It costs Rs.15 or more in clerical costs to handle a purchase requisition and to place a purchase order, so it would help to be able to cut out all the little orders for one or two items or for fifty paise or Rs.1 worth of materials Unfortunately, such items are needed and, worse yet, they may be as badly needed as big items. They, too, can be rush orders.

Most companies let these orders go through the regular procedure cost whatever they may be. Some, however, try to cut the cost down. American Express uses the following policies to reduce small order cost: (I) Don't reorder little things often; order two or three years' supply. It doesn't matter that some day part of the supply of some item may not be needed and may be thrown out. It is still less costly than buying little dribbles all the time (2) Let departments buy directly all things costing less than Rs. 50. Don't bother the purchasing department about them. (3) Place blanket orders with suppliers: then just order by telephone what is wanted now and then without making out a purchase order every time. Cut out the paper work. National Aluminum sends a blank check (valid only up to a limited amount) along with its order and lets the vendor fill it in. Modern computer systems monitor the levels of these items and, when new orders are required, automatically print out the purchase order and even the blank checks.

Follow-up

Keeping large supplies of materials on hand is so costly that no one wants to do it. This means things are not bought, or at least not delivered, until shortly before they are needed. But this also means that if anything goes wrong and the vendor doesn't deliver on time, the customer is in trouble. And vendors do let customers down more often than either they or their customers would like. So buyers "follow up" orders for things that are on a tight schedule. (The factory production control department should keep the buyer informed about which items it is most anxious to get.)

The buyer might call vendor on the telephone or write him a letter and ask him whether the order is coming along all right. He might even "hound" and annoy him and repeatedly remind him that he is counting on getting his order on time. All this helps. The vendor will get the order out just to get the buyer off his back. Likewise he should tell the vendor if the order may be delivered later. This gives the buyer more credibility when he asks to receive his order on time or even earlier than scheduled.

Most purchasing departments have a few expediters who do most of the follow-up, even going to vendor plants to see if the vendor needs any help. Not only does follow-up of this sort get more orders delivered on time, but, if an order is going to be delayed, the customer finds out about it sooner. This gives the customer company more time in which to change its plans.

It might seem that it would be cheaper just to carry a few more items in stock and then not every delay would catch the company short. Actually, however, this often does not pay because it takes too much extra inventory to provide very much protection. Besides, even with the bigger inventory, there will still be occasional stockouts. So it would be necessary to do some follow-up anyway, and the customer would still be out of some material now and then.

Receiving inspection

Purchasing is not complete until the material is in hand. Because receiving usually is not under the purchasing department, purchasing has to be told (it gets a copy of the receiving report) when materials come in as ordered so that it can clear the orders out of its file and tell accounting to pay the bill. The bill (or invoice) has by this time come in by mail to the accounting department. So has the freight bill covering shipping costs. If the material is not right in any way, purchasing has to handle all dealings with the vendor concerning what to do about it.

Yet sometimes it is not possible for receiving inspectors to tell if incoming products pass inspection unless they make special tests-- chemical, electronic, or other. Normally, for example, a receiving clerk can't tell if a shipment of thermostats for stoves is all right. Or picture tubes for television sets. Sometimes he will need to call on engineering or the laboratory to pass final judgment.

How Much Centralization?

When a company has several (or many) plants scattered around the country, it is possible to have one central office do all of the buying or only part of it. There is no pat answer as to which is better. Nearly all companies end up doing some of it centrally and some of it locally. General Motors decentralizes its buying to 52 divisions, which in turn decentralize the actual buying to more than 100 purchasing offices. To aid prospective vendors, GM puts out a directory booklet listing all of its purchasing offices and something about what each one buys.

Buying centrally means dealing in larger volumes, and this sometimes means better prices, possibly up to 10 percent better. And it means more "clout" in periods of materials scarcity. Future supplies are more assured. The total volume of any item is not, of course, increased by central buying. But the volume dealt with on a single contract will be the whole company's volume, not just one plant's volume, so this will probably mean a better price.

More specialized people will be doing the buying when it is done centrally. Buyers don't have to be so all purpose as buyers in small divisions of a company. Also, central buying cuts out duplication of orders and so saves clerical costs. It gives top management tighter control over the whole company's inventory policies, and it forces more standardization in designs. The American Management Association's report that there is a trend toward more centralization of purchasing in large companies.

Against centralization the argument is that it is often slow and too cumbersome for minor items. The thousands of little things can be bought better by separate purchasing departments at the plant level. Also, plant inventories cannot be controlled very well from a central office. The controls are quite likely to become too rigid. Central people just cannot know local needs.

Also, even with central buying it is risky to buy all of any important item from only one supplier. It is well, just as insurance against strikes and other holdups, to divide the orders for most important items and place orders with at least two suppliers. But. of course, if this is done, part of the possible quantity discount expected from centralized purchasing is lost because each supplier gets smaller orders.

Freight is another item. If high-volume orders are placed with only one or two suppliers, and if they ship to all of the customer's plants, long freight hauls may cancel out any quantity discount obtained from volume buying. This does not apply, however, if the vendor is also a multiplant company and can ship to a customer's Midwest plant from its Midwest plant, to the customer's Northwest plant from its Northwest plant, and so on. But if the vendor of any item docs not have plants close by, it will probably pay to give up central buying of that item and let each plant order its needs from a nearby plant just to save freight.

Materials which don't pass inspection and "short" shipments also turn up at times. These can be handled much better locally than centrally. Local buying also gives plant managers more responsibility, and it creates community goodwill.

Large companies usually end up centralizing all buying where large amounts of money are involved or where highly technical knowledge is required. They also centralize most capital expenditure buying because of the enduring nature of the commitment. Buying is also centrally done where reciprocity enters the picture. All other things are bought decentrally in the separate divisions. Often some rupee limit is set for local purchasing, and all contracts for more money must clear through central purchasing. The central purchasing department also sets up policies and procedures for the decentralized groups to use.

Value Analysis

Value analysis tries to reduce the costs of purchased materials by studying the purpose to be served by a part or component being bought and by seeing if there are other less costly ways of accomplishing this purpose. Although the purchasing department is almost always active in this work, value analysis is encompassed in the larger subject of value engineering.

Known Cost

The known-cost idea is very similar to value analysis and usually includes some value analysis work. "Known cost" is a term sometimes use to describe a policy of large retail buyers, such as Sears Roebuck.

The customer company's buyer decides, for complete finished products or for parts, what he can afford to pay for an item, considering his resale price. The customer company may want, for example, a man's shirt which it can sell for Rs. 365. Then the buyer buys them on a set-price basis. He hopes to get good or even fine quality; yet, the price is often set so low (because of the low end product sale price) that there is strong pressure to reduce the item's production costs. Sometimes the supplier can't get his costs down this low without sacrificing quality. If so, a compromise is reached, and the price is raised or the quality is lowered, or both.

The term "known cost" comes from the idea that the customer company knows the price it will pay before negotiations start. The negotiations are concerned more with the quality it can get for the price than with the price which will be paid for a given quality. If either price or quality has to yield, quality - not price - becomes the variable factor.

Mass Production Purchasing

Tata Motor spends over Rs.1.5 billion a month for materials. It takes some 320,000 tons, of steel, costing more than Rs. 90 million for bumpers and springs alone for trucks in one year. But a company does not have to be General Motors to find itself buying many items in million rupee quantities in a year.

These contracts usually are so big that neither buyer nor seller wants to take any chances on price; yet, each wants to be sure of the contract. So the contracts are often written with the price left open, to be settled every now and then during the year. Quantities are also left upon, to be set us the customer orders week by week. Or the price, if the item is a manufactured product, is often subject to negotiation if raw materials prices change. If steel prices go up, Tata Motors pays more for its bumper steel, or the reverse if steel prices go down. That way no one gets hurt much when prices change. Often there are penalty charges if the vendor does not deliver or if the buyer cancels.

Quantities in mass production are so large that neither buyer nor seller wants to carry enough inventory to last more than a few days, so both try to mesh their schedules exactly. Supplier dependability is even more important than price. In busy times Tata trucks eat up steel for bumpers and springs at the rate of more than 1,000 tons a day, which, at 50 tons to a wagon load, means 20 wagon loads a day! Yet the factory rarely carries more than a day or two's supply on hand. In fact, it would want the freight cars of steel to come in at regular intervals all day long rather than all at once. Both the vendor and the railways know this and try to deliver on this kind of schedule.

On the other hand. lead time is very important. To get steel in July, it needs to be rolled in the steel mills in June. Steel mills plan June's production in May, so Tata Motors has to place its order in April. But in April, Tata's July truck-making schedule has not yet been firmed up. Of course everybody knows that trucks will be made in July but not how many or exactly what kinds. Purchasing has to go ahead anyway and place the order and then, in May or even June, ask the vendor to change the quantities to correct for any errors in forecasting. All of this schedule changing makes a great deal of extra work in the purchasing department and in the vendor plant's production control department.

How Many to Buy at One Time

Very few purchases are one-shot items. Nearly everything bought is bought again and again, so there is a question of whether to buy few and often or more at a time and less often. For big day-to-day, bread-and-butter items the answer has already been given: use blanket contracts covering perhaps a year's needs and then get frequent shipments as needed. For the bulk of other items - those bought repetitively but not on blanket contracts - the purchasing department, as we said, usually buys things only in response to specific requests from someone else.

Purchasing should not be too passive, though, in following other people's requests because they may ask for small quantities to be bought often. And it is expensive to order small items in little dribbles. Yet buying more at one time increases inventory carrying costs, so someone should try to balance out these costs, inventory control and purchasing people should work together on problems of how many items to order at a time.

Companies sometimes "speculate" when buying big-volume, regular use raw materials. If they think prices will go up they may contract for even a year's supply in order to take advantage of today's price. This would be risky and would be quite uncommon and would need the approval of the board of directors because of the large financial commitment. Contracting for a year or more needs is generally called speculation, for three months to a year is called forward buying, and for one month to three months ahead is called buying to requirements. Contracting for less than one month is called hand-to-mouth buying and is done only when companies are short of money or when they think prices will go down. Ofcourse, such short-term controlling usually results in higher unit costs for the moment because of the small quantities bought on each order.

Standard quantities

Inventory controllers determine how many of an item they will need in the near future when they ask buyers to buy new supplies. For items which will continue to be used however, the buyers should have some freedom to increase or decrease the quantity asked for to allow for buying standard packages, full barrels, and whole bundles. Nearly always, if an order is for part of a standard package, the price per unit is higher. So the quantities actually ordered should be adjusted when necessary to come out to full standard packages.

On small items, it is often possible to set a fixed quantity (which recognizes standard packages) to reorder every time. Supplies are often ordered this way. So are minor "free issue" items, such as nuts and bolts. Ordering fixed quantities saves clerical time and costs.

This type of savings also applies elsewhere. It often applies where freight or truck rates are consequential. Perhaps the full wagon freight rate for steel applies to orders of 30,000 kgs or more, but the inventory controller wants only 25,000 kgs right now. The shipping rate per pound is higher on all shipments of less than 30,000 kgs. It might even result that the total freight cost on 25,000 kgs at the less-than-wagonload rate would be more than the cost for 30,000 kgs at the full-carload rate.

Unless the company just does not need the extra 5,000 kgs at all, or not for a long time, it may be better off to order 30,000 kgs. The freight cost savings will outweigh the costs of carrying the extra 5,000 kgs a little longer than usual.

Tendering &Vendor Rating

The purchasing department nearly always decides which company to buy from. Equipment buying is an exception; so are some trademarked items that engineering or someone else insists on; and so are reciprocity deals, where top management tells the purchasing department whom to buy from.

To choose vendors intelligently, the purchasing department's buyers need to know which things are sold by which companies. This they learn from salesmen who call on them and from advertisements in technical and trade directories and buyers' guides. Also, they have a file of catalogs of vendor companies and their price and discount lists.

When deciding who gets an order, buyers should consider several things. Price, important though it is, is not the only thing. Reliability usually is more important than small price differences. Can and will the vendor company deliver the order on time? Will the materials pass inspection after they arrive? If they don't, will this vendor fix things up right away without argument? Schedule changes may also be a factor. Will this vendor take care of schedule changes and rush orders? How about service if something goes wrong? Or will he extend credit? Any of these matters might be important.

Assuming that all other factors are equal, often it is still not altogether clear which vendor's price is the lowest. In the following case, for example, from which vendor should the company buy? Each of the companies has submitted a bid in which a separate charge is listed for the special tooling which will be required plus an additional charge per unit.

This problem can be solved by the break-even comparison method. The choice is, in all cases, the source with the lower tool cost for all volumes below the equal cost point and the source with the lower unit cost for

Supplier	Tooling Charge	Cost per Unit	Discount for volumes	
			Price	Volume over
A	Rs. 220	Rs. 0.80	Rs. 0.70	1000
B	Rs. 320	Rs. 0.72	Rs. 0.60	3000
C	Rs. 180	Rs. 0.96	Rs. 0.85	500

Break – even Quality

	B Reg.	*B Disc.*	*C Reg.*	*C Disc.*
A Regular	1,250	500	250	800
A Discount......	- 5,000	1000	154	267
B Regular	....	....	583	1,077
B Discount	....	....	389	560

volumes above the equal cost point.

To compare A and B at regular prices:

$220 + .80x = 320 + .72x \rightarrow x = 1,250$

For volumes below 1,250 units, the choice is A, above 1,250 units it should be B. Actually, this particular comparison yields an irrelevant answer because at 1,250 units, B's volume discount price would be in effect.

In our example there are 12 comparisons needing to be made before a decision can be made. Of these 12, only 2 are useful. The Figure above lists the 12 comparisons. The stars indicate nonapplicable answers, nearly all because the answer is a quantity to which the price used in the calculation does not apply.

In summary, only the two comparisons of A regular prices with C regular prices and C discount prices are left. Because of C's low tool charge, purchases should be made at C's regular prices for volumes up to 250 units. Above 250 units, purchases should go to A at regular prices. At 500 units (this does not show in the Figure above) C's discount price comes into play and orders should be shifted to C. But at 800 units A's lower unit price again comes into play. A should get all orders for quantities above 800. There is no point where B should get any orders at all.

Storage of Materials

Characteristics of a Good Storehouse Operation:

1. The inventory is stored inside a stockroom that has pre assigned bins and an overflow area that is clearly identified.
2. The stockroom has a fence.
3. The fence has a door.
4. The door has a tock on it, and there are very few keys, which are distributed only to authorized people.
5. No unauthorized people ever wander in and out of the stockroom.
6. Service is prompt, and the stockroom hours are known in advance.

7. Every receipt is accompanied by a proper document.
8. Every issue has a corresponding document identified with it.
9. The stockroom people are well turned; a job description available, and there is a break-in period for new people.
10. The objective of zero defects is clearly well understood.
11. Time is allowed every day to reconcile transactions with inventories.
12. Audits are taken periodically, and discrepancies are totally unacceptable.
13. The users have complete confidence in the stockroom's integrity, and that is most important.

The inventory in a company is cash, and the stockroom is the local bank, a company from which we can learn a lot. Is it not remarkable that the average manufacturing company with several million Rupees' worth of parts in inventory - more than your local bank would ever have in cash - does not insist on similarly stringent procedures? Even though it is our money in the bank, we do not walk in and help ourselves but follow definite procedures. A stockroom storing parts must be operated in the same way.

ABC Model of Inventory Control

Many large organizations have to stock and keep track of 10,000 or more different items which are outside of the MRP (Materials Requirements Planning) system and which covers most of the materials used in making products. In most companies the items outside of the MRP system are minor end products, or they are parts or components of end products which are not included in MRP calculations. Some are service parts for products no longer made, or they are supplies, or raw materials for general use, or maintenance items, and items for various other purposes. The investments in such items is substantial, and the record keeping is costly.

They may even be MRP items in that they go into end products covered by the MRP calculation process. But, if they are relatively minor and if they are used in quite a few different end products, it may be more economical not to calculate their needs as part of the MRP process but rather to calculate the needs for each end product and then add all of the demands together. It may be more economical just to replenish these items on a maximum-minimum basis (described in the next few pages).

One purpose of inventory control is to control inventories at the least cost. Some items like paper clips and rubber bands aren't worth keeping detailed records for. It is better just to keep a supply of such items on hand and let people help themselves. It doesn't matter if these little things are used somewhat wastefully because it usually costs less to absorb the waste than to keep the records.

Obviously, loose controls should be limited to unimportant items. This means that a decision has to be made as to which items are little things and which need more careful control. Pareto's "vital few" and "trivial many" concept, the "20-80 principle" mentioned hereunder applies here. The inventory controller should look over the stock records, item by item, and classify them into A, B. and C groups

Pareto's 80/20 Rule

ABC Analysis Or Pareto's Analysis is widely known as the '80/20 Rule'. Italian Sociologist Vilfredo Pareto observed in the early 20th century that about 80% of the time, he liked to put on just 20 % of his shirts. The rest 80 % shirts were not used on more than 20 % occasions. Similarly, 80 % of the time, the family had the same (about 20 % of the total) meals. Exploring the notion further, Pareto found that this rule is widely prevalent in society.

For example, many retailers reported that approximately 80 % of their sales (or Profits) came from just about 20 % of their products. Further, in general about 80 % of the sales come from about 20 % customers too. While there is no sanctity to the figures of 80 % and 20 %, what is implied by this rule is that, an abnormally large part of the sales is usually derived from just a small proportion of the items stocked, or alternatively, just a few customers.

Business Significance: If Management devotes a greater amount of time to controlling the sales of the most important 20% stock items, it is in effect controlling a large proportion of the total value of the firm's sales.

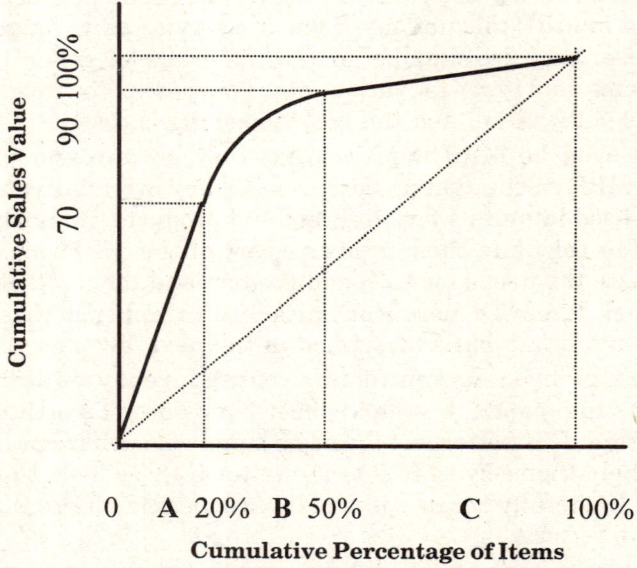

Fig. 4.18.

The '80/20' observation has become a means of classifying items such as Sales, Stock, Customers etc according to their relative importance to the firm. For example, products may be ranked according to their Annual Sales Value. Let us examine the annual sales of a small retailer of children's clothes. Look at Table 1 below:

(1) Serial Number	(2) Cumulative No. of Items	(3) Item Name	(4) Annual Sales	(5) Cumulative Sales of All Items	(6) Item Class
1.	1	Frocks	Rs. 15000/-	Rs. 15,000/-	A
2.	2	Baba Suits	Rs. 6000/-	Rs. 21,000/-	A
3.	3	Dresses	Rs. 4000/-	Rs. 25,000/-	B
4.	4	Half Pants	Rs. 1100/-	Rs. 26,100/-	B
5.	5.	Full Pants	Rs. 900/-	Rs. 27,000/-	B
6.	6	Boy's Vests	Rs. 800/-	Rs. 27,800/-	C
7.	7	Ribbons	Rs. 700/-	Rs. 28,500/-	C
8.	8	Socks	Rs. 600/-	Rs. 29,100/-	C
9.	9	Hankies	Rs. 500/-	Rs. 29,600/-	C
10.	10	Gloves	Rs. 400/-	Rs. 30,000/-	C

The same figures have been plotted in Figure 4.18. The cumulative sales items (from column 2) are plotted on the Horizontal axis and the cumulative sales value (from column 5) on the Vertical axis to show a Pareto Curve. Using this curve, it is possible to place items into three classes:

1. A items, often the first 20% items, which may account for 60-80% of the total annual sales value; (In our case items 1 & 2 account for 70% of the sales and hence are classified as A class.)
2. B items, often the second 30% accounting for perhaps 10-30% of the annual sales value; (In our case items 3,4 & 5 are B class as they together account for 20% of annual sales.) and finally,
3. C items, which might be 50-70% in terms of number of items but account for just 10-30% of the annual sales. (In our case items 6 - 10 are C class as they together account for just 10% sales.)

Having classified items in this manner it is possible to develop Stock Control procedures that are appropriate for each class of items. The rankings can assist management to decide the frequency with which the items can be monitored, for example items A daily, B items weekly, and C items monthly.

Besides annual Sales Value, there can be several other basis of control. Some of these techniques are given in the table 2 below:

S.No.	Title	Basis
1.	*HML* (High, Medium, Low)	Unit Price Of Item
2.	*VED* (Vital, Essential, Desirable)	Criticality of the Item
3.	*FNSD* (Fast, Nominal, Slow, Dead)	Consumption (or sales) Pattern of the Item.
4.	*SDE* (Scarce, Easy, Difficult)	Degree of Difficulty in obtaining the Item.
5.	*ABC* (Always Better Control)	Annual Sales Value

Other Benefits: Similar Rankings can be given to your customers, employees, friends & relatives, clothes, tasks and mail (or email). For example if you have 20 items in your In-tray, first divide them into V (Vital Mail - must attend today), E (Essential Mail - should attend today, if time permits) and D (Desirable to finish, but not necessarily today). This way you will be able to allocate your precious time to the most important items instead of frittering it away in reading junk mail.

Point to Ponder: Look at any product category from toothpaste to TV channels. The top 3 companies in any sector tend to take up 70 - 80% market share in that field. Those that come after them just have to fight for scraps.

Lets construct a Pareto curve. Such a curve would show clearly which items are A, B, and C. Figure A is actually for the usage of materials and parts. And the conclusion is : A few of the items are responsible for most of the cost of all materials and parts used.

"A" items are the large investment items: the vital few. Ten percent of the items commonly account for 70 percent of the amounts spent on materials. A items should be carefully controlled. Their needs should be calculated ahead of time according to the period of use, and their manufacture or purchase should be scheduled so that they arrive just before they are needed. In most cases these items should be ordered a few at a time and frequently, in order to hold down inventories. The inventory levels of A items should be watched very carefully.

"B" items are the 15 to 20 percent of the items which account for some 15 percent of the investment. While they are less important than A items, they are costly enough to make it desirable to keep careful records of their use. Here "maximum-minimum" controls can be used, and past usage, rather than future schedule requirements, can be the basis for reordering. For the most part, MRP methods (which calculate the exact future needs of each item) need not be used for B items. In many cases B items qualify

for MRP treatment in that their needs for end products can be calculated, but it costs more to do this than it is worth.

Minimum stock limits and standard reorder quantities can be set and used. Replenishment reorders can be made out automatically whenever the stock of an item gets down to its reorder point. "Economic order quantities" (see below) can be used to advantage here.

Typical ABC inventory distribution

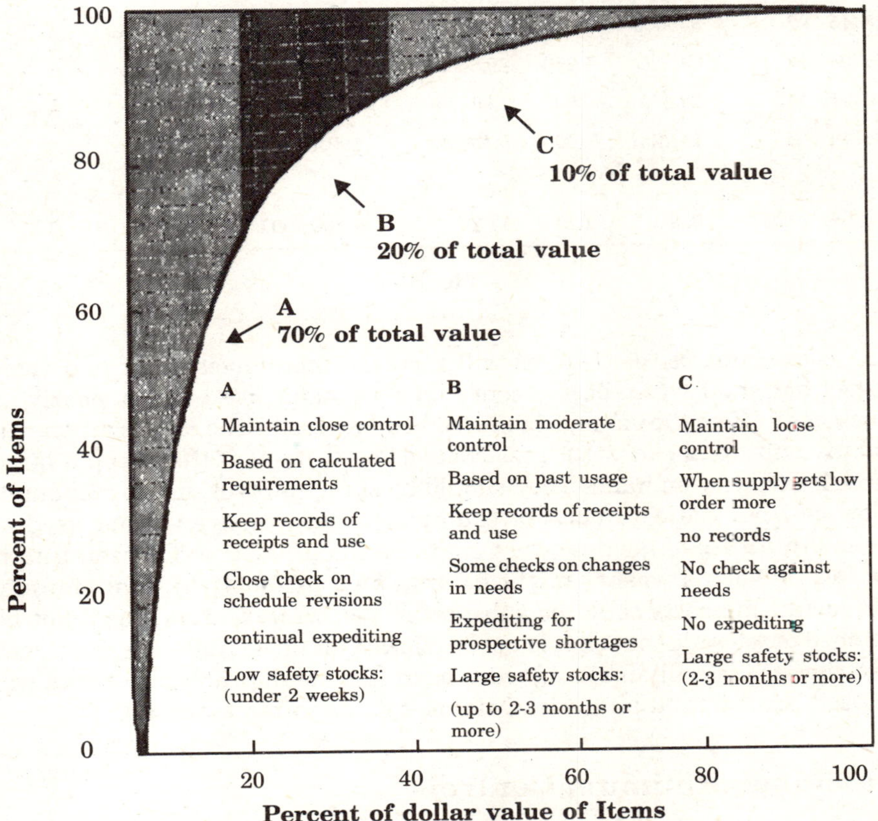

Fig. A

"C" items are the "trivial many." It is not uncommon for 75 percent of the items to account for only 10 percent of the cost of materials. C items should get short shift on planning and records. It is only necessary to order plenty of paper clips, cotter pins. washers, solder, and so on. C items can be put at the operatives' workplaces, where they can help themselves without using requisitions. Future needs of C items usually do not need to be calculated. Nor should they be priced to products individually; they can be charged to an overhead account.

Computer printed for ABC inventory classification

ABC Inventory Classification

Part No.	Rank of item	Usage per year	Unit Cost	Annual Usage (Doll-ARS)	Cumulative usage (dollars)	Cumu-lative percent of usage	ABC group
360467	1	141,500	.620	87,730.00	87,730.00	2.58	A
528445	2	340000	.201	68,340.00	156,070.00	4.59	A
351708	3	24,625	1.200	29,550.00	185,620.00	5.46	A
362401	4	22,823	.350	7,958.05	193,608.05	5.69	A
351748	5	14,725	.400	5,890.00	199,498.05	5.86	A
140868	1250	858	.020	17.16	3,400,000.00	100.00	C

Fig. B

Loose controls of C items will increase their investment and their costs from shelf wear. obsolescence, and wasteful use but not nearly so much as to offset the savings in record keeping costs. The organization will usually end up ahead with loose controls on C items if they keep a large enough quantity on hand. They should be sure, however, not to run out of a low cost but critical item. For example, an inexpensive washer used in the manufacture of lawn mowers might be classified as a "C" item. But, if the lack of such a washer might hold up final assembly of lawn mowers, the down time costs could be substantial. So, while C items need not be watched too closely, they should not be allowed to run out unless replacement lead time is virtually instantaneous or unless an allowable substitute can be used. In the final analysis, C items, too, are often essential.

Maximum-Minimum Controls

People sometimes say that they use "maximum-minimum" inventory control methods in their companies. There is no specific method that goes by the name "maximum-minimum." A person saying this is usually using a system whereby a warning low point is set for each item carried in stock and this warning point serves as a reorder point. When the supply gets down to this danger point (reorder points are discussed in the next few pages), it triggers a reorder.

Paired with this danger point warning is a reorder quantity for each item. This is the amount reordered. The term, "maximum-minimum," actually really ought to be reversed, because the system is really a minimum-maximum method. There is a set minimum stock which serves as the reordering point, but there is no formally set maximum quantity for each item. The maximum depends on how much old stock is left over when a new order comes in.

B items whose use is not keyed directly with demand devolving from end product demand and perhaps some A items should get maximum-minimum control. Normally, however, B items whose demand derives from scheduled end products should be controlled by MRP methods and not maximum-minimum methods.

Investment Limitation Control Methods

Inventory turnover

Inventory turnover is the cycle of using and replacing materials. It is a ratio : the number of "turns" to the investment in a year. If a company sells Rs. 100,000 worth of products a year and has an average inventory valued at Rs. 50,000, it has two turnovers a year. But. if this company could get by with an inventory worth Rs. 25,000, it would have four turns a year. More turns reduce the investment and save carrying costs as well.

Some companies use the turnover ratio as an inventory control method. They insist on a certain number of turns a year. This idea should not be carried very far, however. A high turnover rate means very low inventories, but very low inventories means being out of stock more often. High turnover and low inventories at the same time also force frequent and often uneconomical small reorders which can result in higher unit costs.

Sales volume and reasonable inventory turnover ratios are also related. It is not difficult to obtain more turns when sales volume is high. But, if volume decreases to half and if inventories are also cut in half in order to keep the turnover ratio up, there will be more cases of running out of stock. This could lead to many costly, frequent, and small-quantity re-orders.

Rupee limits

Most companies set rupee limits or budgets on the amount which they will allow to be invested in each class of materials. Each class has an account in the accounting department showing its investments. The inventory control manager is responsible for seeing that the amounts slay within the allowed budgets.

This approach is usually applied only to classes of materials and not to individual items except possibly A items. Otherwise it is just too costly to set rupee limits for each item separately. Rupee limits do not tell inventory controllers when or how much to reorder; all they do is to tell ihem not to exceed an upper investment limit. They have to determine how much of each individual item to provide, while keeping the investment for the item class within the limit.

Rupee limits should be used with discretion when prices or business levels change; otherwise, they automatically tighten or toosen the amount allowed to be carried. If, for example, prices go up and the Rupee limits are not changed, the inventory control manager has to cut the quantities carried. Similarly, if business improves, Rupee limits, if unchanged, hold down the inventories when some increase is really needed to support the added sales. There is need to recognize what the method does to inventory control policies.

Time limits

Time limits are a common way to put Rupee limits into effect. To translate Rupee limits into time limits, it is only necessary to divide the Rupee limit by the Rupee usage per month. A Rs. 20,000 limit is a two-month limit for an item used at a rate of Rs. 10,000 per month.

While Rupee limits can best be used directly to control only A items, time limits can easily be applied to every item. In fact, one single time limit can apply to any number of items at the same time.

Time limits do not directly determine when or how much to order. They merely say, for example, we do not have more than 30 days' supply on hand. Indirectly this sets upper limits on how much can be ordered at one time. To hold the average investment for a class of items down to a month's usage, the inventory controller can never order more than a month's supply of any item on a single order.

For long lead time items, time limits control when reorders go out as well as how much is ordered. If it takes three months to get an item and inventories are limited to one month's supply at one time, it will be necessary to place a new order ever, month for one month's needs, but each order will always be for the third month ahead. There will always be several orders out at the same time. (Items on order do not count in the inventory so far as investment is concerned.)

The inventory "coverage" (the quantity on hand plus the amount on order) is the true available inventory. Assuming reliable lead times, the coverage, in our example, is adequate even though much of it is, for the moment, in the form of open orders rather than stock on hand. The short time limit permitted for stock on hand does not mean that we have to run out of stock of long lead time items.

Time limits are easy to set, easy to change, and easy to operate. And they can be different for different items. If an item's use changes, the time limit can remain unchanged because the reordering quantity can change to reflect the new requirements.

A disadvantage of time limits is that they are not often the very best Production and Inventory planning and control Byat for entire groups of products, although they are usually applied to entire groups. A 30-day limit is probably too much for some items in a group and too little for others. For this reason, both Rupee limits and time limit while commonly used, are not always appropriate.

Fixed Ordering Times

Many, perhaps most, organizations do not order any and every kind of material every day, whenever the need becomes known. Instead, in some cases, they order only once a month (see Figure Below). Warehouses commonly order stock this way. The first week of the month they order all the steel items, the second week all nonferrous items, and the third week, all purchased components, and so on. Ordering entire classes of products together saves clerical work because the order can be just one long listing of requirements.

This method has a disadvantage in that it probably will result in inventories being slightly higher than they need to be. When orders have to be placed, the inventory controller has to look ahead to see if the stock level might get down to a danger point at any time before the next ordering period. If it might run short, he must place his order right now because (except for emergencies) he cannot order more until the next ordering period. So he places the order now, and the new supply will probably come in before it is really needed. This does not have to happen, however, since an order can be placed now and the vendor told when to deliver it.

Economic order quantities (EOQ) and its determination

The best known lot sizing methods are the family of "Economic Order Quantity" or "Economic Lot Size" models. This idea works for both purchased and manufactured items. In theory this idea is simple. The best lot size is the quantity which yields the lowest cost per unit, cost being made up of acquisition costs and costs of possession. The optimum quantity, where the total cost will be the least, is the quantity where the cost of orders plus the cost of carrying inventories are at a minimum. Larger lots run up the costs of possession more than the decline in the cost of acquisition. Smaller lots require more orders which increases acquisition costs.

Figure A shows these relationships in graphic form. It is interesting to see that the total cost curve is almost flat for some distance. This means that it is not necessary to hit the economic lot exactly in order to get low costs. In fact, costs are usually almost as low for reorders up to 25 percent more (or less) than they are for exactly the economic lot.

Since it is unnecessary to hit the EOQ exactly in order to get low costs, most companies that calculate economic lots use simple formulas which leave out such minor factors as the likelihood of obsolescence. Here is the most commonly used formula:

Reporting on a periodic basis results in recorders occurring regardless of the exact quantity on hand at the date for reordering.

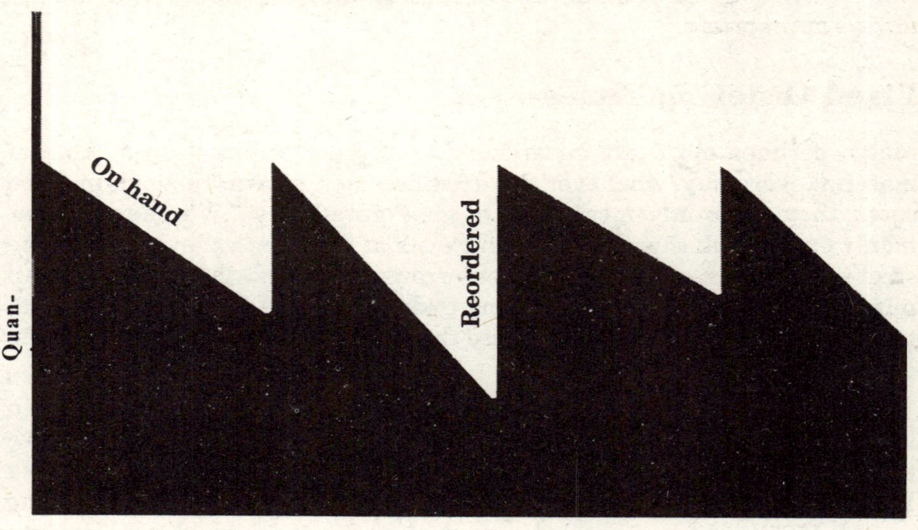

Reordering every month

$$\text{EOQ, in units} = \sqrt{\frac{2 \times \text{the expected annual usage} \times \text{the setup of ordeing cost}}{\text{Labor, material, and overhead cost per piece} \times \text{carrying charge rate}}}$$

Working this out for an expected annual usage of 2,000 units (used more or less steadily throughout the year), an ordering cost of Rs.10 per order, a Rs. 2 per unit value, and an inventory carrying cost of 25 percent, we get:

$$\text{EOQ} = \sqrt{\frac{2 \times 2{,}000 \times \$10}{\text{Rs}2 \times 25\%}} = \sqrt{\frac{40{,}000}{.5}} = 28.3 \text{ units}$$

$$= \sqrt{\frac{6{,}000{,}000}{2}}$$

$$= \sqrt{3{,}000{,}000}$$

$= 1{,}732$, or about $4\frac{1}{3}$ days' usage

Economic Lots With Delivery Over a Period Of Time

Sometimes ordered items do not all arrive at once. This is particularly true with high-volume steadily used items which flow rather regularly and continuously into inventory as well as flowing out at a fairly constant rate. When this condition exists, the formulas previously given will produce too small an answer. They assume that the peak inventory will always include a complete new lot. But actually, since some of the items are being used as they are delivered, the peak inventory will never be that high. Thus the carrying charges are overstated because average inventor) will be smaller.

It is also possible to express all economic lots on a daily use, a daily supply, and n carrying cost per day basis. Doing this does not, however, affect the answer.

EOQs in Managerial Decision Making

So far we have discussed EOQs only with respect to setting the size of manufactured or purchased lots. They can, however, be used to help managers choose the best course of action when there are alternatives.

Although the economic lot can be computed as a specific quantify, total cost is relatively flat over a range of 25 percent above and below the EOQ.

Economic order quantities can also be expressed in terms of month's supply. The formula is just expressed differently:

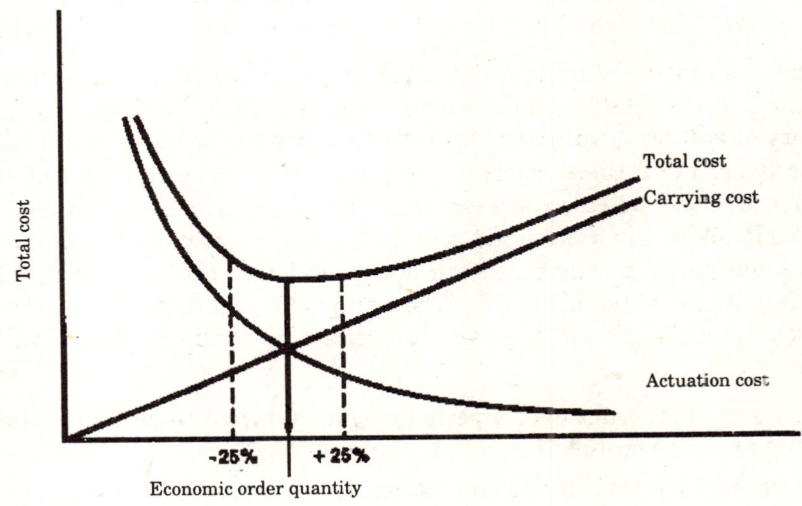

Quantity made in each lot

$$\text{EOQ, in month's supply} = \sqrt{\frac{24 \times \text{the cost to place an order}}{\text{Monthly uasge in dollars} \times \text{carring charge rate}}}$$

Purchasing decisions

Whenever the purchasing department can get quantity discounts, this makes a different EOO for each price offered. But sometimes the economic lot cannot be bought at the price quoted because the vendor does not offer his lower price unless more than the economic quantity is bought. Yet his price cut for larger quantities may save enough to justify buying more than an economic lot.

Suppose, for example, that it costs Rs.10 to place a purchase order and 25 percent a year for carrying costs and that 2,000 units a year are needed. The vendor quotes a price of Rs.2 per unit for all orders under 500 units and Rs.1.95 for 500 or more. How many should be ordered?

To answer this question, it is first necessary to calculate the EOQ for each offer. So far as the buyer's needs are concerned, at Rs.2 the EOO is 283 units and at Rs.1.95 it is 286 units. The price difference is so small that it doesn't change the EOO much. But, actually, the buyer does not get to choose between these two EOQ quantities because he cannot get the Rs.1.95 price unless he buys 500. Will it pay to go up to 500 to get the benefit of the Rs.1.95 price?

If the customer buys 283 units at a time. he will spend, in a year. Rs.71 for 7.1 orders and another Rs.71 to carry an average inventory of 142 pieces valued at Rs.2 each. The total annual cost of this practice will be Rs.142.

The alternative is to buy 500 units at a time for Rs.1.95. With this policy the costs will be Rs.40 for 4 orders and Rs.122 to carry the average inventory of 250 units valued at Rs.1.95 each. This policy will cost S162 a year, or Rs.20 more than ordering the economic lot quantity. But at the Rs.1.95 price there will also be a savings of SIOO in price. This reduces the Rs.162 to Rs.62 as the annual net cost for buying in lots of 500. This saves Rs.80 as compared to buying in the economic lot at the Rs.2 price. The manager's decision should therefore be to buy 500 at a time. If more than one price break is offered, the same procedure as outlined above can be used.

Delivery of an order over a period of time allows it to be used to hold down maximum inventories.

To correct for this in the calculation of the EOQ, it is necessary to adjust the denominator under the square root sign in the EOQ formula by multiplying it by:

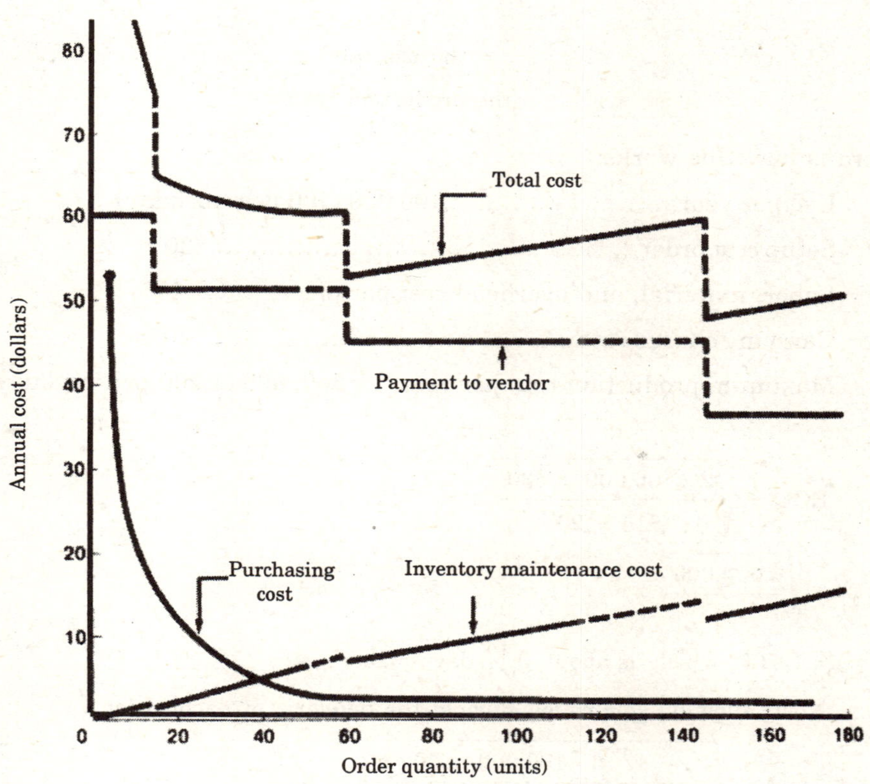
Annual cost (dollars)
80
70
60
50
40
30
20
10
0
Total cost
Payment to vendor
Purchasing cost
Inventory maintenance cost
20
40
60
80
100
120
140
160
180
Order quantity (units)

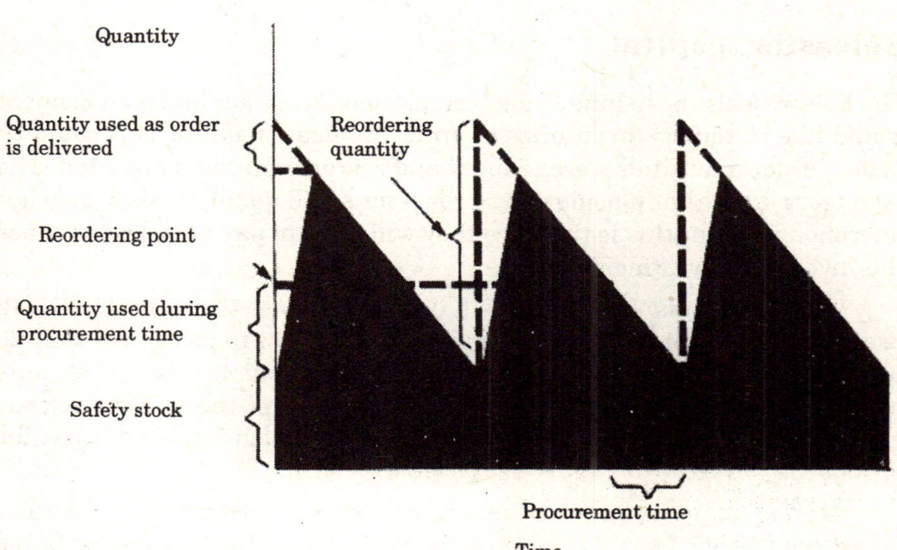
Quantity
Quantity used as order is delivered
Reordering quantity
Reordering point
Quantity used during procurement time
Safety stock
Procurement time
Time

$$1 - \frac{\text{the use rate}}{\text{the production rate}}$$

Here is how this works:

Use per year,........................100,000 (400 per workday)

Setup cost order...$30

Labor, material, and overhead cost per piece..........$15

Carrying charge rate.. 20%

Maximum production rate per year......300, 000 (1,200 per workday)

$$\text{EOQ} = \sqrt{\frac{2 \times 100{,}000 \times \$30}{\$15 \times .20}}$$

$$= \sqrt{\frac{6{,}000{,}000}{3}}$$

= 1,414, which is about $3\frac{1}{2}$ days' uase

Now, allowing for usage during the delivery of each order :

$$\text{EOQ} = \sqrt{\frac{2 \times 100{,}000 \times 30}{15 \times .20 \times (1 - 100{,}000 \div 300{,}000)}}$$

Releasing capital

The EOQ can also be helpful if, for example, money is tight and management would like to reduce inventories in order to release capital. This could be done if order quantities were reduced and reorders placed more often. The managers know that placing extra orders for small quantities is somewhat uneconomical, but this is the price they will have to pay in order to reduce the inventory investment.

The question is: How much will it cost to release the capital? We will use our earlier problem as an example. It cost Rs.10 to place an order, 25 percent a year for carrying costs, and Rs. 2 per unit for the 2,000 units needed in a year. The EOQ was 283 units. If we omit the safety stock the average inventory would be 283 / 2 = 141.5 units, which would have a value of Rs.283.

Management asks: How much will it cost to cut the inventory investment by one fourth, thus releasing Rs. 71 in capital? The new ordering quantity would be 212 units (75 percent of 283). The average inventory would be 106 units, valued at Rs. 212. Ordering 212 units will necessitate 9.43 reorders a year (2,000 / 212 = 9.43), which will cost Rs. 94.30. The carrying charge will be 0.25 X Rs.212 = Rs. 53. So the total costs are Rs. 147.30, which is Rs. 5.30 more than the total of ordering and carrying costs of Rs. 142 if the order quantity were the EOQ of 283. Therefore, an inventory reduction of Rs. 71 can be realized at a cost of Rs. 5.30, the equivalent of a 7.5 percent cost of the capital. This rate seems reasonable, so management should order the inventory reductions.

Actually, order quantities perhaps should often be set at something less possibly as much as 25 percent less, than the EOQ. This is because the curve is relatively flat in the area near the EOQ. Quantities below the EOQ do cost a little more but they release capital.

A manager should be careful, however, when using this kind of analysis. The approach we have just used may be incorrect if the unit price varies for different order quantities. Suppose, for example, that the vendor charges Rs. 2.05 per unit for orders as small as 212 units (as against Rs. 2 when ordering in lots of 283). The extra unit cost would increase total costs by Rs.100. This would entail a total cost of Rs. 105.30 to release Rs. 71 of capital from inventory investment, a 148-percent cost. All of the ramifications of changing an order quantity policy should be considered in this type of analysis.

Enlarging reorder quantities during slack periods

Another instance where EOQ analysis can help may arise during slack periods. The question in this case is whether to make more parts or products than are needed in the immediate future in order to keep the work force busy. We will continue in use the same example, except that the Rs.10 ordering cost is the cost of placing a factory shop order and the Rs. 2 is the cost for direct labour and materials.

Again the EOQ is 283 units and the average inventory is 141.5 units. But, in order to keep the work force busy, management wants to know what it will cost to double the order quantity. This means making lots of Rs. 566, or 3.5 orders, a year. costing Rs. 35. The average inventory would be Rs. 566, which would cost Rs. 141.50 to carry. Total costs would be Rs. 176.50, or Rs. 34.50 more than the total cost using EOQs. Actually, management would not, of course, plan to do this all year long but perhaps only over a short period of one to three months. The actual cost therefore, for the part year involved would probably be less than one quarter of Rs. 34.50, or Rs. 8 more or less. Knowing this cost, managers can decide what to do more intelligently than without this analysis.

EOQs as tests of rule-of-thumb practices

Managers can also use EOQs to test rule-of-thumb practices. One company. for example, which does not use EOQs, uses the following practices in determining reorder quantities for the parts it makes. If setup costs less than Rs. 10, it orders 4 months supply. For setup costs up to Rs. 25, it orders 6 months supply. Above Rs. 25 it orders 8 months supply.

This policy may be more costly than using EOQs. To let it, examples can be worked out. One example might assume a usage of 7,500 units year, setup costs of Rs. 20 and inventory carrying charges of 25 percent with material and direct labour costs being Rs. 3 per unit.

In line with company policy, the inventory controller orders six months supply of this item each time. Thus, he reorders 3,750 units twice a year. The average inventory is 1.875 units, having a value of Rs. 5,635. Inventory carrying costs are Rs. 5,635 × 0.25, or Rs. 1,408.75. Ordering costs are 2 X Rs. 20 = Rs. 40. So the total annual cost for this inventory policy is Rs.1,408.75. Next, the EOQ is calculated:

$$EOQ = \sqrt{\frac{2 \times 7{,}500 \times \$20}{\$3 \times .25}}$$

$$= \sqrt{\frac{300{,}000}{.75}}$$

$$= \sqrt{500{,}000}$$

$$= 632$$

If 632 units are ordered each time, the ordering cost per year is 7,500 / 632 = 11.9 orders per year x Rs. 20 = Rs. 238. Carrying costs would be 632 / 2 = 316 units average inventory X Rs. 3 = Rs. 964 average investment X .25 percent = Rs. 241. The total cost would be Rs. 479.

The company's rule-of-thumb policy is, therefore, in this example, costing an extra Rs. 970 to handle the inventory of this one item in a year (Rs. 1,449 - Rs. 479 = Rs. 970). Similar tests could be made for other examples. If other items are anywhere near comparable to this example, the failure of the company to use EOQs are costing it a great deal of money.

Imputed carrying cost rates

The EOQ approach can be reversed to compute the imputed carrying cost rate for a given inventory order size policy. In the example above, the calculation would be:

$$\text{Imputed rate} = \frac{2 \times \text{annual usage} \times \text{cost to prepare 1 order}}{\text{cost per unit} \times (\text{ordering quantity})^2}$$

$$= \frac{2 \times 7{,}500 \times \$20}{\$3 \times 3{,}750^2}$$

$$= \frac{300{,}000}{3 \times 14{,}062{,}500}$$

$$= \frac{300{,}000}{42{,}187{,}500}$$

$$= .0071$$

The company's reorder policy would produce an EOQ of 3,750 units only if the annual carrying charge rate were 0.7 of 1 percent. But for any higher rate, the EOQ is less than 3.750.

Sensitivity analysis

Managers can also use EOQ calculations to see how sensitive the solution is to changes in any of the factors that go into its calculation. They can change the carrying charges, for example, to see how sensitive the answer is to the size of this factor. (It will usually be found that the formula is not very sensitive to minor changes in any single factor but is quite sensitive to large changes because the change in the EOQ varies according to the square root of changes in individual factors.)

Curiously, using EOQs to aid in decision making scene to be rare. All of the several possible applications given here seem to have greater merit than is recognized.

Reasons For Not Using EOQs

Many companies do not use EOQs, probably because of both practical and technical reasons.

Among the pnictical reasons is the need to use data that are often not available unless money is spent to collect figures. These fieures include the cost of reordering and factory setup costs. Besides, both rates of use and material costs keep changing, and this makes the EOQ keep changing. To stay accurate, EOQs should he recalculated from time to time.

Among the technical reasons is the fact that EOQs are best suited for only B items in any case. Technicians also object to the implicit assumption in the formula of steady use. The formula considers an item's average inventory to be half of the reordering quantity plus the safety stock. But the patterns of use of some items are not like that. Instead, withdrawals from stock are infrequent but large, thus probably invalidating this basic assumption. Obviously. EOQs should not be used for such items if their investment is of consequential proportions.

The EOQ assumption of steady use is also invalid when there are strong seasonal variations in demand. EOO formulas can be adapted to handle seasonal varialions but the mathematics are more complicated.

Another reason for not using EOQs is that they suboptimize, which is not always advantageous to the whole company's operations. This is particularly true in their overuse of capital. Ordering a little less than the EOQ will usually release a certain amount of capital at the equivalent of a very low interest rate.

EOQ methods (and statistical reorder point methods) are generally not applicable to the largest A items nor to most C items. The A items need more careful attention than EOQs and the usual associated ROPs can provide, while C items need less attention than EOQs provide.

Further, the common use of Rupee limits, time limits, and the increasing practice of making parts against known future requirements using MRP methods leaves a smaller area for EOQ use.

Reorder point, Buffer Stock, Safety Stock and Reserve Stock

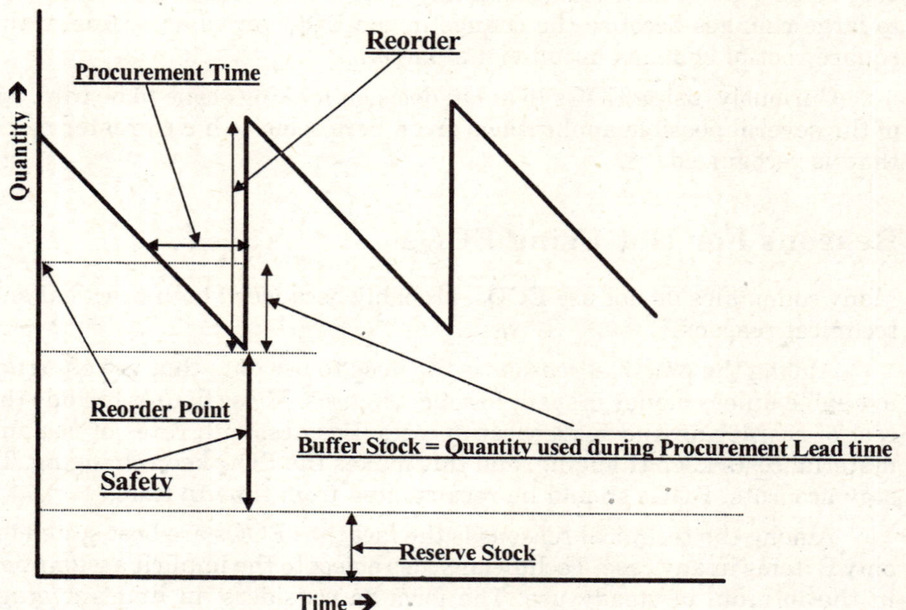

Some Authors think that the MRP approach will continue to reduce the area of EOQ applications. The EOQ is but one of many ways of determining the lot sizes to be ordered. As mentioned earlier, there are several other lot sizing methods that are designed to be used with MRP systems. Each trades off the higher ordering costs of separately ordering each "planned order" quantity against the cost of combining later planned orders with earlier planned ordersthus reducing acquisition costsbut incurring higher inventory carrying costs. However, Burroughs, the computer manufacturer, uses EOQs as the basis for lot sizing when it makes up orders for computer parts, so EOQs are not yet outmoded.

Material Requirements Planning (MRP or MRP-I or MRP)

For a manufacturing company to produce end items to meet demands, the availability of sufficient production capacity must be co-ordinated with the availability of all raw materials and purchased items from which, the end items are to be produced. In other words, there is a need to manage the availability of dependent demand items from which the products are made. Dependent-demand items are the components i.e., materials or purchased items, fabricated parts or sub-assemblies that make up the end product.

One approach to manage the availability of dependent-demand items is to keep a high stock of all the items that might be needed to produce the end items and when the on-hand stock dropped below a present re-order level, the items are produced or bought as the case may be to replenish the stock to the maximum level. However, this approach is costly due to the excessive inventory of components, fabricated parts and sub- assemblies to ensure high service level (i.e., availability of dependent demand items at a short notice).

An alternative approach to managing dependent-demand items is to plan for procurement or manufacture of the specific components that will be required to produce the required quantities of end products as per the production schedule indicated by the master production schedule (MPS). The technique is known as material requirements planning (MRP) technique.

MRP is a computer-based system in which the given MPS is exploded into the required amounts of raw materials, parts and sub-assemblies, needed to produce the end items in each time period (week or month) of the planning horizon. The gross requirement of these materials is reduced to net requirements by taking into account the materials that are in inventory or on order.

A schedule of orders is developed for purchased materials and in-hours manufactured items over the planning horizon based on the knowledge of lead items for procurement or in-house production.

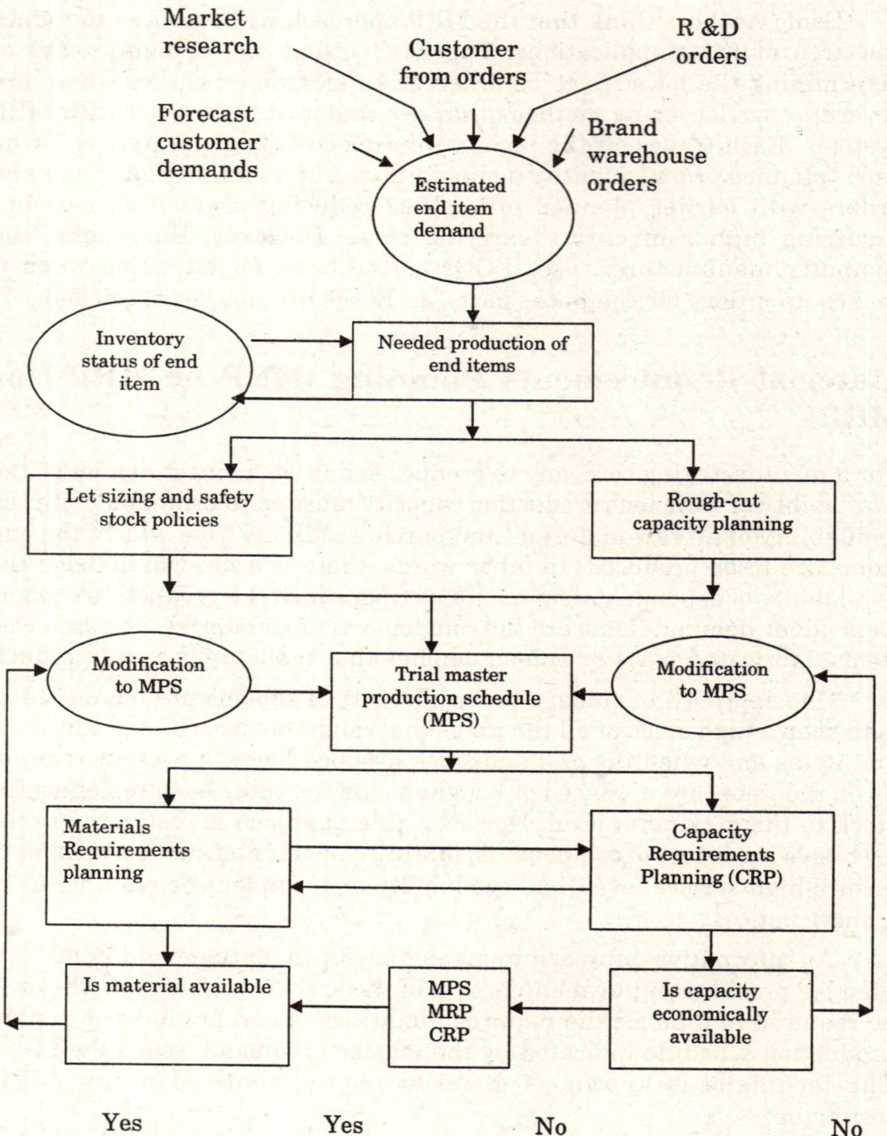

Fig 4.19. Flow chart of Resource requirements planning system or Rough-cut capacity planning process.

Objective of MRP

The objectives of material requirements planning in operations management are :

1. To improve customer service by meeting delivery schedules promised and shortening delivery lead times.

2. To reduce inventory costs by reducing inventory levels.
3. To improve plant operating efficiency by better use of productive resources.

Three facets of MRP technique are :

1. The MRP technique as a requirements calculator
2. MRP - A manufacturing, planning and control system
3. MRP - A manufacturing resource planning system

The MRP technique as a requirements calculator was originally used as an inventory control tool, providing reports that specify how many components should be ordered, when they should be ordered and when they should be procured or produced in-house. Since MRP is a computer-based system, it was possible to expand the system into a manufacturing planning and control system by providing information for planning and controlling both the material and the capacity required to manufacture the products. Hence, MRP serves as a key component in an information system for planning and controlling production operations and procurement of materials. It is the basic foundation for production activity control or shop floor control, for vendor follow-up systems and for detailed capacity requirements planning. When both the MRP and CRP are integrated within one system, the system is known as "Material Requirements Planning", abbreviated as 'MRP' or MRP-I. When MRP is extended to include feed-back from and control of vendor orders and production operations, it is called 'closed-loop MRP' which helps managers achieve effective manufacturing control.

Manufacturing Resource Planning or MRP-II

When the capabilities of closed-loop MRP are extended to integrate financial, accounting, personnel, engineering and marketing information along with the production planning and control activities of the basic MRP system, the resulting broad-based resource-coordination system is known as manufacturing resource planning or MRP-II. MRP-II is the heart of corporate management information system for many companies, as it provides information about inventory investment levels, plant expansion needs, and work-force requirements, that is useful for co-ordinating marketing, financial, engineering and manufacturing efforts to achieve the company's overall business plans.

The projections of what materials and components will be purchased and when, can be used to develop purchase commitments and a projected purchasing budget. The labour hours projected in the capacity requirement plan for each work centre can be aggregated to develop personnel needs and labour budgets. The projected on-hand inventory of material can be used to develop inventory budgets.

Generally Overview of MRP (Material Requirements Planning)

Basically, MRP consists of a set of computer programs that are run periodically (once a week or once a month) to incorporate the latest schedule of production requirements. MRP performs three important functions, viz,

1. Order planning and control, i.e., when to release orders and for what quantity?
2. Priority planning and control i.e., comparison of expected date of availability with the need date of each item.
3. Provision of a basis for planning capacity requirements and development of broad business plans.

MRP is applicable primarily to companies that carry out the fabrication of parts and assembly of standard products in batch quantities.

Figure 4.20 shows a flow chart that provides a general overview of MRP as a means of co-ordinating purchasing activities to support

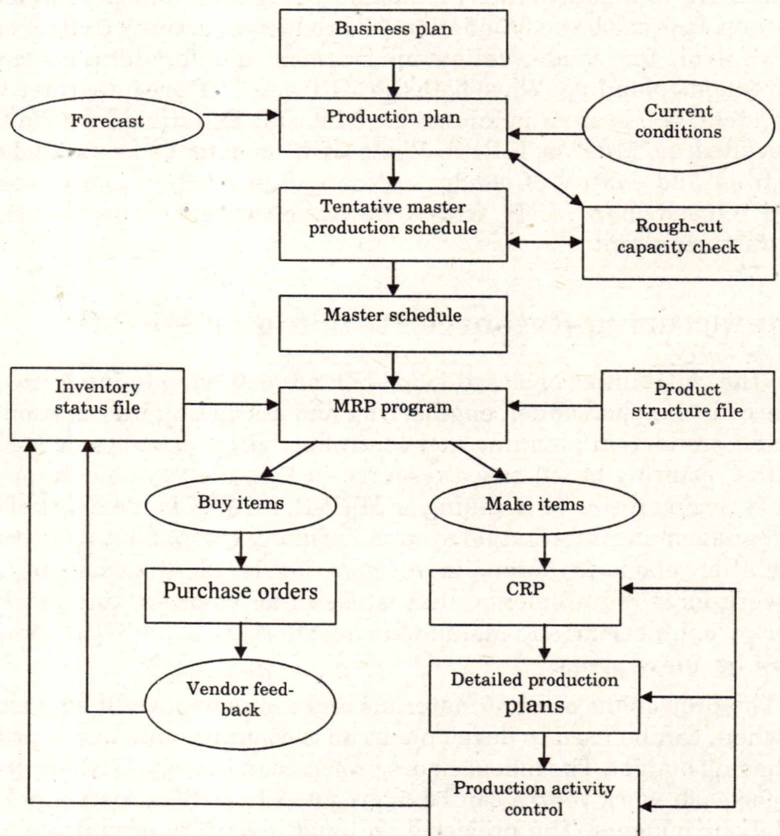

Fig. 4.20. Information flow for planning and controlling with MRP.

manufacturing as well as material requirements and capacity requirements.

Operation of the MRP System

Fig. 4.21 illustrates the operation of MRP system.

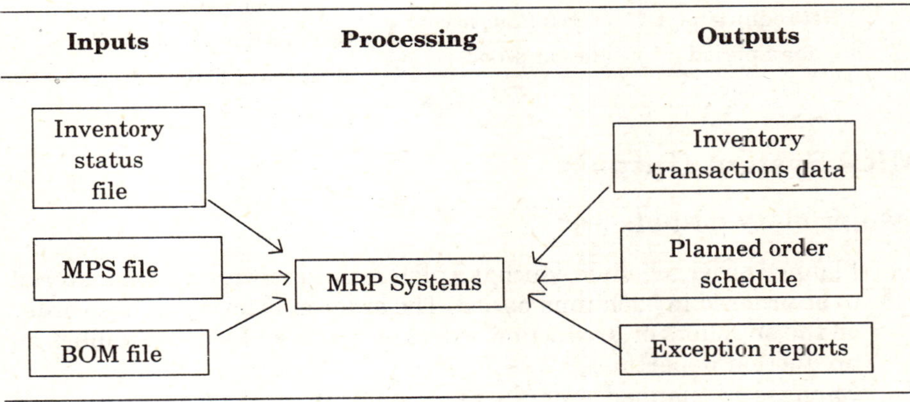

Fig. 4.21. Operation or MRP system

The entire MRP system is driven by the MPS. The bill of materials file and inventory status file are fed in to the MRP computer program to generate the outputs.

MRP System Inputs

1. Master Production Schedule (MPS) : The MPS specifies what end products are to be produced and when. The planning horizon should be long enough to cover the cumulative lead times of all components that must be purchased or manufactured to meet the end product requirements.

2. Bill of Material file BOM or Product Structure file : This file provides the information regarding all the materials, parts and sub-assemblies that go into the end product. The Bill of Materials can be viewed as having a series of levels, each of which represents a stage in the manufacture of the end product. The highest level (or zero level) of the BOM represents the final assembly or end product. The BOM file identifies each component by a unique part number and facilitates processing by exploding the end product requirements into component requirements.

3. Inventory Status file : The inventory status file gives complete and up-to-date information on the on-hand quantities, gross requirements, scheduled receipts and planned order releases for the item. It also includes other information such as lot sizes, lead times, safety stock levels and scrap allowances, etc. The gross requirements are total needs from all resources whereas the net requirements are 'net' after allowing for available

inventory and scheduled receipt. Scheduled receipts are quantities already on order from a vendor or in-house shop. Planned receipts are quantities the quantity and date to initiate the purchase or manufacture of materials that will be received on schedule after the lead time offset.

$$\begin{pmatrix}\text{Net requirement}\\\text{for a period}\end{pmatrix}=\begin{pmatrix}\text{Gross requirement}\\\text{for the period}\end{pmatrix}-\begin{pmatrix}\text{Net requirement}\\\text{period + on hand inventory}\\\text{at the end of the period}\end{pmatrix}$$

MRP System Outputs

Two primary outputs are:

1. Planned order schedule which is a plan of the quantity of each material to be ordered in each time period. The order may be a purchase order on the suppliers or production orders for parts and sub-assemblies on production departments.
2. Changes in planned orders - i.e., modification of previous planned orders. The secondary outputs are:
1. Exception reports which list items requiring management attention to control
2. Performance reports regarding how well the system is operating - eg. Inventory turnovers, percentage of delivery promises kept and stock-out incidences.
3. Planning reports such as inventory forecasts, purchase commitment reports, etc.

Definitions of Terms used in MRP System

1. *Master Production Schedule (MPS) :* This is the schedule of the quantity and timing of all end products to be produced over a specific planning horizon. MPS is developed from customer's firm orders or from forecasts of demand or both. It is an input to the MRP system.

2. *Product structure :* Indicates the level of components required to produce and end product.

3. *Bills of Material :* A list indicating the quantities of all raw materials, parts, components, sub assemblies and major assemblies that go into an end product. It gives details of the build-up of a product. It may also be called as indented parts list.

4. *Bills of Material file :* A bills of material file, also known as product-structure file, is a computerized file listing all finished products, the quantity of raw materials, parts, sub-assemblies and assemblies in each product. The bills of material file must be kept up-to-date as and when the products are redesigned or modified with addition/deletion of some parts, components and sub-assemblies.

5. *Inventory status file :* It is a computerized file with a comprehensive record of each and every material held in inventory. The information included in this file are, materials on hand or on order, planned orders, planned order releases, allocated materials, lot sizes, lead times, safety stock levels, costs and suppliers for each material. The inventory file must be kept up-to-date taking into consideration the daily inventory transactions such as receipts, issues, scrapped materials, planned orders and order releases.

6. *MRP computer program :* It is a computer program, which processes the MRP information. Its inputs are the MPS, inventory status file and bills of material file. The primary outputs are : planned order schedule, planned order releases and changes to planned orders.

7. *Available inventory :* Materials that are held in inventory or which are on order, but are not either safety stock or allocated to other uses.

$$\left.\begin{array}{r}\text{Available inventory}\\ \text{of an item at the end}\\ \text{of a time period}\end{array}\right\} = \left\{\begin{array}{l}\text{[Scheduled receipts + planned}\\ \text{order receipts - gross requirements}\\ \text{for that period] + Quantity available}\\ \text{from the previous period}\end{array}\right.$$

8. *Allocated inventory :* Materials that are held in inventory or on order but which have been allocated to specific production orders (committed for use) in the future. These materials are not available to meet future requirements for use on other orders.

9. *On-hand inventory :* The quantity of a material, physically held in inventory at a point of time. It may include safety stock and allocated inventory except materials on order.

10. *Planning horizon :* The number of time periods (days, weeks or months) included in the MPS, CRP, MRP and departmental schedules.

11. *Action Bucket :* The unit of time measurement in MRP systems. It is a particular period of time in the planning horizon. For example, Bucket # 10 means the tenth period (usually a week in duration) of the planning horizon.

12. *Gross requirements :* The total quantity of an item needed at the end of a period to meet the planned output levels, not considering any availability of the item in inventory or scheduled receipts.

13. *Scheduled receipts* : The quantity of an item that will be received at the beginning of a time period from a supplier as a result of orders already placed (open orders).

14. *Planned order receipts :* The quantity of an item that is planned to be ordered so that, it will be received at the beginning of the time period to meet the net requirements for that time period. The order is yet to be placed.

15. *Planned order releases :* The quantity of an item that is planned to be ordered and the planned time period for releasing this order, so that, the item will be received when needed.

This time schedule is determined by off-setting the planned order receipts schedule to allow for lead times, i.e.,

$$\begin{pmatrix}\text{Planned order release}\\ \text{(time schedule)}\end{pmatrix} = \begin{pmatrix}\text{Planned order receipt}\\ \text{(time schedule)}\end{pmatrix} - (\text{lead time})$$

16. *Net requirements :* The quantity of an item that must be procured to meet the scheduled output for the period.

$$\begin{pmatrix}\text{Net requirements}\\ \text{for the period}\end{pmatrix} = \left[\begin{pmatrix}\text{Gross}\\ \text{requirements for}\\ \text{the period}\end{pmatrix} - \begin{pmatrix}\text{Scheduled}\\ \text{requirements for}\\ \text{the period}\end{pmatrix}\right] - \begin{pmatrix}\text{Qty. available}\\ \text{from the}\\ \text{previous period}\end{pmatrix}$$

or

$$\begin{pmatrix}\text{Net requirements}\\ \text{for the period}\end{pmatrix} = \begin{pmatrix}\text{Gross requirements}\\ \text{for the period}\end{pmatrix} - \begin{pmatrix}\text{Material available}\\ \text{at theperiod}\end{pmatrix}$$

17. *Low-level coding :* It is the coding of each material at the lowest level in any product structure that it appears. A component can appear at more than one level in the product structure. Because MRP computer programs process net requirements calculations for all products, level by level from end items, down to the raw materials, low level coding avoids redundant net requirements calculations.

18. *Lot-sizing decisions* : Whenever there is a need for the net requirement of a material, a decision must be taken regarding the quantity of material to be ordered (either purchase order or production order). Lot-sizing decisions include both the batch or lot-size (quantity) as well as the timing of these lots.

19. *Dependent Demand :* Demand for raw material, part or a component, that is dependent on the demand for the end product in which these materials are used.

20. *Independent demand :* Demand for a material that is independent of the demands for other materials. For example, demand for end products are independent of demand for parts, raw materials or components as their demands are determined, by customers outside the organiation.

21. *Lumpy demand :* If the demand for the materials varies greatly from time period to time period (say week to week), the demand is said to be 'lumpy demand'.

22. *Capacity requirement planning* : The process of reconciling the Master Production Schedule to the available capacities of production departments (viz., machine and labour capacities) over the planning horizon.

23. *Loud Schedules* : A load schedule is a device for comparing the actual labour-hours and machine-hours required to produce the MPS against the available labour-hours and machine-hours in each week.

24. *Net change MRP* : MRP systems that generate outputs emphasizing only the changes to last MRP outputs. Planned order schedules in these systems would indicate only the changes to the previous report and not a completely new schedule.

25. *Regenerative MRP* : MRP systems tend to periodically generate one complete set of MRP outputs. In these systems, a planned order schedule would be a complete report not be comprised solely of changes to an earlier report.

26. *Product Explosion* : The process of determining from the product structure and planned order releases and the gross requirements for components.

27. *Pegging* : The process of tracing through the MRP records and all levels in the product structure to identity how changes in the records of one component will affect the records of other components. Pegging shows the level-by-level linkages among components and their time-phased status in the MRP records.

28. *Cycle counting* : This is counting on-hand inventories at regular intervals to verify inventory quantities shown in the MRP.

29. *Time fence* : A designated length of time that must pass without changing the MPS, to stabilize the MRP system.

30. *Lot-for-lot ordering* : A lot-sizing policy in which, order quantity equals net requirement for the period.

31. Period-order quantity (POQ) method : Also known as part-period method, it is a lot-sizing policy in which, order quantity varies according to a comparison of holding versus ordering costs.

$$\text{POQ} = \frac{\text{No. of weeks per year}}{\text{No. of orders per year (N)}} = \frac{52}{\text{N}} \text{ weeks}$$

$$\text{No. of orders per year (N)} = \frac{\text{Annual Demand (units)}}{\text{Economic Order Quantity}}$$

32. *Frozen MPS* : The early time periods of the MPS that can be assumed to not to be subject to change. Frozen periods of MPS enable managers to commit funds, order materials so such plans, will not need to be subsequently changed.

Potential benefits from MRP

MRP is not just a way of calculating how much material to order and when; but it is a new way of managing manufacturing operations.

MRP is a decision support system or managerial information system, which provides timely and valuable information to operation managers.

When properly developed and implemented, MRP can provide the following benefits to the firm :

1. *Inventory* : The information provided by the MRP system is useful to better coordinate orders for components with production plans for parent items. This results in reduced levels of average inventory for dependent-demand items (i.e., raw materials and work-in-process).

2. *Production :* Information from MRP facilitates better utilization of human and capital resources. Because of more accurate priority information from MRP, it is possible to improve delivery performance. It can also improve flow of work, thereby reducing intermittent delays and reducing the manufacturing cycle time for the jobs.

3. *Sales :* MRP helps to check in advance whether the desired delivery dates are achievable. It improves the company's ability to react to changes in customer orders, improves customer service by helping production, meet assembly dates and helps cut delivery lead times.

4. *Engineering :* MRP helps in planning the time of design releases and design changes.

5. *Planning :* MRP can simulate changes in the MPS for the purpose of evaluation of alternative MPS. It facilities the projection of equipment and facility requirements, workforce planning and procurement expenses for a proposed MPS.

6. *Purchasing :* MRP helps the purchase department by making known the real priorities and recommending changes in due dates for orders so that the purchase staff may expedite or delay the orders placed on vendors. Because of this, the vendor relations can be improved.

7. *Scheduling :* Better scheduling can result from MRP through better knowledge of priorities.

8. *Finance :* MRP can help better planning of cash flow requirements. It can identify time capacity constraints or bottleneck work centres, there by helping operations managers to make better capital investment decisions.

Implementation of MRP

Successful implementation of MRP depends on the following factors

1. *Management commitment :* Top level managers and other managers in all parts of the organization that will be affected by MRP must be aware of the efforts needed to achieve the new way of managing other activities.

2. *User involvement* : A team consisting of people from all those parts of the company that will use the MRP system, will be responsible for the development and implementation of the MRP. This will ensure that the participation of users of the system in its development will make them more familiar with the system and its use.

3. *Education and training* : All the people who work with the MRP system must understand it and must know how to use it. They must know what information to provide and how to provide it, what information to ask and how to obtain it. Hence, it is necessary that all people connected with the MRP system must be trained in its application and use.

4. *Selection of packages* : The potential user must be able to decide about the use of the net change or regenerative MRP package, knowing their advantages and disadvantages. Also the user must decide whether to develop his own programs for MRP system or to purchase and adapt the available packages.

5. *Data accuracy* : After a MRP system is installed, careful attention and discipline must always be exercised to ensure that all data used by the system are accurate. Managers must exert effort to see that, accurate and timely data are supplied to the system.

6. *Realistic MPS* : The MPS developed should be realistic and achievable. The MPS should not overload the plant capacity. The company must develop MPS that effectively uses its capacity without causing bottlenecks or overloads.

Problems in Using MRP

1. *Preparation of MPS*, which is realistic in the midst of uncertainties in market environment and non-availability of adequate lead time from customers for delivery of end products. Frequent changes in MPS aggravate the problem.

2. *Maintaining accurate BOM files* : Changes incorporated in BOM by the design department should be communicated to all users of BOM.

3. *Incorrect stock (inventory) status* : A major problem is to know the correct status of all materials at all stages. Incorrect stock status results in an erroneous net requirement of materials.

4. *Unrealistic lead times* : Most crucial step in the MRP system which minimizes inventory is the time-phasing of requirements and release of orders; advancing by the lead time required, so that, materials arrive just when required.

Problems in Designing the MRP system

1. Inadequacies of software chosen.
2. Deficient system design.

3. Improper and untimely information flow among various related departments.

Solution to overcome the above problems in the design of MRP system are:

1. Careful choice of software package to suit organization's specific needs.
2. Careful planning of activities and scheduling.
3. Assigning work to competent man-power.
4. Continuous monitoring of progress against schedule.
5. Substantial education and training at all levels.
6. Involvement of users at the systems design stage itself.
7. Maximum attention at the stage of creating the database.

Problem in Managing the MRP system

1. Need for formal systems and role of systems
2. Need for proper organization of functions viz., production planning and control, materials, production, quality, engineering, etc.
3. Importance of proper appreciation of planning and control systems.
4. Timeliness of generating information required in managing the plant.
5. Effective communication system
6. Proper motivation of people concerned with the implementation of the system.
7. Right leadership.

Evaluation of MRP

The advantages of the MRP system over conventional inventory-planning approaches viz., fixed order quantity system (Q system) and fixed order-point system (P system) are

(a) improved customer service,
(b) reduced inventory levels and
(c) improved operating efficiencies of production departments

However, MRP systems cannot be used in all the production systems. Conventionally, MRP is applied only to manufacturing system which process discrete products for which BOM can be generated. MRP is seldom used in service systems viz., petroleum refineries, retailing, retailing systems, transportation firms and other non-manufacturing systems.

The production systems suitable for MRP should have the following desirable characteristics:

1. An effective computer system,
2. Computerized BOM files and inventory status file for all end products and materials with the highest possible accuracy.

3. A production system that manufactures discrete products made up of raw materials, parts, sub-assemblies and major assemblies which are processed through several production steps of operations.
4. Production processes or operations requiring long processing times.
5. Short and reliable lead time for procurement of raw materials and components from vendors.
6. The time fence for the frozen MPS should be sufficient to procure materials without undue expediting effort.
7. Support and commitment of the top management.

MRP is more useful in process-focussed system that have long processing times and complex multi-stage production steps. It simplifies production and inventory planning in process-focussed systems by its ability to offset planned order receipts to planned order releases to account for long lead times for in-house processed items or raw materials and components purchased from suppliers.

For MRP to be effective, supplier lead times must be short and reliable and the MPS must be frozen before the start of actual production to the MPS. What is to be produced (i.e., the MPS) must be known with certainty and quantity and timing of receipts of raw materials and components must be dependable. MRP offers advantages in inventory planning when lot-sizes are small and demand is highly variable.

However, it should be remembered that MRP is not a panacea to solve all our inventory planning problems. MRP is a computerized information system for production and operations managers. MRP will not be of much help when computer systems are ineffective, inventory status and BOM files are inaccurate and MPS are unrealistic. MRP is best applied when production systems are well managed and when a comprehensive production and inventory planning system is needed.

11

Statistical Quality Control

Introduction

Statistical Quality Control (SQC) is the application of statistical techniques to accept or reject products already produced, or to control the process and, therefore, product quality while the part is being made. While the latter is called process control, the former is named acceptance sampling.

Statistical quality control (SQC) applies the theory of probability to sample testing, or inspection. A great deal of inspection work has always been done by sampling; a small part of a certain lot of products is inspected and its quality is assumed to be the quality of the lot. This is called statistical inference. The characteristics of the whole lot or "population" are inferred to be like the sample. Sampling, however, is risky because it is always possible that a sample will not have exactly the same characteristics as the lot.

Years ago, before statistical quality control methods were developed, no one knew how much risk was involved. Often larger samples than necessary were inspected. These entailed wasted inspection costs. For other items, higher risks than realized were taken, resulting in, at times, more defects than desired being passed by inspectors. This allowed costs for defects to be too high. With statistical quality control, inspection is more reliable, and it allows for balancing off of these costs at their least costly combination.

Statistical quality Control

Statistical quality control deals with samples and their reliability as indicators of lot characteristics. Sampling inspection, where it can be used satisfactorily, eliminates most of the cost of 100 percent inspection, and it is the only possible method for products which must be tested until they fail or break (as in tests of length of life or tensile strength). Sampling is also the only way to test the chemical or physical characteristics of liquids and powdered or granulated material, or the thickness gage of sheet metal. paper, and cloth.

Sampling is therefore desirable in many cases; because it saves money. And in other cases there is no other way to inspect.

Statistical quality control does not create risks, nor does it eliminate risks. With or without statistical quality control, there is always some chance that any sample from a lot will not be exactly like the rest of a lot. The objectives of statistical quality control are to show how reliable the sample is and how to control the risks. It lets managers decide the risks they are willing to take (that bad products will slip by or that good products will be rejected). They can then decide whether it will cost more to catch the possible bad products or to let them go and save inspection costs. They can make a conscious decision about how much risk they want to assume. SQC also helps control processing by warning managers if machines are getting out of adjustment so that they can be reset before many defective products are made.

The quality production Interaction system

Production operations
Output
Inspection and test
Quality information
Corrective action
Organize quality information
Process out of control
Decide corrective action
Process out of control
Evaluate quality Information against standards

SQC procedures which check products already completed is called "acceptance" sampling. This is where most of the "risk controlling" applies. But SQC (still using samples and still dealing in risks) can also be used to control processes while things are being made. Not only does SQC indicate when a process is out of adjustment and turning out bad work, but it warns the operator if the machine is getting out of adjustment. It monitors operations and indicates drifts toward defectives. This helps prevent defectives and cuts losses due to scrap.

Areas of Use

Statistical quality control has three general uses: (1) to control the quality of work done on individual operations while the work is being done, (2) to decide whether to accept or reject lots of products already produced (whether purchased or made within the company), and (3) to furnish management with a quality audit of the company's products. A fourth result checking the reasonableness of the quality standards and setup specifications is generally accomplished, more or less, as a by-product of SQC in operation.

Quality Control

One of the major achievement of the Industrial Revolution has been the ability to mass produce goods of uniform quality. This achievement flourished till recently. It recent years, poor quality has been causing problems and an embarrassment to industry owners. Quality control has, therefore, become highly relevant.

Definitions

Quality

Quality refers to the sum of the attributes or properties that describe a product. These are generally expressed in terms of specific product characteristics such as length, width, colour, specific gravity and the like. To be meaningful in an industrial sense, these characteristics must be quantitatively expressed in terms, that can be objectively measured or observed. There are instances where, subjective measures will be necessary, but such cases are generally held to an absolute minimum.

The need for quality needs no special emphasis. One benefit of quality i,s increased productivity. Better quality means reduced costs for repairs, instruction, scrap, rework and product warranties. Increased productivity results in better profits and builds customer loyalty.

Quality also results in sustained profits. Earning profit in one year and incurring loss the very next year will not speak high about an organisation. What is needed is sustained profit over a long period of time. This is possible when the organisation is able to maintain persistent quality for its products.

The need for quality is felt more in our country than anywhere. For too long, we have been the victims of poor quality goods. Take for example, razor blades. A packet has five blades. Not all the five have uniform quality. Two or three of them give better shave and the rest are fit only for one use each. Take shirtings, you pay hefty sum of Rs. 100 per metre of cloth. After one wash, the shirt sheds enormous fuzz and the piece looks like a 20 years old one. Take electrical fittings in your house! How long will they last?

Maximum five years. After this, you have to replace all fittings. Same is the story with all the products we buy and use. Ironically, our manufacturers are not poor in claims. For them, all blades give best me shave, detergents wash whitest and cream makes your skin smoothest. It is time that we stop these claims and improve quality first. We should realize we are facing strategic competition from foreign brands. Quality is the only weapon to fight competition.

Quality Creation : Those activities involved in the selection of the specific characteristics, required to achieve the desired quality and the processing or fabrication of materials to conform to the specific characteristics selected. Quality creation involves almost all organisational elements of the enterprise and is the basic objective towards which most activity is directed.

Quality Control : Those activities which assure that quality creation is performed in such a manner that, the resulting produce will in fact perform its intended function. When used in this sense, quality control can be divided into two fundamental endeavours: Assurance that the product characteristics selected will achieve the intended result and assurance that, items produced contain the specified characteristics.

In a more limited sense, quality control is frequently used to refer to a specific organisation within the industrial enterprise which is assigned responsibility for many of the activities necessary to achieve quality objectives.

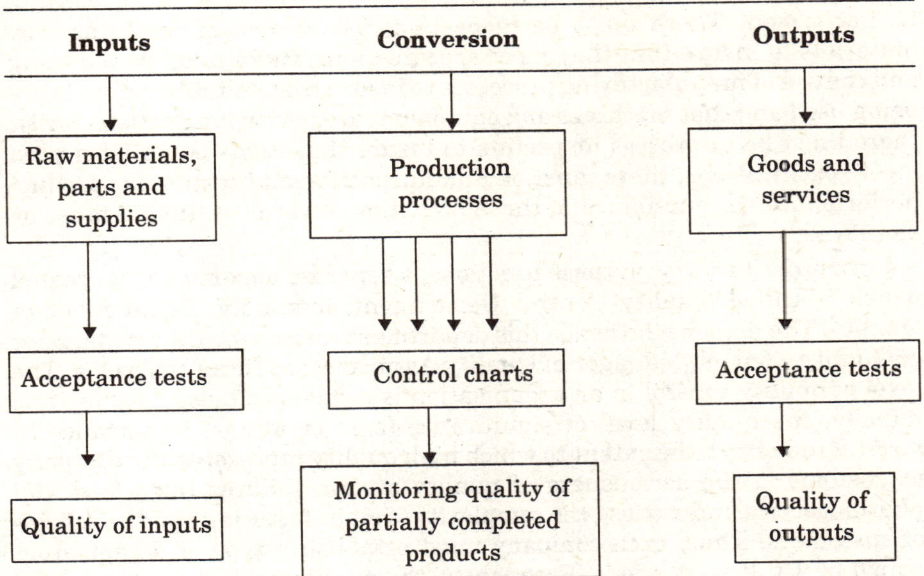

Fig. 5.1. Quality Control through production systems

Contrary to popular perception, quality control does not begin after the goods are produced. Rather, it begins long before goods and services are delivered to customers. As Fig. 5.1 shows, early in the production system, raw materials, parts and supplies must be of acceptable quality before they are allowed to be used. Materials must meet the appropriate specification - strength, size, colour, finish, appearance, chemical content, weight, and other characteristics. As the inputs of the production system proceed through production, the quality of these - partly finished units is monitored to determine whether the system is operating on the expected lines. This monitoring is necessary to alert operating managers to institute corrective action before poor quality goods and services are produced. Thereafter, finished goods and services are inspected to determine their acceptability.

Quality Assurance : Is another expression which needs a mention in this context. Quality assurance includes quality control and also refers to emphasis on quality in the design of the products, processes, and jobs, and in personnel selection and training.

Of all the expressions, it is quality control, which is widely used in the literature on quality. The following sections in this chapter are, therefore, devoted to quality control.

Organisation for Quality Control

Quality control is a staff function concerned with the prevention of defects in manufacturing so that, items may be made right at the first time and not to be rejected later. In order to achieve this end, several activities need to be performed. There must be inspection and control of incoming raw materials to insure that they meet specifications; there must be planning and control of manufacturing processes to insure that suitable methods are being used and that machines and equipment are performing satisfactorily; there must be in-process inspection to insure that items being fabricated meet specifications; there must be final inspection and testing for product performance. In pursuance of these activities, several technique must be employed.

In order to carry on these functions, a separate department is created which is called Quality Control Department or simply, Department of Quality. The person who heads this department carries the title of Manager of Quality Control, Manager of Quality Assurance, or Chief Inspector. The level of quality control in an organisation is influenced by several factors, namely, the quality level of significance (e.g., of utmost importance in aircraft industry), the extent to which high quality represents the company to customers, the seriousness of quality system failures (e.g., food and pharmaceutical industries), the complexity of manufacturing and the policies of customers. Thus, each company must establish a type of organisation which best fulfils its needs. Frequently, the quality control department is composed of a quality engineering function, an inspection function and a laboratory function.

It should be stated that, quality control is not the responsibility of personnel in the quality control department. Everybody in the organisation must be equally responsible to ensure quality of the end product.

Quality involves the members of the management who set the quality policies, the salesman who contract to sell the products of a certain quality, the design engineers who set the product specifications, the buyers who purchase raw materials of the right quality and the manufacturing personnel who are responsible for making the product according to the prescribed specification. It is only through the whole hearted co-operation of all the people that a sustained quality control programme can be maintained.

Ensuring Quality

Ensuring quality involves action on several fronts. To be specific, quality control involves the following steps:

Control of engineering quality

(i) Assist in the evaluation of customer requirements to arrive at a clear understanding of the product quality objectives.

(ii) Review design documentation for conformance to design standards and practice and for identification of potential quality problems.

(iii) Validate the accuracy and completeness of design proof tests and qualification tests.

(iv) Audit the release and distribution of design documents to assure that all drawings and specifications in use are current and correct.

(v) Provide information on previous quality problems encountered for consideration in new product designs or current product improvements.

Control of purchased material quality

(vi) Assist in the evaluation and selection of potential suppliers or sub-contractors.

(vii) Review purchase orders and sub-contracts for correctness and completeness of quality requirements.

(viii) Assure that purchased material conforms to the requirements of purchase orders and specifications.

(ix) Initiate corrective action with supplies and sub-contractors when purchased material is not of an acceptable quality level.

B. Control of manufacturing quality

(i) Evaluate and approve manufacturing equipment, processes, testing and test equipment.

(ii) Assure that measuring and test equipment is properly calibrated and maintained.

(iii) Establish points of inspection and tests at selected points in the production processes.
(iv) Perform inspection and tests at selected points in the production processes.
(v) Collect and analyse inspection and test data and provide information on process and product quality levels.
(vi) Initiate corrective action on out-of-control condition and related quality problems.
(vii) Conduct follow-up to assure that corrective action is accomplished in a timely manner.
(viii) Control the handling, preservation, and packaging of material and equipment from receipt through shipment of the final product.

C. Actions supporting the product after delivery

(i) Assure that product service specifications are clear and correct.
(ii) Assure that spare parts conform to quality requirements.
(iii) Assure that repair and modification are performed in accordance with company quality requirements.
(iv) Gather and analyse complaint data from the field to measure the degree of customer satisfaction and initiate appropriate corrective action.

Quality Control Techniques

Various techniques of quality control have been developed. More prominent of them are: Just-In-Time, quality at the source, quality circles, inspection, statistical quality control and total quality management. A brief explanation of each, follows.

1. Just-In-Time (JIT)

JIT has different interpretations. For some, it is buying materials on time, for some others, it means planning and controlling production on the shop floor, and for others it is a philosophy of production that permeates every facet of organisations. For our purpose, JIT is viewed as a technique of quality control. Just as JIT has different interpretations, it has varied names too. For some companies, IBM for example, continuous flow manufacture; for some others, Hewlett-Packard, for example, it is called stockless production and repetitive manufacturing system; GE calls it management by sight; and many Japanese firms use the term Toyota system instead of JIT.

JIT helps achieve quality, because, it is philosophy, that seeks to constantly improve production processes and methods. Specifically, JIT contributes to high product quality in the following ways:

1. Production is highly standardised. Workers perform standard tasks every day. They are familiar with their tasks. Familiarity ensures high quality.
2. In-process inventories are drastically reduced by cutting lot-sizes. Any interruption, therefore, causes production to stop until the problem has been solved. In this way, JIT has been called a system of enforced problem solving. Now, this stoppage in production forces everybody to solve the quality problem, so that the defect will not repeat. Hence, high product quality is ensured.
3. Suppliers of materials, under the JIT system, supply materials of perfect quality. Many companies do not even inspect suppliers' deliveries of materials; rather, the emphasis is on working with suppliers to produce perfect parts and materials.
4. JIT system envisages the use of automated equipment and robots in production processes. Use of such sophisticated machines will ensure high product quality.
5. JIT system also envisages the use of intensive preventive maintenance programmes in order to prevent any machine break-down. This results in machines producing parts of perfect quality.
6. Workers are responsible for producing parts of perfect quality or with zero defects, before they are passed on the next production operation.

2. Quality at the Source

Where workers are made responsible to produce parts of perfect quality, before they are passed on the next operation, the concept of quality at the source emerges. The worker is put in the driver's seat in controlling product quality. The principles underlying quality at the source are:

1. Every worker's job becomes a quality control station. The worker is responsible for inspecting his own work, identifying any defects and reworking them into non-defectives, and correcting any cause of defect.
2. Statistical quality control techniques are used to monitor the quality of parts produced at each work station, and easy-to-understand charts and graphs are used to communicate progress to workers and managers.
3. Each worker is given the right to stop the production line to avoid producing defective parts.
4. Workers and managers are organised into quality circles -groups of people who analyse quality problems, work to solve the problems and implement programmes to improve product quality.

3. Inspection

The act of determining conformance or non-conformance of the expected performance is the function of inspection. In other words, by inspection, a manager seeks to determine the acceptability or non-acceptability of the parts, products or services. The basis for inspection is usually a specification, which is called inspection standard. Inspection is made by comparing the quality of the product to the standard.

How often inspection should be conducted? The answer depends on comparing the cost of inspection with the cost of not inspecting. The challenge is to keep inspection costs minimum, yet realise expected quality. In certain cases, every part is inspected, in which case, it is called 100 per cent inspection. When it is less than 100 per cent, it is called partial or sampling inspection. Parts with high value and those having tendency to run into large number of rejects are normally subject to 100% inspection.

When to inspect is the next relevant question. In general, inspection is desired at -

(i) Finished products and parts to know that, correct parts are to be assembled or products are right when shipped;
(ii) Before an expensive processing,
(iii) The output of automatic machine periodically, so that, possible errors are confined to small quantities, and
(iv) Before an operation that cannot be undone, for example, in mixing paint.

Where to inspect is also a related question. Inspection may be performed in one of several basic locations: inspection scripts, at inspection stations in the production line, or a series of production locations serviced on a rowing basis.

Crib inspection involves moving of lot quantities of parts to specific locations, set apart for inspection. These lots are inspected and returned to the next production line. Crib inspection results is followed when, production flows from operation to operation on production line. In such cases, it is desirable to locate inspection stations at selected points along the line. One problem with this arrangement is that, bottlenecks may develop if, inspection efforts do not balance with the flow of production. If flow of production does not match with inspection, there might be idle time of the latter. This method is desirable, when the item to be inspected is large and difficult to move. In such a case, it is desirable that the inspector moves to the location of the work. The inspector may periodically visit the work place - or may go to the location of the work, when required.

Statistical Quality Control (SQC) for Process Control

Mainly, SQC is used for controlling quality during production in mass production industries which produce standard products. SQC for process control is based on the probability theory. It is common knowledge that, when several identical parts are manufactured, some are a little large and some a little small, but most will be approximately the same. The middle or average will be the most frequent, with smaller and larger sizes as extremes from the average. When the frequency or count of the items by size is plotted with size on the horizontal scale and count on the vertical scale, a normal or bell-shaped curve of the type given in Fig. 5.2 is obtained.

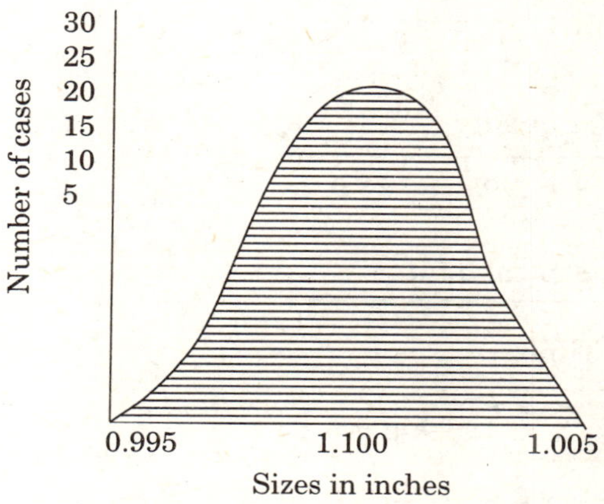

Fig. 5.2. Bell Shaped Curve

Variations in size between 0.995 inches and 1.005 inches, with most measuring 1.000 inches are due to chance causes. Chance causes are inherent and cannot be controlled or prevented. Chance causes are ignored because any effort to eliminate them is uneconomical and may be counter-productive too. However, if the size measures beyond 1.005 inches or below 0.995 inches, it is not due to chance causes but because of assignable causes. In other words, the part is not normal. Assignable causes include internal temperature and wear and tear of the machine parts, a worn-out-tool, improper dimension of raw material, or the setting of the machine being changed unintentionally. When it is known that an improper size is made as a result of an assignable cause, it is possible to stop, detect the cause and rectify it.

In practice, SQC for process control manifests through control charts. Control charts, first developed by Dr. Walter A. Shewhart of the Bell Telephone Laboratories during the 1920s, are horizontal extensions of the bell-shaped curve.

A typical control chart consists of a central line corresponding to the average quality oat which the process is to perform and two other lines corresponding to the upper and lower control limits, also called the tolerate limits. The vertical scale indicates the quality variations and the horizontal scale has time. Samples of product are taken at specified time intervals, quality checked, measured, averaged and plotted on the chart. If the values plotted are within the control limits, the processing is said to be under control. If the values move away from control limits, the process must be improved. In the Fig. 5.3, values are within control limits. Naturally, the process is under control.

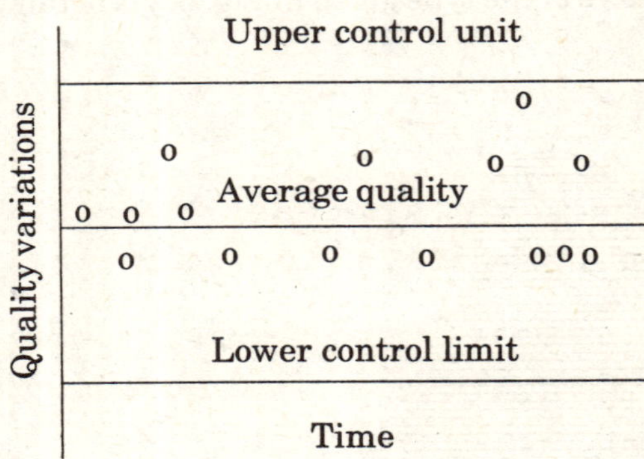

Fig. 5.3.

(This is the bell-shaped curves are adapted form Principle of Management by George R. Terry)

Quality Control Charts

When statistical quality control is used to control operations, samples of products are checked from time to time, and their measurements are plotted on "control charts." Since it is impossible to make two absolutely identical products, some minor variations in measurement always occur, even when the machines are in adjustment. A machine will occasionally produce an unacceptable item, even when it is in adjustment. Control charts show when operations are producing too many unacceptable products and indicate to operators when they need to reset their machines.

Statistical quality control for accepting or rejecting entire lots of products ("acceptance" sampling) usually deals with the proportion of rejects found in a sample. When a lot contains considerably more or considerably less than the allowable proportion of rejects, this will almost surely be revealed by even a small sample. Additional samples need be taken only when the small initial sample provides borderline (or near borderline) results.

Statistical quality control for quality auditing also operates on a sample basis. Faults in samples of completed products are classified according to their seriousness, and demerits are assigned (see Chart below). Major defects -- those which will interfere with the product's salability or its operation or which might be dangerous may be assigned, say, 25 to 50 demerits, depending on the seriousness of the defects. Minor defects, which might shorten the life of the product or increase its maintenance costs, may be assigned 10 demerits. Incidental defects, such as appearance blemishes, may be given 5 (or even only 1) demerits, depending on their seriousness. Ratios of the numbers of demerits found, per unit of product inspected, can be compared for products made at different periods of time. Ratios can also be combined to get departmentor even plant-wide-averages to use in further comparisons.

Quality audits are not just limited to defects detected before they are sold. Hewlett-Packard, for example, maintains a worldwide product defect surveillance system which classifies product failures in the field. This information is fed back so SQC, engineering design, and manufacturing can take corrective action.

An SQC by-product is the evaluation of the reasonableness of tolerances and specifications. SQC may reveal that the standards cannot be met satisfactorily with the company's existing labour skill levels and machines. If so. the labour force may need to be trained or upgraded, or the company may have to invest in better machines. Or, finally, if the rejects are still high, the managers may have to relax the standards or simply "live with" high reject rates.

SQC may also show that the design itself is faulty. If individual', parts meet all the quality standards but the finished product still does not perform well then the fault is in the design and not in the manufacturing processes.

Demerit List-Step by Step Switch Mechanisms

Attributes and Variables

When inspectors look at a product and say "It passes" or "It is a reject," they are dealing with "attributes." But if they measure "how much," "how thick," "how round," and so on, they are dealing with "variables."

A distinction needs to be made between attributes and variables because they require different statistical procedures. Attributes deal with percentages (or proportions) of products rejected. Variables deal with averages of measurements and the extent of the deviations. Attribute inspection is most important in acceptance sampling inspecting products away from the operation and after considerable quantities have been made - as in the case of purchased items. Variable inspection is more important in controlling operations as they are being performed because most of it is done at the job.

Attribute inspection is used (1) when items are obviously good or bad (an alarm stock rings or it doesn't; or (2) when the characteristics cannot be easily measured, thus forcing an inspector to judge them (as in the degree of shine on a polished surface or deciding whether a soldered connection is good enough); or (3) when a characteristic can be measured but the exact amount is not needed (as when go/no-go gages are used to

DEMERIT LIST – STEP BY STEP SWITCH MECHANISMS

Item	Dem.	Defect description	Item	Dem.	Defect description
	1.	*ELECTRICAL*			Rotary Pawl springs:
101 B	50	Breakdown Between (parts) on (specified) voltage	2010C	10	Opening in loop exceeds specified limit
		Cross or ground between (parts):	2011C	10	Rotary Pawl play: rotary pawl binds
102A	100	Affecting circuit, not readily corrected			Vertical position of rotary armature:
102B	50	Affecting circuit, readily corrected	2012B	50	no overlap
			2012C	10	overlap not as specified
			2013C	10	Rotary pawl position not as specified
103C	10	Clearance between insulated parts insufficient			Rotary magnet position:
		Open circuit:	2014C	10	rotary dog and ratchet
104A	100	not readily corrected			tooth clearance not as specified
104B	50	readily corrected Current flow; release magnet coil:	2015C	10	armature does not strike both magnet cores
105B	50	more than 10% outside of specified value	2016C	10	clearance between rotary pawl and front stop not as specified
106C	10	armature does not release after operation on specified current	2017C	10	Rotary pawl guide position: rotary pawl tip does not strike tooth as specified
107B	50	Contacts dirty; breaking continuity	2018C	10	Normal pin position: rotary pawl does not strike first tooth in same relative position as other teeth
	2.	*MECHANICAL*			
2001C	10	Bank or wiper contacts not cleaned or treated			

inspect for size). Most inspection of metal, glass, cloth, or painted surfaces for cracks, scratches, or surface irregularities, and most inspection of cotor finish are attribute inspections.

Most measurements of dimensions, however, as well as all types of length-of-life tests, are inspection of variables. The tested items always differ somewhat, and it is necessary to tabulate and analyze the frequency of each measurement.

Representative Samples

As mentioned earlier, the entire lot from which a sample is taken is called the "inspection lot." the "total population." the "parent population," or the "universe."

If statistical quality control is to operate successfully, samples must be "representative." meaning they must have about the same characteristics as the lots from which they are taken. In SQC, the word "sample" always refers to a representative sample. It does not mean a non-representative, non-typical, or poor sample. When samples are referred to as "random" samples, the intent has been to obtain a representative sample. It does not mean a non-representative, non-typical, or poor sample. When samples are referred to as "random" samples, the intent has been to obtain a representative sample. A random sample from a barrel of material would include materials taken from the top, middle, bottom, outside and inside of the barrel. A random sample of automatically machined products should include items taken at the end.

Products being sampled should be, and usually are, homogenous (the same throughout). If they are not -- if some boxes of parts have more bad items in them than other boxes -- the inspector must be very careful to see that he gets a representative sample. He should, for example, draw part of the sample from every box or at least allow each box to have an equal chance of being included in the sample, in fact. the inspector should always do this, whether he suspects that the various boxfuls are of unequal quality or not.

In factory inspection, ordinarily only one universe, such as a shipment of products received from one vendor or one run of products from an automatic machine, needs to be considered at a time. It is desirable, however, to consider each day's output from automatic machines as a separate lot. A random sample of each day's, or each hour's, output should be inspected separately in order to catch gradual changes in the products which might be caused by tool wear or by the machine's gradually getting out of adjustment.

Size of Sample

It seems logical that large samples should be more reliable than small samples. One might even suspect that if one sample is twice as large as another it would be twice as reliable. Large samples are more representative of the population but not at all proportionally better. We can't say exactly how much better a large sample is because, whereas a sample of 20 is considerably more reliable than 10, there is almost no gain in reliability if a sample of 1,000 is increased to 2.000 yet, in each case the sample size is doubled. In fact, in the inspection of variables, the gain in reliability from inspecting a sample of 300 instead of 200 is rarely worth the added inspection costs. Sample sizes in the hundreds are all quite reliable, depending, of course, on how much variability there is in the population being sampled and how tightly the item is to be controlled. From there on, little reliability is added by inspecting more pieces. For attribute inspection, typical sample sizes need to be a little higher, but they too become quite reliable at the 300 or 400 level.

Even small samples are almost completely reliable for lots which are quite good or quite bad. When inspecting variables, a sample size of 25 will produce virtually conclusive results if it is found to be much better or much worse than the limit of acceptability because it is very unlikely that a sample will be very good or very bad when the entire lot is not correspondingly good or bad. A sample of 100 pieces, in such a case, would add little to the reliability of the results found in the smaller sample. But, if a 25-piece sample turns out to be of borderline quality, it is not so certain whether the whole lot should pass. Inspecting a 100-piece sample adds a great deal of certainty that the lot is borderline good or borderline bad.

Another matter is the size of the sample as it relates to the universe. The reliability of a sample does not depend on its proportion of the universe: its reliability is almost entirely dependent on its own numerical size. The size of the whole lot has little effect on the sample's reliability. A sample of 200 taken from a lot of 5,000 is almost as reliable an indicator of the whole 5,000 as a sample of 200 taken from a lot of 1,000. Yet. in the first case it is a 4-percent sample as against 20 percent in the second case. This fact, used in sampling inspection, permits considerable inspection cost savings by confining the sample to the smallest practicable quantity. Only very small samples, proportionately, need to be inspected from large lots.

Eastman Kodak sets the sample size for much of its inspection by using the following formula (in which n is the sample size and N is the whole lot):

$$n = \sqrt{2n}$$

Using this formula, a sample of 200 would suffice for a lot of 20,000. Eastman inspects larger samples for products it thinks might he of uneven quality. But the largest samples, even if Eastman suspects that a lot is of uneven quality, are limited to 2.5 times the usual sample or 500 in the case of a 20,000 lot.

Sometimes, no matter how large a sample is taken and how sophisticated the quality control system is, enough "bad" items slip through which can be disastrous. For example, the Wall Street Journal reported that in 1975 H. J, Heinz shut down its production process for instant dry baby cereal because of the fourth complaint over metal particles found in the food. Heinz "recalled" about 600,000 boxes from the market. The total cost of the recall was $ 250,000.

The Normal Curve and the Standard Deviation

Statistical quality control is based on the concept that no two things are exactly alike. And that when either people or nature try to make identical products, their actual sizes will vary from small to large with most items being ctose to the middle size. The most frequent size will be the middle size with less frequent items being at the larger and smaller extremes.

The count of items by size, when plotted on a chart, nearly always approximates a "normal" or "bell-shaped" curve. Occasionally the curve is pulled off to one side ("skewed"), showing that there are more extreme deviations above the norm or more extreme deviations smaller than the norm. If there is an extremely pronounced variation from the normal distribution, different statistical procedures need to be used to analyze the data and the usual kind of statistical quality control methods should not be used.

In a normal distribution there is a progressive tapering off of the number of items above and below the point of greatest frequency, which itself is the highest point on the curve and is in the middle of the curve. This highest point is the average measurement (the "arithmetic mean") of the series. Expected variations in measurements of individual items from the mean can be determined on the basis of the way the data vary when the overall pattern follows the normal curve.

SQC deals with samples, not entire lots. Each item of a sample is measured. Then a tabulation of the frequency of each measurement can be made up. tabulated, and plotted on a chart. Almost always this chart will turn out to be a bell-shaped curve but based on perhaps 50 to 100 measurements rather than 10,000 measurements for an entire lot. The distribution of measurements between large and small in the sample will be about the same as in the parent population. If the sample is of reasonable size and is random, it will be representative of the whole population.

In statistical quality control it is first necessary to calculate the "standard deviation".

The standard deviation for a sample is usually indicated by the Greek letter sigma, "σ". The letter sigma refers to the standard deviation for the while population, which is actually never known when samples are used. When a sample is used, the standard deviation of the measurements of the items in the sample is denoted "S." When subsamples are used, then each subsample has its own arithmetic mean and the measure of variability of these several subsample means is Sx. It is called the "standard error of the mean of the sampling distribution." Its calculation formula is:

$$S_i = \frac{S}{\sqrt{n}}$$

The normal curve distribution pattern which lies behind statistical quality control

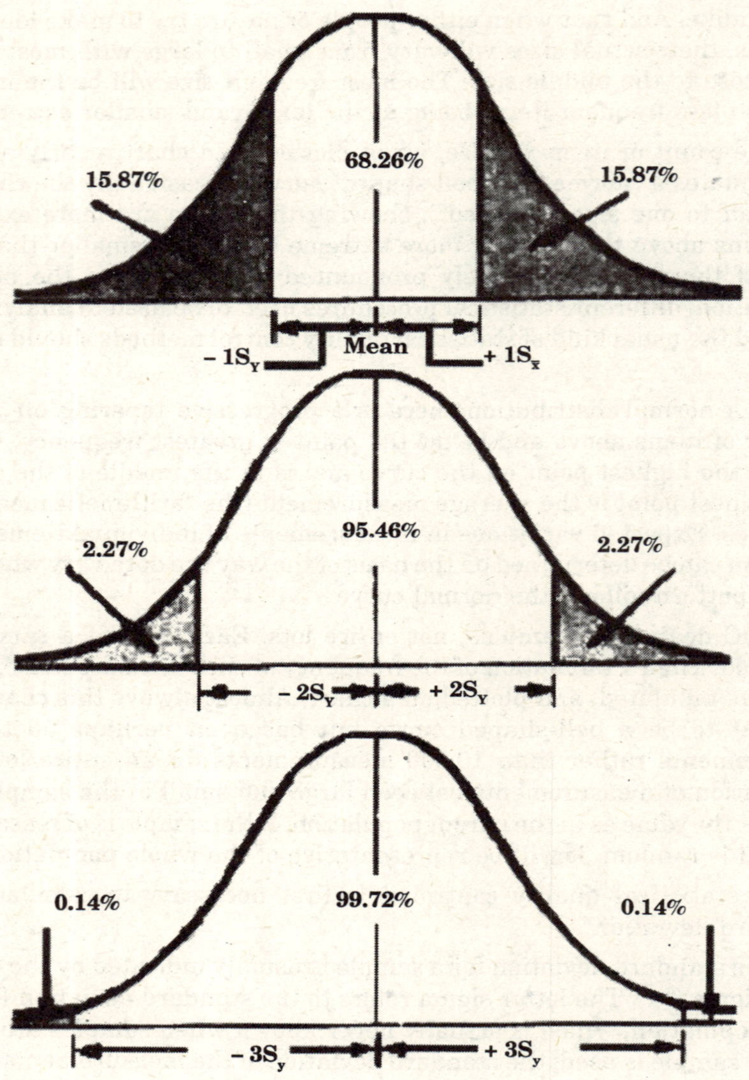

where n is the sample size

In a normal distribution, as shown in Figure above, the mean 1 Sx sets limits between 68.3 percent of the measures of the sampled products fall. The mean 2 Sx set limits which include 95.5 percent of the cases, while 3 Sx sets limits which include 99.7 percent of the cases.

An example will show how this works. If a pan 4 inches long is being manufactured, close measurement will show that the parts vary in size, most of them being close to but not exactly 4 inches long. The arithmetic mean of the pieces in our sample, however, ought to be almost exactly 4 inches. We will say that the mean length of the parts in our sample is exactly 4 inches and Sx is .002 inches. Therefore 4 inches + and -1 Sx is 4.002 and 3.998 inches respectively; so 68.3 percent of the sample measurements for very close to it are between these limits. Measuring out 2 Sx produces measurements of 4.004 and 3.996 inches. These measurements will include 95.5 percent of the cases. Three Sx out each way, Or 4.006 and 3.994 inches, will include 99.7 percent of the cases.

Statisticians have developed short-cut methods for doing the calculations. An example demonstrating a short-cut for setting control limits for control charts is shown in Table One below. SQC is also helpful in the cases where extremes are important, as for example, with the weakest link in a chain. It is all very good for the average strength of each link in a chain to be well above the minimum, but, if even if one link is too weak, the chain breaks. Charts can be set up so that attention is focused on such extremes.

In other cases consistency is more important. Suppose a company buys two lots of 1/8 inch (0.1250 inches) diameter ball bearings. And suppose lot A's mean is .1248 inches but lot B's mean is exactly .1250 inches. But within lot A the individual balls range between .1247 and .1251 inches, while in lot B, with the perfect mean, the individual size range from .1240 to .1260 inches. Which lot would probably work out best? Probably lot A, because no ball bearing varies more than 3/10,000 of an inch from the specified 1/8 inch size, while in lot B some vary as much as 10/10,000 of an inch. Many SQC applications deal with this matter of consistency.

Whether the interest is in means, extremes, standard errors, or percentages, statistical quality control is directed (I) towards obtaining measurements, test scores, or percent defectives of items in the sample; (2) to computing the combined measures for the sample: (3) to comparing the combined sample measures to preset scales showing the limits of acceptability; and (4) if the measures exceed the limits of acceptability, some action must be taken to remedy the situation.

Control Charts for Operations

Books on statistical quality control do not furnish precomputed control charts for general use. Instead, they explain how to set up and use control charts. This is because every control chart has to be unique for the operation it serves.

Figure below shows the steps to go through for setting up control charts the end product of a process that starts with collecting and analyzing certain figures about an operation. This has to be done separately for every job where control charts are to be used.

Step 1

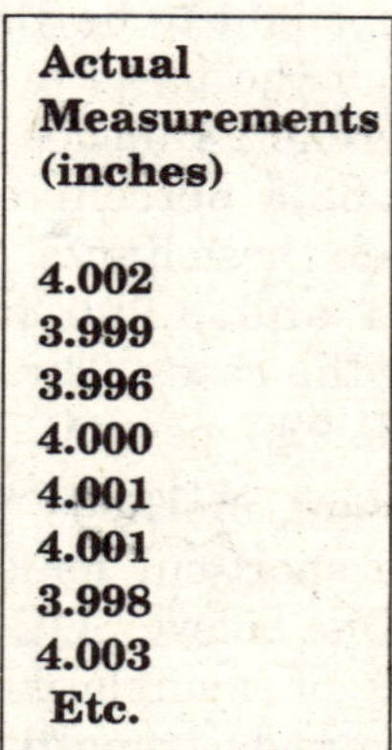

Step 2

Compute X, the arithmetic mean of the measurements

Step 3

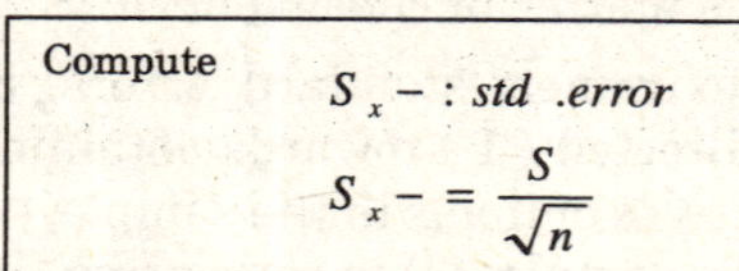

Step 4

Compute

$$S_x - : std\ .error$$

$$S_x - = \frac{S}{\sqrt{n}}$$

Step 5

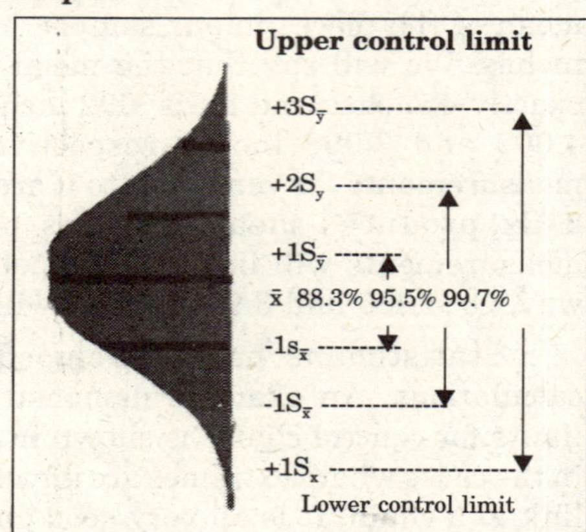

Step 6

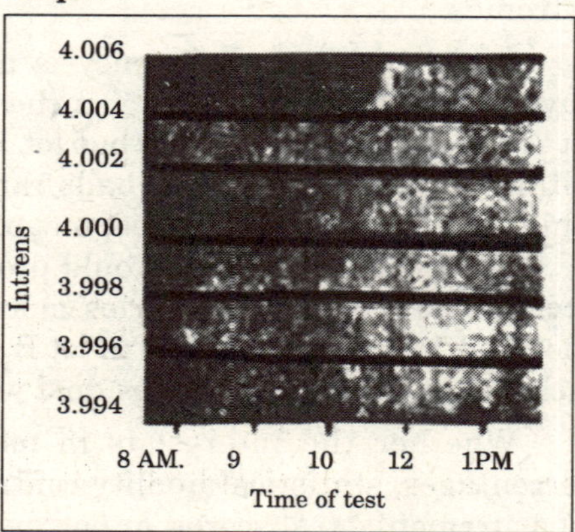

To make a control chart, it is first necessary to measure each item of a random sample of items made by an operation. Suppose that 40 such measurements are made of parts intended to be 4 inches long. The mean of the 40 proves to be 4 inches exactly and Sx is .002 inches, as in our earlier example. The 3 Sx control limits (3.994 and 4.006 inches respectively) are then plotted in along a vertical measurement scale, as done in Fig below.

Horizontal lines are drawn across to the right to "fence in" the area of acceptable measurements . The horizontal scale is a time scale for plotting the measurements taken periodically throughout the day.

Before using a control chart, however, it should be checked against the job's specified tolerance limits. The 3 Sx, limits are 4.006 and 3.994 inches respectively. If the specification says 4 inches 0.010, then the operation can proceed because all of the production is well within the 4.010

Table showing relationship between sample size n and the Control limits.

Number in each small sample	Factor
2	1.88
3	1.02
4	.73
5	.58
6	.48
7	.42
8	.37
9	.34
10	.31

and 3.990 limits. But if the specification says 4 inches 0.004. then only 95 percent of the products will pass. The operation will probably have to be improved.

Now that the control chart is set up, it is used by having the inspector in the factory mea-sure a very small sample of products (as few as three to five every half hour or so) and plot the mean of these measurements on the chart, as is done in Figure B below. If one of these means falls outside the control limits, something is almost certainly wrong with the production process. This is called assignable variation because almost always the variation can be said to be caused by the machine being out of adjustment.

If the mean fluctuates within the control limits, these fluctuations are called chance variations and are regarded just as normal variability representing the best that the machine can do.

The point is that when the point being plotted falls outside the control limits, this serves as a signal, and the inspector and the operator are warned to stop the machine and get it back into adjustment. Some companies also show lines on the chart for 2 standard errors. When the means being plotted get beyond these limits, this serves as a warning that the machine is getting out of adjustment, and although it is not yet off far enough as to be producing rejects, it is moving that way.

As we said, however, statisticians have developed a short-cut method for determining control limits for control charts. Suppose we plan to inspect a sample of four every half hoar after the chart is set up. First it is necessary to take a random sample of items, say as many as 40. These measurements should not be sorted into any order (as from large to small). They should be used just as they come.

For each set of four, its mean measurement is calculated, as is its range (the difference between the largest and smallest item in the set of four). This produces ten means and ten ranges. Next, the mean should be calculated (by adding the ten such sample means together and dividing by ten).

Reference can now be made to the table above. Reading down to four, the number in our subsample, we find the factor (F) = 0.73.

The upper control limit is obtained by multiplying the mean range by .73 and adding the result to the grand mean. The same amount is subtracted from the grand mean to get the lower control limit. Let us assume that the pieces are supposed to be 4 inches and the mean range of the 10 samples is .009 inches. Multiplying .009 by .73 gives .006. Adding this to - and subtracting it from - 4 inches establishes control limits of 4.006 and 3.994 inches. We can now plot these lines as the control limits on the control chart.

We have been talking about controlling the means of sub samples, but there is usually a need to control variability as well. Two pieces, one 3 inches long and one 5 inches long, average 4 inches long. But this is not much comfort to an assembler who wants two pieces each 4 inches long.

Variability is controlled by paying attention to the range (the difference between the largest and smallest items in the samples). Control charts to monitor the range are developed in almost exactly the same way as charts to control means. Short-cut methods are also available to allow these charts to be set up in a matter of minutes.

Advantage of SQC

SQC offers several advantages to its users. Hence, it is being increasingly used in the industrial field. Some of the advantages of SQC are:

1. It helps prevent defects from being made. Assignments causes signifying deviations in quality are detected and rectified. Costly rework, rejection and scrap are avoided.
2. It also helps avoidance of the risk of accepting a bad lot.
3. Emphasising on inspection of only samples, SQC avoids inspection of the entire lot.
4. It ensures the maintenance of high standards of quality and enables the users to build up their goodwill.
5. Another important reason for using SQC is to supply an audit of quality regarding the producers' products. A universally understood measurement is supplied. In addition, the reasonableness of the quality standards established are checked. Frequently, this is a 'free extra', but in some cases, quite important information is heeded.

As process control and acceptance sampling are two prominent techniques of quality control, it is proposed to discuss them in greater detail. Two terms need to be clarified before the detailed discussion. They are : (i) sampling and (ii) central limit theorem.

Sampling : It is the process of selecting and measuring (or inspecting) representative units of output, termed sample units. A set of sample units is termed sample. The sample units are drawn from the lot (universe or population) at random. A random sample is one in which each unit in the lot has an equal chance of being included in the sample and the sample is likely to be representative of the lot.

Central limit theorem : This theorem is stated as 'Sampling distributions can be assumed to be normally distributed even though the population distributions are not normal.'

Figure 5.4 compares a population distribution with its sampling distribution of sample means.

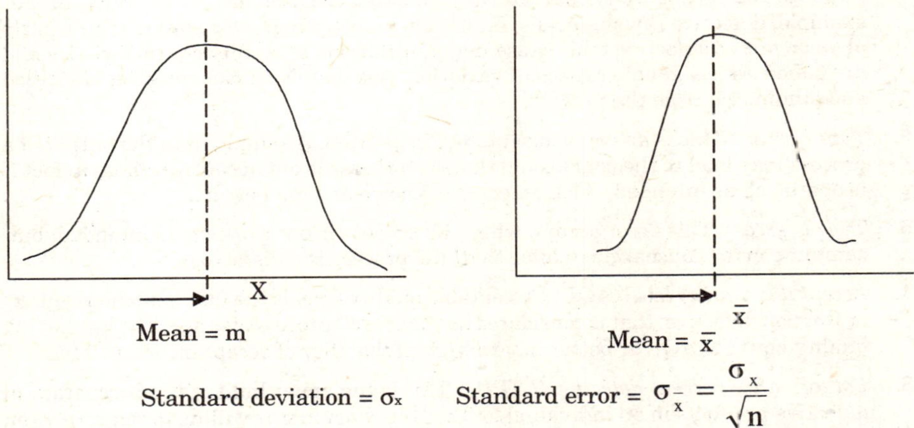

Fig. 5.4. A comparison of population and sampling distributions

The following generalisations are made about sampling distributions:

1. The sampling distribution can be assumed to be normally distributed unless the sample size (n) is extremely small (i.e., less than five).
2. The mean of the sampling distribution ($\bar{\bar{x}}$) is equal to the population mean (μ).
3. The standard error of the sampling distribution ($\sigma_{\bar{x}}$) is smaller than the population standard deviation (σx) by a factor of ($\frac{1}{\sqrt{n}}$

Table 5.1: lists some of the terms used under statistical process control and acceptance sampling techniques.

Table 5.1. Definition of Terms used in SQC Techniques.

1. *Variables :* Variables are quality characteristics that can be measured on a continuous scale. For example, the diameter of a shaft can be measured by a dial micrometer before taking a decision regarding the quality i.e., whether the diameter is within the permissible limits of variation.

2. *Attributes* : Attributes are quality characteristics which can be classified into one of the two categories namely good or bad, defective or non-defective. For example, a painted surface is good or bad depending on the quality of the workmanship of the painter and the quality of the paint used.

3. *Chance causes of variation :* Chance causes are reasons for minor variations in the quality characteristics that are inspected. These causes do not cause the item to be rejected as the variation are within the limits (i.e. tolerance limits). Chance causes of variation are inherent in the process.

4. *Assignable causes of variation :* These causes are external to the process and cause large variations in quality characteristics making the item liable to be rejected. For example, defective raw materials, faulty machine settings, worn out machine parts or worn out or defective tools cause major variations in quality characteristics and are called as assignable causes of variation. Assignable causes must be identified and eliminated from the process.

5. *Type I error :* This is an error in sampling inspection. A sample from the output of a process may lead to the conclusion, that the process is out of control when, in fact it is operating as intended. Such an error is known as type I error.

6. *Type II error :* This error occurs, when the process is not working as intended, but, sampling error causes one to infer that, the process is satisfactory.

7. *Acceptable quality level (AQL) :* Acceptable quality level is the maximum percentage or fraction defective, that is considered as the overall process average. The lots having quality equal to AQL or better have a high probability of acceptance (i.e., 0.95)

8. *Lot tolerance percent defective (LTPD) :* This is the upper limit of the percentage of defective products in an individual lot that the consumer is willing to tolerate, even if the process average is acceptable. This is also known as limiting quality level (LQL). Lots having quality equal to LTPD or worse have a very low probability of acceptance (i.e., 0.10)

9. *Producer's Risk (a) :* This is the risk of getting a sample which has a higher proportion of defectives than the lot as a whole and thereby rejecting a good lot based on sample evidence, i.e. a lot as good as AQL will be rejected by use of a particular sampling plan. While using acceptance sampling plans, producers hope to keep this risk (a) as low as 5%.

10. *Consumer's Risk (ß) :* This is the risk getting a sample which has a lower proportion of defectives than the lot as a whole and thereby accepting a bad lot as a good lot. i.e. it is the probability that a lot with a percentage of defective equal to the LTPD will be accepted by the sampling plan. While using sampling plans, consumers want to keep this risk (ß) as low as 10%.

11. Average outgoing quality (AOQ) : In a production process, if the lots that are produced have an average fraction defection p' and if some of the lots which are rejected based on sample evidence are inspected 100 percent and the defective units are either simply removed or replaced with nondefective ones, the average quality of the outgoing lots after inspection improves. This average level of quality leaving the inspection operation is called average outgoing quality (AOQ).

Table 5.2. Basic types of control charts and control limits.

Quality Characteristic	Applicable control chart	Formula to compute control control limits
Variables	$\bar{X}$ - R chart (Mean – Range chart)	a) For chart control line CL = $\bar{X}$ Upper control limit $UCL_{\bar{x}} = \bar{\bar{X}} - A_2\bar{R}$ Lower control limit $LCL_{\bar{x}} = \bar{\bar{X}} - A_2\bar{R}$ For 'R' chart: central line CL = $\bar{R}$ b) Upper control limit $UCL_{\bar{R}} = D_4\bar{R}$ Lower control limit $LCL_{\bar{R}} = D_3\bar{R}$, Where A_2, D_3 and D_4 are constants whoe value depends on the sample size 'n' (Refer Table 20.3 for values of constants)
Attributes	i) 'np' chart ("Number of defective charts", for constant sample size 'n')	i) Central line $CL = n\bar{p}$ $UCL = n\bar{p} + 3\sqrt{n\bar{p}(1-\bar{p})}$ $LCL = n\bar{p} - 3\sqrt{n\bar{p}(1-\bar{p})}$ LCL = 0 if its value is negative.
	ii) 'p' chart ("Fraction defective chart" for varying sample size	ii) $CL = \bar{p}$ $UCL = \bar{p} + 3\sqrt{\frac{\bar{p}(1-\bar{p})}{\text{sample size}}}$ $LCL = \bar{p} - 3\sqrt{\frac{\bar{p}(1-\bar{p})}{\text{sample size}}}$ LCL = 0 if its value is negative.
	iii) 'c' chart ("Number of defects chart" for constant sample size	iii) $CL = \bar{c}$ $UCL = \bar{c} + 3\sqrt{\bar{c}}$ $LCL = \bar{c} - 3\sqrt{\bar{c}}$ LCL = 0 if its value is negative
	iv) 'u' chart ("number of defects per unit" chart for varying sample size	iv) $CL = \bar{u}$ $UCL = \bar{u} + 3\sqrt{\frac{\bar{u}}{\text{sample size}}}$ $LCL = \bar{u} - 3\sqrt{\frac{\bar{u}}{\text{sample size}}}$ LCL = 0 if its value is negative

Table 5.3. Values of Constants for $\overline{X}$ – R Chart (Also refer Anexure-A).

Sample size 'n'	A_2	D_2	D_4	Sample size 'n'	A_2	D_2	D_4
2	1.880	0	3.267	10	0.308	0.223	1.777
3	1.023	0	2.575	15	0.223	0.348	1.652
4	0.729	0	2.282	20	0.180	0.414	1.586
5	0.577	0	2.116	25	0.153	0.459	1.541

Types of Control Charts

The way that control charts are constructed differs according to the quality characteristics that are controlled. Accordingly control charts can be broadly classified as

(a) Control charts for variables.

(b) Control charts for attributes.

Table 20.2 gives the basic types of control charts and the control limits for the same

Construction of Control Charts

A control chart is a graphic comparison of process performance and data with computed control limits drawn as limit lines on a chart. Measurements taken from product quality are plotted on a graph sheet on which three limit lines are drawn viz, (i) a central line indication the desired process average (i.e. the average level of the quality characteristic) (ii) two lines equi-spaced from the central line, indicating upper control limit and lower control limits. After there three limit lines are established, they become the bench-marks against which to compare future samples.

The control chart distinguishes between chance causes and assignable causes of variations by fixing the natural limits of variation viz., the upper control limit and the lower control limit. If the process operates under chance causes of variation only, the probability of actual variation to exceed the control limits is very low. If actual variation exceeds control limits, it gives a signal that assignable causes have entered into the process and action is required for controlling the process.

Usually, two kinds of information are available from control charts

(i) Whether the process is running under stable condition or not i.e., whether the process is under the 'state of statistical control' or not.

(ii) Whether the process is meeting the desired quality standards or not. If statistical control does not exist, it has to be established through technical control.

Construction of $\overline{X}$ - R(Mean-range Chart) (for variable quality characteristics).

There are two viz $\overline{X}$ chart and 'R' chart employed in analyzing a variable data. There is no meaningful interpretation obtained if the $\overline{X}$ chart or 'R' chart are analysed individually, ' $\overline{X}$ - R' charts have to exist as a 'pair' - Interpretation regarding the quality of the on-going process has to be done analyzing both the charts simultaneously.

The various steps involved in the constructions of $\overline{X}$ and R charts are listed below.

Step No. 1 : Choice of variable (X) - choose the quality characteristic C variable which gives maximum possible scope for cost reduction through control of the process. Also ensure that the quality characteristic can be measured quantitatively.

Step No. 2 : Selection of rational sub-groups: rational sub-groups are homogeneous observations grouped into small groups (sample size varying from 3 to 20, 4 or 5 being ideal)

Step No. 3 : Choice of frequency: Frequency is the time interval between successive measurements of quality characteristics of sub groups. Usually, it is determined as a percentage of the quantity of products measured or as a percentage of the total duration of the manufacturing process.

Step No. 4 : Collect about 'K' number of sub-groups (usually K = 25) each of convenient sample size 'n' (say 4 to 10)

Step No. 5 : For each sub-group, calculate, mean

$$\overline{X} = \frac{\Sigma X}{n} = \frac{X_1 + X_2 + \ldots X_n}{n}$$

And Range $R = X_{max} - X_{min}$

Step No. 6 : Calculate the average of different ranges for 'K' sub-groups i.e., $\overline{R} = \frac{\Sigma R}{K} = \frac{R_1 + R_2 + R_k}{K}$

Step No. 7 : Compute central line ($\overline{R}$), upper control limit and lower control limit for Range Chart using the formulae.

Central line $\overline{R} = \frac{\Sigma R}{K} = \frac{R_1 + R_2 + R_k}{K}$

Upper control limit $UCL_R = D_4 \overline{R}$

Lower control limit $LCL_R = D_3 \overline{R}$,

Step No. 8 : Test for homogeneity. Compare all individual range values for 'K' sub-groups with the values of UCL_R and LCL_R. If these individual range values fall in between the values of UCL_R and LCL_R, all range values are said to be 'homogeneous' and then the sub-groups are known as 'rational' sub-groups.

Step No. 9 : If the sub-groups are not homogeneous, remove the sample results which are out of the range limits (i.e., UCL_R and LCL_R) compute modified $\overline{R}$, modified UCL_R and modified LCL_R till homogeneity is obtained.

Step No. 10 :For the homogenized sub-groups (say)

Calculate, $\overline{\overline{X}} = \frac{\Sigma\overline{X}}{K_1} = \frac{X_1 + X_2 + ...X_{K_1}}{K_1}$

and compute upper control limit and lower control limit using the formulae

$ULC_{\overline{X}} = \overline{\overline{X}} + A_2\overline{R}$ and $LCL_{\overline{X}} = \overline{\overline{X}} + A_2\overline{R}$

Step No. 11 : Test for homogeneity : Compare all individual values of $\overline{x}$ for K_1 sub-groups with the values of $ULC_{\overline{X}}$ and . $LCL_{\overline{X}}$

If these individual values of $\overline{X}$ fall in between the values of $ULC_{\overline{X}}$ and $LCL_{\overline{X}}$, these $\overline{X}$ values of are homogenous and K_1 sub-groups are known as rational sub-groups.

Step No. 12 :If the above condition for homogeneity is not satisfied, remove sample results for which $\overline{X}$ values fall outside the control limits and re-calculate the values of modified $\overline{X}$, modified $ULC_{\overline{X}}$ and modified $LCL_{\overline{X}}$ till homogeneity is achieved.

Step No. 13 :Construct $\overline{X}$ chart and 'R' chart for the rational sub-groups obtained after testing homogeneity. The charts are drawn as shown in Figure 5.5 below.

Step No. 14 :

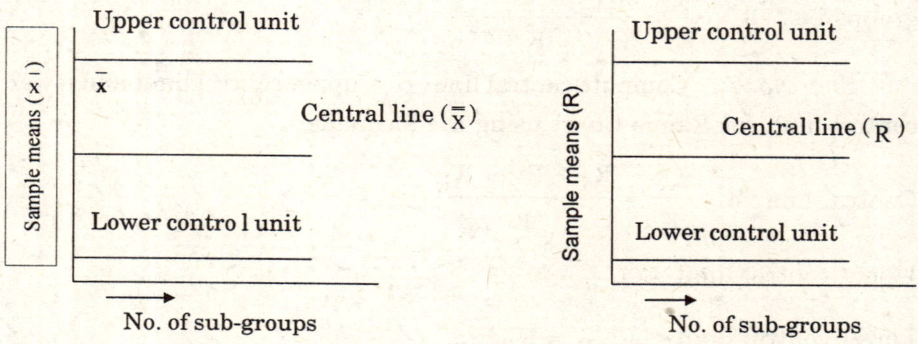

Fig. 5.5(a) Mean chart ($\overline{X}$ chart) **Fig. 5.5(b)** Range chart ($\overline{R}$ chart)

Illustration of construction of $\overline{X}$- R Chart

Product - Wirebonded transistor

Parameter (variable quality characteristic which is measured) - Bond strength.

Specification limit : 3 grams.

Number of samples per subgroup = n = 3.

No. of sub-groups K = 26.

Data collected for 26 sub-group are as below:

	Bond strength in grams				Bond strength in grams		
Sub-group Number	Sample 1	Sample 2	Sample 3	Sub-group Number	Sample 1	Sample 2	Sample 3
1	6.5	6.5	5.0	14	6.0	4.5	4.5
2	6.5	6.0	7.0	15	4.0	6.5	5.5
3	7.0	5.5	5.5	16	4.0	7.0	7.0
4	4.0	3.0	3.5	17	5.0	6.0	4.0
5	2.0	0	1.0	18	3.0	6.0	6.0
6	6.0	6.0	6.0	19	5.5	5.0	7.5
7	6.0	4.0	4.0	20	7.0	6.0	5.0
8	6.0	4.0	6.0	21	5.0	5.0	5.0
9	5.5	5.0	4.5	22	5.0	2.5	3.5
10	7.0	6.0	6.0	23	4.0	5.0	5.0
11	4.0	3.0	3.5	24	4.0	0	2.0
12	4.0	3.5	3.0	25	5.0	3.0	3.5
13	5.0	3.5	5.0	26	2.5	5.0	3.0

Calculation of Mean ($\overline{X}$) and Range (R)

Sub-group No.	Mean ( )	Range (R)	Sub-group No.	Mean ( )	Range (R)
1	6.0	1.5	14	5.0	1.5
2	6.5	1.0	15	5.3	2.5
3	6.0	1.5	16	6.0	3.0
4	3.5	1.0	17	5.0	2.0
5	1.0	2.0	18	5.0	3.0
6	6.0	0	19	6.0	2.5
7	4.6	2.0	20	6.0	2.0
8	5.3	2.0	21	5.0	0
9	5.0	1.0	22	3.6	2.5
10	6.3	1.0	23	4.8	1.5
11	3.5	1.0	24	2.0	4.0
12	3.5	1.0	25	3.8	2.0
13	4.5	1.5	26	3.5	2.5

$$\Sigma \overline{X} = \overline{X_1} + \overline{X_2} + \ldots \overline{X_K} \quad \text{(where K = 26)}$$

$$= \quad 122.7$$

$$\Sigma R = R_1 + R_2 + \ldots R_K \quad \text{(where K = 26)}$$

$$= 45.5$$

$$\overline{\overline{x}} = \frac{\Sigma \overline{X}}{K} = \frac{122.7}{26} = 4.72$$

$$\overline{R} = \frac{\Sigma R}{K} = \frac{45.5}{26} = 1.75$$

$$ULC_{\overline{X}} = \overline{\overline{X}} + A_2 \overline{R} \qquad \left.\begin{array}{r}\text{Value of constat } A_2 \text{ for} \\ \text{for sample size n = 3}\end{array}\right\} = 1.02$$

$$= 4.72 + 1.02 \; 1.75 = 6.50$$

$$LCL_{\overline{X}} = \overline{\overline{X}} + A_2 \overline{R}$$

$$= 4.72 - 1.02 \; 1.75$$

$$= 4.72 - 1.785 = 2.935 = 2.94$$

$$UCL_R = D_4 \overline{R} \qquad \left.\begin{array}{r}\text{Value of constat } D_4 \\ \text{for sample size n = 3}\end{array}\right\} = 2.57$$

$$= 2.57 \; 1.75 \qquad \left.\begin{array}{r}\text{Value of constat } D_3 \\ \text{for sample size n = 3}\end{array}\right\} = \text{Nil}$$

$$= 4.497 = 4.50$$

$$LCL_R = D_3 \overline{R} \;\; \text{Nil}$$

Test for Homogeneity

(i) Since all values of range (R) for 26 sub groups fall in between zero and 4.5 (values of UCL_R and LCL_R), range values are homogeneous.

(ii) $\overline{X}$ values for sub group No.5 and 24 are lower than the value of (i.e., $LCL_{\overline{X}}$ 2.94).

For homogeneity delete the sample results for sub-groups number 5 and 24 and calculate modified values of $CL_{\overline{X}}$, $UCL_{\overline{X}}$, and $LCL_{\overline{X}}$ as below:

Modified $\overline{\overline{X}} = \dfrac{\Sigma \overline{X}}{24} = 4.99$; Modified $\overline{R} = \dfrac{\Sigma R}{24} = 1.64$

Modified $UCL_{\overline{X}} = 6.67$; Modified $LCL_{\overline{X}} = 3.31$

Modified $UCL_R = 4.21$; Modified $LCL_R = \text{Nil}$

Now it may be noted that these 24 sub-groups are homogeneous. The charts are drawn as shown below:

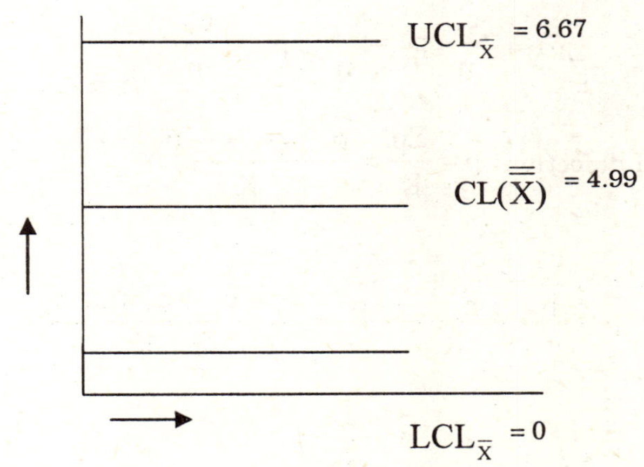

$\overline{X}$ (mean) chart

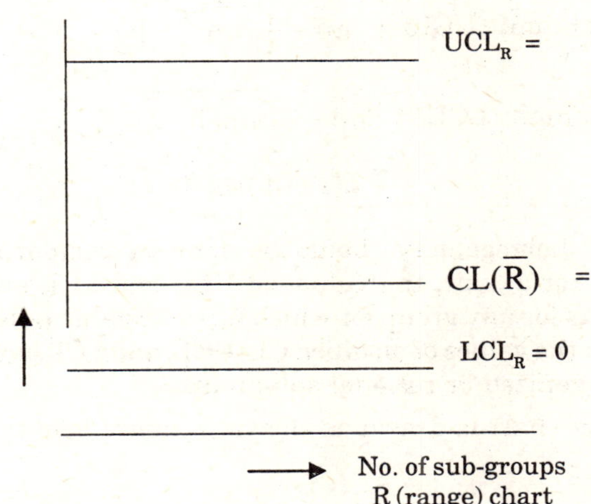

R (range) chart

Control Charts for Attributes

(i) Construction of 'np' chart (Number of defectives chart) for constant sample size 'n':

Sample size = n. Number of sub-groups = K

Number of defectives per sub-group = c

Fraction defective $p = \frac{c}{n}$, calculated for each of K sub-groups i.e,

$$p1 = \frac{c_1}{n}, p_2 = \frac{c_2}{n} \ldots p_K = \frac{c_K}{n}$$

Average fraction defective $\bar{p} = \frac{\Sigma p}{K} = \frac{p_1 + p_2 + \text{--} p_K}{K}$

$$\bar{p} = \frac{\frac{c_1}{n} + \frac{c_2}{n} + \ldots \frac{c_K}{n}}{K} = \frac{c_1 + c_2 + c_3 + \ldots c_K}{n \times K}$$

$$\bar{p} = \frac{\Sigma c}{nK}$$

$$\text{Central line,} = n \times \frac{\Sigma c}{n \times K} = \frac{\Sigma c}{K}$$

Upper control limit (UCL) = $n\bar{p} + 3\sqrt{n\bar{p}(1 - \bar{p})}$

Level control limit (LCL) = $n\bar{p} - 3\sqrt{n\bar{p}(1 - \bar{p})}$

= Zero (if negative)

Test for homogeneity should be done by comparing all individual values of np (or c) with the values of UCL and LCL and discarding the sample results for any group for which np (or c) value falls outside the limit values. Again the values of modified CL, UCL, and LCL have to be calculated for the homogenized or rational sub-groups.

The 'np' chart is drawn as shown in figure below:

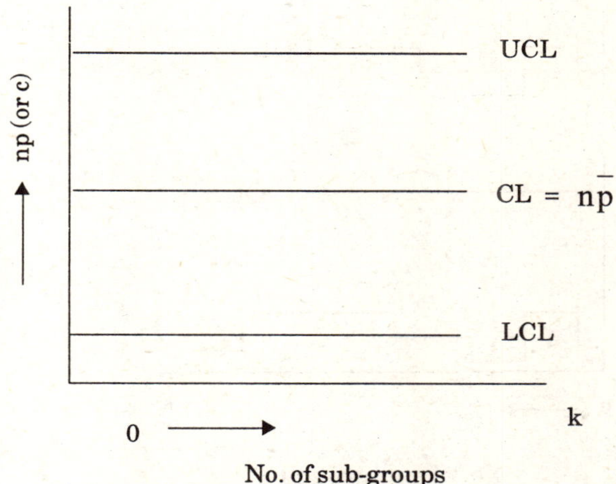

(ii) Construction of 'p' chart (fraction defective chart) for varying sample size:

The data collected gives the sample size ($n_1, + n_2 \ldots n_k$) for k sub groups, and values of number of defectives ($c_1, + c_2 \ldots c_k$) for k sub groups. Fraction defective for each sub-group are calculated as P1 = $\frac{c_1}{n_1}, p_2 = \frac{c_2}{n_2} \ldots p_k = \frac{c_k}{n_k}$

$$\text{Central line } \bar{p} = \frac{\Sigma p}{k} = \frac{p_1 + p_2 + p_k}{k}$$

$$\left.\begin{matrix}\text{Upper control limit (UCL)} \\ \text{for each sub - group}\end{matrix}\right\} = \bar{p} + 3\sqrt{\frac{\bar{p}(1-\bar{p})}{\text{Sample size}}}$$

$$\left.\begin{matrix}\text{Lower control limit (LCL)} \\ \text{for each sub - group}\end{matrix}\right\} = \bar{p} - 3\sqrt{\frac{\bar{p}(1-\bar{p})}{\text{Sample size}}}$$

Since sample size varies for each sub-group; there will be as many values of LCL and UCL as the number of values of sample size. (i.e.)

The chart is drawn as shown.

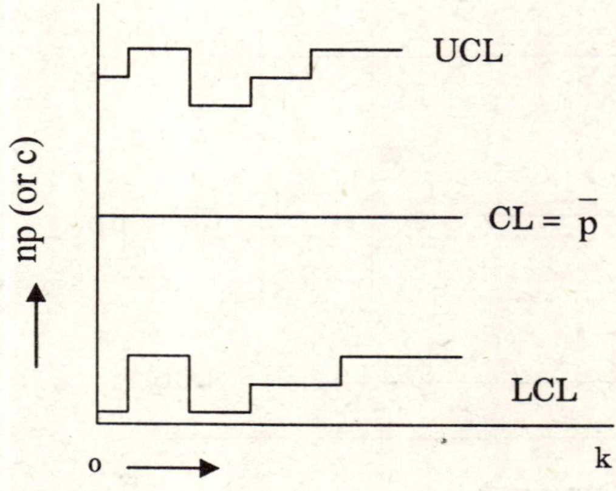

(iii) Construction of 'C' chart ('Number of defects' chart)

The data regarding the number of defects existing in all the samples in each sub-groups are collected for 'K' sub-groups each of sample size n. The number of $c_1, + c_2, \dots c_K$. defects per sub-groups are say

Then central line (CL) $\bar{c} = \frac{\Sigma c}{K} = \frac{c_1 + c_2 \dots c_K}{K}$

$$\left.\begin{array}{r}\text{Upper control limit (UCL)}\\ \text{for each sub - group}\end{array}\right\} = \bar{c} - 3\sqrt{c}$$

$$\left.\begin{array}{r}\text{Lower control limit (LCL)}\\ \text{for each sub - group}\end{array}\right\} = \bar{c} - 3\sqrt{c}$$

Test for homogeneity is done by comparing the individual values of $c_1 + c_2 \dots c_K$ with the control limit values and discarding, the sub-groups for which values of 'c' fall beyond the limit values. For the remaining sub-group, modified values of $\bar{c}$, UCL and LCL are calculated till homogeneity is obtained. The chart is drawn as below:

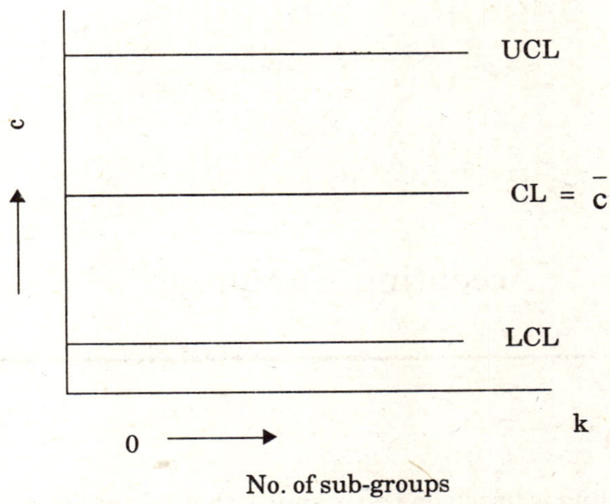

(iv) Construction of 'u' chart ('No. of defects per unit' chart for varying sample size)

Data regarding the sample size and the number of defects in all the samples in each sub-groups are collected for K sub-groups. Let $c_1 + c_2 \ldots c_K$ n_1 ;... to n_K .be the number of defects per sub-group for K sub-groups each having sample size varying from

$$\text{No. of defects per sub-group } u = \frac{c}{n} \text{ or } \frac{c}{\text{sample size}}$$

$$\text{i.e.,} \quad u1 = \frac{c_1}{n_1}, u_2 = \frac{c_2}{n_2} \ldots u_K = \frac{c_K}{n_K}$$

$$\text{Central line (CL), } \bar{u} = \frac{\Sigma u}{K} = \frac{u_1 + u_2 + \text{-}\text{-} u_K}{K}$$

$$\left.\begin{array}{r}\text{Upper control limit (UCL)}\\ \text{for each sub - group}\end{array}\right\} = \bar{u} + 3\sqrt{\frac{\bar{u}}{\text{Sample size}}}$$

$$\left.\begin{array}{r}\text{Lower control limit (LCL)}\\ \text{for each sub - group}\end{array}\right\} = \bar{u} - 3\sqrt{\frac{\bar{u}}{\text{Sample size}}}$$

12

Accepting Sampling

Introduction

Acceptance sampling is based on the premise, that a sample represents the whole lot from which the former is drawn. In this method, samples are taken out and are carefully inspected to detect defects. On the basis of number of defects found, the lot is accepted or rejected. If defects are few, lot is accepted. It is rejected when defects are more. Thus, acceptance sampling is used to take a decision regarding acceptance or rejection of a lot without having to examine the entire lot, thereby providing economy of inspection. It may be used at any point in a plant, but is most often found in incoming inspection and as such, it is an important part of the overall quality control programme of a plant. The acceptance sampling technique is discussed in detail later in this chapter.

Acceptance Sampling Technique

When 100% inspection is not practical (i.e., either too costly and time consuming or when the inspection is of destructive nature) sampling inspection is the best way of estimating the quality of incoming or outgoing lots.

Random sampling provides each element with an equal chance of being selected and permit logical inferences to be made about the lot (population or universe in statistical terms) quality on the basis of sample evidence.

Acceptance sampling inspection can be either sampling by attributes or *sampling by variables*.

Sampling plans for attributes or variables

Quality control inspectors are normally forced to resort to sampling inspection of lots because of the cost of 100% inspection and/or the destructive nature of inspection or testing which rules out 100% inspection.

Since the decision to accept or reject a lot must be made on the basis of sample evidence, we must be willing to accept some risks of rejecting good lots or accepting bad lots.

Acceptance Sampling by Attributes

Acceptance Sampling by attributes involves extracting a random sample from the lot to determine whether to accept or reject the entire lot based on the quality of the sample, or whether to subject the lot for 100% inspection and separate the good from the bad. This process many be used in inwards goods or receiving inspection for raw materials or bought-out components, in process inspection for semi finished products and finished product inspection or final inspection. The sampling may be single sampling, double sampling or sequential sampling, depending on the sampling procedure and the number of samples drawn from a single lot for inspection,

Acceptance sampling plans have two important concepts as background when the characteristics being measured are attributes. They are:

(a) Average outgoing quality curves and

(b) Operating characteristic curves which are described below.

Average Outgoing Quality (AOQ) Curves : Acceptance sampling plans provides managers with the assurance that the average quality level or percent defectives actually going to customer will not exceed a certain limit. Figure 5.6 demonstrates this concept.

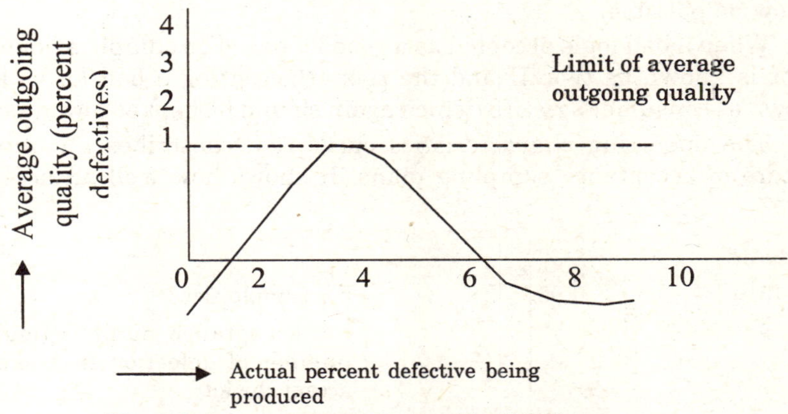

Fig. 5.6. An average outgoing quality (AOQ) curve

It can be observed from the AOQ curve that as the actual percent defectives in a production process increase, initially the effect for the lots to be passed even though the number of defectives has increased and the percent defectives going to the customer increases. If this trend increases, the acceptance plan begin to reject lots and when lots are rejected, the lots are usually inspected 100% and defective units are replaced by good ones. The net effect is to improve the average quality of the outgoing lots because the rejected lots that are ultimately accepted contain all non - defective (due to 100% inspection)

As the actual percent defectives increases, the average outgoing quality improves because more and more lots rejected. At the extreme condition, when all lots are rejected, the percent defectives going to customers approach zero.

This concept of AOQ curves show that acceptance plans protect an organisation through limiting the percentage of defective products that go to the customers.

Operating Characteristic (OC) Curves

The following can happen when we go for acceptance sampling plans

1. We accept goods lots.
2. We reject bad lots.
3. We may accept bad lots.
4. We may reject good lots.

In the vast majority of cases, we do accept good lots and reject bad lots when we apply acceptance sampling plans. On rare occasions, we may accept bad lots even though sampling inspection shows the quality of the lot as good, based on sample evidence. On the other hand, we may reject good lots as bad lots based on sample evidence. When a good lot is rejected, the error is known as type - I error and the risk of rejecting a good lot based on sample evidence is known as producer's risk (a) which should be kept as low as possible.

When a bad lot is accepted as a good lot based on sample evidence, the error is known as type II and the risk of accepting a bad lot as good is known as consumer's risk (ß) which again should be kept as low as possible.

The operating characteristics curve (OC) describes an important feature of acceptance sampling plans. It shows how well an acceptance

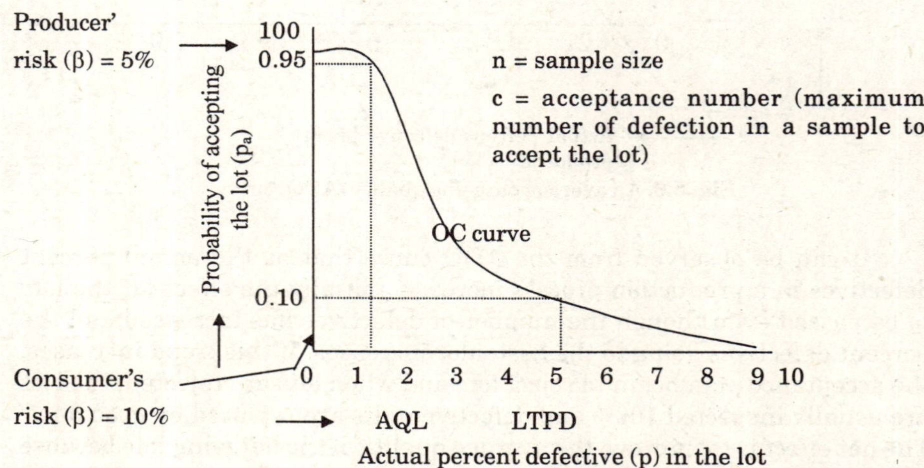

Fig. 5.7. Operating Characteristics curve

plan discriminates between good and bad lots. Figure 5.7 shows an OC curve.

In this figure, let us say, that we define a good lot as any lot having no more than 1 percent defectives. This is called the acceptable quality level (AQL). If there is 1% actual defectives in a lot, the probability of accepting the lot should be as high as 95% and then the probability of rejecting a good lot is 5%. The probability of rejecting a lot at the AQL quality is known as producer's risk (a).

Let us say that we define a bad lot as any having 5% or more defectives. This is known as lot tolerance percent defective (LTPD). The probability of a accepting a lot with 5% defectives should be as low as 10%. That is called the consumer's risk (ß). But the probability of rejecting a lot with 5% defectives or more is 90%.

We want acceptance plans that accept good lots and reject bad lots, i.e. acceptance plans that discriminate between good and bad lots. Sampling plans do not provide perfect discrimination between good and bad lots. Some lots of low quality may be accepted while some lots of very good quality may be rejected due to sample evidence.

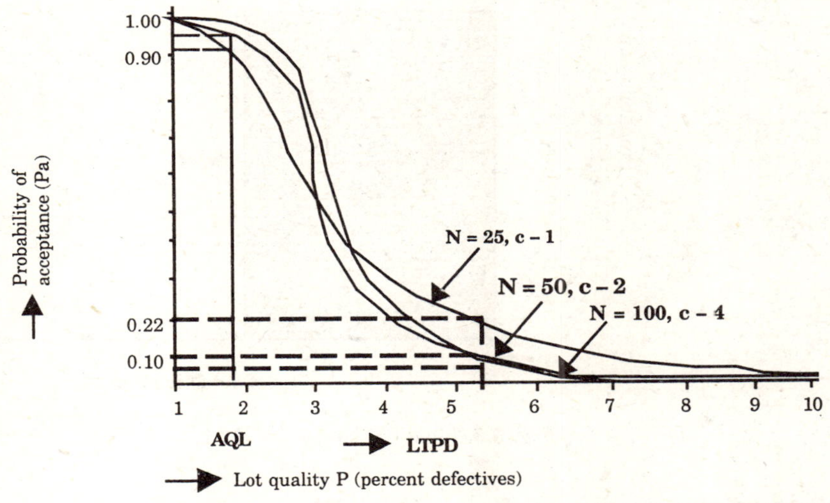

Fig. 5.8. OC curves for different sample sizes

The degree to which a sampling plan discriminates between good and bad lots is a function of the steepness of the OC curve.

Figure 5.8 shows the OC curve for various values of sample size 'n' and acceptance number 'c'. It can be observed that for the same percentage defectives as the maximum allowable for an acceptable lot, the larger the sample size, the greater is the discriminating power. On the other hand, it is seen that, acceptance plans with smaller sample sizes reject more good lots and accept more bad lots. However, it should be noted that, higher the sample sizě, higher the inspection costs. Therefore, we must make trade-off decision when designing acceptance plans.

Ideal OC Curve

If perfect discrimination is required between a good lot and a bad lot, say for example, in a lot of a product of size N = 100 units, if the quantity of defective units is less than 2.0%, the lots is to be accepted and if the quantity of defectives in greater than 2.0 %, the lots is to be rejected. Then the OC curve drawn is as shown in figure 20.9. This kind of perfect discrimination is possible only by 100% inspection and this O.C curve is known as ideal OC curve.

However, in practice as we cannot go for 100% inspection big lots, the OC curve selected should ensure that, as the lot quality decreased (i.e. percent defectives increase) the probability of acceptance of such lots should decrease, although, the relationship is not linear.

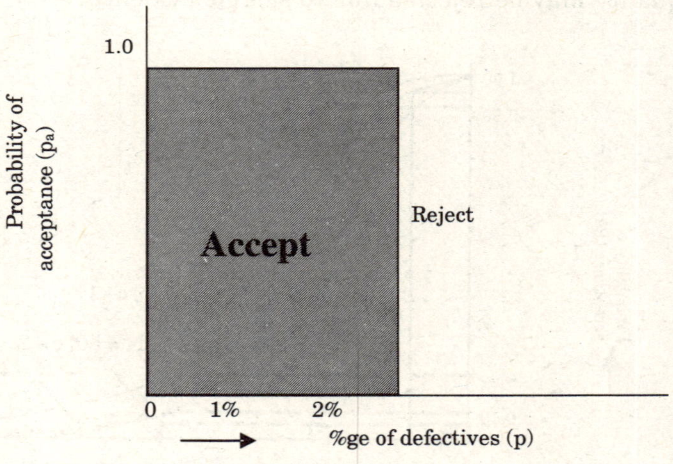

Fig. 5.9. Ideal OC curve

Design of Acceptance Sampling Plans

OC curves are not used to make day-to-day decisions about accepting or rejecting lots. They simply depict graphically how a particular acceptance plan discriminates between good and bad lots. In practice, all that operations managers must know to make accept-or-reject decisions about attributes in lots of materials in the sample size (n) and the maximum number of defectives in a sample to accept the lot (c) for each material. To determine sample size (n) and acceptance number (c), operations managers first use judgement in setting the values of producer's risk (a), consumer's risk (ß), acceptance quality level (AQL) or the percent defectives in good lots and lot-tolerance percent defective (LTPD) or the percent defectives in a bad lot, for each material. Then the values of 'n' and 'c' can be found out for the selected values of a, ß, AQL & LTPD from Thorndike Chart (Refer Annexure-B)

Types of Acceptance Sampling Plans

Single sampling

A sampling plan for a single sample is specified by two numbers n and c. the number of items that should be included in a single random sample from the lot being inspected is the sample size n. The acceptance number 'c' specifies the maximum number of Figure 5.10 illustrates the operation of single sampling plans

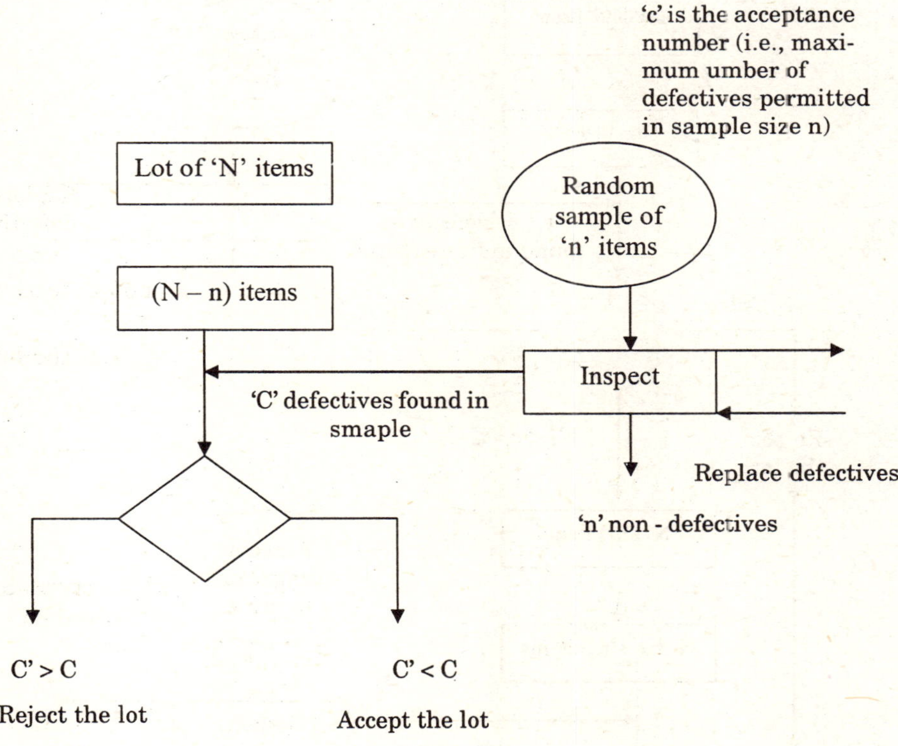

Fig. 5.10. Single sampling plans

defectives that may be permitted in the sample if the lot is to be accepted. If the number of defectives found in the sample is more than 'c', the entire lot will be rejected or inspected 100 percent.

Double sampling

In double sampling, one small sample is drawn initially. Two acceptance numbers $C_1$and C_2(i.e, $C_2 > C_1$)are selected. If the number of defectives (C'_1) in the first sample of size (n_1) is less than or equal to C_1, the lot is accepted. If the number of defectives (C'_1) is greater than C_2 , the lot is rejected. If the number of defectives more than C_1 but less than C'_2, second larger sample of size n_2 (i.e $n_2 > n_1$,) is taken and inspected. If the number of defectives in the second sample is C'_2, then the total number of defectives $(C^1_1 + C^1_2)$ from the two samples is compared with C_2. $C'_1 + C'_2 > C_2$, If the lot is rejected and if $C'_1 + C'_2 \leq C_2$, the lot is accepted

Figure 5.11 illustrates how double sampling plant opetrates.

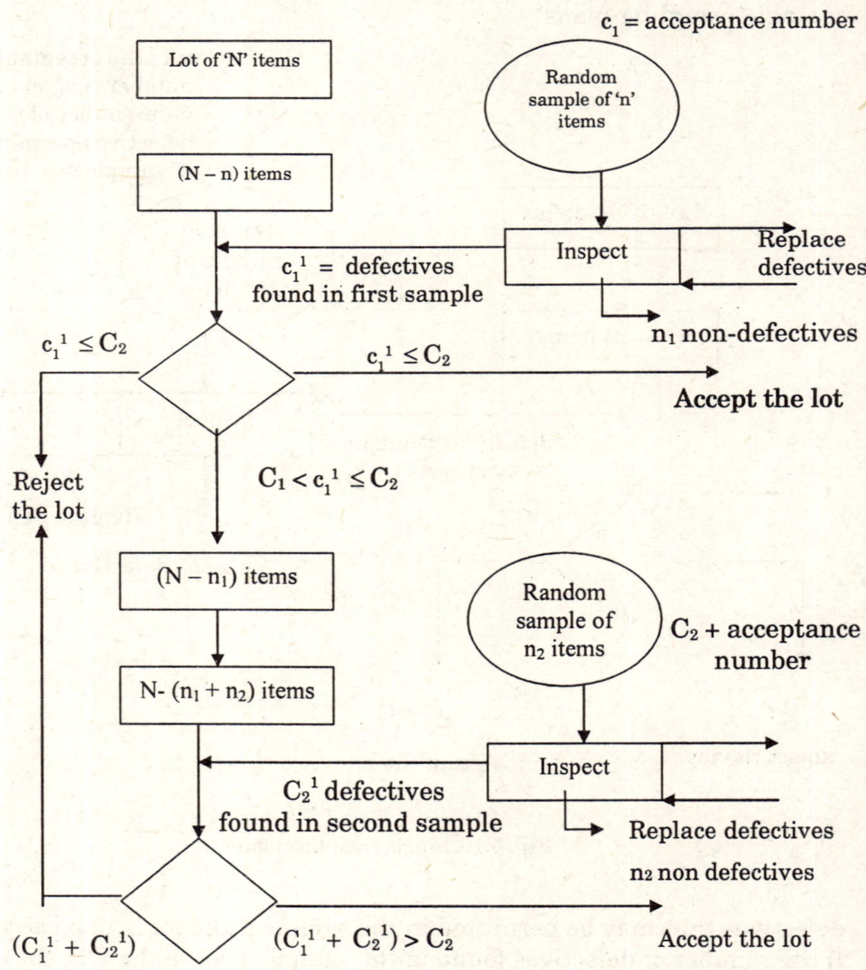

Fig. 5.11. Double sampling plan

(Source : Norman Gaither, Production and Operations Management, 4th Edition, p.703)

Sequential sampling

In sequential sampling plan, units are randomly selected from the lot and tested one by one. After each one is tested a reject, accept or continuous sampling decision is made. This process continues until the lot is accepted or rejected.

Figure 5.12 illustrates how such plans operate.

Suppose, when units are randomly drawn and inspected, the first defective is the 15th unit, which is in the 'continue sampling' zone in the figure, and so we continue to sample further units from the lot. If the second defective is the 25th unit which is again in the 'continue sampling' zone, and we still continue sampling if the 4th defective is the 40th unit which put in the reject lot zone, therefore the lot is rejected.

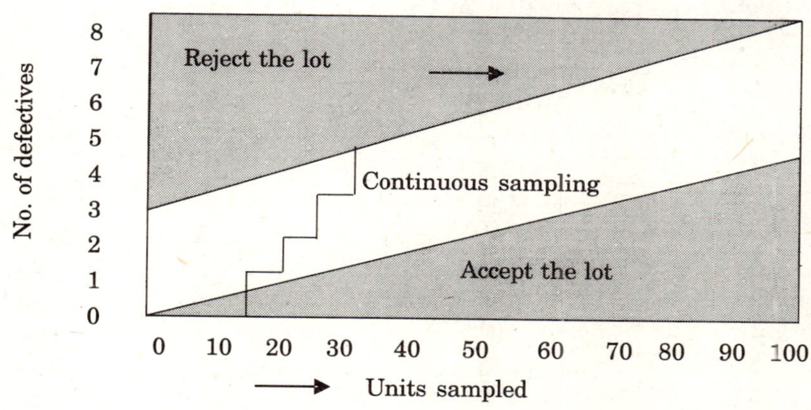

Fig. 5.12. Sequential sampling

Illustration of design of single acceptance sampling plan

Let the values of AQL, α, LTPD and β selected by operations managers for a particular material as below :

AQL = 2 percent α = 5 percent

LTPD = 8 percent β= 10 percent

To design the sampling plan, we have to select an OC cure which passes through these four points viz., AQL, α, LTPD and β, for a particular value of sample size (n) and acceptance number (c). to determine these values of n and c, we can use the Thorndike chart as explained beow:

Tabulate value of for = $\frac{PD \times n}{100}$ (1 - P_a) = 95 percent and = b = 1Da percent for each value of c say 1, 2, 3, 4 etc., from the Thorndike chart.

For example, for P_a = 95 percent and c = 1, read the value of $\frac{PD \times n}{100}$ from Thorndike P_a chart as 0.36 and for = 10 percent and c = 1, read $\frac{PD \times n}{100}$ 3.9 from the same chart.

Similarly, find the value of $\frac{PD \times n}{100}$ for various values of c (i.e. c = 2, 3, 4 ... 8) and tabulate the same as shown below:

Acceptance number P_a = 95 percent (AQL)	**Value of $\frac{PD \times n}{100}$ at Pa = 10 percent (LTPD)**	**Value of $\frac{PD \times n}{100}$ at**	**Ratio of LTPD/AQL**
1	0.36	3.9 5.3	$\frac{3.9}{0.36} = 10.83$
2	0.80	6.7	6.63
3	0.35	8.0	4.96
4	1.97	9.3	4.06
5	2.60	10.5	3.58
6	3.30		3.18

Step No. 2 : Compare the ratio of LTPD/AQL computed in step no.1 for various values c with the ratio of $\frac{LTPD}{AQL}$ desired for the selected sampling plan. In this example, the selected $\frac{LTPD}{AQL}$ ratio of is 8/2 = 4.

The ratio 4 falls between 4.06 and 3.58 at c = 4 and 5 respectively as shown in the table in step no. 1. Since 4.06 is nearer to 4 than 3.58, the value of 'c' to be selected is 4.

Step No. 3 : Compute sample size as shown in table below, deciding whether to hold a fixed and let β float or vice versa.

c fixed at 4		c fixed at 5	
α = 5 percent β floats	β = 10 percent α floats	α = 5 percent β floats	β = 10 percent α floats
$n = 1.97 \times \frac{100}{2} = 99$	$n = 8 \times \frac{100}{8} = 100$	$n = \frac{2.60 \times 100}{2} = 130$	$n = \frac{9.3 \times 100}{8} = 115$
β = 10.5 percent	α = 5.5 percent	β = 5 percent	α = 3 percent

For example, selecting c = 4 and holding a at 5 percent,

$$\text{Then } \frac{PD \times n}{100} = AQL \times \frac{n}{100} = 1.97 \quad n = \frac{1.97 \times 100}{AQL} = \frac{1.97 \times 100}{2} = 99$$

The sampling plan is n = 99; c =4.
Calculation in the same manner, the four plans are

plan 1	n = 99	c = 4	α = 5%	α = 10.5%
plan 2	n = 100	c = 4	β = 10%	β = 5.5%
plan 3	n = 130	c = 5	α = 5%	α = 5%
plan 4	n = 115	c = 5	β = 10%	β= 3%

Since the desired a is 5% and ß is 10 %, plan 1 and 2 come closest to the desired sampling plan.

Quality Circles (QC)

It was quality circles which gave birth to TQM. A quality circle is a group of employees whose assignment is to identify problems, formulate solutions, and present their results to the management with suggestions for implementation.

The definition given by the Union of Japanese Scientists and Engineers (UJSE) is more revealing. To quote the definition: "the QC is a small group that voluntarily performs quality control activities within the shop, where its members work, the small group carrying out its work continuously as part of a company-wide programme of quality control, self-development, mutual development, flow-control and improvement within workshop. By engaging in QC activities, the circle members gain valuable experience in communication with colleagues, working together to solve problems and sharing their findings, not only among themselves but with other circles at other companies."

As in TQM, popular perception about QC is that, it deals with only product quality. Far from it, QC also aims at individual and group development. In other words, QC has quality of life as its primary objective. But in reality, QC is perceived to be an instrument to achieve high product quality.

Although simple in concept, successful implementation of quality circles programme requires a massive effort on the part of management. The support structure usually consists of a steering committee of top management officials, facilitators, circle leaders and circle members.

Steering Committee : Provide overall guidance, suggest problems for the circle to address, receive recommendations from the circles and follow up on implementation. The steering committee must make sure that, the circles receive the support they need, to be effective.

Facilitators : One facilitator is assigned to several circles. They provide training for the leaders and support the training programmes for the members. When the circle requests information, the facilitator's responsibility is to provide it. A facilitator must be well connected in the organisation and requires strong backing from the top management.

Circle Leaders : Often an area supervisor, a leader has responsibilities that include training the circle members in problem identification and solution methods, and preparing an effective presentation for the management. This is considered as an excellent preparation for someone, who is likely to be promoted, since they become indoctrinated in the philosophy that a manager's function is to facilitate the tasks of the workers.

Circle Members : These are volunteers from the regular work force. They are given one hour of company time weekly to carry out their discussions and projects. Trained in techniques of brain-storming and identifying causes, they keep the facilitator busy by requesting information about various problems of their choice. Based on preliminary findings, the group focuses on a problem and works out a solution and a strategy to implement it. If the recommendation is accepted by the steering committee, the circle is kept posted on its progress. If the recommendation is rejected, it is the responsibility of the steering committee to explain in detail why it was rejected.

Started first in Japan, quality circles have become a strategic global phenomena. In Japan, there are more than 170,000 QCs officially registered with UJSE and probably twice that many operating independently of UJSE. Since the typical circle has six to ten members, it is estimated that, there are at least three million workers in Japan directly involved in some kind of official QC activity.

The QC activities are inter-connected in a nationwide network, and QC members have easy access to what other people are doing in other industries. There are more than 1,000 volunteer QC leaders in Japan co-operating in organizing local and national meetings to promote the flow of information among members.

Elsewhere, companies like J.C. Penny and Co., US Navy, Armstrong Cork, GE Co., Ford, Firestone, Bendix Corporation, Victor Business Machines, General Motors and Lockheeds, have employed QC approach in their respective plants.

Nearer at home, BHEL, BEL, BFW, Shriram Fibres Ltd., ECI, Durgapur Steel Plant, Kirloskar Electric Co., L&T, HMT, TELCO, Hindustan Antibiotics Ltd., and Essar Industries have QCs in their respective organisations.

Developing a QC Programme

Most QC programmes are developed in an identical way, though difference do exist. Before describing the pattern of development, three points need to be stressed. First, membership in the circle is voluntary both for leaders as well as for members. Second, the creation of QCs is usually preceded by in-house training for leaders, and these session typically last for two or three days. Most of the time is devoted to discussions of group dynamics, leadership skills and QC philosophies. A day is spent on the different approaches to problem-solving. Employees are usually given one day of intensive training and problem-solving techniques. The workers also receive an explanation of the leader's role and information on the quality circle concept. Third, the circle is permitted to select the problems it, wants to tackle. Management may suggest problems of concern, but the group is empowered to decide which one to select. Ideally, the selection process is not by democratic vote but is carried out by a consensus, whereby every one agrees on the problems to be tackled.

Coming to the formation of a QC, it may be stated that, the programme involves six phases. They are: (1) start-up, (2) initial problem solving, (3) presentation and approval of initial suggestions, (4) implementation of solutions, (5) expansion and continued problem-solving and (6) decline. Table 20.4 lists the major activities which take place in each phase and destructive forces which might exist. Most QCs exist for several years, usually until the members run out of problems to tackle or lose interest in the programme.

Benefits of a QC Programme

QC programmes can be used in a variety of ways, including -

1. Collecting ideas for work improvement from those closest to the work itself, eg., the work group,

Table 5.4. Development aspects of a QC.

	Phase	Activity	Destructive Forces
1.	Start-up	Publicise. Obtain funds and train volunteers	Low volunteers rate. Inadequate funding. Inability to learn group processes and problem solving skills.
2.	Initial problem solving	Identify and solve problems.	Disagreement on problems. Lack of knowledge of operations.
3.	Approval of initial suggestions	Present and have initial suggestion accepted.	Resistance by staff groups and middle management. Poor presentation and suggestions because of limited knowledge.
4.	Implementation	Relevant groups. Act on suggestions.	Prohibitive costs. Resistance by groups that must implement.
5.	Expansion and problem-solving	From new groups. Old groups continue.	Member-non-member conflict. Raised aspirations. Lack of problems. Expense of parallel organisation. Savings not realised. Rewards wanted.
6.	Decline	Fewer groups meet.	Cynicism about programme. Burnout

2. Providing opportunities for problem-solving,
3. Dealing with special projects on a temporary basis,
4. Enhancing personal and professional growth of QC members.
5. Team building and
6. Helping the organisation make the transition to a more participative culture.

Towards Better QC Programmes

A variety of suggestions have been given for ensuring that QCs are used effectively in organisations. They include -

- Obtain managerial support and involvement for the programme.

- Do not expect the QC programme to solve all problems in the organisation.
- Make sure that the managers realise that any change will take time.
- Inform all employees about the philosophy and goals of the programme.
- Keep the programme voluntary.
- Select group members based on their technical expertise and their support of the programme's goals.
- Prepare individuals for their new roles in a participative culture.
- Provide ongoing training for managers as leaders.
- Provide training for support staff who will serve as facilitators.
- Start with a pilot test of the programme in a supportive department.
- Implement the suggestions made by employees.
- Provide recognition for the employees.
- Provide recognition for the employees' efforts.

Solved problems

1. Last week's visual inspection carried out to find defects in a manufactured item revealed the following data for a sample size of 30 numbers.

   This week, 30 pieces were again inspected on each of the two occasions and 6 pieces and 9 pieces were found to be defective in each case respectively. Determine whether the process is under statistical control or not, this week.

Solution

Since sample size (n) is constant for all the 30 sub-groups, we have to construct the np chart (i.e., Number of defectives chart) and establish the central line, upper control limit and lower control limit values for the number of defectives (c) per sub-group.

Central line = $n\bar{p}$

Where $\bar{p}$ is the average fraction defective

$$\bar{p} = \frac{\text{sum of all the defectives}}{\text{Number of sub-groups} \times \text{sample size (n)}}$$

$$= \frac{\Sigma np}{K \times n}$$

Sub-group number	Number of defectives	Sub-group number	Number of defectives
1	5	11	5
2	4	12	7
3	4	13	4
4	4	14	5
5	7	15	4
6	4	16	5
7	5	17	5
8	6	18	7
9	4	19	6
10	5	20	4

Where K = number of sub-groups ; n = Sample size

In this problem, K = 20, n = 30

Fraction defective $p = \frac{c}{n}$ where 'c' is the number of defectives

c = np $\quad \therefore \quad \bar{p} = \frac{\Sigma np}{K \times n} = \frac{\Sigma c}{K \times n}$

Σc = ∴ 5+4+4+5+7+4+5+6+4+5+5+7+4+5+4+5+5+7+6+4]

= 101

$$\bar{p} = \frac{101}{20 \times 30} = \frac{101}{600} = 0.168$$

Central line = $n\bar{p} = \frac{101}{600} \times 30 = \frac{101}{20} = 5.05$

Upper control limit UCL = $n\bar{p} + 3\sqrt{n\bar{p}(1-\bar{p})}$

= 5.05 + 3 $\sqrt{5.05(1-0.168)}$

= 5.05 + 3 $\sqrt{5.05 \times 0.832} = 5.05 + 3\sqrt{4.20}$

= 5.05 3 2.05

= 5.05 + 6.15 = 9.20

Lower control limit = $n\bar{p} - 3\sqrt{n\bar{p}(1-\bar{p})}$

= 5.05 - 6.15 = - 1.10

= 0 (if negative)

For 2 sub-groups from which samples are inspected this week, the defectives found were 6 nos. and 9 nos. Since these values of defections are less than the upper central limit (i.e., 9 - 2) and more than lower control limit (i.e., zero), the process is under statistical control.

Assume constant values A_2 = 0.73, D_4 = 2.28

2. Construct both $\bar{X}$ and R chart from the following data

Sub-group number		R	Sub-group number		R
1	6.36	0.10	11	6.32	0.18
2	6.38	0.18	12	6.30	0.10
3	6.35	0.17	13	6.34	0.11
4	6.39	0.20	14	6.39	0.14
5	6.32	0.15	15	6.37	0.17
6	6.34	0.16	16	6.36	0.15
7	6.40	0.13	17	6.35	0.18
8	6.33	0.18	18	6.35	0.13
9	6.37	0.16	19	6.34	0.18
10	6.33	0.13	20	6.34	0.16

Solution

For the construction of $\bar{X}$ - R chart

The following formulae are used.

(a) For mean chart ($\bar{X}$ Chart) :

Central line,

Where K = number of sub-groups = 20 $\bar{X} = \frac{\Sigma\bar{X}}{K}$

$$\bar{\bar{X}} = \frac{127.03}{20} = 6.351 \qquad \bar{R} = \frac{\Sigma R}{K} = \frac{3.06}{20} = 0.153$$

Upper control limit $UCL_{\bar{X}} = \bar{\bar{X}} + A_2\bar{R}$

$$UCL_{\bar{X}} = \bar{\bar{X}} + A_2\bar{R} \; UCL_{\bar{X}} = \bar{\bar{X}} + A_2\bar{R}$$

= 6.351 + 0.73 0.153

= 6.351 + 0.112 = 6.463

Lower control limit $LCL_{\bar{X}} = \bar{\bar{X}} - A_2\bar{R}$

= 6.351 - 0.112 = 6.239

(b) For Range chart (R chart)

Central line = $\bar{R}$ = 0.153

Upper control limit (UCL_R) = $D_4\bar{R}$

= 2.28 0.153 = 0.349

Lower control limit (LCL_R) = $D_3\bar{R}$

= Nil

Total Quality Management (TQM)

The quality control system explained till now has been a passive approach. Quality is considered a by-product of the manufacturing system; that is, each individual process has some variation that will lead to the production of some defective parts. If the resulting defective rate is too high, compared to the established quality standards, quality inspectors will identify and sent them for rework. The approach is expensive and does not guarantee the desired quality, because quality maintaining and ensuring itself cannot be inspected into a product. This approach assigns the responsibility for quality to quality control managers.

A more enlightened approach to quality, emphasizes building quality into the product by studying and improving activities that affect quality, from marketing through design to manufacturing. This new approach is referred to as total quality management (TQM). It is an active approach, encompassing a company-wide operating philosophy and system for continuous improvement of quality. It demands co-operation from everyone in the company, from the top management down to the workers.

TQM owes its origin to two Americans -W. Edwards Deming and J.M. Juran - who launched it first in Japan which was on the process of rebuilding its economy devastated by World War - II.

One of Juran's key ideas was to define quality as 'fitness for use', a phrase that referred to how well a product or service satisfied a customer's real needs. By focusing on these real needs, Juran felt, managers and workers could concentrate their efforts, where it really mattered. Deming, perhaps the most widely recognized American in Japanese manufacturing circles, questioned the basic assumption, that high quality means higher prices. He felt that 'constancy of purpose' - an unwavering focus on an organisation's mission - combined with statistical quality control, would lead to ever-improving quality at lower costs. Moreover, Deming believed that the manager's job is to seek out and correct the causes of failure, rather than merely identify failures on designing, operations system that produced products with extremely small margins of errors and mistakes.

The famous 14 principles of quality advocated by Deming speak about his quality philosophy. The 14 principles are:

1. Create constancy of purpose towards improving products and services, allocating resources to provide for long-range needs rather than short-term profitability.
2. Adopt the new philosophy for economic stability by refusing to allow commonly accepted levels of delays, mistakes, defective materials and defective workmanship.
3. Cease dependence on mass inspection by requiring statistical evidence of built-in quality in both manufacturing and purchasing functions.
4. Reduce the number of suppliers for the same item by eliminating those, that do not qualify with statistical evidence of quality. End the practice of awarding business solely on the basis of price.
5. Search continually for problems in the system to constantly improve processes.
6. Institute modern methods of training to make better use of all employees.
7. Focus supervision on helping people to a better job. Ensure that immediate action is taken on report of defects, maintenance requirements, poor tools, inadequate operating definitions, or other conditions detrimental to the product's quality.
8. Encourage effective two-way communication and other means to drive out fear throughout the organisation and help people work more productively.
9. Break down barriers between departments by encouraging problem-solving through teamwork, combining the efforts of people from different areas such as research, design, sales and production.
10. Eliminate the use of numerical goals, posters and slogans for the workforce that ask for new levels of productivity without providing methods.

11. Use statistical methods for continuing improvement of quality and productivity, and eliminate work standards that prescribe numerical quotas.
12. Remove all barriers that inhibit the worker's right to pride of workmanship.
13. Institute a vigorous programme of education and re-training to keep up with changes in materials, methods, product design and machinery.
14. Clearly define top management's permanent commitment to quality and productivity and its obligation to implement all these principles.

The philosophy of TQM extends beyond product quality and covers quality of life of people. In fact, the primary concern of TQM is people and then comes the product. 'When speaking of quality.' writes Masaki Imai, 'One tends to think first to terms of product quality'. Nothing could be further from the truth. In TQM, the first and foremost concern is with the quality of people. Instilling quality into people has always been fundamental to TQM. A company able to build quality into its people is already halfway towards producing quality products.

'The three building blocks of business are hardware, software, and humanware. TQM starts with humanware. Only after the humanware is squarely in placed, should the hardware and software aspects of business he considered.'

But in practice, quality of product is stressed more in TQM than the quality of life of people.

Total Quality Management (TQM) is an enhancement to the traditional way of doing business. It is a proven technique to guarantee survival in world-class competition. Only by changing the actions of management will be culture and actions of an entire organization be transformed. TQM is for the most part common sense. Analyzing the three words, we have

Total-Made up of the whole.

Quality - Degree of excellence a product or service provides.

Management - Act, art, or manner of handling, controlling, directing, etc.

Therefore, TQM, is the art of managing the whole to achieve excellence. The Golden Rule is a simple but effective way to explain it: Do unto others as your would have them do unto you.

TQM is defined as both a philosophy and a set of guiding principles that represent the foundation of a continuously improving organization. It is the application of quantitative methods and human resources to improve all the processes with an organization and exceed customer needs now and in the future. TQM integrates fundamental management techniques, existing improvement efforts, and technical tools under a disciplined approach.

Basic Approach

TQM requires six basic concepts:

1. A committed and involved management to provide long-term top-to-bottom organizational support.
2. An unwavering focus on the customer, both internally and externally.
3. Effective involvement and utilization of the entire work force.
4. Continuous improvement of the business and production process.
5. Treating suppliers as partners.
6. Establish performance measures for the processes.

These concept outline and excellent way to run an organization. A brief paragraph on each of them is given here. The next six chapters cover these concepts in greater detail.

1. Management must participate in the quality program. A quality council must be established to develop a clear vision, set long-term goals, and direct the program. Quality goals are included in the business plan. An annual quality improvement program is established and involves input from the entire work force. Managers participate on quality improvement teams and also act as coaches to other teams. TQM is a continual activity that must be entrenched in thee culture-it is not just a one-shot program. TQM must be communicated to all people.

2. The key to an effective TQM program is its focus on the customer. An excellent place to start is by satisfying internal customers. We must listen to the "voice of the customer" and emphasize design quality and defect prevention. Do it right the first time and every time, for customer satisfaction is the most important consideration.

3. TQM is an organization-wide challenge that is everyone's responsibility. All personnel must be trained in TQM, statistical process control (SPC), and other appropriate quality improvement skills so they can effectively participate on project teams. Including internal customers and, for that matter, internal suppliers on project teams is an excellent approach. Those affected by the plan must be involved in its development and implementation. They understand the process better than anyone else. Changing behavior is the goal. People must come to work not only to do their jobs, but also to think about how to improve their jobs. People must be empowered at the lowest possible level to perform processes in an optimum manner.

4. There must be a continual striving to improve all business and production processes. Quality improvement projects, such as on-time delivery, order entry efficiency, billing error rate, customer satisfaction, cycle time, scrap reduction, and supplier management, are good places to begin. Technical techniques such as SPC, benchmarking, quality function deployment, ISO 9000, and designed experiments are excellent for problem solving.

5. On the average 40% of the sales dollar is purchased product or service; therefore, the supplier quality must be outstanding. A partnering relationship rather than an adversarial one must be developed. Both parties have as much to gain or lose based on the success or failure of the product or service. The focus should be on quality and life-cycle costs rather than price. Suppliers should be few in number so that true partnering can occur.

6. Performance measures such as uptime, percent nonconforming, absenteeism, and customer satisfaction should be determined for each functional area. These measures should be posted for everyone to see. Quantitative data are necessary to measure the continuous quality improvement activity.

The purpose of TQM is to provide a quality product and/or service to customers, which will, in turn, increase productivity and lower cost. With a higher quality product and lower price, competitive position in the marketplace will be enhanced. This series of events will allow the organization to achieve the objective of profit and growth with greater ease. In addition, the work force will have job security, which will create a satisfying place to work.

As previously stated, TQM requires a cultural change. Table 5.5 compares the previous state with the TQM State for typical quality elements. This change is substantial and will not be accomplished in a short period of time. Small organizations will be able to make the transformation much faster than large organizations.

Table 5.5. New and old cultures.

Quality Element	Previous State	TQM
Definition	Product-oriented	Customer-oriented
Priorities	Second to service and cost	First among equals of service and cost
Decisions	Short-term	Long-term
Emphasis	Detection	Prevention
Errors	Operations	System
Responsibility	Quality control	Everyone
Problem Solving	Managers	Teams
Procurement	Price	Life-cycle costs, partnership
Manager's Role	Plan, assign, control, and enforce	Delegate, coach, facilitate, and mentor

Gurus of Total Quality Management

Shewhart

Walter A. Shewhart, Ph.D., spent his professional career at Western Electric and Bell Telephone Laboratories, both divisions of AT&T. He developed control chart theory with control limits, assignable and chance causes of var0ation, and rational subgroups . In 1931, he authored Economic Control of Quality of Manufactured product, which is regarded as a complete and thorough work of the basic principles of quality control. He also developed the PDSA cycle for learning and improvement .

Deming

W.Edwards Deming, PhD, was a protégé of Shewhart. In 1950, he taught statistical process control and the importance of quality to the leading CEOs of Japanese industry. He is credited with providing the foundation for the Japanese quality miracle and resurgence as an economic power. Deming is the best-known quality expert in the world. His 14 points provide a theory for management to improve quality, productivity, and conpetitive position (see Chapter 2). He has authored a number of books including Out of the Crisis and Quality, Productivity, and Competitive Position as well as 161 shoclarly studies.

Juran

Joseph M. Juran, PhD worked at Western Electric from 1924 to 1941. There he was exposed to the concepts of Shewhart. Juran traveled to Japan in 1954 to teach quality management. He emphasized the necessity for management at all levels to be committed to the quality effort with hands-on involvement. He recommended project improvements based on return on investment to achieve breakthrough results. The Juran Trilogy (see Chapter 6) for managing quality is carried out by the three interrelated processes of planning, control, and improvement. In 1951, the first edition of Juran's Quality Control Handbook was published.

Feiganbaum

Armand V. Feigenbaum, PhD, argues that total quality control is necessary to achieve productivity, market penetration, and competitive advantage. Quality begins by identifying the customer's requirements and ends with a product or service in the hands of a satisfied customer. In addition to customer satisfaction, some of Feigenbaum's quality principles are genuine management involvement, employee involvement, first-line supervision leadership, and company-wide quality control. In 1951, he authored Total Quality Control.

Ishikawa

Kaoru Ishikawa, PhD, studied under Deming, Juran, and Feigenbaum. He borrowed the total quality control concept and adapted it for the Japanese.

In addition, he authored SPC texts in Japanese and in English. Ishikawa is best known for the development of the cause and effect diagram (see Chapter 18), which is sometimes called an Ishikawa diagram. He developed the quality circle concept (see Chapter 4) in Japan, whereby work groups, including their supervisor, were trained in SPC concepts. The groups then met to identify and solve quality problems in their work environment.

Crosby

Philllip B. Crosby authored his first book, Quality ifs Free, in 1979, which was translated into 15 languages. It sold 1.5 million copies and changed the way management looked a t quality. He argued that "doing it right the first time" is less expensive than the costs of detecting and correcting nonconformities. In 1984, he authored Quality Without Tears, which contained his four absolutes of quality management. These absolutes are: quality is conformance to requirements, prevention of nonconformance is the objective not appraisal, the performance standard is zero defects not "that's close enough," and the measurement of quality is the cost of nonconformance.

Taguchi

Genichi Taguchi, PhD, developed his loss function concept that combines cost, target, and variation into one metric. Because the loss function is reactive, he developed the signal to noise ratio as a proactive equivalent. The cornerstone of Taguchi's philosophy is the robust design of parameters and tolerances. It is built on the simplification and use of traditional design of experiments.

TQM Framework

Figure 5.13 shows the framework for the TQM system. It begins with the knowledge provided by gurus of quality: Shewhart, Deming, Juran, Figenbaum, Ishikawa, Crosby, and Taguchi,. As the figure shows, they contributed to the development of principles and practices and/or the tools and techniques. Leadership, customer satisfaction, employee involvement, continuous process improvement, supplier partnership and performance measures provide information on principle & practices of TQM. Some of these tools and techniques are used in the product and/or service realization activity. Feedback from internal/external customers or interested parties provides information to continually improve the organization's system, product and/or service.

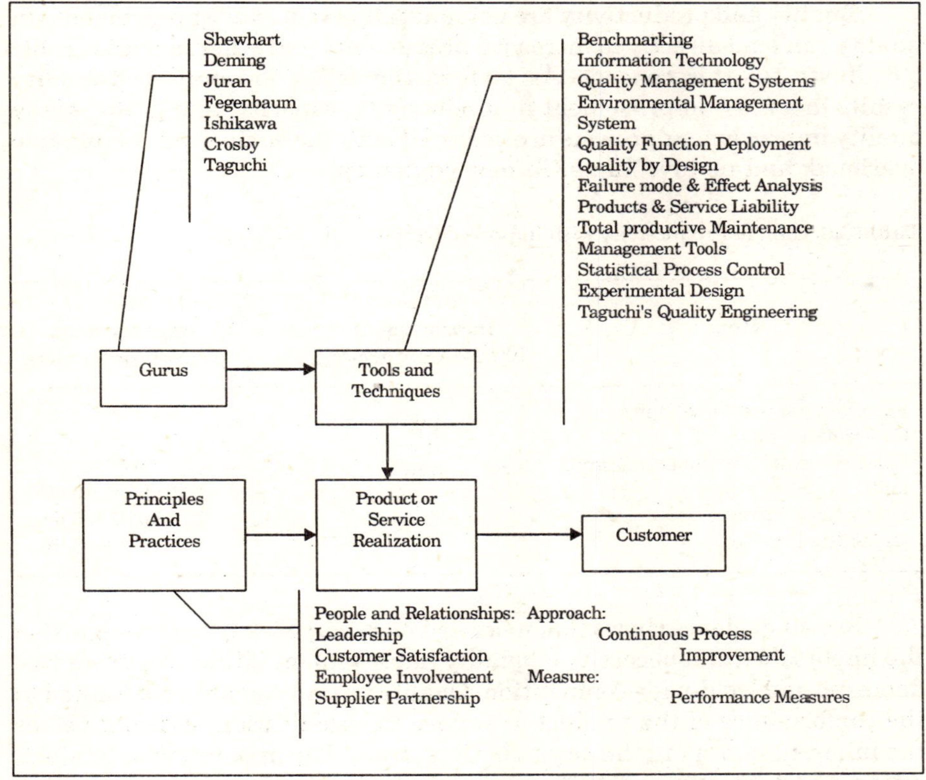

Fig. 5.13. TQM Framework

Awareness

An organization will not begin the transformation to TQM unit it is aware that the quality of the product or service must be improved. Awareness comes about when an organization loses market share or realizes that quality and productivity go hand-in-hand. It also occurs if TQM is mandated by the customer or if management realizes that TQM is a better way to run a business and compete in domestic and world markets.

Automation and other productivity enhancements might not help a corporation if it is unable to market its product or service because the quality is poor. The Japanese leaned this fact from practical experience. Prior to World War II, they could sell their products only at ridiculously low prices, and even then it was difficult to secure repeat sales. Until recently, corporations have not recognized the importance of quality. However, a new attitude has emerged - quality first among the equals of cost and service. To sum it up, the customer wants value.

Quality and productivity are not mutually exclusive. Improvements in quality can lead directly to increased productivity and other benefits. Table 5.6 illustrates this concept. As seen in the table, the improved quality results in a 5.6% improvement in productivity, capacity, and profit. Many quality improvement projects are achieved with the same work force, same overhead, and no investment in new equipment.

Table 5.6. Gain in Productivity with Improved Quality

Item	Before Improvement 10% Nonconforming	After Improvement 5% Nonconforming
Relative total cost for 20 units	1.00	1.00
Conforming units	18	19
Relative cost for nonconforming units	0.10	0.05
		(100) (1/18) = 5.6%
Productivity increase		(100) (1/18) = 5.6%
Capability increase		(100) (1/18) = 5.6%

Recent evidence shows that more and more corporations are recognizing the importance and necessity of quality improvement if they are to survive domestic and wold-wide competition. Quality improvement is not limited to the conformance of the product or service to specification; it also involves the inherent quality in the design of the system. The prevention of product, service, and process problems is a more desirable objective than taking corrective action after the product is manufactured or a service rendered.

TQM does not occur overnight; there are no quick remedies. It takes a long time to build the appropriate emphasis and techniques into the culture. Overemphasis on short-term results and profits must be set aside so long-term planning and constancy of purpose will prevail.

Defining Quality

When the expression "quality" is used, we usually think in terms of an excellent product or service that fulfils or exceeds our expectations. These expectations are based on the intended use and the selling price. For example, a customer expects a different performance from a plain steel washer than from a chrome-plated steel washer because they are a different grade. When a product surpasses our expectations we consider that quality. Thus, It is somewhat of an intangible based on perception. Quality can be quantified as follows:

$$Q = P\ I\ E$$

Where Q = Quality

P = performance

E = expectations

If Q is greater than 1.0, then the customer has a good feeling about the product or service. Of course, the determination of P and E will most likely be based on perception with the organization determining performance and the customer determining expectations.

A more definitive definition of quality is given in ISO 9000:2000. It is defined as the degree to which a set of inherent characteristic fulfills requirements. Degree means that quality can be sued with adjectives such as poor, good, and excellent. Inherent is defined as existing in something, especially as a permanent characteristic. Characteristics can be quantitative or qualitative. Requirement is a need or expectation that is stated; generally implied by the organization, its customers, and other interested parties or obligatory.

Quality has nine different dimensions. Table 5.7 shows these nine dimensions of quality with their meanings and explanations in terms of a slide projector.

These dimensions are somewhat independent; therefore, a product can be excellent in one dimension and average or poor in another. Very few, if any, products excel in all nine dimensions. For example, the Japanese were cited for high-quality cars in the 1970s based only on the dimension of reliability, conformance, and aesthetics. Therefore, quality products can be determined by using a few of the dimensions of quality.

Marketing has the responsibility of identifying the relative importance

Table 5.7. The dimensions of Quality.

Dimension	Meaning and Example
Performance	Primary product characteristics, such as the brightness of the picture
Features	Secondary characteristics, added features, such as remote control
Conformance	Meeting specifications or industry standard, workmanship
Reliability	Consistency of performance over time, average time for the unit to fail
Durability	Useful life, includes repair
Service	Resolution of problems and complaints, ease of repair
Response	Human-to-human interface, such as the courtesy of the dealer
Aesthetics	Sensory characteristics, such, as exterior finish
Reputation	Past performance and other intangibles, such as being ranked first.

of each dimension of quality. These dimensions are then translated into the requirements for the development of a new product or the improvement of an existing one.

Historical Review

The history of quality control is undoubtedly as old as industry itself. During the Middle Ages, quality was to a large extent controlled why the long periods of training required by the guilds. This training instilled pride in workers for quality of a product.

The concept of specialization of labor was introduced during the Industrial Revolution. As a result, a worker no longer made the entire product, only a portion. This change brought about a decline in workmanship. Because most products manufacture during that early period were not complicated, quality was not greatly affected. In fact, because productivity improved there was a decrease in cost, which resulted in lower customer expectations. As products became more complicated and jobs more specialized, it became necessary to inspect products after manufacture.

In 1924, W.A. Shewhart of Bell Telephone Laboratories developed a statistical chart for the control of product variables. This chart is considered to be the beginning of statistical quality control. Later in the same decade, H.F. Dodge and H.G. Romig, both of Bell Telephone Laboratories, developed the area of acceptance sampling as a substitute for 100% inspection. Recognition of the value of statistical quality control became apparent by 1942. Unfortunately, U.S. managers failed to recognize its value.

In 1946, the American Society for Quality Control was formed. Recently, the name was changed to American Society for Quality (ASQ). This organization, through its publications, conferences, and training sessions, has promoted the use of quality for all types of production and service.

1950, W. Edwards Deming, who leaned statistical quality control from Shewhart, gave a series of lectures on statistical methods to Japanese engineers and on quality responsibility to the CEOs of the largest organization in Japan. Joseph M. Juran made his first trip to Japan in 1954 and further emphasized management's responsibility to achieve quality. Using these concepts the Japanese set the quality standards for the rest of the world to follow.

In 1960, the first quality control circles were formed for the purpose of quality improvement. Simple statistical techniques were learned and applied by Japanese workers.

By the late 1970s and early 1980s, U.S. managers were making frequent trips to Japan to learn about the Japanese miracle. These trips were really not necessary - they could have read the writings of Deming and Juran. Nevertheless, a quality renaissance began to occur in U.S. products and services, and by the middle of 1980 the concepts of TQM were being publicized.

In the late 1980s the automotive industry began to emphasize statistical process control (SPC). Suppliers and their suppliers were required to use these techniques. Other industries and the Department of Defense also implemented SPC. The Malconlm Baldridge National Quality Award was established and became the means to measure TQM. Genechi Taguchi introduced his concepts of parameter and tolerance design and brought about a resurgence of design of experiments (DOE) as a valuable quality improvement tool.

Emphasis on quality continued in the auto industry in the 1990s when the Saturn automobile ranked first in customer satisfaction (1996). In addition, ISO 9000 became the world wide model for a quality management system. ISO 14000 was approved as the worldwide model for environmental management systems.

The new millenium brought about increased emphasis on world wide quality and the Internet.

Obstacles

Implementation of TQM is described in the next chapter, on leadership. This section gives information concerning the obstacles associated with implementation.

Many organization's, especially small ones with a niche, are comfortable with their current state. They are satisfied with the amount of work being performed, the profits realized, and the perception that the customers are satisfied. Organizations with this culture will see little need for TQM, there will be obstacles to its successful in implementation. The first eight most common were determined by Robert J. Masters after an extensive literature search and the last obstacle added by the authors. They are gives below.

Lack of Management Commitment

In order for any organizational effort to succeed, there must be a substantial management commitment of management time and organizational resources. The purpose must be clearly and continuously communicated to all personnel. Management must consistently apply the principles of TQM.

Robert Galvin of Motorola said that only the CEO can ensure, even in times of great pressure, that quality and customer satisfaction are preserved. In a survey of 188 quality professionals, 66% reported that management's compensation is not linked to quality goals such as failure costs, customer complaints, and cycle time reduction.

Inability to Change Organizational Culture

Changing an organization's culture is difficult and will require as much as five years. Individuals resist change-they become accustomed to doing a particular process and it becomes the preferred way. Management must understand and utilize the basic concepts of change. They are:

1. People change when they want to and to meet their own needs.
2. Never expect anyone to engage in behavior that serves the organization's values unless adequate reason (why) has been given.
3. For change to be accepted, people must be moved from a state of fear to trust.

It is difficult for individuals to change their way of doing things; it is much more difficult for an organization to make a cultural change.

Management by exhortation and inspiration will fail. Speeches, slogans, and campaigns that are supposed to motivate people are only effective for a short period of time. Impediments to a cultural change are the lack of effective communication and emphasizes on short-term results. Organizations that spend more time planning for the cultural aspects of implementing a TQM program will improve their chances of success.

Improper Planning

All constituents of the organization must be involved in the development of the implementation plan and nay modifications that occur as the plan evolves. Of particular importance is the two-way communication of ideas by all personnel during the development of the plan and its implementation. Customer satisfaction should be the goal rather than financial or sales goals. Peterson Products, a metal stamping firm near Chicago, improved o-time delivery, which resulted in a 25% increase in sales. Focus on quality and the other goals will follow.

Lack of Continuous Training and Education

Training and education is an ongoing process for everyone in the organization. Needs must be determined and a plan developed to achieve those needs. Training and education are most effective when senior management conducts the training on the principles of TQM. Informal training occurs by communicating the TQM effort to all personnel on a continual basis.

In the study by Tamimi and Sebastianelli previously cited, lack of training in group discussion and communication techniques, quality improvement skills, problem identification, and the problem-solving method was the second most important obstacle.

Incompatible Organizational Structure and Isolated Individuals and Departments

Differences between departments and individuals can create implementation problem. The use of multifunctional terms will help to break down long-standing barriers.

Restructuring to make the organization more responsive to customer needs may be needed. Individuals who do not embrace the new philosophy can be required to leave the organization. Adherence to the six basic concepts will minimize the problems over time.

At Spartan Light Metal Products, Inc. in Sparta, IL, product support teams composed of three members from design, quality, and production are assigned to each customer segment.

Ineffective Measurement Techniques and Lack of Access to Data and Results

Key characteristics of the organization should be measured so that effective decisions can be made. In order to improve a process you need to measure the effect of improvement ideas. Access to data and quick retrieval is necessary for effective processes.

People Bank of Bridgeport, CT found that extra inspection, training, and management encouragement did not help a high error rate. Finally the bank investigated the rood causes of the problem and corrected them, which virtually eliminated the problems.

Paying Inadequate Attention to Internal and External Customers

Organizations need to understand the changing needs and expectations of their customers. Effective feedback mechanisms that provide data for decision making are necessary for this understanding. One way to overcome this obstacle is to give the right people direct access to the customers. Ingersol Rand of Princeton, NJ hd its design team of marketing, engineering, and manufacturing conduct focus groups of customers throughout the country with the result that it was able to develop a new grinder in one-third the usual cycle time. When an organization fails to empower individuals and teams, it cannot hold them responsible for producing results.

Inadequate Use of Empowerment and Teamwork

Team need to have the proper training and, at least in the beginning, a facilitator. Wherever possible, the team's recommendations should be followed. Individuals should be empowered to make decisions that affect the efficiency of their process or he satisfaction of their customers. Solar Turbines, Inc. flattened its organization by restructuring into work teams and delegating authority to the point of customer contact or to the work performed.

Failure to Continually Improve

It is tempting to sit back and rest on your laurels. However, a lack of continuous improvement of the processes, and/or service will even leave the leader of the pack in the dust. Will Rogers said it best, "Even if you're on the right track, you'll get run over if you just sit there." Even though Champion Mortgage's 1998 business volume increased 59% , it continues to address culture, staff, and service issues.

Benefits of TQM

According to a survey of manufacturing firms in Georgia, the benefits of TQM are improved quality, employee participation, teamwork, working relationships, customer satisfaction, employee satisfaction, productivity, communication, profitability, and market share.

TQM is a good investment as shown by a ten-year study by Hendricks and Singhai. They showed that there is a strong link between TQM and financial performance. The researchers selected a group of 600 publicly traded organizations that had won awards for effectively implementing TQM. They then selected a control group similar in size and industry to the award winners. Performance of both groups was compared during the five years prior to the award and five-year after winning the award. No difference was shown between the two groups prior to the award. However, as shown below the award group far outstripped the control group during the five-year period after the award.

Description	Control	Award
Growth in Operating Income	43%	91%
Increase in Sales	32%	69%
Increase in Total Assets	37%	79%

The study also showed that stock price performance for the award winners was 114% while the S&P was 80%. In addition, the study showed that small organizations out performed larger organizations. Recent studies have shown that only about 30% of manufacturing organizations have successfully implemented TQM.

Leadership

Definitions

There is no universal definition of leadership and indeed many books have been devoted to the topic of leadership. In his book Leadership, James MacGregor Burns describes a leader as one who instills purposes, not one who controls by brute force. A leader strengthens and inspires the followers to accomplish shared goals. Leaders shape the organization's values, promote the organization's values, protect the organization's values and exemplify the organization's values. Ultimately, Burns says, "Leaders and followers raise one another to higher levels of motivation and morality.......leadership becomes moral in that it raises the level of human conduct and ethical aspiration of both the leader and the led, and thus has a transforming effect on both. " Similarly, Daimler Chrysler's CEO Bob Eaton defines a leader as ".......someone who can take a group of people to a place they don't think they can go. " Leadership is we, not me; mission, not my show; vision, not division; and community, not domicile". As the above illustrates, leadership is difficult to define in anything other than lofty words.

The Malcolm Baldrige National Quality Award has a more grounded definition of leadership in its core values. As stated in its core values and concepts, visionary leadership is :

"An organization's senior leaders should set directions and create a customer focus, clear and visible values, and high expectations. The directions, values, and expectations should balance the needs of all your stakeholders. Your leaders should ensure the creation of strategies, systems, and methods for achieving excellence, stimulating innovation, and building knowledge and capabilities. The values and strategies should help guide all activities and decisions of your organization. Senior leaders should inspire and motivate your entire workforce and should encourage all employees to contribute, to develop and learn, to be innovative, and to be creative.

Senior leaders should serve as role models through their ethical behavior and their personal involvement in planning communications, coaching, development of future leaders,review of organizational performance, and employee recognition. As role models, they can reinforce values and expectations while building leadership, commitment,and initiative throughout your organization."

Leadership can be difficult to define. However, successful quality leaders tend to have certain characteristics.

Characteristics of Quality Leaders

There are 12 behaviors or characteristics that successful quality leaders demonstrate.

1. They give priority attention to external and internal customers and their needs. Leaders place themselves in the customers' shoes and service their needs from that perspective. They continually evaluate the customers' changing requirements.

2. They empower, rather than control, subordinates. Leaders have trust and confidence in the performance of their subordinates. They provide the resources, training, and work environment to help subordinates do

their jobs. However, the decision to accept responsibility lies with the individual.

3. They emphasize improvement rather than maintenance. Leaders use the phrase " If it isn't perfect, improve it " rather than " If it ain't broke, don't fix it. " There is always room for improvement, even if the improvement is small. Major breakthrough sometimes happen, but it's the little ones that keep the continuous process improvement on a positive track.

4. They emphasize prevention. " An ounce of prevention is worth a proud of cure" is certainly true. It is also true that perfection can be the enemy of creativity. We can't always wait until we have created the perfect process or product. There must be a balance between preventing problems and developing better, but not perfect, processes.

5. They encourage collaboration rather than competition. When functional areas, departments, or work groups are in competition, they may find subtle ways of working against each other or withholding information. Instead, there must be collaboration among and within units.

6. They train and coach, rather than direct and supervise. Leaders know that the development of the human resource is a necessity. As coaches, they help their subordinates learn to do a better job.

7. They learn from problems. When a problem exists, it is treated as an opportunity rather than something to be minimized or covered up. " What caused it ?" and " How can we prevent it in the future ?" are the questions quality leaders ask.

8. They continually try to improve communications. Leaders continually disseminate information about the TQM effort. They make it evident that TQM is not just a slogan. Communication is two way----ideas will be generated by people when leaders encourage them and act upon them. For example, on the eve of Desert Storm, General Colin Powell solicited enlisted men and women for advice on winning the war. Communication is the glue that holds a TQM organization together.

9. They continually demonstrate their commitment to quality. Leaders walk their talk-----their actions, rather than their words, communicate their level of commitment. They let the quality statements be their decision-making guide.

10. They choose suppliers on the basis of quality, not price. Suppliers are encouraged to participate on project teams and become involved. Leaders know that quality begins with the quality materials and the true measure is the life-cycle cost.

11. They establish organizational systems to support the quality effort. At the senior management level a quality council is provided, and at the first-line supervisor level, work groups and project teams are organized to improve the process.

12. They encourage and recognize team effort. They encourage, provide recognition, and reward individuals and teams. Leaders know that people

like to know that their contributions are appreciated and important. This action is one of the leader's most powerful tools.

Leadership Concepts

In order to become successful, leadership requires an intuitive understanding of human nature-the basic needs, wants, and abilities of people. To be effective, a leader understands that:

1. People, paradoxically, need security and independence at the same time.
2. People are sensitive to external rewards and punishments and yet are also strongly self-motivated.
3. People like to hear a kind word of praise. Catch people doing something right, so you can pat them on the back.
4. People can process only a few facts at a time; thus, a leader needs to keep things simple.
5. People trust their gut reaction more than statistical data.
6. People distrust a leader's rhetoric if the words are inconsistent with the leader's action's

Leaders need to give their employees independence and yet provide a secure working environment --- one that encourages and rewards successes. A working environment must be provided that fosters employee creativity and risk-taking by not penalizing mistakes.

A leader will focus on a few key values and objectives. Focusing on a few values or objectives gives the employees the ability to discern on a daily basis what is important and what is not. Employees, upon understanding the objectives, must be given personal control over the task in order to make the task their own and, thereby, something to which they can commit. A leader, by giving the employee a measure of control over an important task, will tap into the employee's inner drive. Employees, led by the manager can become excited participants in the organization.

Having a worthwhile cause such as total quality management is not always enough to get employees to participate.People, (and, in turn, employees) follow a leader,not a cause. Indeed, when people like the leader but not the vision, they will try to change the vision or reconcile their vision to the leader's vision. If the leader is liked, people will not look for another leader. This is especially evident in politics. If the leader is trusted and liked, then the employees will participate in the total quality management cause. Therefore, it is particularly important that a leader's character and competence, which is developed by good habits and ethics, be above reproach. Effective leadership begins on the inside and moves out.

Customer Satisfaction

Introduction

The most important asset of any organization is its customers. An organization's success depends on how many customers it has, how much they buy, and how often they buy. Customers that are satisfied will increase in number, buy more, and buy more frequently. Satisfied customers also pay their bills promptly, which greatly improves cash flow the lifeblood of any organization. The organizational diagram in Figure 5.14 best exemplified just how important the customer is to any organization.

Increasingly, manufacturing and service organizations are using customer satisfaction as the measure of quality. The importance of customer satisfaction is not only due to national competition but also due to worldwide competition. This fact is reflected in the Malcolm Baldrige National Quality Award, where customer satisfaction accounts for 30 percent of the total points. Similarly, customer satisfaction standards are woven throughout ISO 9000:2000. Customer satisfaction is one of the major purposes of a quality management system.

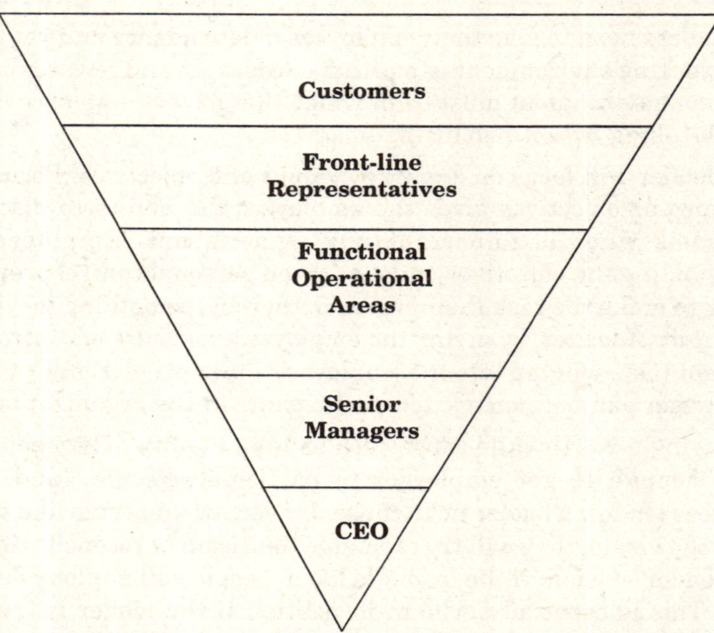

Fig. 5.14. Customer Satisfaction Organizational Diagram

Total Quality Management (TQM) implies an organizational obsession with meeting or exceeding customer expectations, so that customers are delighted. Understanding the customer's needs and expectations is essential to winning new business and keeping excising business. An organization must give its customers a quality product or service that meets their needs at a reasonable price, which includes on-time delivery and outstanding service. To attain this level, the organization needs to continually examine their quality system to see if it is responsive to ever-changing customer requirement and expectations.

The most successful TQM programs begin by defining quality from the customer's perspective. We know that quality means meeting or exceeding the customer's expectations. Dr. Deming added that quality also means anticipating the future needs of the customer. Customer satisfaction, not increasing profits, must be the primary goal of the organization. It is the most important consideration, because satisfied customers will lead to increased profits.

A simplistic definition of customer satisfaction is illustrated by the Teboul model, which is shown in Figure 5.15. The customer/'s needs are represented by the circle, and the square depicts the product or service offered by the organization. Total satisfaction is achieved when the offer matches the need, or the circle is superimposed on the square. The goal is to cover the expected performance level better than the competitors.

That part of the square that lies within the circle is perceived by the customer as satisfying, and the part of the square outside the circle is perceived as unnecessary. It is important that the organization listen to the "voice of the customer" and ensure that its marketing, design, production, and distribution processes truly meet the expectations of the customer.

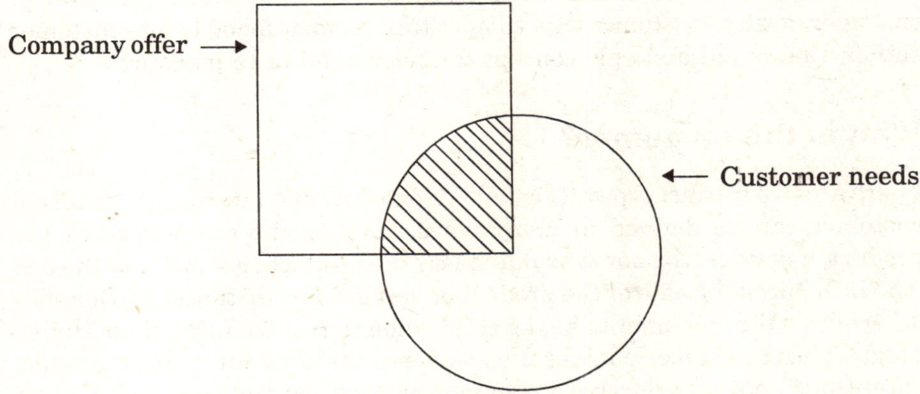

Fig 5.15. Customer Satisfaction Model

Customer satisfaction seems simple enough, and yet it is far from simple. Customer satisfaction is not an objective statistic but more of a feeling or attitude. Although certain statistical patterns can be developed to represent customer satisfaction, it is best to remember that people's opinions and attitudes are subjective by nature.

Because customer satisfaction is subjective, it is hard to measure. There are so many facets to a customer's experience with a product or service that need to be measured individually to get an accurate total picture of customer satisfaction. Whether or not a customer is satisfied cannot be classed as a yes or no answer. Errors can occur when customer satisfaction is simplified too much. The Teboul model, for instance, describes customer satisfaction as the degree to which the customer's experience of a service or product matches her expectations. Using this model, a customer's satisfaction level would be the same if the experience were mediocre in the context of low expectations, or if the experience were superior in the context of high expectations. Customer satisfaction's focus is creating superior experiences, not mediocre experiences.

Since customer satisfaction is hard to measure, the measurement often is not precise. As with most attitudes, there is variability among people, and often within the same person at different times. Often, due to the difficulty of measuring feelings, customer satisfaction strategies are developed around clearly stated, logical customer opinions, and the emotional issues of a purchase are disregarded. This can be a costly mistake.

Customer satisfaction should not be viewed in a vacuum. For example, a customer may be satisfied with a product or service and therefore rate the product or service highly in a survey, and yet that same customer may buy another product or service. It is of little benefit to understand a customer's views about a product or service if the customer's views about competitors' product or service are not understood. The value customers place on one product compared to another may be a better indicator of customer loyalty. Customer with competitors. As mentioned before customer satisfaction is not a simple concept to understand or to measure.

Who is the customer?

There are two distinct types of customers-external and internal. An external customer can be defined in many ways, such as the one who uses the product or service, the one who purchases the product or service, or the one who influences the sale of the product or service. For instance, McDonald's determined the customer to be the child when they introduced their Happy Meals. The child never paid for the meals but the child influenced the sale. Oftentimes, parents purchase lawnmowers and yet the teenage children use the lawnmowers. The identify of the external customer is not always easy to determine.

An external customer exists outside the organization and generallly falls into three categories: current, prospective, and lost customers. Each category provides valuable customer satisfaction information for the organization. Every employee in the organization must know how their job enhances the total satisfaction of the external customer. Performance must be continually improved in order to retain existing customers and to aim new ones.

An internal customer is just s important. Every function, whether it be engineering order processing, or production, has an internal customer-each receives a product or service and, in exchange, provides a product or service. Every person in a process is considered a customer of the preceding operation. Each worker's goal is to make sure that the quality meets the expectations of the next person. When that happens throughout the manufacturing, sales, and distribution chain, the satisfaction of the external customer should be assured.

All processes have outputs, which are used by internal or external customers, and inputs, which are provided by internal or external suppliers. Each supplier performs work that produces some service or product that is used by another customer. As shown by Figure 5.16, each forms a link in the customer/supplier chain, where every chain ends with an external customer and starts with an external supplier. Every employee throughout the organization is part of the chain of internal customers and suppliers.

One basic concept of TQM is an unwavering focus on customers, both internal and external. Most employees know about the external customer or end user buy may not think of other employees as internal customers of their output.

In the ideal organization, every employee would have direct contact with customers and be effective at meeting their needs. But the reality is that most employees are shielded from customers by organizational layers. For example, the first-line supervisor in a computer factory may never speak with the businessperson who buys and depends on the organization's product. However, that supervisor and countless other employees who lack direct contact must still contribute to the businessperson's satisfaction.

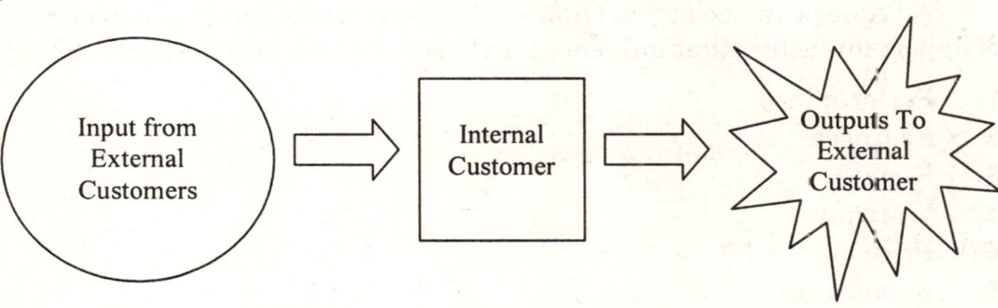

Fig. 5.16. Customer/Supplier Chain

The formula for successful internal customer/supplier relationships varies. But it always begins with people asking their internal customers three basic questions:

1. What do you need from me ?
2. What do you do with my output?
3. Are there any gaps between what you need and what you get?

The leader's role is to process work through the internal customer-supplier chain by helping workers guarantee that the end product or service fully satisfies the end user. Rather than strive for personal objectives, each individual or group must identify and satisfy the internal customer (s) while fostering a team effort where all people help the organization. Each department must determine what activities are important to both external and internal customers and manage quality every step of the way. All quality management systems start with the basic need of ensuring that the external customer's requirements are adequately documented. Similarly, the organization must document explicitly what each internal customer expects. In addition, clear criteria must be provided for measuring success in meeting the expectations of both internal and external customers.

Customer Perception of Quality

One of the basic concepts of the TQM philosophy is continuous process improvement. This concept implies that there is no acceptable quality level because the customer's needs, values, and expectations are constantly changing and becoming more demanding.

Before making a major purchase, some people check consumer magazines that rate product quality. During the period 1980 to 1988, the quality of the product and its performance ranked first, price was second, and service was third. During the period 1989 to 1992, product quality remained the most important factor, but service ranked about price in importance.

An American Society for Quality (ASQ) survey on end user perceptions of important factors that influence purchases showed the following ranking:

1. Performance
2. Features
3. Service
4. Warranty
5. Price
6. Reputation

The factors performance, features, service, and warranty are part of the product or service quality; therefore, it is evident that product quality and service are more important than price. Although this information is based on the retail customer, it appears, to some extent, to be true for the commercial customer also.

Performance

Performance involves "fitness for use" - a phrase that indicates that the product and service is ready for the customer's use at the time of sale. Other considerations are (1) availability, which is the probability that a product will operate when needed; (2) reliability which is freedom from failure over time; and (3) maintainability, which is the ease of keeping the product operable.

Features

Identifiable features or attributes of a product or service are psychological, time-oriented, contractual, ethical, and technological. Features are secondary characteristics of the product or service. For example, the primary function of an automobile is transportation, whereas a car stereo system is a feature of an automobile.

Service

An emphasis on customer service is emerging as a method for organizations to give the customer-added value. However, customer service is an intangible - it is made up of many small things, all geared to changing the customer's perception. Intangible characteristics are those traits that are not quantifiable, yet contribute greatly to customer satisfaction. Providing excellent customer service is different from the more difficult to achieve than excellent product quality. Organizations that emphasize service never stop looking for and finding ways to serve their customers better, even if their customers are not complaining. For instance, at Baptist Hospital in Pensacola, FL, janitors, after cleaning a room, ask if there is anything they can do for the patient. Often patients will have a request for a window shade to be drawn or a door closed.

Warranty

The product warranty represents an organization's public promise of a quality product backed up by a guarantee of customer satisfaction. Ideally, it also represents a public commitment to guarantee a level of service sufficient to satisfy the customer.

A warranty forces the organization to focus on the customer's definition of product and service quality. An organization has to identify the characteristics of product and service quality and the importance the customer attaches to each of those characteristics. A warranty generates feedback by providing information on the product and service quality. It also forces the organization to develop a corrective action system.

Finally, a warranty builds marketing muscle. The warranty encourages customers to buy a service by reducing the risk of the purchase decision, and it generates more sales from existing customers by enhancing loyalty.

Price

Today's customer is willing to pay a higher price to obtain value. Customers are constantly evaluating one organization's products and services against those of its competitors to determine who provides the greatest value. However, in our highly competitive environment, each customer's concept of value is continually changing. On going efforts must be made by everyone having contact with customers to identify, verify, and update each customer's perception of value in relation to each product and service.

Reputation

Most of us find ourselves rating organizations by our overall experience with them. Total customer satisfaction is based on the entire experience with the organization, not just the product. Good experiences are repeated to six people and bad experiences are repeated to 15 people; therefore, it is more difficult to create a favorable reputation.

Customers are willing to pay a premium for a known or trusted brand name and often become customers for life. Because it costs five times as much to win a new customer as it does to keep an existing one, customer retention is an important economic strategy for any organization. Although it is difficult for an organization to quantify improved customer satisfaction, it is very easy to quantify an increase in customer retention. Investment in customer retention can be a more effective bottom-line approach than concentrating on lowering operational costs. An effective marketing retention strategy is achieved through using feedback from information collecting tools.

Feedback

Customer feedback must be continually solicited and monitored. Customers continually change. They change their minds, their expectations, and thei suppliers. Customer feedback is not a one-time effort; it is an ongoing and active probing of the customers' mind. Feedback enables the organization to:

Discover customer dissatisfaction.

Discover relative priorities of quality.

Compare performance with the competition,.

Identify customers' needs.

Determine opportunities for improvement.

Even in service industries, such as insurance and banking, customer feedback has become so important that it derives new product development. There are programs to identify and analyze errors, take corrective action, and make ongoing enhancements. All these efforts are justified when the consumers' expectation levels are very high. Effective organizations take the time to listen to the voice of the customer and feed that information back to the idea stage. For instance, listening to the voice of the customer changed how the Internal Revenue Service does business. Previously, the IRS thought that good customer service was mailing tax forms out right after New year's Day. Then, the IRS asked its customers what good customer service was. The IRS found out that the customers wanted fast refunds and very little contact with the IRS. Now, about 20 million taxpayers can forget using the 1040EZ form and file on their touch-tone phone. There is no contact with the IRS, it takes about six minutes, and the phone system does the math. Refunds are received within 21 days.

Listening to the voice of the customer can be accomplished by numerous information-collecting tools. The principal ones are comment cards, questionnaires, focus groups, toll-free telephone lines, customer visits, report cards, the Internet, employee feedback, mass customization and the American Customer Satisfaction Index.

Employee Involvement

Introduction

Employee involvement is one approach to improving quality ad productivity. Its use is credited for contribution to the success enjoyed by the Japanese in the world market-place. Employee involvement is not a replacement for management nor is it the final word in quality improvement. It is a means to better meet the organization's goals for quality and productivity at all levels of an organization.

Motivation

Knowledge of motivation helps us to understand the utilization of employee involvement to achieve process improvement.

Maslow's Hierarchy of Needs

One of the first and most popular motivational theories was developed by Abraham Maslow. He stated that motivation could best be explained in terms of a hierarchy of needs and that there were five levels. These levels are survival, security, social, esteem, and self-actualization. They are shown in Figure 5.17. Once a given level is satisfied, it can no longer motivate a person.

Relating these needs to motivation, we know that Level 1 (survival) means food, clothing, and shelter, which is usually provided by a job. In the workplace, Level 1 needs include proper lighting, heating/air conditioning, ventilation, phone system, data/voice access, and computer information system. Level 2 (security) can mean a safe place to work and job security, which are very important to employees. When the organization demonstrates an interest in the personal well-being of employees, it is a motivating factor. A threat of losing one's job certainly does not enhance motivation. Level 2 is not limited to job security. It also includes having privacy on the job such as being able to lock one's office door or having lockable storage for personal items, as well as having a safe work environment that may include ergonomic adjustable furniture.

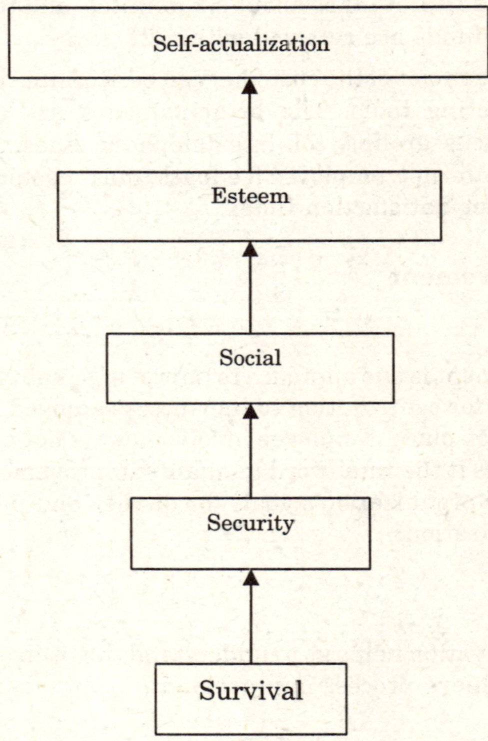

Fig. 5.17. Maslow's Hierarchy of Needs

Because we are social animals, Level 3 (social) relates to our need to belong. It has been said that cutting someone out of the group is devastating to that individual. Isolation is an effective punishment. Conversely, giving an individual the opportunity to be part of the group by feeling important and needed will motivate that person. If possible, employees should be provided with both formal social areas such as a cafeteria and conference rooms and informal areas such as water coolers and bulleting boards. Being a member of a team is a good way to bring employees into the group. Level 4 (esteem) relates to pride and self-worth. Everyone, regardless of position or job assignment, wants to be recognized as a person of value to the organization. Where possible, employees should be given offices or personal spaces with aesthetics. Business cards, workspace size, and office protocols also provide employees with a certain level of self-esteem within an organization. Seeking advice or input into business or production processes is a good way of telling employees that they are of value. This activity requires giving employees control and freedom of their jobs by providing trust. Level 5 (self-actualization) says that individuals must be given the opportunity to go as far as their abilities will take them. Many organizations have a policy of promoting from within. It is true that some employees do not want to move up the corporate ladder, which is understandable. However, those who do want to move up must know that it is possible.

It is important to note that as employees move up the hierarchy, they will immediately revert back to the previous level if they feel threatened. For example, if an employee is satisfied in Level 3, a rumor of downsizing may cause an immediate return to Level 2.

Herzberg's Two-Factor Theory

Frederick Herzberg extended the general work of Maslow by using empirical research to develop his theory on employee motivation. He found that people were motivated by recognition, responsibility, achievement, advancement, and the work itself. These factors were labeled motivators. In addition, his research showed that bad feelings were associated with low salary, minimal fringe benefits, poor working conditions, ill-defined organizational policies, and mediocre technical supervision. These job-related factors were labeled dissatisfies or hygiene factors, which implies they are preventable. It is important to realize that dissatisfies are often extrinsic in nature and motivators are intrinsic. The presence of the extrinsic conditions does not necessary motivate employees; however, their absence results in dissatisfaction among employees. Absence of motivating factors does no make employees dissatisfied, but when there are motivating factors present, they do provide strong levels of motivation that result in good job performance for the individual and the organization. In general, dissatisfies must be taken care of before motivator can be actuated. Herzberg's dissatisfies are roughly equivalent to Maslow's lower levels, and the motivators are similar to the upper levels.

Employee Wants

While management thinks that good pay is the number one want of the employee, survey results show that this factor is usually in the middle of the ranking. Table 5.8 shows employee wants and manager perceptions of employee wants. Employee wants tend to follow the theories of Maslow and Herzberg. It is interesting to note that the managers' perceptions are much different. By involving employee's through the use of teams in meaningful work and by providing the proper reward and recognition, managers can reap the advantages of greater quality and productivity along with employee satisfaction. Here this is described how

Table 5.8. What Employees Want.

Factor	Employee Rating	Manager Rating
Interesting work	1	5
Appreciation	2	8
Involvement	3	10
Job security	4	2
Good pay	5	1
Promotion/growth	6	3
Good working conditions	7	4
Loyal to employees	8	7
Help with personal problems	9	9
Tactful discipline	10	6

managers can develop employee motivation and how they can involve their employees through empowerment. If managers are to effectively motivate employees, they must align their actions closer to the motivators.

Achieving a Motivated Work Force

The building of a motivated work force is for the most part an indirect process. Managers at all levels cannot cause an employee to become motivated; they must create the environment for individuals to motivate themselves. Concepts to achieve a motivated work force are as follows:

1. Know thyself. Managers must understand their own motivations, strengths, and weaknesses. This understanding can best be obtained by having peers and employees anonymously appraise the manager's performance. Motivating managers know that the most valuable resource is people and that their success largely depends on employees achieving their goals.

2. Know your employees. Most people like to talk about themselves; therefore, the motivating manager will ask questions and listen to answers. With knowledge of the employees' interests, the manager can help achieve them within the business context. As the manager learns more about the

employee, he/she can assist the employee in directing their efforts toward satisfying their goals and well-being. This knowledge will also enable the manager to utilize their strengths.

3. Establish a positive attitude. A positive action-oriented attitude permeates the work unit. Managers are responsible for generating attitudes that lead to positive actions. Feedback should, for the most part (say, 87%), be positive and constructive. Respect and sensitivity toward others is essential to the development of positive attitudes. Asking employees for their opinions concerning job-related problems is an effective way to build a cooperative atmosphere. Managers should treat ideas and suggestions as priceless treasures and implement them immediately whenever possible.

4. Share the goals. A motivated work force needs well-defined goals that address both individual and organizational needs. Information on goal setting is given in Chapter 2.

5. Monitor progress. The process of goal-setting should include a road map detailing the journey with periodic milestones and individual assignment. Managers should periodically review performance.

6. Develop interesting work. Managers should consider altering the employees' assignments by means of job rotation, job enlargement, and job enrichment.

Job rotation permits employees to switch jobs within a work unit for a prescribed period of time. This activity reduces boredom and provides knowledge of the entire process and the affect of the sub-process. Thus, quality consciousness is raised, which may lead to process improvement.

Job enlargement combines tasks horizontally so that the employee performs a number of jobs sequentially. Thus, the employee is responsible for a greater portion of the product or service, which may also lead to process improvement.

Job enrichment combines tasks vertically by adding managerial elements such as planning, scheduling, and inspection. This contributes to the employees' sense of autonomy and control over their work, which may lead to process improvement.

7. Communicate effectively. Effective communication provides employees with knowledge about their work unit and the organization rather than "grapevine" information. Communication is covered in greater detail in Chapter 2.

8. Celebrate success. Recognizing employee achievements is the most powerful tool in the manager's toolbox. Additional information is given in the recognition and reward section of this chapter.

These eight concepts can be used at al l managerial levels of the organization.

Employee Surveys

As described in the previous section, an initial step a manger should take in initiating employee empowerment is to survey their employees to determine their current level of perceived empowerment. Employee surveys help managers assess the current state of employee relations, identify trends, measure the effectiveness of program implementation, identify needed improvements, and increase communication effectiveness. The success of the survey is directly related to the quality of the planning. An organization should no plan, develop, and administer the survey unless managers are willing to use the results and work towards empowering their employees.

The first step is for the quality council to create a multifunctional team with responsibilities as previously described. In addition, the team will determine the objective and develop a plan to communicate results, encourage root cause analysis, and encourage corrective action.

Next, the team will develop the survey instrument using in-house and external expertise. Identifiers such as location, sex, age, seniority, and work unit are absolutely essential to analyze the results. If the entire population is not surveyed, then the sampling procedure should be determined for the initial and subsequent ones. The survey is pilot tested and revised as needed.

Other constructs to address in the survey include personality characteristics, management styles, job attitudes, and the work. Examples of each include:

- Personality characteristics - anxiety, self-esteem in the organization, and ability to participate in the organization.
- Management styles - consideration of subordinates, initiating structure, commitment to quality.
- Job attitudes - job satisfaction, social support at work and co-worker's commitment to quality.
- The work-task variety, autonomy and importance.

Several employee empowerment questionnaires exist in the literature.

The third step is to administer the survey. This activity begins by communicating to the employees the purpose, schedule of events, and employee expectation. The survey should be administered by an outside group to maintain anonymity. Written comments should be typed with names disguised. Employees should be given time to complete the questionnaire, preferably during normal work hours in a large area such as the cafeteria. Surveys are administered every 12 to 18 months.

Next, the results are compiled and analyzed, and a report is prepared for the quality council in a timely manager. This report is shared with the entire organization, including a mechanism for input of reactions and suggestions.

The last step is to determine areas for improvement. Such areas for improvement will occur at the work unit level, cross boundaries among work groups such as between engineering design and marketing, and cover the entire organization.

By listening to the voice of the employee, the organization can receive feedback to help ensure a thriving TQM effort.

Continuous Process Improvement

Introduction

Quality-based organizations should strive to achieve perfection by continuously improving the business and production processes., Of course, perfection is impossible because the race is never over; however, we must continually strive for its attainment.

Improvement is made by

- Viewing all work as a process, whether it is associated with production or business activities.
- Making all processes effective, efficient, and adaptable.
- Anticipating changing customer needs.
- Controlling in-process performance using measures such as scrap reduction, cycle time, control charts, and so forth.
- Maintaining constructive dissatisfaction with the present level of performance.
- Eliminating waste and rework wherever it occurs.
- Investigating activities that do not add value to the product or service, with the aim of eliminating those activities.
- Eliminating nonconformities in all phases of everyone's work, even if the increment of improvement is small.
- Using benchmarking to improve competitive advantage.
- Innovating to achieve breakthroughs.
- Incorporating lessons learned into future activities.
- Using technical tools such as statistical process control (SPC), experimental design, benchmarking, quality function deployment (QFD), and so forth.

Continuous process improvement is designed to utilize the resources of the organization to achieve a quality-driven culture. Individuals must think, act, and speak quality. An organization attempts to reach a single-minded link between quality and work execution by educating its constituents to "continuously" analyze and improve their own work, the processes, and their work group.

Process

Process refers to business and production activities on an organization. Business processes such as purchasing, engineering, accounting, and marketing are areas where nonconformance can represent an opportunity for substantial improvement. Figure 5.18 shows a process model.

Inputs may be materials, money, information, data, etc. Outputs may be information, data, products, service, etc. The output of one process also can be the input to another process. Outputs usually require performance measures. They are designed to achieve certain desirable outcomes such as customer satisfaction. Feedback is provided in order to improve the process.

The process is the interaction of some combination of people, materials, equipment method, measurement, and the environment to produce an outcome such as a product, a service, or an input to another process. In addition to having measurable input and output, a process must have value-added activities and repeatability. It must be effective, efficient, under control, and adaptable. In addition, it must adhere to certain conditions imposed by policies and constraints or regulations. Examples of such conditions may include constraints related to union-based job descriptions of employees, state and federal regulations related to storage of environmental waste, or bio-ethical policies related to patient care.

Process definition begins with defining the internal and/or external customers. The customer defines the purpose of the organization and every process within it. Because the organization exists to serve the customer, process improvements must be defined in terms of increased customer satisfaction as a result of higher quality products and services.

All processes have at least one owner. In some cases, the owner is obvious, because there is only one person performing the activity. However, frequently the process will cross multiple organizational boundaries, and supporting sub-processes will be owned by individuals within each of the organizations. Thus, ownership should be part of the process improvement initiatives.

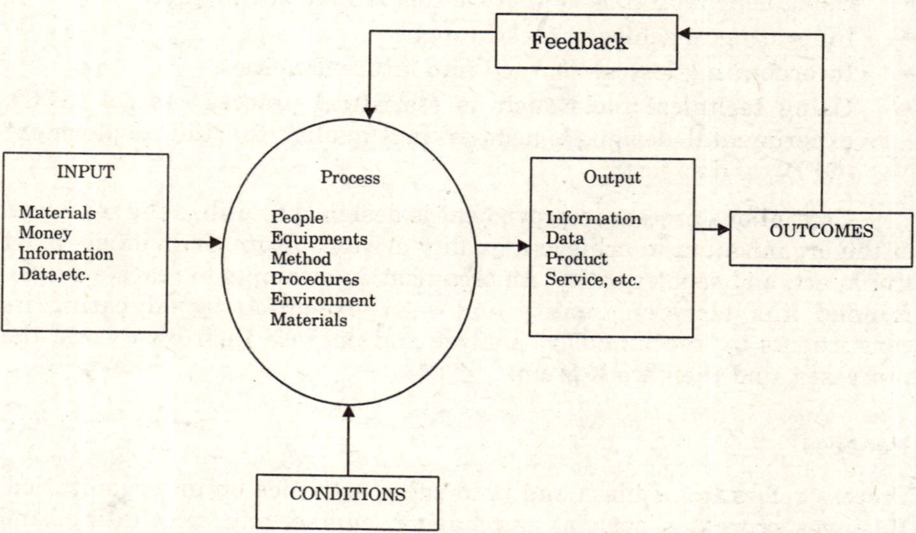

Fig- 5.18. Input/Output Process Model

At this point it is important to define an improvement. There are five basic ways to improve: (1) reduce resources, (2) reduce errors, (3) meet or exceed expectations of downstream customers, (4) make the process safer, and (5) make the process more satisfying to the person doing it.

First, process that uses more resources than necessary is wasteful. Reports that are distributed to more people than necessary wastes copying and distribution time, material, user read time, and, eventually, file space.

Second, for the most part, errors are a sign of poor workmanship and require rework. Typing errors that are detected after the computer printout require opining the file, making the correction, and printing the revised document.

Third, by meeting or exceeding expectations of downstream customers, the process is improved. For example, the better the weld, the less grinding required, making the appearance of a finish paint more pleasing.

The fourth was a process can be improved is by making it safer. A safer workplace is a more productive one with fewer lost-time accidents and less workers' compensation claims.

The fifth way to improve a process is to increase the satisfaction of the individual performing the process. Sometimes a little change, such as an ergonomically correct chair, can make a substantial change in a person's attitude toward their work.

This chapter presents several different approaches towards continuous process improvement. The first, Juran's Trilogy, approaches quality improvement from a cost-oriented perspective. The second is Shewhart's Plan-Do-Study-Act cycle. This approach is basically the engineering scientific method applied to continuous improvement and quality. A more in-depth description of the problem solving method is provided to further explain how to carry out the approach. The third is Kaizen, the Japanese approach to improvement. The Kaizen approach focuses on making small incremental improvements to the individual and the organization. It is actually more behavioral in nature than the other two approaches describe, as it often focuses on improving the individual and their individual job; thus, improvements to the organization as a whole are realized. The Chapter concludes with a short discussion of reengineering and six-sigma concepts. These two approaches are becoming more popular in business, and they provide many of the basic concepts presented in the chapter.

The Juran Trilogy

Process improvement involves planning. One of the best approaches is the one developed by Dr. Joseph Juran. It has three components: planning, control, and improvement, and is referred to as the Juran Trilogy. It is based loosely on financial processes such as budgeting (planning), expense measurement (control), and cost reduction (improvement).

Planning

The planning component begins with external customers. Once quality goals are established, marketing determines the external customers, and all organizational personnel (managers, members of multifunctional teams, or work groups) determine the internal customers. External customers may be quite numerous, as is the case of a bank supply organization, where they include tellers, financial planners, loan officers, auditors, managers, and the bank's customers. Where there are numerous customers, a Pareto diagram might be useful to determine the vital few.

Once the customers are determined, their needs are discovered. This activity requires the customers to state needs in there own words and from their own viewpoint; however, real needs may differ from stated needs. For example, a stated need may be an automobile, whereas the real need is transportation or a status symbol. In addition, internal customers may not wish to voic3 real needs out of fear of the consequences. One might discover these needs by (1) being a user of the product or service, (2) communicating with customers through product or service satisfaction and dissatisfaction information, or (3) simulation in the laboratory. Because customer needs are stated from their viewpoint, they should be translated to requirements that are understandable to the organization and its suppliers.

The next step in the planning process it to develop product and/or service featu4res that respond to customer needs, meet the needs of the organization and its suppliers, are competitive, and optimize the costs of all stakeholders. This step typically is performed by a multifunctional team. Quality function deployment Taguchi's quality engineering and quality by design are some of the approaches that can be used. It is important that the design team, rather than a single department, approve the final design and that the team be composed of all functional areas within an organization as well as customers and suppliers.

The fourth step is to develop the processes able to produce the product and/or service features. Some of this planning would have occurred during the previous step. This step is also performed by a multifunctional team with a liaison to the design team. Activities include determining the necessary facilities, training, and operation, control, and maintenance of the facilities. Of particular concern will be the "scaling up" from the laboratory or prototype environment to the rear process environment. Additional activities include process capability evaluation and process control type and location.

Transferring plans to operations is the final step of the planning process. Once again, a multifunctional team with a liaison to the other teams is used. When training is necessary, it should be performed by members of the process planning team. Process validation is necessary to ensure, with a high degree of assurance, that a process will consistently produce a product or service meeting requirements. Positrol and process certification, discussed later in the chapter, are excellent techniques to use to help validate the process.

Control

Control is used by operating forces to help meet the product, process, and service requirements. It uses the feedback loop and consists of the following steps:

1. Determine items/subjects to be controlled and their units of measure.
2. Set goals for the controls and determine what sensors need to be put in place to measure the product, process, or service.
3. Measure actual performance.
4. Compare actual performance to goals.
5. Act on the difference.

Statistical process control is the primary technique for achieving control. The basic statistical process control (SPC) tools are Pareto diagrams, flow diagrams, cause-and-effect diagrams, check sheets, histograms, control charts, and scatter diagrams. In addition, process capability information such as Cp and Cpk are used to determine if the process is capable and is centered.

Improvement

The third part of the trilogy aims to attain levels of performance that are significantly higher than current levels. Process improvements begin with the establishment of an effective infrastructure such as the quality council. Two of the duties of the council are to identify the improvement projects and establish the project teams with a project owner. In addition, the quality council needs to provide the teams with the resources to determine the causes, create solutions, and establish controls to hold the gains. The problem-solving method described in a later section may be applied to improve the process, while the quality council is the driver that ensures that improvement is continuous and never-ending. Process improvement can be incremental or breakthrough.

Figure 5.19 provides an example of how the three continuos improvement processes interrelate. In the figure, Juran provides a distinction between sporadic waste and chronic waste. The sporadic wasted can be identified and corrected through quality control. The chronic waste requires an improvement process. As a solution is found through the improvement process, lessons learned are bought back to the quality planning process so that new goals for the organization may be established.

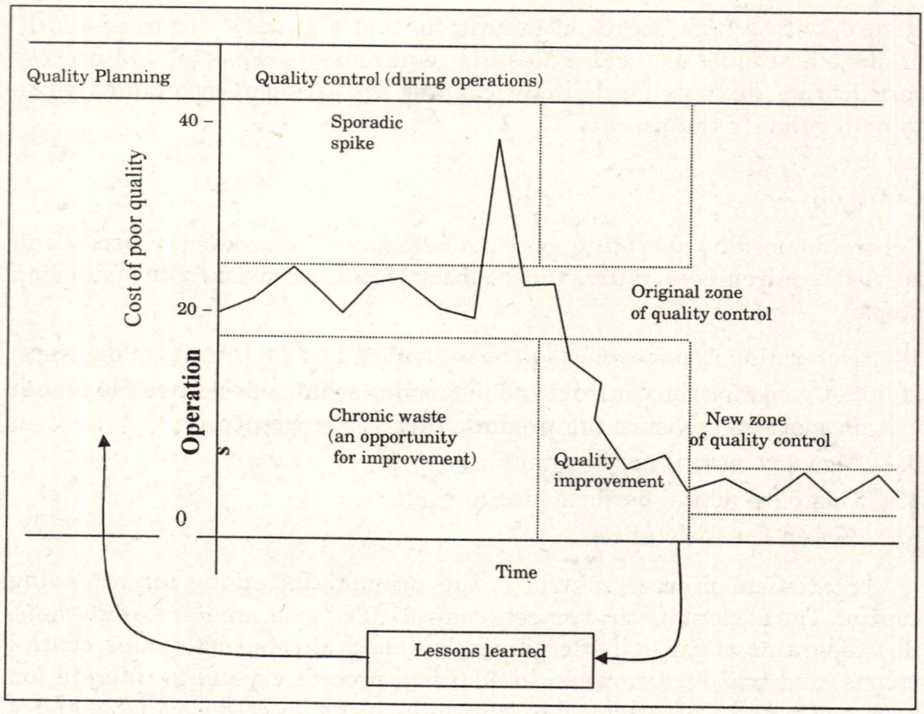

Fig. 5.19. The Juran Trilogy Diagram

Supplier Partnership

Introduction

An organization spends a substantial portion of every sales dollar on the purchase of raw materials, components, and services. In fact, 60% of the cost of goods sold in 2000 consisted of purchased goods. This is an increase from 20% in 1970.! Therefore, supplier quality can substantially affect the overall cost of a product or service. One of the keys to obtaining high-quality products and services is for the customer to work with the suppliers in a partnering atmosphere to achieve the same quality level as attained within the organization.

Customers and suppliers have the same goal---to satisfy the end user. The better the supplier's quality, the better the supplier's long- term position, because the customer will have better quality. Because both the customer and the supplier have limited resources, they must work together as partners to maximize their return on investment.

There have been a number of forces that have changed supplier relations. Prior to the 1980s procurement decision were typically based on price, thereby awarding contracts to the lowest bidder. As a result, quality and timely delivery were sacrificed. One force, Deming's fourth point, addressed this problem. He stated that customers must stop awarding business based on the low bidder because price has no basis without quality. In addition, he advocated single suppliers for each item to help develop long-term relationship of loyalty and trust. These action will lead to improved products and services.

Another force changing supplier relations was the introduction of the just-in-time (JIT) concept. It calls for raw materials and components to reach the production operation in small quantities when they are needed and not before. The benefit of JIT is that inventory-related costs are kept to a minimum. Procurement lots are small and delivery is frequent. As a result, the supplier will have many more process setups, thus becoming a JIT organization itself. The supplier must drastically reduce setup time or its costs will increase. Because there is little or no inventory, the quality of incoming materials must be very good or the production line will be shut down. To be successful, JIT require exceptional quality and reduced setup times.

The practice of continuous process improvement has also caused many suppliers to develop partnerships with their customers. Citing the company's effective use of Kaizen, the CEO of Freudenber-NOK approached Chrysler to implement a Kaizen project for every part it supplied to the automaker to reduce "controllable/variable" costs. The company freed 30% of its floor-space and increased revenues by 300% resulting in a strong alliance with its customer.

Because approximately half of all revenues currently generated in the U.S.economy are derived from products and services developed in the last five years, many original equipment manufacturers (OEMs) are developing strategic partnerships with their suppliers. Suppliers are now taking on increased product-development responsibilities. In the development of new products, many suppliers are becoming involved in product design and complexity, formation of specifications, and component testing.

A final force is ISO 9000, and in particular QS 9000 (ISO/TS 16949), which is mandated by the major automotive assembly firms. Specifically, first tier and tiers subsequent to the OEMs must maintain supply chain development through three key factors: zero defects, 100% on-time delivery, and a process for continuous improvement.

These forces have changed adversarial customer-supplier relationships into mutually beneficial partnerships. Joint efforts improve quality, reduce costs, and increase market share for both parties.

Principles of Customer/Supplier Relations

Dr. Kaoru Ishikawa has suggested ten principles to ensure quality products and services and eliminate unsatisfactory conditions between the customer and the supplier:

1. Both the customer and the supplier are fully responsible for the control of quality.
2. Both the customer and the supplier should be independent of each other and respect each other's independence.
3. The customer is responsible for providing the supplier with clear and sufficient requirements so that the supplier can know precisely what to produce.
4. Both the customer and the supplier should enter into a nonadversarial contract with respect to quality, quantity, price, delivery method, and terms of payments.
5. The supplier is responsible for providing the quality that will satisfy the customer and submitting necessary data upon the customer's request.
6. Both the customer and the supplier should decide the method to evaluate the quality of the product or service to the satisfaction of both parties.
7. Both the customer and the supplier should establish in the contract the method by which they can reach an amicable settlement of any disputes that may arise.
8. Both the customer and the supplier should continually exchange information, sometimes using multifunctional teams, I order to improve the product or service quality.
9. Both the customer and the supplier should perform business activities such as procurement, production and inventory planning, clerical work, and systems so that an amicable and satisfactory relationship is maintained.
10. When dealing with business transactions, both the customer and the supplier should always have the best interest of the end user in mind.

Although most of these principles are common sense, a close scrutiny shows that a true partnering relationship exists with long-term commitment, trust, and shared vision. Ishikawa, like Deming, preaches a family-type relationship, where each party preserves their identity and independence.

Partnering

Partnering is a long-term commitment between two or more organizations for the purpose of achieving specific business goals and objectives by maximizing the effectiveness of each participant" resources. The relationship is based upon trust, dedication to common goals and objectives and an understanding of each participant" expectations and values. Benefits include improved quality, increased efficiency, low cost, increased opportunity for innovation, and the continuous improvement of products and services. Partnering is a multifaceted relationship requiring constant nurturing to achieve continuous improvement and maximum benefit.

There are three key elements to a partnering relationship: long-term commitment, trust, and shared vision.

1. Long-Term Commitment. Experience has shown that the benefits of partnering are not achieved quickly. Problems require time to solve or processes need constant improvement. Long-term commitment provides the needed environment for both parties to work toward continuous improvement. There must be total organizational involvement from the CEO to the workers.

Each party contributes its unique strengths to the processes. When these strengths are not sufficient, investment in nee equipment, systems, or personnel may be required. The parties take risks that are commensurate with their regards and the degree of the relationship. A supplier might not take these risks, such as acquiring new equipment or systems, without a long-term commitment.

Chrysler requires about 70 percent of the manufacturing tools it uses to be used by its suppliers as well. Chrysler works early in the supplier relationship to expose and train the supplier to use CAE, CAD, and CAM software tools. Without supplier involvement, the use of advanced technologi8es within Chrysler would have had only marginal impact on the competition.

2. Trust. Trust enables the resources and knowledge of each partner to the combined to eliminate an adversarial relationship. Partners are then able to share information and accept reduced control. Mutual trust forms the basis for a strong working relationship. It should be viewed a s a business paradigm shift and begins with the purchase contract that is nonadversarial. The purchasing function of the organization must be subordinate to the overall relationship goals and objectives. Open and frequent communication avoids misdirection and disputes while strengthening the relationship.

The parties should have access to each other's business plans and technical information, such as product and process parameters. In addition, they may share or integrate resources such as training activities, administrative systems, and equipment.

The strength of partnering is based on fairness and parity. Both parties become mutually motivate d when "win-win" solutions are sought rather than "win-lose" solutions.

3. Shared Vision. Each of the partnering organizations must understand the need to satisfy the final customer. To achieve this vision, there should be an open and candid exchange of needs and expectation. Shared goals and objectives ensure a common direction and must be aligned with each party's mission. Employees of both parties should think and act for their common good. Each partner must understand the other partner's business so that equitable decisions are made. These decisions must be formulated and implemented as a team. Thus, the sharing of business plans aids in mutual strategic planning.

Sourcing

There are three types of sourcing: sole, multiple, and single. A sole source of supply implies that the organization is forced to use only one supplier. This situation is due to factors such as patents, technical specifications, raw material location, only one organization producing the item, or the item being produced by another plant or division of the organization. Partnering is a natural consequence of this type of sourcing, provided the supplier is willing to work together to satisfy the end user.

Multiple sourcing is the use of two or more suppliers for an item. Usually three suppliers are chosen, and their portion of the business is a function of their performance in terms of price, quality, and delivery. The theory of multiple sourcing is that competition will result in better quality, lower costs, and better service. However, in practice , an adversarial relationship may result without the claimed advantages. Multiple sourcing also eliminates disruption of supply due to strikes and other problems.

Single sourcing is a planned decision by the organization to select one supplier for an item when several sources are available. It results in large, long-term contracts and a partnering relationship. With a guaranteed future volume, the supplier can direct its resources to improve the processes. For the organization, the advantages are reduced business and production cost, complete accountability, supplier loyalty, and a better end product with less variability. Delivery disruption is always a problem and is even more so with JIT implementation. For the supplier, the advantages are new business from the customer and reduced cost of business and production processes because of economies of scale. Single sourcing has allowed organizations to reduce their supplier base. For example, Xerox eliminated 90% of its suppliers and improved supplier quality from 92% to 99.97% in six years. Through supplier consolidation, Merck cut its supplier base 75% in eight years; and Whirlpool reduced its suppliers 50% in four years.

Supplier Selection

Before discussing supplier activities, it must be decided whether to produce or outsource a particular item. This decision is a strategic one that must be made during the design stage. The following three questions need to be answered:

1. How critical is the item to the design of the product or service?
2. Does the organization have the technical knowledge to produce the items internally? If not, should that knowledge be developed?
3. Are there suppliers who specialize in producing the item? If not, is the organization willing to develop such a specialized supplier?

These questions must be answered in terms of cost, delivery, quality, safety, and the acquisition of technical knowledge. One organization outsourced their trucking operation, warehousing, and accounts payable because it could be done better and cheaper.

Once the decision has been made to outsource, then the supplier must be selected. Following are ten conditions for selection and evaluation of suppliers.

1. The supplier understands and appreciates the management philosophy of the organization.
2. The supplier has a stable management system. In determining this condition, several questions should be asked: Is there a quality policy statement that includes objectives for quality and its commitment to quality? Is the policy implemented and understood at all levels of the organization? Is there documentation that indicates who is in charge and responsible for quality in the organization? Is there a member of top management with the authority to execute a quality system? Does the management have scheduled reviews of its quality system to determine its effectiveness?
3. The Supplier maintains high technical standards and has the capability of dealing with future technological innovations.
4. The Supplier can provide those raw materials and parts required by the purchaser, and those supplied meet the quality specifications.
5. The supplier has the capability to produce the amount of production needed or can attain that capability.
6. There is no danger of the supplier breaching corporate secrets.
7. The price is right and the delivery dates can be met. In addition, the supplier is easily accessible in terms of transportation and communication. There must also be a system to trace the product or lot from receipt and all changes of production delivery.
8. The supplier is sincere in implementing the contract provisions. Does the supplier have a system for contract review, and does that system include a contract review of requirements and how differences between the contract and/or accepted order requirements should be resolved? Further, does the system allow the inclusion of amendments? Also, does the system include maintaining records of reviewed contracts?
9. The supplier has an effective quality system and improvement program such as ISO/QS 9000.
10. The supplier has a track record of customer satisfaction and organization credibility. A recent study by Andersen, the University of Cambridge, and Cardiff Business School found Japan to be the leader in the number of world class automotive supplier plants, but the U.S. held the top three supplier positions. Of the 13 supplier plants identified as "world class," five were from Japan.

The preceding conditions go beyond evaluating a supplier on the basis of quality, price, and delivery. It is recommended that a large organization send a multifunctional team to assess these supplier conditions. The team may wish to score each condition on a scale of 1 to 5. Small organizations may wish to use a written questionnaire and survey potential suppliers by mail.

Performance Measures

Introduction

The sixth and final concept of Total Quality Measurement (TQM } is performance measures. One of the Malcolm Baldrige National Quality Award core values is managing by fact rather than by gut feeling. Managing an organization without performance measures is like a captain of a ship navigating without instrumentation. The ship would most likely end up traveling in circles, as would an organization. Measures play a vital part in the success or failure of an organization.

Basic Concepts

Objectives

Performance measures are used to achieve one or more of the following seven objectives:

1. Establish baseline measures and reveal trends.
2. Determine which processes need to be improved.
3. Indicate process gains and losses.
4. Compare goals with actual performance.
5. Provide information for individual and team evaluation.
6. Provide information to make informed decisions.
7. Determine the overall performance of the organization.

Typical Measurements

What should be measured is frequently asked by managers and teams. The information below suggests some items that can be measured.

Human Resources

Lost time due to accidents, absenteeism, turnover, employee satisfaction index, number of suggestions for improvement, number of suggestions implemented, number of training hours per employee, training cost per employee, number of active teams, number of grievances.

Customers

Number of complaints, number of on-time deliveries, warranty data such as parts replacement, customer satisfaction index, time to resolve complaints, telephone data such as response time, mean time to repair, dealer satisfaction, report cards.

Production

Inventory turns, SPC charts, Cp / CPK amount of scrap/rework, non-conformities per million units, software errors per 1000 lines of code, percent of flights that arrive on time, process yield, machine downtime, actual performance to goal, number of products returned, cost per unit.

Research and Development

New product time to market, design change orders, R&D spending to sales, average time, to process proposal, recall data, cost estimating errors.

Suppliers

SPC charts, Cp / CPK on-time delivery, service rating, quality performance, billing accuracy, average lead time, percent of suppliers that are error free, just-in-time delivery target.

Marketing/Sales

Sales expense to revenue, order accuracy, introduction cost to development cost, new product sales to total sales, new customers, gained or lost accounts, sales income to number of salespeople, number of successful calls per week.

Administration

Revenue per employee, expense to revenue, cost of poor quality, percent of payroll distributed on time, number of days accounts receivable past due, number of accounts payable past due, office equipment up-time, purchase order errors, vehicle fleet data, order entry/billing accuracy.

A good metric compares the measurement of interest to the total possible outcomes, such as rework hours to total hours.

Criteria

All organizations have some measurements in place that can be adapted for TQM. However, some measurements may need to be added. In order to evaluate the existing measures or add new ones, the following ten criteria are recommended:

1. Simple : Measures should be understandable by those who will use them.

2. Few in number: The important measures must be distinguished from the unimportant once so that users can concentrate on just a few. Two or three measures should be sufficient for any work group, with the number increasing for departments, functional areas, plants and corporations. Quality councils may wish to use composite measures such as a customer satisfaction index. It is composed of several-weighted metrics such as on-time delivery, cost, product or service quality, and complaints.

3. Developed by users: In order to ensure ownership of the measures, they must be developed by the user. Measures dictated by a higher authority will usually not receive support from downstream units. However, in some cases, measures are mandated by the customer.

4. Relevance to customer: Measures must be relevant to the needs of internal or external customers. Control over important changes should be vested in the people who are held responsible for the performance measure. They also decide what measures to use and set target goals.

5. Improvement: Although correcting non-conformances and making current decisions are important, the focus should be on improvement, prevention, and strategic long-term planning and goal setting. Measures are used to promote improvement, not to identify poor performance and penalize the low performers. They should be sensitive to the improvements made.

6. Cost: Of course, the bottom line is that cost and profit must reflect an improved financial picture, as shown by the cost of poor quality system and other financial data. In addition, the cost of measurement should be considered.

7. Visible: Facility-wide measures should be posted in a central location, such as the lunch or break room, where everyone can see them. Likewise, unit measures should be posted at the machine or work center.

8. Timely: Financial and accounting data are often presented too late to be actionable. This may require that measurements are taken hourly, daily, or weekly rather than monthly or quarterly as in traditional accounting systems.A significant portion of measurements need to be operational rather than financial. Data needs to be measured, analyzed, and evaluated with respect to the desired goals so that the information can be used effectively in decision making.

9. Aligned: A comprehensive set of measures and indicators tied to customer and organizational performance requirements provides a way to align all activities with organizational goals.

10. Results: Key result measures need to be guided and balanced by the interests of all stakeholders---customers, employees, stockholders, suppliers, the public, and the community.

Use of these criteria will improve the suitability of the selected measures.

Quality Management Systems

Introduction

The International Organization for Standardization (ISO) was founded in 1946 in Geneva, Switzerland, where it is still based. Its mandate is to promote the development of international standards to facilitate the exchange of goods and services worldwide. ISO is composed of more than 90 member countries.The United States representative is the American National Standards Institute (ANSI).

The ISO Technical Committee (TC) 176 developed a series of international standards for quality systems, which were first published in 1987. The standards (ISO 9000, 9001,and 9004) were intended to be advisory and were developed for use in two-party contractual situations and internal auditing. However, with their adoption by the European Community (EC) and a worldwide emphasis on quality and economic competitiveness, the standards have become universally accepted.

Most countries have adopted the ISO 9000 series as their national standards. Like-wise, thousands of organizations throughout the world have quality systems registered to the standard. In the United States, the national standards are published by the American National Institute/ American Society for Quality (ANSI/ ASQ) as the ANSI/ ASQQ9000 series. Government bodies throughout the world, including the United States, are also using the series are the Department of Defense (DOD) and the Food and Drug Administration (FDA)

In a two-party system, the supplier of a product or service would develop a quality system that conformed to the standard. The customers would then audit the system for acceptability. This two-party system results in both the supplier and customer having to participate in multiple audits, which can be extremely costly. This practice is replaced by a third-party registration system.

A quality system registration involves the assessment and periodic surveillance audit of the adequacy of a supplier's quality system by a third party, who is a registrar. When a system conforms to the registrar's interpretation of the standard, the registrar issues a certificate of registration to the supplier. This registration ensures customers or potential customers that a supplier has a quality system in place and it is being monitored.

Benefits of ISO Registration

There are various reasons for implementing a quality system that conforms to an ISO standard. The primary reason is that customers or marketing are suggesting or demanding compliance to a quality system. Other reasons are needed improvement in processes or systems and a desire for global deployment of products and services. As more and more organizations become registered, they are requiring their subcontractors or suppliers to be registered, creating a snowball effect. Consequently, in order to maintain or increase market share, many organizations are finding they must be in conformance with an ISO standard. Internal benefits that can be received from developing and implementing a well-documented quality system can far outweigh the external pressures.

A study of 100 Italian manufacturing firms was undertaking to determine if there was any improvement in performance after registration. Significant improvement was noted in:

Internal quality as measured by the percent of scrap, rework, and nonconformities at final inspection.

Production reliability as measured by the number of breakdowns per month, percent of time dedicated to emergencies, and percent of downtime per shift.

External quality as measured by product accepted by customers without inspection, claims of nonconforming product, and returned product.

Time performance as measured by item to market, on-time delivery, and throughput time.

Cost of poor quality as measured by external nonconformities, scrap, and rework

On the negative side, prevention and appraisal costs increased.

Additional examples of benefits after registration are:

The American Institute of Certified Public Accountants (AICPA) now has a quality system that works, and there was a 4% improvement in gross margins, which was the largest improvement in their history.

North town Ford automobile dealership in Toronto, Ontario raised customer satisfaction and loyalty by 20%, and it had a 55% increase in c customers who would recommend the dealership.

United Airlines reduced the average engine overhaul cycle time from 120 days to 60 days.

Cleveland Center for Joint Reconstruction has experienced lower costs and more control and consistency in the care it provides.

ISO 9000 Series of Standards

The ISO 9000 Series of Standards is generic in scope. By design, the series can be tailored to fit any organization's needs, whether it is large or small, a manufacturer or a service organization. It can be applied to construction, engineering, health care, legal, and other professional services as well as the manufacturing of anything from nuts and bolts to spacecraft. Its purpose is to unify quality terms and definitions used by industrialized nations and use those terms to demonstrate a supplier's capability of controlling its processes. In very simplified terms, the standards required an organization to say what it is doing to ensure quality, then do what it says, and, finally, document or prove that it has done what it said.

The three standards of the series are described briefly in the following paragraphs:

ISO 9000:2000-Quality Management Systems (QMS) -v fundamentals and vocabulary discusses the fundamental concepts related to the QMS and provides the terminology used in the other two standards.

ISO 9001:20000-Qaulity Management Systems (QMS)-requirements is the standard used for registration by demonstrating conformity of the QMS to customers, regulatory, and the organization's own requirements.

ISO 9004:20000-Quality Management Systems (QMS)-guidelines for performance improvement provides guidelines that an organization can use to establish a QMS focussed on improving performance.

Sector-specific Standards

The ISO 9000 system is designed as a simple system that could be used by any industry. Other systems have been developed that are specific to a particular industry such as automotive or aerospace. These systems use the ISO 9001 as the basic framework and modify it to their needs. There are currently three other quality systems: AS9100, ISO/TS 16949, and TL 9000.

One of the problems with sector-specific standards is the need for suppliers with customers in different industries to set up quality systems to meet each sector's requirements. For example, a packaging supplier that services the aerospace, automobile, and telecommunications industries would need to set up its system to accommodate not only ISO 9001 but three other standards. In addition, the Registration Accreditation Board (RAB) points out that sector-specific standards have created a need for specialized auditors and training courses. On the positive side, the standardization of requirements beyond ISO 9001 makes compliance by key suppliers and implementation by major customers much easier?